Newswriter's Handbook

An Introduction to Journalism

SECOND EDITION

M.L. Stein, Susan F. Paterno
and R. Christopher Burnett

Blackwell
Publishing

M. L. "Mike" Stein has more than 40 years of experience as a journalist, author and teacher. After 16 years as a reporter for mid-size and metropolitan dailies as well as national magazines, Stein served as professor and chairman of the Department of Journalism and Mass Communications at New York University and the Department of Journalism at California State University, Long Beach. He also has reported from overseas. Stein is the author of several books on journalism and general writing skills.

Susan F. Paterno, director of the journalism program at Chapman University in Orange, Calif., is an award-winning journalist with more than 20 years experience as a reporter, writer and columnist. A senior writer for *American Journalism Review,* Paterno has also written for the *Los Angeles Times,* the *New York Times, U.S. News & World Report, Parenting,* and many other publications. For nearly a decade, Paterno served on the staff of the Orange County Register, where she won numerous awards for writing and reporting, and several fellowships for post-graduate study.

R. Christopher Burnett, Ph.D., is an assistant professor of journalism at California State University, Long Beach. Burnett worked for more than a decade as a political reporter in Washington, D.C. He also has worked in public relations, on political campaigns, and as an editor and a reporter on newspapers in Colorado, Michigan, New York, and Ohio. He still works as a freelance writer.

© 2006 Blackwell Publishing

Blackwell Publishing Professional
2121 State Avenue, Ames, Iowa 50014, USA

Orders: 1-800-862-6657
Office: 1-515-292-0140
Fax: 1-515-292-3348
Web site: www.blackwellprofessional.com

Blackwell Publishing Ltd
9600 Garsington Road, Oxford OX4 2DQ, UK
Tel.: +44 (0)1865 776868

Blackwell Publishing Asia
550 Swanston Street, Carlton, Victoria 3053, Australia
Tel.: +61 (0)3 8359 1011

Authorization to photocopy items for internal or personal use, or the internal or personal use of specific clients, is granted by Blackwell Publishing, provided that the base fee is paid directly to the Copyright Clearance Center, 222 Rosewood Drive, Danvers, MA 01923. For those organizations that have been granted a photocopy license by CCC, a separate system of payments has been arranged. The fee code for users of the Transactional Reporting Service is ISBN-13: 978-0-8138-2721-6/2006.

First edition, 1998
Second edition, 2006

Library of Congress Cataloging-in-Publication Data

Stein, M. L. (Meyer L.)
    Newswriter's handbook : an introduction to journalism / M.L. Stein, Susan F. Paterno, and R. Christopher Burnett.—2nd ed.
        p. cm.
    Includes index.
    ISBN-13: 978-0-8138-2721-6 (alk. paper)
    ISBN-10: 0-8138-2721-3 (alk. paper)
    1. Journalism—Vocational guidance.   I. Paterno, Susan.   II. Burnett, R. Christopher   III. Title.

PN4797.S67 2006
070.4023—dc22

                                                                2005027820

The last digit is the print number: 9 8 7 6 5 4 3 2

Contents

Preface

In the 21st century, the demands placed on news professionals are greater than ever. Not only must journalists adhere to traditional standards of accuracy and fairness, but rapidly advancing technology and a more skeptical public are requiring that journalists be quick, be able to handle multiple tasks at the same time, and adhere to ever higher standards of ethical behavior. Under the banner of convergence, students studying journalism today must prepare to write stories that will appear in print and online versions of their publication, and then also be prepared to appear on camera to report before a television audience.

This can be daunting to some students who begin studying journalism thinking they want to write magazine articles on things that already interest them or travel the world for publications such as *National Geographic*. Of course there are jobs such as these, but the vast majority of young news professionals will launch their careers on small daily or weekly publications, or report for small-market television or radio stations. On these publications the most important sought-after quality—good writing and editing skills—remains the same as a generation ago.

Thus, one of this book's main objectives is to teach writing and reporting skills necessary in the job market. Another objective is to give students an understanding of the reporting process and the demands it makes in terms of accuracy, fairness, and that subtle but extremely important element called *news judgment*.

The authors also hope that the reader will realize the importance of being an ethical journalist, one who reports fairly and leaves his or her biases out of the story. In an increasingly partisan political environment, in which reporters are being held to higher standards than ever before in covering government, ethics are of paramount importance.

The book emphasizes these qualities and provides insights from professional journalists who have done it all. Some stories cited as illustrations of good writing and reporting in this second edition are from professionals working on the nation's leading newspapers such as the *New York Times* and *Los Angeles Times*. Other stories come from respected state capital city publications like the *Sacramento* (Calif.) *Bee* and *Columbus* (Ohio) *Dispatch*.

However, this edition also highlights the work of excellent young reporters writing for papers like the *Ashland* (Ohio) *Times-Gazette* and *Long Beach* (Calif.) *Press-Telegram*. Most recent journalism school graduates get hired at papers such as these, and it is here that they get the opportunities to make significant differences in their community and even win reporting awards. Some talented reporters and editors make entire careers working at these smaller and mid-sized publications.

The second edition of this textbook also provides greater emphasis on recent legal trends involving journalism and focuses attention on ethical scandals that in recent years have strained the credibility of news organizations large and small. A new section on obituary writing is added, and greater emphasis is given to opportunities on the World Wide Web.

However, neither this text nor any other can, by itself, mold one into a competent journalist. Aspiring reporters and editors are urged to read newspapers, magazines and books, both in hard copy and online versions. Knowledge of government and business, still under-reported by most news organizations, is critically important. Knowing how the system works is crucial in journalism if reporters are to go beyond the superficial.

We also suggest that reporting classes encourage students both to write for their school newspapers and explore writing opportunities and internships off campus. Two stories in this textbook were written by students for campus newspapers. Student newspapers are crucial training grounds, as are internships that give students the opportunity to see first-hand whether journalism is for them. Here, more than in the classroom, students can get real-world experience meeting deadlines and putting together stories using multiple sources.

Finally, this book is designed to excite students about the possibilities that come with committing to a career in the news business. Journalists, more than any other professional, get a first-hand, eyewitness view of the world and get paid to write about events in a way that can make a difference in their communities. The challenges in this task are great, but the rewards are many for those who strive to make careers reporting accurately and fairly.

Acknowledgments

"Are Red-Light Cameras the Ticket to Safety?" by Wendy Thomas Russell, April 21,2003, Long Beach *Press-Telegram*. Copyright 2003 by the Long Beach Press-Telegram. Reprinted by permission.

"Our View: Tuition Fees Not Unfair," by Jeff Overley, March 29, 2004, *Daily Forty-Niner*. Copyright 2004 by Forty-Niner Publications, California State University at Long Beach. Reprinted by permission.

"Slicing the L.B. Pie: Council Members' Budgets Differ on Staffing, Car Expenses," by Jason Gewirtz, Sept. 7, 2003, Long Beach *Press-Telegram*. Copyright 2003 by the Long Beach Press-Telegram. Reprinted by permission.

"A Hard Lesson: Clintonville Preschool is Focusing on Safety After Death of Child," by Tim Doulin, April 22, 2005, *The Columbus Dispatch*. Copyright 2005 by the Dispatch Printing Company. Reprinted by permission.

"Gates Puts Patient behind Bars," by Mary Ann Milbourn, Jan. 3, 1996, *Orange County Register*. Reprinted with permission of the Orange County Register, copyright 1996.

"Support for Bush, War, Starting to Slip," by Joe Hallett, May 2, 2004, *The Columbus Dispatch*. Copyright 2004 by the Dispatch Printing Company. Reprinted by permission.

"Getting Organized," by Jack Hart, Apr. 8, 1995, *Editor & Publisher*. Copyright 1995 Jack Hart. Reprinted by permission.

"Absence Shifted Marriage Vote," by Jason Gewirtz, June 3, 2004, Long Beach *Press-Telegram*. Copyright 2004 by the Long Beach Press-Telegram. Reprinted by permission.

"Over the Brink and Into Poverty," by Alan Johnson, Catherine Candisky and Jonathan Riskind, June 6, 2004, *The Columbus Dispatch*. Copyright 2004 by the Dispatch Printing Company. Reprinted by permission.

"The Sex Offender Next Door," by Paul Young, Sept. 22, 2002, Long Beach *Press-Telegram*. Copyright 2002 by the Long Beach Press-Telegram. Reprinted by permission.

"Rabin and Arafat Seal Their Accord: Old Warriors Now Face Task of Building upon Foundation," by Thomas L. Friedman, Sept. 14, 1993, *New York Times*. Copyright by The New York Times Co. Reprinted by permission.

"15 to Life: Bruce Koklich Sentenced for Killing His Wife," by Wendy Thomas Russell, March 17, 2004, Long Beach *Press-Telegram*. Copyright 2004 by the Long Beach Press-Telegram. Reprinted by permission.

"Graduation Stole Raises Tensions," by Marlo Jo Fisher, June 18, 2004, *The Orange County Register*. Copyright 2004 by the *Orange County Register*. Reprinted by permission.

"Builders Approve Code to Child-Proof Swimming Pools," by Jeffrey Miller, Sept. 20 1990, *The Orange County Register*. Reprinted with permission of the Orange County Register, copyright 1990.

"Getting It Right," by Keith Shelton, Apr. 16, 1994, *Editor & Publisher*. Copyright 1994 Keith Shelton. Reprinted by permission.

"Medical Pot Smokers Sway City Council," by Jason Gewirtz, June 15, 2004, Long Beach *Press-Telegram*. Copyright 2004, the Long Beach Press-Telegram. Reprinted by permission.

"Mothers Rally to Halt Gang Killings," by Geoffrey Mohan, Oct. 8, 1995, *Los Angeles Times*. Copyright 1995 Geoffrey Mohan. Reprinted by permission.

"Neighbors up in Arms over Marines' Aircraft Noise," by James W. Crawley, Oct. 19, 1995, *San Diego Union-Tribune*. Copyright 1996 The San Diego Union-Tribune. Reprinted by permission of the publisher.

"A Life Story: Garden Grove Native Kept Gardens Growing," by Robin Hinch, April 28, 2002, *Orange County Register*. Reprinted by permission of the Orange County Register, Copyright 2002.

"Program to Aid Minority Teachers Is in Peril," by Jolayne Houtz, Nov. 9, 1995, *Seattle Times*. Copyright 1995 Seattle Times Company.

"One City's Tale of Economic Development," by Jocelyn Allison, Feb. 24, 2005, *Ashland* (Ohio) *Times-Gazette*. Reprinted by permission.

"Seniors Face Eviction from San Francisco Complex," by Catherine Bowman, *San Francisco Chronicle*. Copyright San Francisco Chronicle. Reprinted by permission.

Code of Ethics of the Society of Professional Journalists. Reprinted by permission.

"31 Arrested in Investigation of Theft Ring," by Kevin Mayhood and Evan Goodenow, April 23, 2005, *The Columbus* (Ohio) *Dispatch*. Copyright 2005 by the Dispatch Printing Company. Reprinted by permission.

"Animal Rights Activists Draw Convictions," by Stuart Pfeifer, Jan. 18, 1996, *Orange County Register*. Reprinted with the permission of the Orange County Register, copyright 1996.

"Honor Student Gets Four Months in Traffic Death," by Vicki Allen, Feb. 28, 1984, *The Sacramento Bee*. Reprinted by permission of the Sacramento Bee.

"Deputies' Intolerance Alleged in Trial," by Edgar Sanchez, Jan. 13, 1996, *The Sacramento Bee*. Reprinted by permission of the Sacramento Bee.

"$50,000 in Billings Focus of Dispute. Sullivan Trustees Release Attorney's Memo or Department Lawsuit," by Darcie Loreno, *Ashland* (Ohio) *Times-Gazette*. April 23, 2005. Reprinted by permission.

"Claims Would Bankrupt Garcia Estate, Lawyers Say," by Torri Minton, Jan. 24, 1996, *San Francisco Chronicle*. San Francisco Chronicle. Reprinted by permission.

"Savannah's Secret of Success: Residents Credit Community's Closeness to Strong Sense of Volunteerism," by Jocelyn Allison, Aug. 19, 2003, *Ashland* (Ohio) *Times-Gazette*. Copyright 2003 by the Ashland Times-Gazette.

"Ashland Boy Preparing for Third Heart Surgery," by Jarred Opatz, April 13, 2005, *Ashland* (Ohio) *Times-Gazette*. Copyright 2003 by the Ashland Times-Gazette.

"Importance of Pap Smears," by Beth Francis, *Best of Gannett Magazine, 1994 edition, P-26* (originally in Fort Myers [Fla.] *News-Press*). Copyright 1994 Best of Gannett Magazine. Reprinted by permission of the publisher.

"A Member for Life," by Gary Krino, *Orange County Register*. Reprinted with permission of The Orange County Register, copyrighted 1996.

"Powter Keg," by Jeannine Stein, Sept. 14, 1994, *Los Angeles Times*. Copyright, 1994, Los Angeles Times. Reprinted by permission.

"The Main Man: Fathers Play a Key Role in the Development of Sons and Daughters," by Cheryl Rosenberg Neubert, June 20, 2004, the *Orange County Register*. Reprinted by permission of the Orange County Register.

"Some Commonsense Pointers," Feb. 1996, *University of California at Berkeley Wellness Letter*. Reprinted with permission from the University of California at Berkeley Wellness Letter, Health Letter Associates, 1996.

"Gene Mutation, Not Chance, May Be Behind Some Cancers," by Misti Crane, April 21, 2005, the *Columbus* (Ohio) *Dispatch*. Copyright 2005 by the Dispatch Printing Company. Reprinted by permission.

"$250 a Semester for Textbooks? You Can Believe It," by David J. Smollar, Jan. 15, 1996, *Orange County Register*. Reprinted with permission of the Orange County Register, copyright 1996.

"Wells Finally Snags First Interstate," by Peter Stinton, Jan. 25, 1996, *San Francisco Chronicle*. San Francisco Chronicle. Reprinted by permission.

"Job Losses Lead Women to New Careers," by Karen Hanna, Feb. 24, 2005, the *Ashland* (Ohio) *Times-Gazette*. Reprinted by permission.

"Hornet Rivals Return to Nest: Wildcasts Look to End Sac State's Year for Third-Straight Season," by Jimmy Spencer, March 2, 2005, *The State Hornet*. Reprinted with permission, the State Hornet of Sacramento State University, 2005.

"U.S.-Gulp—Favored in Soccer," by Mark Zeigler, Jan. 10, 1996, *San Diego Union-Tribune*. Copyright 1996 The San Diego Union-Tribune. Reprinted by permission of the publisher.

"An Atmosphere for Learning: State Standards Mean Preschool Activities All Must Have Purpose," by Karen Hanna, Jan. 5, 2005, the *Ashland* (Ohio) *Times-Gazette*. Reprinted by permission.

"Where the TV News Jobs Are: Fox, Cable," by Lou Prato, Oct. 1991, *American Journalism Review*. Reprinted by permission of the American Journalism Review.

Newswriter's Handbook

SECOND EDITION

1

What Is News?

When asked to describe pornography, Supreme Court Justice Potter Stewart said simply: "I know it when I see it." Many editors use a similar litmus test to decide what news is, what to cover and what to pass over based on years spent developing "news judgment," an almost indefinable instinct. As a student of journalism, you must immediately begin developing a news instinct. Good ideas allow you to write stories that appeal to readers and to advance to better and higher-paying jobs. Without ideas, you will fail. Without enterprise, you will fail. Without discipline and devotion, you will fail. But the converse is also true: Anyone with ideas, enterprise and a willingness to work hard can succeed in the media business.

So, where do ideas come from? Some people are lucky. They were born curious. They see in every encounter the germ of an idea. When a casual conversation in the dining hall turns to confessions of widespread cheating on exams, these folks see a story. When a couple of students holding placards in front of the college president's office begin chanting derogatory slogans, these folks start asking questions. When police officers arrive at the dorms to break up a domestic dispute, these folks take out notebooks and start interviewing. For others, though, the task of finding a story idea is more oppressive than taking an exam. "Where do I go? Whom do I talk to? Why won't *you* give me an idea?" some journalism students whine. The last thing your boss wants to hear from you is, "Won't you do the work for me?"

So, here's where we start: We're going to help you develop news judgment, a skill that will take years of reporting and writing to master.

Start reading the newspaper daily, listening to all-news radio, watching TV news, and reading news on the Web. Become an active thinker instead of a passive reader or listener. Why did a story show up in the newspaper and not on TV? Which stories appear in all these media? Why do you suppose that some stories merit widespread media attention and others appear only in the paper, or on the radio or on TV? Why does TV devote 10 seconds to a story about a local municipal bankruptcy while the newspaper devotes 45 inches? Why does TV devote five minutes to a story about a local model's murder while the newspaper gives it five inches?

By thinking critically about the stories you're reading and hearing, you can begin to think critically about the media. And you can also begin looking for trends that tell you what professionals consider newsworthy. Professional news judgments change, too, as editors and news directors seek to discover what their readers and viewers want to know. Obviously, some editors—especially those at supermarket tabloids—go straight to the cheap seats without apology, sell sensationalism, sex and scandal, make a bundle of money and successfully defend their First Amendment right to do so. But a great many purveyors of news also believe that the media—the only businesses in America protected by the Constitution—have to serve the public as well as the bottom line. As a consequence, editors try to strike a balance between their need to sell news and their public service responsibility to protect democracy by serving as a watchdog of government.

Spot or Hard or Straight News, Features, News Features, Editorials and Opinions

Before you can start developing news judgment, you need to recognize the different sorts of stories that appear in your newspaper and on TV. They differ in how they're written and their graphic treatment—that is, how they look on the page or on the screen. Pick up a copy of your local newspaper. The front page usually showcases four to eight stories, deemed by editors to be the most important news of the day. A local newspaper such as the *Press-Telegram,* in Long Beach, California, will choose to highlight the local issues its editors believe most important to its local readers. A national newspaper like the *New York Times* will highlight stories its editors believe most essential to its national, more sophisticated, audience. Each publication bases its news judgment on the wants and needs of its particular audience, just as you should as you begin formulating story ideas for your campus newspaper or TV news show.

The *Long Beach Press-Telegram* and the *New York Times* have a few things in common, too: They, as do most American newspapers, put a mix of spot news, features and news features on Page One. Sometimes telling the difference is as easy as noticing how each story looks on the page. Often, features are accompanied by large photographs, are run across three or four columns and appear in a box. Straight news, by contrast, tends to run without photos, often across one or two columns. But the opposite can be true, too: Spot news, particularly the story that appears above the fold, might run across five columns and come with several photos, charts and graphs. A better way to tell the difference is by reading the story's lead, the first few paragraphs that explain the story's focus.

Spot news, also called hard news or straight news, is easiest to recognize. A plane crashes. Terrorists blow up a federal building. A drug bust occurs on campus. A fire burns down a day care center, killing several small children. Spot news usually happens within a 24-hour time frame. Reporters respond to those events, interview officials, victims and witnesses, collect details from the scene, and then follow a fairly standard and useful formula for writing the story, putting the most important details in the beginning, or lead, of the story.

How do reporters decide what's most important? By answering the following questions: Who? What? When? Where? Why? How? Why is this information or event important? How will this issue affect my readers' lives?

If you don't have answers to those questions, you're not done reporting. Go back and ask more questions. As soon as you have the answers, sit down and ask yourself, What's the absolute most important one of those answers? From that answer, you will craft your lead. The most important questions in disaster stories—plane crashes, fires, freeway wrecks, earthquakes, bomb blasts, for example—are, How many died? How many survived? How many were injured?

> Six people survived a plane crash that killed 214 Tuesday at 7:30 p.m. when an American Airlines jet, en route from Miami and off course as it prepared for landing, slammed into a remote mountainside 14 miles from the international airport in Cali, Colombia.
> Officials at the crash site offered no explanation for the accident. They hope a transcript of the cockpit crew's conversation at the time of the crash, contained in a flight recorder recovered from the wreckage, would provide answers in the coming days, they said.
> It was the worst air disaster involving an American carrier since 1988.

"Who?" Six people survived . . .

"What?" . . . a plane crash that killed 214 . . .

"When?" Tuesday at 7:30 p.m. . . .

"How?" (did it happen?) after an American Airlines jet, off course as it prepared for landing, slammed into a remote mountainside

"Where?" 14 miles from the airport in Cali, Colombia.

"Why?" Officials at the crash site offered no explanation for the accident, and said they hope a transcript of the cockpit crew's conversation at the time of the crash, contained in a flight recorder recovered from the wreckage, would provide answers in the coming days.

"Why is this event important?" It was the worst air disaster involving an American carrier since 1988.

The writer's job is to keep the reader wanting more. Straight news usually informs readers quickly, clearly and concisely in a "just the facts, ma'am" writing style that holds interest because it imparts vital information in a simple, easy-to-understand way.

Features demand the same—and often more—attention to facts and details, but they also ask the reporter to use more sophisticated storytelling devices, narrative techniques free of purple prose, muddled adjectives, clichés and stereotypes. Often, a well-crafted feature will start with an anecdotal lead and include answers to Who? What? When? Where? Why? How? Who cares? in the first five or six paragraphs. Features run on Page One of the city or metro section and in sports, entertainment or special lifestyle sections.

Good reporting and writing can be found in all papers, from the campus weekly or small-town daily to major metropolitan newspapers such as the *Los Angeles Times* or *Washington Post*. In fact, some of the best writing is found in the hundreds of medium and small dailies across the country that offer the best opportunities for young journalists fresh from the college campus. The following feature from the *Long Beach* (Calif.) *Press-Telegram* starts with an anecdote about a college student, a woman who symbolizes the story's focus, who has run a red light and received a traffic ticket. The story's focus is contained in the paragraph known as the "nut graph" and is summed up usually in one or two paragraphs. Look, too, for the cosmic quote, a quote high in the story, often from an expert, that supports the nut graph.

By Wendy Thomas Russell

LONG BEACH—When college student Alexia Arbuckle ran a red light at Bellflower Boulevard and Willow Street last summer, she didn't see the set of digital-video cameras stationed above the intersection. But they saw her. Now, the 20-year-old watches silently as her violation is displayed in full color inside a wood-paneled bungalow that doubles as Long Beach Superior Court's traffic division.

At a judge's instruction, Long Beach Police Detective Dave Lauro plays the tape in slow motion, showing the signals turning from green to yellow to red. A moment later, a white car appears in the frame—no less than 30 feet behind the limit line. It passes through the intersection without slowing. Lauro pushes a button to reveal a still photograph of the car's interior.

"This is a close-up of the driver, who does appear to be the defendant on my right," he says.

It's what prosecutors might call a slam-dunk case. Arbuckle is convicted and fined on the spot.

Thousands of drivers have been cited so far under the city's 18-month-old red-light camera program. But whether the cameras are doing their job is still a matter of considerable debate.

For years, critics have argued that red-light technology invades drivers' privacy and uses law enforcement to line the pockets of private companies. The cameras are more about revenue, they say, and less about safety.

To that, supporters point to a long list of cities that swear by their red-light programs. They say the cameras have reduced accidents—and traffic violations—by 20, 30, even 50 percent. . .

—Long Beach *Press-Telegram*

In this story, the focus, or "nut graf," is summarized in a paragraph that takes the reader from the anecdote about Arbuckle's conviction to the story's more general emphasis on drivers' experiences with red-light radar:

> Thousands of drivers have been cited so far under the city's
> 18-month-old red-light camera program. But whether the cameras
> are doing their job is still a matter of considerable debate.

The previous story uses an individual to personify an issue. Frequently, writers of profiles, a type of feature that showcases an individual, use anecdotal leads as well. Profiles almost always have a news hook, a significant reason to put the person in the news. The profile might highlight a public figure—a politician, important business executive, student leader, college president or actor; it also might put the spotlight on a lesser known, but equally important, average person doing extraordinary things.

Don't confuse news and feature writing with editorial and opinion writing. While reporting, or gathering information, for news and feature stories, journalists follow an industry-wide convention of writing the most fair and balanced piece they can. To do this, journalists interview as many sources as there are points of view on any given issue (at least two but usually many more) and report fairly and without bias their news sources' opinions, with facts, statistics and anecdotes for supporting evidence.

The editorial or opinion piece, by contrast, makes no pretense of being fair, though writers strive to argue their case well enough—using accurate facts and statistics—to change other people's minds. In most newspapers, you'll find editorial and opinion pieces in one place: the editorial and op-ed page (so called because of its placement opposite the editorial page). Editorials are usually unsigned columns voicing the opinion of the newspaper's owners, penned by staff members hired specifically to champion or criticize causes and initiatives from a partisan perspective. Opinion pieces usually run on the op-ed page, are written by guest or staff columnists and often, though not always, reinforce the beliefs of the editorial writers. Editorials and opinion pieces are never forums for uninformed, ignorant rantings; the writers of these columns spend as much time reporting their pieces as do news and feature writers.

The following piece, written by Jeff Overley, the opinion editor of the *Daily Forty-Niner,* the student newspaper at California State University in Long Beach, California, illustrates how students can write insightful editorials on issues of direct relevance to a college-age population. As is the case with nearly all editorials, the opinion piece did not carry his name. This is the case because it is assumed that the piece reflects the opinion of the publication, not just the writer. The editorial ran in 2004, when students across California were protesting tuition fee hikes to help reduce the state's higher education spending deficit. The editorial argues that the fee hikes are fair, a position contrary to that held by many students. The story ran in the *Daily Forty-Niner* with the headline "Tuition Fees Not Unfair."

By Jeff Overly

If we lived in a utopia, all the things vital to human welfare would be free, higher education among them. We instead reside in a capitalist waste that provides complimentary elementary and secondary schooling while charging for a college education.

No viable mass movement in the United States has even protested college costs on the grounds that such schooling should be free to everyone. Nor do we ever hear about mass rallies praising states that are able to make public universities more affordable. But when prices go up, so do the placards and picket signs denouncing elevated fees.

This has been the scene across the country during the past year, as state budget deficits become ubiquitous and force a reduction in subsidization of education. The protests are certainly understandable. For one thing, no one likes to pay for anything they have become accustomed to receiving at a lower cost.

Oftentimes, a sense of injustice arises that perceives higher prices as inherently unfair and always the result of a greedy government with misplaced prerogatives. And when it comes to a critical social good such as education, people tend to equate rising costs with neglecting the country's future.

It is unclear if these sentiments are justified in some U.S. states, but one thing is certain: for Americans desiring reasonably priced higher education, California is about as close to utopia as it gets.

The state's community colleges, despite fast rising fees, are the lowest priced in the nation. One year ago they charged $11 per unit; costs are currently $18 per unit and stand to rise to $24 per unit next semester in an effort to raise state revenue in a time of fiscal calamity.

Assuming the hike is approved, community college attendees will face an annual tuition payment of about $800. If this seems equitable on the surface, it becomes a bargain basement buy when one notices the national community college tuition average of $1,905.

Then there are the four-year public universities. California's state universities carry an almost $2,400 annual price tag, while the schools of its more prestigious University of California system average about $5,300. Averaging the two gives a figure of about $3,850, which compares favorably with the national average of $4,700.

So, a California student who attends two years of community college and two years at an "average" university will end up paying a total of $9,300 in tuition fees. A student paying the national average will spend $13,210.

California's students, and students across the nation for that matter, should also recognize the fact that the fees they pay cover only a fraction of the cost of higher education. In California in 2003, the state spent almost $3,000 on every community college student, nearly $10,000 on every state university enrollee and almost $20,000 for every student in the University of California system.

Even in light of such generosity on behalf of the state, protest has its merits. It can show that the university population is responsive, can force careful and fair decision-making on the part of top administrators and may help to bring costs back down once the budget nightmare subsides.

But as they hit the pavement and chant their slogans, protesters should remember that climate isn't the only thing that makes California utopian.

—Daily Forty-Niner

For the beginning journalism student, opinion pieces can serve as a source of story ideas. In the previous piece, for example, the writer asks a key question: "What makes a hike in tuition fair or unfair? Is it enough to simply compare last year's prices with the upcoming year's prices and generalize?"

Astute young journalists would take that germ of an idea and localize it to their own school's situation. How does the tuition situation in your state compare with that in California? Are tuition rates above, or below, the national average? And what would tuition fee hikes, if approved, specifically pay for that would benefit students?

Remember, too, the importance of what have come to be called "Hey Martha" stories. "Hey Martha" stories make readers stand up and take notice, as in the case of the hypothetical husband calling to his wife: "Hey Martha, did ya see that story about the horse that mated with the zebra? They got a zorse!" But even those stories often contain conflict. In the case of the zorse, a true story, breeders created a faster racehorse by combining the speedy zebra with a quarter horse. Will it be allowed to run in quarter horse races? How do quarter horse owners feel about the possibility of losing prize money to a genetically altered breed? They likely will have some objections.

If your editor assigns you a story, you can assume it's news. But news is never that simple. Reporters are expected to make news judgments on the spot, often without the assistance of a more knowledgeable editor. A political candidate makes a statement at a press conference. Is it really news or has she said it before? The city manager announces "new" noise-level requirements for air traffic. Are they new or were the same rules assigned two years ago and often violated? A federal official issues rosy figures on employment or wholesale pricing. Do they represent gains or is someone merely playing a numbers game to make the agency look good?

The answers are frequently hard to unravel, given the tendency of some bureaucrats to hype facts. To gain the knowledge and experience you'll need to learn to separate news from zeal requires asking tough questions that probe beyond exaggeration and public relations double-talk. Before starting any story, get the clips: Research it by seeking from the library previous stories written on the same topic. By doing your homework, you can avoid big mistakes that might cost you a job.

Take, for example, the story of the young reporter who went to a routine student government meeting, returned and told his editor nothing happened.

"What do you mean nothing happened?" the surprised editor asked.

"Five minutes after the meeting started, the president told everybody to leave, so we all left."

"Why?" the editor asked.

"Because she said they were holding a closed door session to discuss a senator's impeachment."

The reporter never bothered to inquire on what grounds the president was closing the meeting. Had he asked, he would have learned the student government was violating its constitution by closing the meeting. At the very least, the reporter should have informed the paper's readers of the student government's blatant disregard for its own constitution. He also should have followed up with questions about the impending impeachment: Who was being impeached and for what?

It is always a story when government officials oust reporters. The ousting becomes the story.

To help you begin honing your judgment, we're including a checklist so that you can figure out whether your story is newsworthy. News is:

1. Out of the ordinary, a departure from routine or convention.
2. Topical and timely. News has a short life span.
3. Significant in terms of human progress or failure.
4. Of local interest.
5. Emotional; an event that will make people laugh or cry.
6. Of widespread interest. The more people affected by the news, the more important it becomes.
7. Crime, disaster and upheaval.
8. Government and political proceedings.
9. Pocketbook issues such as taxes, inflation and cost of living that affect people's lives.
10. Prominent. Famous or well-known people, both nationally and locally, make the news.
11. What people are talking about.
12. Change. The passing of an era, old landmarks being torn down, new lifestyles replacing old, new attitudes on old questions, anniversaries of major events.

Suggested Assignments

1. Bring a copy of your local newspaper to class and identify the type of stories on Page One. Which ones are straight news? Features?

2. Identify an editorial and an opinion piece. How do opinion pieces differ from news and features? How are they similar?
3. Propose a straight news story that you might write for your campus newspaper.
4. Propose a news or feature story about date rape on campus. Who would you interview for the story and why?

Finding Stories

2

All stories boil down to a handful of themes that illustrate the fundamental conflicts of life: birth and death. Triumph over human suffering. Heroism and cowardice. Selflessness and greed. Crime and the quest for justice. Honor and corruption. Freedom and oppression. One person's fight against the tyranny of the majority. Sacrifice for the greater good. Love against all odds. The action of fate, or chance, in the world.

Within the context of these universal themes, American journalists also historically have acted as guardians of democracy, serving as a watchdog of the government, ferreting out official malfeasance and corruption, giving voters the information they need to cast aside incompetents through the election process. The journalists' task, it has been said, is to write the rough draft of history. Whereas it was once sufficient to simply record government proceedings, journalists today must explain official action, always mindful of answering the question: How will this affect my readers' lives?

In a newsroom, there are usually more stories on any given day than reporters to cover them. Based on news judgment, assigning editors decide which stories to cover. The most straightforward stories come from police scanners and press releases; others come from journalists assigned to beats, specific areas of expertise. Hurricanes, fires involving death or large monetary losses, earthquakes, homicides—especially when the victim is even remotely well-known in the community—are easy to recognize. But the majority of what beginning reporters cover centers on governments, cops, courts, pets, weather, ethnic festivals and holidays. The most successful starters are expected to find stories that go beyond routine coverage. How? By looking at people and events in terms of the universal themes we've discussed. In any gathering of human beings, you will find compelling stories.

First, look for something out of place. Let's say you're assigned to cover the student council meeting, in which next year's budget is under discussion. As you review the figures, you notice a discrepancy. Most campus clubs of similar size have received roughly the same amount of funding, but you notice that the radio station has a budget $20,000 more than that of any other organization. You ask why and discover that the president of the student council is also the director of the radio station. He plans to join four other students on an all-expense-paid trip to Radio City Music Hall in New York City. He also asked for and received funds to bankroll a publicity stunt that includes nude skydivers. You write a story explaining to students how their fees are being spent, leaving it up to your readers and the editorial writers to decide whether the information warrants a recall election. A less curious reporter would never have noticed the discrepancy, would never have asked why and would have written a substandard story that never answered the basic question: How will this affect my readers?

The late Scott Newhall, former editor of the *San Francisco Chronicle* before he retired to edit the *Newhall Signal* in Santa Clarita, California, used to routinely tell wet-behind-the-ears reporters one true thing about journalism: "There are no boring stories, just boring writers." With a quick mind, enterprise and hard work, reporters can frame any story to reflect the universal themes that touch us all.

When President John F. Kennedy was assassinated in 1963, for example, journalist Jimmy Breslin left the reporters at the Capitol Rotunda and interviewed the grave digger. It was Breslin's ability to see great stories that others missed that eventually led to his lucrative, prestigious and powerful career as a New York City columnist. In another instance of creative journalism, a *Des Moines* (Iowa) *Register* reporter noticed a spate of briefs in his paper about farmers dying or being maimed in farming accidents. His curiosity led him to the discovery that farming had become the nation's most dangerous occupation. The story he wrote about it won him the Pulitzer Prize.

"The best stories are often the most obvious; they're the ones that everyone else has missed," award-winning reporter and writer Ken Fuson said in the industry trade publication *Editor & Publisher.* "The quickest way to succeed in this business is to figure which way everyone else is headed, then go in the opposite direction. And always, always be open to the obvious."

Look for fresh angles, Fuson suggests. The year in which "Sesame Street" creator Jim Henson died, many reporters did routine stories that included spending the morning interviewing four-year-olds as they watched Sesame Street. One quick-thinking reporter realized that the children who were four when the show started were now in college, and she interviewed them about Henson's effect on their lives.

"Look everywhere for ideas and listen for them, too," Fuson went on. "I have trained myself to immediately ask, 'Is this a story?' Whenever you find yourself laughing at a situation, or shaking your head, or saying to someone, 'Listen to this,' you've probably got a story." If the story has been done, he says, don't do it again. "If it's been done before and I have to do it, then I want to do it better than it was done before." The best stories, he said, "have conflict and resolution."

Some other suggestions on where to find ideas:

1. **Ask people what makes them mad, sad or happy.** Talk to them about problems that concern or affect them; ask how they would fix the problem if given the opportunity. Listen to conversations in restaurants, in the dining hall, in waiting rooms or study halls. What are people talking about?

2. **Read voraciously, listen to radio and TV news and zero in on controversies that also may be happening in your own community.** Then, localize the story and demonstrate how your community is trying to grapple with the issue or problem. Copying the story is plagiarism, but finding a new angle unique to your community is good journalism.

3. **Ask yourself: What are the major problems in my community?** Then report on how the people charged with solving those problems are succeeding. If the problems are not being solved, write a story about why not.

4. **Look for watchdog stories.** Are the people who govern you and your readers successfully doing the job they were elected or assigned to do? Are they spending the tax dollars or student fees they collect wisely and responsibly? If not, why not?

5. **Make use of news releases.** News releases come from public relations people who want to publicize a cause or event. Generally biased and often factually incorrect, news releases should never be reprinted verbatim, but they can serve as an excellent source for story ideas. Double-check all information in a news release before publishing.

6. **Comfort the afflicted and afflict the comfortable.** How do powerful leaders in your community deal with the less fortunate?

7. **Find stories in the newspaper.** Many times, news reporters fail to follow up on what might make a terrific story. Here's an example of what a reporter can turn up: A brief news story appeared in the local paper about an illegal immigrant from Mexico falling off a train and under its wheels. His leg was severed. A homeless man saved him and took him to a local hospital. After reading the story in her paper, a reporter visited the victim in the hospital and discovered a much bigger story: He had stowed away on the freight train in a desperate attempt to enter the United States, seeking work. The reporter found statistics to support a huge increase in the number of immigrant stowaways being crushed and maimed on freight trains; she documented official attempts to grapple with the problem. The story first appeared in the *Orange County Register* but was reprinted on the wires and was read throughout the nation.

    In another case, a reporter saw a small item in her paper from a hearing in probate court about a 38-year-old deaf man whose lawyer was protesting his reincarceration in a mental hospital where he had spent the last 30 years of his life. After a six-month investigation, the reporter wrote a story about an overburdened, underfunded mental health agency that wrongly incarcerated the man as a young boy because he was deaf and then failed to educate or socialize him, leaving him without language and with no hope of escape. After the story ran, the man was freed from the institution and awarded a multimillion-dollar legal settlement.

8. **Look for trends. Document change over time.** Make sense of everyday news stories and put them into context. If you report on a series of rapes on and

around your campus, ask the police what the crimes have in common. To spot trends, ask yourself and others what isolated news events might mean in a larger context; do they signal a change in mainstream assumptions?

9. **Watch for world records, important anniversaries, weird people and potatoes that bear an uncanny resemblance to Liza Minnelli; they make good stories.** Or, as discussed in the previous chapter, look for anything that makes that hypothetical husband shout: "Hey, Martha!"

10. **Scan advertisements.** Some weird stuff turns up in the personals, but don't stop there. One student reporter noticed an ad looking for intelligent men willing to donate sperm for money. The student wrote an award-winning, first-person account of his trials and tribulations as a would-be donor.

Story Meetings

When you have gathered a list of story ideas, you're expected to present them at a story meeting, a gathering of your assigning editor and his or her staff of reporters; there, ideas are focused on and tested. At story meetings, reporters and editors discuss the ideas and offer suggestions on angles to pursue and sources to contact. Sometimes, as in the case of breaking news, story meetings consist of a five-minute briefing session with your editor before you're sent off to the scene of a car wreck, fire, double homicide or hastily called news conference. Never leave on an assignment without a clear idea of your editor's expectation. Never be afraid, of course, to dispute the angle your editor gave you on a story, especially if your interviews and field research tell you the story needs an entirely different focus. Editors depend on the news judgment of reporters and expect them to change the story's direction when the facts lead to a different conclusion.

Finding Sources

Now that you have an idea, you'll begin the arduous task of reporting, gathering the information you'll need to write a balanced, fair and accurate account of the issue, problem or controversy. Reporting entails collecting evidence—facts, statistics, anecdotes and quotes from people with differing viewpoints—that support your story's focus. Begin reporting with the story's premise or focus in mind and always be aware that your reporting will likely require you to change your point of view as the facts twist and turn in different directions.

The most important part of reporting is interviewing sources. Try to interview:

- The official most directly involved in the problem.
- Someone who disagrees with the handling of the problem.
- A victim hurt by the problem.
- A person helped by the problem, if applicable.
- An outside expert to lend perspective on the problem and the way it's being handled by officials.

Quotes and Attributions

The quality of your finished product will depend largely on two things: the depth and thoroughness of your reporting and your ability to collect quotes, or, for TV, sound bites. Identifying what constitutes a good quote requires experience and skill. If, when interviewing a source, a little voice in your head exclaims, "Gee, I've never heard it put quite that way before!" you probably have a good quote. Write it down. Quotes used correctly function as exclamation points, conveying opinion or moving the story forward in a surprising way.

Paragraph after paragraph of boring quotes that state facts you never bothered to corroborate with other sources will compel readers to turn to the comics. That's why skilled writers paraphrase information in concise language, boiling it down to what is most essential, careful not to lose the meaning of what the source was trying to say. Rarely should statistics, for example, be in quotes. Instead, paraphrase the information and attribute it to its source. The same holds true for most factual information. The writer of the following news story from the *Long Beach Press-Telegram* about office spending by city council members decided to paraphrase statistics rather than put the figures in direct quotes and attribute everything to the proposed city budget released by the mayor's office. Reporter Jason Gewirtz uses quotes from council members to convey information he is unable to restate more clearly and add color to the story. Note the richness of detail in this story, which is especially significant because it performs the local media's watchdog function over government spending. Further detail on each council member's spending accompanies the story in a graphic titled with the headline, "Who's Spending What?"

By Jason Gewirtz

LONG BEACH—City Council members each represent roughly the same number of people. But when it comes to their budgets, their spending is all over the map.

In the proposed 2004 city budget, the nine council members' office budgets range from a low of $287,984 to a high of $365,324. Mayor Beverly O'Neill, meanwhile, reports an $810,586 spending plan.

Overall, the costs are 5 percent lower than during the fiscal year that ends Sept. 30.

A breakdown of these expenses shows that most of the office costs, as is the case in all city departments, come from employee salaries, benefits and insurance. But the budgets also reveal different spending priorities for different districts, from car expenses to field office rents.

With the city in the middle of a massive fiscal shortfall, the individual office budgets of elected officials—who have final say over the entire $1.6 billion city budget—have received increased attention. A citizen's advisory committee that O'Neill formed last year recommended that council district budgets be equal to the average of all nine budgets. Citizens also suggested equal budgets in the unscientific "Voice Your Choice" survey the city commissioned last year.

Among the elected leaders, however, there's disagreement over whether all districts should be equal when it comes to spending.

"It's like saying every household should have the same budget," said Councilwoman Bonnie Lowenthal, who has the third-smallest budget on the council.

But Councilwoman Jackie Kell, whose proposed office budget is the lowest, questioned those offices that require more money than the average.

"When you're serving the same amount of people, more or less, what are they doing with that money, self aggrandizement or what?" she asked.

—Long Beach *Press-Telegram*

Not all stories, of course, are about budgets, taxes and spending, and other serious subjects. Stories exist even in the most commonplace of events, such as the daily weekday ritual in which parents drop their children off at school. For many readers, these stories hit a lot closer to home than more complex meeting stories.

In the following story, notice how the writer weaves direct quotes with a description of the scene at the parking lot where preschool children are being dropped off in the Clintonville neighborhood of Columbus, Ohio.

By Tim Doulin

As vehicles pull up to Overbrook Weekday Preschool to drop off children, Warren Powell stands at the ready.

Wearing an orange vest and carrying a traffic wand, Powell helps shepherd vehicles through the busy parking lot.

"We're just an extra set of eyes," said Powell, a 71-year-old retired chemist who volunteers to help direct traffic at the Clintonville school.

"We're just roving around the parking lot making sure there aren't any kids around."

Safety was a lesson learned the hard way at Overbrook.

In March 2004, 3-year-old Michael Breschi died after he wandered behind a sport-utility vehicle backing up in the parking lot.

After Michael's death, school officials, parents and volunteers from Overbrook Presbyterian Church—which houses the school—rallied to make sure nothing like that happens again.

With the help of a safety consultant and Columbus police, the school implemented a safer system this year for dropping off and picking up children.

At the curbside drop-off, a school official or volunteer helps children from their vehicles and leads them by the hand inside.

Parents who want to take their children inside the school can drive through a second entrance at the opposite end of the parking lot and park. Parents are told to hold their children's hands.

During pickups, parents park their vehicles and go inside to get their children.

The school, which teaches about 200 children, stresses a holding-hands philosophy, said Stacey Houser, whose 4-year-old son, Will, attends the school. There are school T-shirts that sport a big hand holding a small hand.

"After what happened, everybody keeps a tight hold," said Houser, a parking-lot volunteer.

Michael was struck in a parking area near the drop-off zone that requires vehicles to back out of parking spaces. Those spaces now are reserved for staff members.

Parents are encouraged to park in such a way that they don't have to back out of spaces.

Volunteers offer another set of eyes for drivers who must back up.

"Kids can be behind them," Powell said. "The parents like to know it is clear."

Vehicles must leave the parking lot through a designated exit. An enlarged crosswalk and directional markings have been added to the parking-lot pavement.

Drivers also must follow a set of rules, which include no chatting on cell phones, no drinking beverages and no passing other vehicles.

"We have made these changes which . . . I think are making the place safer," said Joyce Matthews, director of the school.

Maryan DeBrosse's daughter, Abigail, now 5, was in Michael's class.

"To this day, she still asks about him," said DeBrosse, whose 3-year-old son, Michael, also attends Overbrook.

DeBrosse said Michael's death had an impact on Abigail.

"She is very safety conscious," she said.

The school recently held a silent auction that raised more than $4,000. Some of the money, Matthews said, will be used to buy playground equipment in Michael's name.

—The Columbus Dispatch

Rather than start the story with a lead like "More than a year has passed since a 3-year-old boy died after wandering behind a sport-utility vehicle backing up at the Overday Weekday Preschool in Clintonville," the writer sets the scene to draw the reader in. The writer starts his story focusing on an adult directing traffic in the school's parking lot. Only in the fifth paragraph, after a couple paragraphs of direct quotes, does the reader learn the key point of the story—that "safety was a lesson learned the hard way" at the school through the death of a child.

This simple story illustrates how stories can be found in everyday events. And they are far from trivial fillers. For parents of school-age children, this story is most likely more important than a story about politicians spending tax money. Room exists for both kinds of news in the daily digest of stories that routinely fill America's newspapers.

Suggested Assignments

1. Submit five focused story ideas that you could write for your campus newspaper. Identify them as news or feature stories.
2. For each of those five ideas, submit the names and phone numbers of at least three sources you plan to contact. Explain what you hope to learn from those sources.
3. Explain how you would get an interview with a source who refuses to return your phone calls.
4. Explain what you would do if a key source refused to grant you an interview.
5. Identify the news hook in each of the news and feature stories reprinted in this chapter.
6. Identify the nut graph in each of those stories.

Basic Reporting

No matter how well you write, you will never be able to compensate for a badly reported story. Explaining an issue or a problem well requires becoming an expert in it; becoming an expert means mastering far more detail than your readers need to know. Often, experienced reporters use about 10 percent of the information gathered. Does that mean you're collecting 90 percent more information than you need? Not at all. The knowledge you gain from the details will give you the confidence you need to write a fair and accurate story. Without that knowledge you become one of the mediocre reporters who fail to understand the problem they're writing about and simply recite fact after quote after fact without any context or synthesis (otherwise known as the "dumping your notebook" approach).

First-rate reporters critically analyze a problem before they write about it. If you think through a problem, you're more likely to leave no questions unanswered. The following story is full of unanswered questions, even though it ran on the front page of the metro section in one of the country's largest dailies. The story details the struggles of an old rancher who, ignoring the protests of his wealthy neighbors, allowed the poor to build a squatter's settlement on his land. (It is a story, as discussed in Chapter 1, of "one person's fight against the tyranny of the majority.") Careful readers want more answers than they'll find in the story and will be frustrated by the reporter's carelessness. When readers and viewers become frustrated, they find the media less useful, lose trust in it and eventually stop reading the paper or viewing the broadcast.

> TRABUCO CANYON—For years, Sam Porter cast himself as the fighter for the little guy.
>
> He fought the county, he fought his neighbors and he fought almost anybody else who dared tell him what he could do on his sprawling 233-acre ranch.
>
> At age 68, Porter has another battle on his hands, but this time, he's being held back by failing health.
>
> A stroke in March left him partially paralyzed. And a gate erected by the Trabuco Canyon Community Association to resolve a longtime dispute has left him a virtual prisoner on his property.
>
> Porter curses and shakes his head under his trademark straw cowboy hat.

He can't say much these days. The stroke affected his speech. But mention his problems with the homeowners association and the hellfire blazes in his ice-blue eyes.

The locked gate blocks the only entrance to Porter's property. For a while, Porter gave keys to a friend who came to help him.

In November, he turned to the Dayle McIntosh Center for the Disabled, which arranged meals and therapy. But Meals on Wheels volunteers, who change every day, could not trade keys, so they couldn't get in.

Occupational, physical and speech therapists faced waits of up to 45 minutes to get in with needed treatment. Some of them left.

Anything that blocks Porter's access to government services is a violation of the Americans with Disabilities Act, said Juda Carter, an advocate with the Dayle McIntosh Center's Laguna Niguel office. She said repeated calls and letters to the homeowners association have gone unanswered.

Porter's wife, Jeanne, who is separated from Porter but still lives on the ranch and helps out, says the association is dragging its feet out of revenge.

"I don't think they are interested in cooperating," she said.

Porter and the association have been sparring since the 1980s, when Porter opened his property to illegal Mexican immigrants who formed a hodge-podge settlement of rented shacks and trailers dubbed Porterville.

The only way into his ranch was through Trabuco Highlands, a development of $250,000 homes overlooking Porter's property and the Cleveland Forest beyond.

Trabuco Highland neighbors, unhappy about the Porterville residents coming through their neighborhood, sued.

The upshot was a wrought-iron gate at the entrance to the ranch on Shadow Rock Lane that locked the shantytown residents in. Only Porter, his immediate family, and contractors working on his property would have a key to get in and out. Eventually, Porterville closed, but the gate stayed.

Mike Safranski, homeowners association president, said the past is past. He blamed the current delays on a misunderstanding. He said he thought Porter wanted a new electronically operated gate—a major expense to the homeowners.

"We know we need to make a reasonable accommodation quickly," Safranski said.

Late Tuesday, Safranski said a real estate lock box with a combination lock would be installed. Those with the combination will be able to open it and get a key to the gate.

"I want to see it happen," Carter said. "I've been told in the past this is going to be worked out, and nothing happened."

Porter, leaning on a cane, his right hand hanging limply at his side, glowered past the bars on the gate.

—Orange County Register

Let's examine the unanswered questions, looking at the paragraphs that contain them.

"A stroke in March left him partially paralyzed. And a gate erected by the Trabuco Canyon Community Association to resolve a longtime dispute has left him a virtual prisoner on his property."

How can a housing association make anyone a prisoner? When reporters make such statements, they are obliged to explain them in the following paragraph. But this reporter never did.

"In November, he turned to the Dayle McIntosh Center for the Disabled, which arranged meals and therapy. But Meals on Wheels volunteers, who change every day, could not trade keys, so they couldn't get in."

Is Porter a member of this housing association? If not, then doesn't he have the right to refuse to follow the rules it imposes? And besides, on what legal grounds can a housing association prevent homeowners from allowing invited guests on their property?

Anything that blocks Porter's access to government services is a violation of the Americans with Disabilities Act, said Juda Carter, an advocate with the Dayle McIntosh Center's Laguna Niguel office. She said repeated calls and letters to the homeowners association have gone unanswered.

If this organization is breaking the law, why hasn't anyone called the police? If the organization is breaking a federal law, why hasn't anyone called the Justice Department? Are there any consequences for the perpetrators of such crimes? Does anyone enforce this law?

"Porter and the association have been sparring since the 1980s, when Porter opened his property to illegal Mexican immigrants who formed a hodge-podge settlement of rented shacks and trailers dubbed Porterville."

Wait a minute. Is Porter a hero or a slumlord? Did he allow these people to live on his land so that he could overcharge them for rent while providing them with few services?

"The upshot was a wrought-iron gate at the entrance to the ranch on Shadow Rock Lane that locked the shantytown residents in. Only Porter, his immediate family, and contractors working on his property would have a key to get in and out. Eventually, Porterville closed, but the gate stayed."

The upshot of what? A court decision? An out-of-court settlement? If Porter agreed to this, why is he complaining now? If he didn't agree to the decision and a judge forced it upon him, the question remains: How can this be legal? How can a housing association dictate to property owners who they can allow to live on their property, especially if Porter doesn't belong to this association?

Why does Porter have no authority over this gate on his property? How can a housing association prohibit residents from using Shadow Rock Lane, presumably a public street? Or is it? Maybe it's a private street. Then, perhaps, the association might legally be able to restrict access to it. The story never tells us.

For whatever reason, the reporter and editor failed to anticipate and answer the readers' questions. Perhaps the reporter had the answers in her notebook but never understood the issue well enough to know to include them in her story. Perhaps her editor is at fault for failing to read the story carefully enough to note its deficiencies so that the reporter could have fixed them before publication. Whatever the reason, it is imperative that you learn the art of self-editing while you are mastering reporting. It is rare indeed to find an editor these days with the time and patience to teach you; much of your success will depend on your ability to teach yourself.

Where Do Answers Come From?

They come from reporting, from people, from observation and from documents—the sources you'll use in nearly every story. Let's start with the most important part of information gathering: the interview.

Preparing for the Interview

In Chapter 2, we discussed story ideas. Once you have an idea and you've developed its focus, it's time to develop a reporting strategy.

Before you leave on the assignment, think about what you hope to achieve in each interview, discuss your approach with your editor or another reporter and ask for advice on potential sources. Jot down questions you want to ask to help you stay on track during the interview. Remember to remain flexible. If you want to find out from the mayor why she fired the police chief and she blurts out that he once arrested her for prostitution, make sure you digress. To save time, talk to as many office-bound officials as possible over the phone and use field observations and interviews to bolster or disprove what they tell you.

Other tips to help you get started with reporting:

1. When you call your source to arrange an interview, identify yourself as a reporter writing a story and make clear your story's focus.
2. Allow as much lead time as possible when calling news sources to arrange interviews. After the interview, thank them for the time they spent with you. Before you leave, arrange for a time and place to call back in case you realize later that there were a few more questions you wished you'd asked.
3. Except in extreme cases, never agree to provide a list of questions before the interview. In those extreme cases, make sure you discuss your intention with an editor. Most sources want questions ahead of time to have control over the direction of the story.

4. When arranging interviews, make sure you speak to the official in charge. The official's secretary or the receptionist or the student worker who happens to pick up the phone is an inappropriate source, unless this person can tell you President VIP took the endowment fund and is on his way to the Bahamas.

5. Be on the lookout for officials at the scene of a news event who, hoping to avoid bad publicity, refer you for comment to their boss, who refers you to the next boss, who refers you to the next boss. Administrative officials subordinate to the provost or president, for example, are well-qualified sources on issues related to the university.

6. Seek out the most senior source available for interviews.

7. If one source says, "Sorry, can't help you," ask: "If you can't, who can?" Never hang up the phone without another source to call.

8. Never stop at no. A large part of a reporter's job is getting information from people who'd rather not give it. Think of rejection as a challenge to overcome rather than a failure. If you call the provost's office on Monday and the secretary insists that the provost can't see you until after your Friday deadline, inform the secretary that you will write the story anyway, and phone the provost's boss to politely inform her of the provost's inaccessibility. Try to interview the source's supervisor, if possible. If you're stuck without the boss or the source, gather as much information as you can from other sources and state in the story: "Provost VIP, in Europe for the annual convention of university provosts, was unavailable for comment." Or, "Provost VIP refused to return repeated phone calls to his office." After the story's publication, consider doing a follow-up with comment from Provost VIP.

   In the interest of fairness, you must make a good-faith effort to reach officials key to the story. If you're given an assignment on Monday with a Friday deadline and you wait until Thursday to call Provost VIP, who just left the office, you blew it. You cannot responsibly write that the provost refused to return your phone call. A good-faith effort means calling every day or every hour if necessary, noting the time and date of each call and the name and response of the person answering the phone.

9. One of the easiest ways to reach hard-to-reach sources is calling directory assistance for home phone numbers. Many officials, particularly at colleges and universities, list their numbers in the phone book. Always ask for a home phone number if someone is difficult to reach. You never know when a secretary or associate will give it to you. As a reporter, no question you ask is out of bounds. Sources who prefer to keep the information secret will simply say, "I don't want to tell you." You've lost nothing for trying. And in some cases, when it works, you've found a shortcut to finishing your story.

10. Do your homework. Research the subject and the person you intend to interview. Never ever leave for an interview with the idea that "my source will tell me what the focus of my story is." Unfocused reporting leads to hours-long, unfocused interviews that usually yield little information for the story. Worse, a sophisticated source may manipulate an unsophisticated, unfocused reporter,

who may then produce a biased and inaccurate story. Though no question is too dumb to ask, some questions merely showcase a reporter's laziness. If you were lucky enough to land an interview with the president of the United States, would you begin by asking: "So when were you elected, anyway?" You should never insult your sources, or waste their time, by asking questions you should have researched and nailed down before the interview. The easiest and most essential homework you can do is check the clips. Go to the library and find articles already written about the person, event, problem or issue and formulate questions based on new angles.

11. Use computer databases. Understanding how a library works is essential to becoming a good reporter. There are myriad electronic databases available to find information on your topic. If you don't know how to use these databases, sign up for a library research strategies workshop. The workshop should teach you basic research skills, how to use the Internet and various commercial databases such as Lexis-Nexus. Become friends with research librarians and seek help from them often.

Even students writing for campus publications can check clips before an assignment; most college and university libraries keep copies of the campus paper arranged chronologically by date in the periodicals section. If you're writing about a riot that occurred on campus recently and someone mentions that another such riot occurred two years previously, go back to the campus paper and check out what was written to get proper background on the event.

Unless a fact is common knowledge—presidential elections in the United State occur every four years, for instance—never assume that information you find in periodicals is accurate. Always double-check what you want to use with human sources.

Interviewing

Interviewing can be a disorienting and overwhelming task if you attempt to write down every word your source utters. Stop and listen; then write. Continue asking questions until the meaning of what your source is trying to say is crystal clear. If that means putting down your pen and asking for an explanation in plain English, do it. Process what you hear; don't act like a tape recorder. In your notebook, use your own abbreviated shorthand to jot down concepts, ideas, statistics and pithy quotes.

As the reporter, you must decide where to do the interview. In today's journalism, most interviews take place over the phone. Phone interviews save lots of time, but you also run the risk of your source's being less than candid. The type of story you're working on will dictate where the interview should take place. If, for instance, you're working night cops at 10:30 p.m. and you hear about a double homicide that occurred 50 miles away from your office, you likely won't be able to get to the scene and phone in the information by your 11 p.m. deadline. Instead, find out the address of the murder scene and refer to the reverse or "crisscross" directory, a reference book that lists a house's phone number by its address. Then call the victims' neighbors and interview them over the phone. You might even try calling the victims' phone numbers. Sometimes the investigating officer or a family member will pick up the phone. Start asking questions. It might be a few minutes before they hang up on you, and you'll have the information you need for your story.

That leads to an often-asked question: Is it morally defensible to interview family members of a homicide victim in the midst of their grief? Psychologists say those who lose loved ones to tragedy often want to talk to the media to share their grief and to let others know how they felt about the dead relative or friend. A good rule to follow is this: When interviewing victims of tragedy, politely ask whether they'd like to share some of what was good about their loved one, and during the course of the interview, ask how and why the tragedy occurred. If those left grieving choose not to grant interviews, never push yourself on them. Thank them for their time and offer your condolences. Beware, though, if you fail to land the interview and your editor sees an exclusive with the grieving relatives on TV or in a competing media. That sort of blunder is enough to warrant permanent placement on night cops, or a demotion to a distant bureau.

When more time permits, go to the scene, especially for crime, accident or disaster stories. If that double homicide happened during the day, you and the legions of other local media would descend upon the victims' neighborhood and attempt to wrench details from the cops and neighbors. In competitive news situations, getting to the scene first is foremost. Imagine how you'd feel if you found out about the homicide two hours after the local TV crews and the competing papers? By the time you got around to knocking on the neighbors' doors, they'd either be gone or more than likely ready to turn down your request for information with a terse: "But I already talked to reporters from channels 5, 9, 11, the *Bugle* and the *Times*. I'm beat." Remember, your editor doesn't care about your problems or the reason you were late to the scene. Editors care about beating the competition and spelling the names correctly. What saves you in gut-wrenching, competitive situations is your interviewing skills, your ability to convince sources to talk to you when they'd rather not and your ability to get more thorough and compelling information from those sources than other reporters do.

Successful Interviewing

Before you arrange for an interview, prepare. Ask yourself: What's my story about? How will I focus my reporting? Try to boil down your story idea to one or two focused sentences that illuminate the issue, problem or controversy. Then make a list of people you need or want to interview. To figure out who those people might be, ask yourself some more questions: Who are the main characters in my story? What are they doing? Who are their critics? What are the names of experts who can provide facts and evidence to explain questions raised by the main characters and their critics? Which government or regulatory officials might provide facts or evidence to support the claims of supporters or opponents? Finally, remember to interview average, everyday people who might be affected by the problem or controversy.

Begin your preparation by doing your homework. After you've got a story idea, seek out supporters, opponents and experts. Go the library and search the Internet. Collect all the clips you can find on your subject. Whenever you're walking through an office, get to know the clerks, workers and secretaries. They can often be your best source for documents.

- **Learn the vocabulary and the workings of the office or industry you're writing about.** "I spent a whole year reading *Turkey World* magazine for a series on the department of agriculture," says veteran investigative reporter Mike McGraw. "Gather as many documents— and as much knowledge—as you can."

- **Get organized.** Create a source list—in a paper file or your computer. Include sources' address, office and home telephone number, as well as other relevant information, such as birthday, social security number, job title, expertise etc. Don't rule out anybody who might have information that you need. Pick names from newspaper clippings and documents. Ask everyone you talk to whether he or she can think of other people you should approach. Every time someone says something significant, ask the question, "How do you know that?" The answer often leads to other sources. Who will you interview and in what order? Sometimes you have to catch people quickly before they're scared off. Other times you have to circle them, talking to their friends and associates before you interview them.

  Sometimes it makes sense to ask the source to provide you with any research materials that might help you. You should also find the best reference librarians in your local or university library and use them often. They'll show you volumes upon volumes of reference books to help you find out about a particular person or subject. They'll also help you figure out how to use the Internet for research; ask them how you can access the library's reference materials from your computer at home. When you've found a few particularly helpful librarians, treat them well and bring them small treats. They will prove invaluable to your reporting.

  When you have the evidence you need to ask intelligent questions, start formulating an angle or hypothesis, a one- or two-sentence focus around which you can begin your interviewing strategies. After you have the story focus in mind, and you've figured out the people you want to interview to test your hypothesis, how will you begin the interview?

- **Prepare to get started.** The first question sets the tone, so spend some beforehand thinking about what you want to say. One reporter, assigned to profile a journalist known for her withering interviewing style, started with the question: "If you were interviewing yourself, what would you ask?" Avoid close-ended questions, or questions a source can respond to with "yes" or "no." Instead, ask questions beginning with what, how and why. These open-ended questions will help you understand what happened, how it happened and why.

Write down the questions you want to ask and then note the crucial questions. If your source tries to cut the interview short, switch to what you must have to understand the issue or problem. Especially if you're interviewing busy people, you'll want to prepare crucial questions before you pick up the phone to set up the interview.

Celebrities, politicians, public relations people, high-ranking government officials, executives and professional athletes usually have done so many interviews that they come determined to get their message across.

- **Prepare before you call.** Frequently, when you call busy people, they'll tell you, "I can talk for a few minutes right now." Usually, that means now or never. If you haven't prepared, you'll be a position to decline the interview, hoping it can be rescheduled (which often it can't) or you'll end up asking uninformed questions.
- **Never start an interview with a stupid statement.** If you're unprepared, apologize for being uninformed and then appeal to your source's desire to have the story told fairly and accurately. You might say: "Help me understand what happened. I'm not the expert; you are. Because so many thousands of people will read (or see) this, let's get it right." Tell your sources that you'll likely call them back to check your story's facts and to make sure that what you've written is accurate. Most sources appreciate that kind of attention to details.
- **Organize your questions.** To keep track of questions, some reporters jot them down on a separate sheet of paper; others suggest writing single-word clues on the flap of your notebook to remind you of issues you want to cover. Pick a good seat, as close to the subject as possible but far enough away so that neither the subject nor his associates can see your notes or documents.
- **Get out of the newsroom.** To find sources—and stories—you need to climb a few stairs. In a piece he wrote for *Editor & Publisher* magazine, veteran editor Bill Gloede seconded the sentiments of a newspaper owner who says that the biggest problem he faces "is getting the reporters off their asses and out into the communities they are supposed to be covering."

If you're writing about a problem or controversy, make sure that you've got a list of sources that includes supporters, opponents and experts. Experts are disinterested observers who can provide objective evidence to help you sort through conflicting opinions and facts provided by the supporter and opponents. You should write no single-source stories. If the source is the central focus of the story—a profile of someone, for instance—you still have to interview that person's friends and foes.

Go into every interview with a clear goal. Make sure that you've discussed the angle and the type of story with your editor. Is it hard news? Feature? News feature? Profile? Is it 500 words? Five thousand words? Remember, too, that your objective—and your focus—may change as you interview your sources. Be ready to go in any direction that will make yours a better angle, focus and, ultimately, story.

With your story's focus in mind, consider what you hope to achieve in your interviews. Something brought you to this person. What was it?

When you approach people to ask for an interview, say as little as possible, advises John Sawatsky, a writing consultant. "Identify who you are, who you represent, what the subject is, and shut up. They may ask questions. Be honest. But don't volunteer information. Make your answers as general as possible without being misleading."

When the interview begins—which is as soon as you've identified yourself as a reporter working on a story—never lecture your sources, argue or debate with them; keep personal opinions and comments to yourself. Keep your anger—or any other emotion besides cheerful interest—in check. Many sources will cut short interviews or refuse to talk to you again if you show bias or behave inappropriately. By maintaining distance and staying in control, you'll avoid having your source intimidate you or put you on the defensive.

Remember, an interview is not a conversation, says Sawatsky. In a conversation, you exchange information. In an interview, you gather information. The difference is subtle, but important. Too many journalists try to browbeat their sources into an admission of wrong-doing, or attempt to seduce them as they would a lover, with a single goal in mind: "to lure the subject into saying something he or she shouldn't," writes David Fryxell in *Writer's Digest*. "If the interview is for television rather than print, the ideal seems to be to reduce the subject to tears." Occasionally, you can get people to rise to the bait. But that's the exception, he adds. It's also the old way of interviewing, an approach that no longer works. Anyone who has had any experience dealing with reporters has figured out the standard tricks reporters use. In the last decade media trainers have become such a growth industry that "you can even find them among small businessmen in Newfoundland," Sawatsky says, teaching politicians and executives "how to run circles around journalists. It's a sophisticated battle for control," he says, with journalists too often relying on outdated, conventional approaches to interviewing.

Sawatsky denounces standard interviewing techniques as "the old methodology," often characterized as a power struggle between interviewer and subject, as a battle of wills, a game to be won or lost. Sawatsky advises changing the framework, taking the mystery out of what most journalists have always believed is a mystical, serendipitous experience, likened to "lovemaking" by reporter Claudia Dreifus in a recent book on interviewing.

The conventional method represents an irrational belief "in magic," says Sawatsky. "If an interview goes well, then we say it's magic. But it's not magic. It happens for an understandable reason. It's rational. It's a skill. It's easy to teach someone skills."

Journalists are often trained to appear to be tough by asking accusatory questions, the prosecutorial method of interviewing. Reportorial victories of the previous three decades—the Watergate scandal, the Pentagon Papers, the My Lai massacre—empowered journalists, galvanizing them to ambush and grill unsuspecting sources, who responded with stonewalling or outright hostility. Oriana Fallaci, Mike Wallace, Barbara Walters and Larry King took center stage; the source became the enemy to defeat at any cost.

In 1990, writer Janet Malcolm unleashed a professional tempest when she compared journalists to "a kind of confidence man, preying on people's vanity, ignorance or loneliness, gaining their trust and betraying them without remorse." Malcolm gave voice to conventional interviewing at its worst, and it touched a raw nerve. Based on competition and coercion, the old way often leads journalist and subject to an unavoidable moral impasse. At its best, it leaves information gathering to chance, allowing spin meisters to control what the public learns. In any case, the old way puts journalists in a defensive crouch, attacked by those who believe the media are biased, left leaning, and agenda driven. "People are pretty savvy; they know when they're being coerced. And they don't like it. With competition, the goal becomes winning. The more we win, the more they lose. That's a lousy way to get openness. If we thought about it, we'd do it differently," Sawatsky says. "But we don't think; we react."

Interviewing Traps to Avoid

Sometimes seemingly innocuous questions elicit over-the-top responses. That's usually because the reporter has used loaded words, often without realizing it. In the following example, a reporter begins interviewing media tycoon and business executive Jack Kent Cook with what seems like a reasonable question. But the question angers Cook, and he refuses to answer it and the subsequent questions as well.

> Reporter: "What's the biggest mistake you've ever made?
> Cook: "I'm not answering that."
> Reporter: "What's your greatest failing?"
> Cook: "Failing? Mistake? To hell with my greatest failing. I'm not going to answer that, either."
> Reporter: "Well, then, what's your greatest regret?"
> Cook: "Regret? It's the same damn thing, Bob. You can't snare me with that."

The reporter used value-laden, subjective language that offended Cook. If you have to ask a negative question, start first with a positive. "What have been your greatest successes?" After answering the first question, the source will likely be more inclined to answer the second, more negative one. In the course of answering the first question, in fact, the source may allude to a failure. At that point, follow up with: "You mentioned failing. What has been your greatest failing?"

Eliminate subjective values from your questions and the source will feel compelled to fill in the blanks you left behind. Instead of: "Were you surprised?" (surprised is subjective), ask: "How did you react?" Instead of: "Did you feel sick?" ask: "How did you feel?" Instead of: "It must have been tough in the early years," ask: "What were the early years like?" The answers become unpredictable. "That's the secret to getting surprising answers from people," says Sawatsky. Questions should arouse the source's need to tell us more.

"Interviewing is about people. They're not chemical compounds, and they don't always act predictably. But there is a predictable part." Ask a close-ended question—one that can be answered with a yes or a no—and sources "will confirm or deny 98 percent of the time," Sawatsky says. "That's the science." The unpredictable part is what happens next. "Socially, people are taught to add a post script to a confirmation or a denial. As journalists, we hope the P.S. will describe or explain the issue we've raised. That's interviewing by accident. If you get somebody who doesn't want to play, you're in trouble."

Most of the time, in friendly interviews, the source adds the P.S. "out of charity. Because our social instincts tell us to be nice. Their charity—not the question—delivers the answer. We're relying on them to help us out. Relying on people's charity to get answers is not a good practice. The ones we need charity from the most are the least likely to give it—the people who stand to lose something." And certain people rarely give charity: "People who go by the book—cops, bureaucrats, lawyers—people who take questions literally, people who are nervous. The last thing fearful people do is open up. They shut down. Professional answer givers, sophisticated politicians and business executives, frequently defeat journalists by answering a close-ended question with a curt 'No, not at all' or a disingenuous 'Gosh, I hope not!' before switching to a prepackaged 'message track,' the spiel they had planned to use to answer any uncomfortable questions."

Sawatsky suggests using the interviewing strategies described in the following sections.

1. Ask Neutral, Open-Ended Questions   Start questions with what, how and why; they demand the most from sources, requiring them to describe causes (what happened?), processes (how did it happen?) and motivation (why did you do it?). Fill in the blanks with questions beginning with who, where and when. Beware the two basic traps that reporters are prone to fall into when they fail to keep the questions open ended enough.

Avoid Asking "How Do You Feel?"   Reporters too often ask a mother who has just lost a child or a worker whose factory just closed down or an athlete who just won a big game, "How do you feel?" In the immediate aftermath of an event, this question almost always fails to evoke a meaningful response. Why? "They don't know how they feel. It's too soon for them to articulate how they feel," Sawatsky explains. Wait until the source has had ample time to reflect on what happened. Then "the question works quite well."

The Problem of Counterbalancing Sources nearly always make up for a lack of neutrality by counterbalancing, that is, counteracting overblown questions with modest responses. One example is a Larry King interview with the late John F. Kennedy, Jr. "You don't have a normal life," King tells him.

> JFK, Jr. responds: "I have a pretty normal life."
> King: "Is it hard being the son of a legend?"
> JFK, Jr.: "No, it's not hard."

The source "feels compelled to give arguments for the other side." King should have asked, "What's it like being the son of JFK?" The source in this situation most likely will feel compelled to fill in the blank.

2. Tough Issues Make Tough Questions When she owned the Cincinnati Reds' baseball team, the late Marge Schott was accused of being a racist. How should reporters handle interviewing Schott about her alleged racist remarks? Asking her, "Are you a racist?" is an easy question that sounds tough. She'll almost certainly answer no. Race, though, is a tough issue for Schott. Asking her focused, open-ended questions about race will yield surprising results. By contrast, asking her open-ended questions about easy issues—safe, unthreatening topics, such as her favorite color or charity—will produce predictable responses or a predetermined message track.

3. The More a Question Huffs and Puffs, the More It Blows The more information journalists put into questions, the more information sources leave out. Less is more: Short questions produce succinct, dramatic, focused responses. Long, rambling questions usually get long, rambling answers or curt, confused responses.

4. Open People Up through Strategy Strategy becomes especially important when the issue is difficult for the source. Ask yourself, What's the goal? Then devise a strategy to achieve it. A reporter came to Sawatsky with a statistic she wanted to humanize: One third of the school children in Edmonton, Canada, were going without breakfast. Asking the children directly: "Did you eat breakfast this morning?" would likely produce a less than truthful response since even small children are socialized to avoid admitting that they're hungry and poor. Ask instead a series of questions designed to get a truthful response: "What's the first thing you did when you got up this morning? Then what? Then what? Then what?" Keep asking to the point of the child's having arrived at school. If the child made no mention of breakfast, you ask: What about breakfast? Why didn't you eat anything? What happens to you when you don't eat breakfast?"

5. Establish Agreement   The reporter and source must agree on basic facts; there are no exceptions. Without agreement, reporters spend most of the interview trying to force the source to accept their version of events, usually resorting to coercion and leading questions. When reporters had evidence that President Bill Clinton was having sex with an intern, they should have forced Clinton to agree to a definition of what constitutes sexual relations. Clinton was able to deny his dalliance precisely because he stubbornly refused to define what he did as "sexual relations."

6. Build the Interview on Answers, Not Questions   People find it easier to volunteer information than to admit to it. When the source makes an original assertion, follow up with a question asking for evidence to support it. "When (sources) own the statement, they become accountable. It's hard to force them to take ownership of our statements."

7. Put the Burden of Proof on the Source   Make no original assertions in the interview. Either we require the source to provide the evidence to substantiate subjective statements, or we bring our own values and subjectivity into the interview and risk being forced by a savvy source to prove ourselves and defend our statements. A question beginning with "how" pushes sources to go further or exposes them, forcing them to respond. If a source, for instance, insists, "There was no crime," ask, "How do you know that?" If a source says, "I can't remember" ask, "Why can't you remember?"

Activate the burden of proof with deadly precision. There are no innocuous statements in questions. To focus your questions, pick a key phrase you want to probe. Repeat it. Ask a what, how, or why question. If, in describing his marriage, Ted Kennedy says, "We've had difficult times," respond, "What do you mean by difficult times?"

Caveats:

- Use the source's exact words. If you change the words even a little, the source no longer owns the statement.
- Stay in the moment. Sawatsky advises against dredging up old clips and asking a source to defend an illuminating revelation made months, weeks or even days earlier. "If you give sources time to think, they'll usually disown what they've said."
- Never repeat phrases in your question from a source's message track; doing so will always result in more message track.

Sawatsky also has compiled a list he calls the "Seven Deadly Sins," or what to avoid in an interview.

1. **Failing to ask a question.** If you're making a statement, you're not asking a question. Your job is to get information from sources, not to impress them with your superior knowledge. When reporters make statements, they allow sources to avoid answering questions.

2. **Asking two questions simultaneously, also known as asking "double barrel" questions.** Example of a double-barrel question: "Who did you like interviewing least and what's your most impressive interviewing coup?" Sources will naturally gravitate to answering questions that make them look best and avoid those whose answers might be less than flattering to their reputations.

3. **Overloading questions.** By putting too much information into a question, the source with something to hide can easily keep it hidden. For example, when reporters were trying to find out whether President Bill Clinton had had a longstanding affair with a woman named Gennifer Flowers, a well-known television reporter misused his opportunity by asking an overloaded question.

> Reporter: "Was Gennifer Flowers your alleged lover for 12 years?"
> Clinton: "That allegation is false."

Which allegation is false? That she was his lover? Or that she was his lover for 12 years? Maybe she was his lover for 11 years or seven years, in which case, Clinton answered truthfully. By asking imprecise questions, reporters allow sources to wriggle out of responding to issues that are difficult for them.

4. **Adding statements or comments to questions.** Even adding an innocuous statement can derail a good question. Instead of answering the question, the source answers the comment. A good example of a lost opportunity can be seen in an interview with former American hostage Terry Anderson. Anderson, who spent seven years as a hostage in Lebanon, shared his prison cell with other hostages. After he was released, Anderson did dozens of interviews, answering questions about what his life as a hostage had been like. During one television interview, the reporter asked him, "What would go through your mind in the quiet times? Because there must have been times when you didn't talk to each other."

Anderson replied, "Oh, sure, there were times when we didn't talk to each other; we had to get out of that room by getting out of our minds."

Instead of answering the excellent question—"What went through your mind?"—Anderson answered the comment, "There must have been times when you didn't talk to each other."

The interviewer's comment was about as benign as they come, which is precisely Sawatsky's point. The content of the statement doesn't matter. Most people will respond to the last phrase out of the interviewer's mouth. As a consequence, we never learned what went through Anderson's mind, and we missed an opportunity to find out first hand what hostages think about when being held in captivity for seven years. By interjecting statements, Sawatsky explains, "we lose our ability to get precise comments."

5. **Using loaded or "trigger" words in questions.** Some words are obviously loaded. Let's say your university's president has proposed replacing the English department with a school of journalism. You've been assigned the story. You begin the interview by asking: "How will you sell this scheme to the board of trustees?" More than likely, the president will respond by attacking your use of the word *scheme*; he will respond not to the question, but to the

trigger word: "This is not a scheme. This is a well-thought-out plan." By using the word *scheme,* you've allowed the president to ignore an important question: How will he convince the board of trustees to go along with the plan? Moreover, it gives the president a forum—free publicity, really—to sell an uncritical version of his controversial plan to your readers or viewers.

6. **Using hyperbole, or asking hyperbolic questions.** When reporters ask sources hyperbolic questions—"What does it feel like to be a sex god?" "What does it feel like to be a superstar?" "What does it feel like to be a hero?"—we can predict that the response will almost always be modest, says Sawatsky. Sources tend to want to counterbalance hyperbolic questions with humble responses. Instead of using generalizations, ask your sources to answer specific questions focusing on evidence that suggests that they're a sex god, a superstar or a hero.

7. **Asking closed-ended questions.** Sources with something to hide, or a message to get across, will usually answer a closed-ended question with a curt "No, not at all," "Gosh, I hope not!" or "Sure, but. . ." followed by their prepared message or defense. When baseball team owner Marge Schott made statements that led to accusations that she was a racist, she appeared on a network news show. "Are you a racist?" the reporter asked. The answer was predictable. She said: "No, not at all," and preceded to offer for the network's viewers the message she wanted them to hear. "Of course she's going to deny," says Sawatsky. The reporters "are trying by magic to confront her, hoping she'll reveal something of herself. Once she denies that she's a racist, where does that leave the reporter?"

Successful Stalling

During your first few interviews, you'll feel as though you barely have the process under control. Asking questions, listening carefully to responses, thinking about what you've missed and formulating more questions to fill the holes in the source's responses, all while attempting to write down the essence of what's being said, will test the limits of your abilities. Sometimes you'll catch the tail end of what you know is a great quote after the source is on another subject. Meanwhile, you're still writing down something that was said a minute previously. Your mind goes blank.

Stop the interview and say: "You know, that point you were making is a good one. Would you mind repeating it?" Or, "Will you explain that point? It's unclear to me." Never be afraid to stop an interview to ask for clarification. Sources appreciate a reporter's effort to get the facts straight and the quotes in context.

Other stalling techniques are useful. If you don't want to call attention to what your source just said but you need more time to write it down and to think about the next question, ask an innocuous question that will engage the source long enough for you to get your bearings. Maybe comment on your source's tie or a photograph in her office. Don't forget, though, once you're in control again, to bring the interview back to the story's focus.

Problem Interviews

Listening to sources but not really understanding what they're saying is another problem that beginning reporters often face. Sometimes the reason is as simple as a reporter's failing to do the appropriate homework beforehand or failing to pay attention carefully during the interview. But sometimes sources like to confuse reporters with a well-worn trick: phrasing answers in the bloated jargon of their profession. This is especially true of computer company officials, financial bureaucrats and anyone in the education profession.

Never let such a source erode your confidence. Simply ask for answers in plain English. Some will dodge direct questions with such a flourish that you won't realize you don't have the answer until you're writing the story. Stay alert during the interview and keep rephrasing the question until your source adequately answers it or blows up and says, "I'm not going to answer that." Then you quote him saying just that.

It is always the reporter's responsibility to understand fully what the source is trying to say. Learn from the mistake of the young reporter who turned in a story about the launch of a problem-plagued campus program. When her editor began asking her questions about the quotes from one of her sources, she responded, "I don't really know what he was trying to say. He was really confusing." The reporter failed to accomplish her most basic task: to understand a problem and to explain it well to readers.

Often, sources will tell inconsistent versions of the same event. You get a tip that the university president is about to fire the dean of humanities. During an interview, the president denies the rumor. But you notice the dean's personnel file on the president's desk. The file itself isn't a story. It's a sign that you have lots more reporting to do. Keep investigating. Reporters should never simply report what was said. Instead, verify the truth. Who's telling it? Who's lying? Is the truth somewhere in the middle? Keep interviewing and digging until you find the answer. Don't be surprised if a source goes on the offensive, trying to throw you off track by attacking your intelligence or your credibility. In instances in which you know you're right, stand your ground and don't leave the interview until your source has answered the key questions or tells you she never intends to respond. If you think you may be off base, thank the source politely, contact your editor and try to redirect your reporting. It is not unusual, though, for sources to intentionally withhold information or even lie. If you suspect that your source is lying, you must continue searching for other sources until you feel reasonably sure that you have uncovered the truth.

Beware the Pauses

Humans seem inclined to fill uncomfortable pauses in conversation. Skilled interviewers know this and use it to their advantage. Hold your tongue and let your sources fill the silence. While they're thinking about answering, observe the scene for color and detail, noting how your sources fit into their environment and how that environment affects the focus of your story.

Remember, reporting means being aware of your five senses: hearing, seeing, tasting, smelling and feeling. Reporter Larry Campbell, part of a team that won the 1989 Pulitzer Prize for the Anchorage (Ala.) *Daily News,* told *Editor & Publisher* that a key for him is noting his surroundings. On a classroom visit, for example:

> "I might sense the aroma of wet snow pants dumped in the wardrobe after recess or see a boy in a red-striped shirt rhythmically kicking a buddy's chair in front of him. Are the walls bare, or a cacophony of construction paper Thanksgiving turkeys, or Halloween pumpkins?"

Campbell added that his memories of people help him complete the picture. He takes notes on these memories to jog his memory later. For example, a woman's perfume might remind him of a high-school girlfriend, whereas a "jowly, red-haired, red-bearded man reminds me of a basset hound." Later, as he sits down to write, these images "snap the whole scene back into my head and make it real for me all over again," Campbell said.

Thinking on Your Feet

One of journalism's most important missions is to act as watchdog of the government, to keep citizens informed of decisions made on their behalf by elected officials. As a student reporter, you should cover the student government regularly, especially those issues related to the way student fees are spent. In a few cases, such as the release of a student's academic or discipline records, privacy laws may prevent officials from releasing the information you want. Most information, though, is a matter of public record, which means you're entitled to share it with your readers. When an official refuses to release the information you want, make sure you get the source's name, title and phone number. Find out whether the information you seek is a matter of public record; if it is, return to the source and inform her of her legal obligation to release it.

Let's say, though, that a particular meeting is a student conduct board hearing to evaluate a charge that a student provoked a security guard into harassing and hitting him. You ask to attend the meeting and are told it is closed. You appeal to administrators, who show you case law attesting to the legal validity of making this a closed hearing. You call a lawyer and confirm that the university has the right to shut the hearing.

You can—and should—report on the hearing.

The names of those sitting on the student conduct board are easy enough to find. Interview each of them. Try to find out the name of the alleged victim and the alleged perpetrator, either from the board members or from other sources close to the investigation. Interview each. Such a story should never go unreported just because the meeting is closed to students.

More commonly, student government officials and student journalists become antagonists, especially if student journalists do their job and report the peccadillos of their government representatives. Tough reporting often brings retaliation, including student government officials excluding reporters from meetings or threatening to withhold funding.

Before that happens to you, make sure you understand the provisions of your student constitution; most provide for open meetings in all matters. If you're asked to leave a student government meeting or told that what occurs is off-the-record, protest politely. Tell the presiding officer that the constitution provides for open meetings and you plan to report the proceedings to your readers. Don't leave. Chances are, one of two things will occur: Student officials will adjourn, postpone or move the meeting to another location (follow closely behind). Or, they'll eject you.

Make sure the record shows you left politely under protest. Then write a story about having been ejected, pointing out that student officials violated the constitution. Don't forget to find out what exactly was so important that warranted a closed-door discussion. Even without the details, the story should focus on why and how officials are abusing power.

Anecdotes and Statistics

Collecting anecdotes while interviewing is particularly important for profiles and feature stories, though anecdotes also appear in news and newsfeature stories. An anecdote, as we discussed in Chapter 2, is a story within your story. Anecdotal evidence usually puts a human face on the facts and figures you've collected to illuminate your story's focus.

Anecdotal evidence helps reporters find stories, but more important, it helps reporters humanize facts. This is how one *Columbus* (Ohio) *Dispatch* reporter led a story about slippage in support for President George W. Bush in spring 2004 due to the war in Iraq:

By Joe Hallett

Ken Thomas is the face of polls that show an erosion of support for President Bush and the war in Iraq as the conflict turned deadlier in the past couple of months.

Thomas, 53, a microbiologist for the Ohio Department of Agriculture, voted for Bush in 2000 "mainly because he's pro-gun."

But on Nov. 2, Thomas said he will vote for the presumptive Democratic presidential candidate, Massachusetts Sen. John Kerry, mainly because "he's not Bush."

"I do regret voting for Bush," the Democrat said. "We never should have gone into Iraq in the first place. Now that we're there, Bush doesn't have an exit strategy. He's taken this country in the wrong direction. He's leading us into wars that aren't necessary."

Across Columbus Ward 62, a *Dispatch* Poll in February of 842 likely voters showed 53 percent of respondents approved of Bush's handling of the war and 47 percent disapproved.

As the war turned bloodier, national polls show support for Bush waning.

A *New York Times*/CBS News Poll released Thursday—and largely mirrored by an Associated Press poll posted April 23—showed 47 percent of respondents now think U.S. military action against Iraq was warranted, down from 58 percent a month earlier and 63 percent in December.

The poll also showed Bush's approval rating at 46 percent, the lowest of his presidency.

—Columbus Dispatch

Note how the writer uses the anecdotal lead, focusing on the views of one voter, to illustrate the trend shown by the statistics. Thomas lives in Ward 62, where voters divided almost evenly in 2000 between Bush and Democrat Al Gore. The writer cites figures from that voting ward as well as state and national poll results. The lead puts a human face on what otherwise could be a story filled with numbers. Keep in mind that some sources manipulate statistics to achieve their own ends as easily as they manipulate reporters. It's up to you to discern when statistics are accurate or bogus, to confirm statistics with others and to reject those that seem improbable.

After citing the statistical evidence backing up the lead, the writer supported the figures further with more quotes from Ward 62 residents. To help give the story balance, the next quote is from a Bush supporter. The story continues:

Interviews last week with Ward 62 voters who know at least one U.S. soldier in Iraq echoed the conflicting opinions that appear to be increasingly dividing the nation.

"I believe that al-Qaida is very much behind the fighting going on over there, and I believe 9/11 and Iraq are connected," said Sharon Freeman, 35, a stay-at-home mom and Bush supporter.

"We haven't had any attacks at home since the war's been going on. As long as the battles are being fought, it's better to have our trained men and women fighting over there than to have our citizens blown up at home. . .I trust the president and his administration. I trust that they know what they are doing and they are protecting our country."

Others, however, contend that April's morbid statistics belie the "Mission Accomplished" banner strung above Bush a year ago yesterday as he stood on the deck of the aircraft carrier Abraham Lincoln and proclaimed the end of major combat operations in Iraq.

With 136 U.S. troops killed and at least 900 injured, along with 1,361 Iraqis killed, April is the deadliest month of the war.

"Every morning when I wake up, when I get home after work, every minute of the day it seems, you see it, the reports of more dead," said Diana Bowens, 49, who analyzes traffic statistics for the state.

"When I saw the picture of all the caskets last week, that wasn't the way it was supposed to be. We were supposed to go over there, clean house and come out. The president made us think it was going to be a piece of cake. Now it's true hell over there. The people are fighting each other, and they are fighting us."

How did the reporter collect these anecdotes? Is the placement of the quotes in the story purely random? No. During the interviews, he sought out supporters of both candidates, likely interviewing many more than he used in his story. He asked the sources to share specific views that helped illustrate the overall focus. Note, too, that the reporter asked those interviewed how old they were. This is something many new reporters are reluctant to do, figuring that is an unnecessary intrusion of their source's privacy. Some reporters also figure this will make sources uncomfortable. But if age appears to be a key part of the story, as it is here and in nearly all personality profile stories, the question of how old the source is must be asked.

Critical Thinking

Critically analyzing a response to one of your questions is key to getting to the truth behind the bluster. You're a reporter, not a recorder. Know the difference between fact and opinion and critically analyze what a source tells you.

Let's say that a student wants you to do a story about a professor he claims discriminated against him because he is a white male. The evidence he brings to you is a D he received in the class. Other white males in the class also received D's, he tells you, for the same reason. You confirm that three of the six white males in the class received D's and the five women in the class received passing marks.

Is white male discrimination rampant in the class? Yes, say some of the students, even a few of the women who received passing marks.

That's their opinion. Now you need facts. What evidence do the students who allege discrimination have to support their view? This is the conversation that took place between reporter and source:

Source: "The class required a midterm, a final and project, and the men received D's on all three." (Fact)

Reporter: "How is that discriminatory?"

Source: "The professor grades women more leniently than men." (Opinion)

Reporter: "How did you reach that conclusion?"

> Source: "Well, she's married, and she still uses her maiden name, which means she's a feminist and everybody knows all feminists favor women over men." (Opinion)

Opinions are value judgments. Facts are verifiable. Critical thinking means understanding the difference between the two and being able to determine the reliability of each. Every story you do requires critical thinking skills, since most sources try to sway news coverage to favor their own bias or version of the truth. To help you determine the validity of your sources' claims, use the following critical thinking checklist published in the Phi Delta Kappa newsletter. Your goal in every interview with every source is to:

1. Determine the accuracy of a statement.
2. Distinguish between legitimate and illegitimate claims.
3. Distinguish between relevant and irrelevant information, claims or reasons.
4. Detect bias.
5. Identify stated and unstated assumptions.
6. Identify ambiguous or equivocal claims or arguments.
7. Recognize logical inconsistencies in an argument.

Make sure you quote the correct sources; consider that most problems or issues have many more than two sides. Your job is to seek out majority and minority viewpoints, to master and understand them and to present them clearly and precisely. To do this, you must understand what people are saying and their motive for saying it.

And, of course, you must always allow people to rebut charges made against them. Let's say that a disabled student accuses an administrator of suggesting she either stop complaining about a lack of on-campus handicap access or transfer to another school. It is not only bad journalism but potentially libelous to print the allegation without giving the administrator ample opportunity to respond.

When Is an Interview Over?

Always end an interview with the question, "What have I forgotten to ask?" A source often will tell you something you never considered or forgot to ask. Invariably, the dullest of interviews will get lively after you've closed your notebook and put away your pen. Always keep both handy and start writing again when the source loosens up and starts talking.

Calling Back

You'll do interviews, forget to ask the crucial question and fail to realize it until you get back to the office and your editor asks, "Well, why did the president fire the dean?"

You know when, where, how and what but you realize right then that you never asked directly: Why? Yikes! Good thing you have the president's home phone number. Call back sources as soon as you realize you forgot to ask something, even if it means calling back 10 times. The more reporting you do, the less likely you'll be to forget to ask important questions. But even seasoned professionals make mistakes, and they know that calling back is part of the job.

It often happens, too, that your notes are illegible and you're not sure whether the president said she fired the dean because he had embezzled $5,000 or $5,800 from the scholarship fund. Call back. Any time you're hazy on a fact, figure or opinion, call back and clarify it with your source.

Spot News: What Am I Looking For?

Spot news stories—the kind that happen suddenly—make reporting an exciting vocation, but it's important that you're not carried away by the event to the point of not thinking straight. A cool head is paramount, or you become just another stimulated spectator at the scene of an air crash, riot or mine cave-in. You are there to get information, not gawk. You must absorb detail, talk to the right sources and make sure your facts are accurate.

The scene of a spot news story is usually frantic and chaotic, as victims, witnesses, rescue workers and officials slog through the wreckage of an auto accident, mine disaster, fire, murder, riot, drug bust or plane crash. Police, paramedics and other officials make their way through crowds of bystanders who frequently hamper their efforts. Sirens scream as more patrol cars and ambulances arrive. Streets are roped off to allow police and firefighters to do their jobs.

Before you begin asking questions, study the overall picture to orient yourself. If you're covering an event, seek out the best possible vantage point and don't forget to interview people on the fringes; for example, interview sign-carrying protesters at a political rally or bystanders at a campus demonstration. Note the color and detail you may want to incorporate into the story.

After orienting yourself, seek out police, fire and other officials for information. Ask specific questions and take notes. Be careful not to bother a fire captain directing a crew battling a blaze or a police officer taking fingerprints. Wait until the source has a moment to talk to you. If a response seems vague, ask the question again or rephrase it. Make sure you understand everything said and that you've double-checked the correct spelling of names. Don't try to spell a name phonetically.

Normally, police and other officials are cooperative with the media. Now and then, expect trouble. Some cops don't like reporters and treat them poorly or refuse to divulge information they are legally required to make public. In other situations, security or the danger of hordes of newshounds trampling evidence may prompt even the most benign officials to clamp a lid on information and access. Attempt to work out a compromise with authorities for release of information at a more convenient time. If a compromise appears hopeless and you sense that information is being withheld for no good reason, protest vigorously, as experienced reporters do.

Some sources insist on secrecy, particularly if their own incompetence, blundering or malfeasance is involved. When officials agree to on-the-scene interviews, note their names and ranks and get phone numbers, including home phones, so you can call with more questions or for more current information. (For more specific suggestions of questions to ask during fire or police emergencies, see Chapter 10.)

Speeches, news conferences and meetings constitute another sort of spot news story, one we explore in greater depth in Chapter 6. The fact that a group had a meeting is usually not news. What the members of a group do or say at the meeting is news, especially if they vote and take action on an issue or problem. Let's say that you're assigned to a routine meeting of the student council. After a rather lengthy and boring session in which the council voted to fund the photo club and to provide costumes for the next student play, members quickly voted to abolish the constitution, awarded themselves funds remaining in the coffers and adjourned the meeting. The lead for your story would reflect the most dramatic or unusual action, the action with the most wide-reaching impact on readers, *even though it was only a small part of the meeting.*

The most important rule when covering stories with no apparent focus: Look for the news. Focus on what's new, different or dramatic about what the speech maker is saying. When General H. Norman Schwarzkopf, the commander of U.S. troops during the first Persian Gulf War, was invited to speak at a local university, he was asked to address "War, Peace and Justice." A campus reporter wrote a rambling, unfocused chronological account of the 45-minute speech, mistakenly believing that the story's focus must be the glories of America's youth because the retired general focused the bulk of his remarks on that subject.

But a *Los Angeles Times* reporter recognized the news of the story immediately and landed on it, even though it wasn't the focus of the speech. The reporter instead focused on the fact that Schwarzkopf had said the war was fought to protect oil supplies, something far more newsworthy than general reflections on the glories of youth. This statement was especially newsworthy given that Schwarzkopf was contradicting statements by then President George H.W. Bush.

Color and Details

Color and detail come from the reporter's observation of sounds, reaction, appearance, smell, taste and feel. Especially in features and profiles, the color and detail you note should illuminate the story's focus. If you're doing a profile of an absent-minded professor, for instance, and her office is so cluttered you can't find a place to put down a cup of coffee, you would want to use that observation in your story. (For more on the importance of color and detail, especially in features, see Chapter 11.) In news stories, detail and color help readers understand the event in its context.

Editors

Use yours. Editors, because they are busy, can be gruff and unreceptive to questions or problems. Even so, you must insist that your editor help you; rarely will one object if asked directly. But always be mindful of their schedules. The time to ask for help is not when they're on deadline or about to walk into a news meeting. If they're unavailable at the moment, set up a time to meet and persist until they find the time to help you. Sometimes you have to treat editors as you would an evasive source, but it's worth the trouble. A good editor can be enormously useful in helping you formulate a focus as you go along and assisting you in framing the questions you'll need to ask. Anytime you encounter a problem and need advice on how to continue, whom to talk to or how to get the information that eludes you, seek out your editor immediately.

Off-the-Record and On-Background Comments

If a source says: "This is off-the-record," that means you should publish nothing of what you've been told. If, however, your source tells you the information is "on background," that means you may publish the comments but must attribute them to an anonymous source.

Journalists have differing opinions about on-background and off-the-record comments. A good journalist is willing to accept any information from any source, as long as it remains nothing more than a tip that will lead to someone willing to go on the record. Fewer and fewer news organizations are willing to write stories with anonymous sources since many times sources hide behind anonymity as a way to manipulate a news event or a journalist. Always ask a source, "If you can't tell me on the record, who can?" Or, "If you can't tell me on the record, will you provide me with a document to corroborate what you're saying? If you can't, who can?"

Notetaking and Tape Recorders

Don't write everything down. A lot of what you'll collect is background information, what you need to know to understand the story. Listening carefully and critically is crucial to getting the information you need to write the story. Understand what your sources are saying; figure out their bias. When you've done that, start thinking about what you'll need to support the story's focus. Jot down sentences that sum up your source's perspective in a nutshell or sound bite.

A tape recorder is a useful tool that ensures that your quotes will be accurate and in context. But taping interviews poses particular problems, especially for beginners.

First off, beginners often use tape recorders as a crutch, an excuse to stop paying attention and stop taking notes during an interview. Ever tried to transcribe an hour-long interview? It takes about three hours. Multiply that by three sources, and you've missed your 5 p.m. deadline. Worse, the more students rely on tape recorders, the easier it is to put off learning the crucial skill of note taking, which is best mastered, like the rest of journalism, by practice.

Except to double-check the accuracy of selected quotes, forget the tape recorder until you're a skilled interviewer and note taker. If you must use one, pretend it's not there and take notes as usual. If the machine malfunctions, you'll have the information you need. Also, and perhaps most important, written notes will help you determine what's essential to transcribe and what you can leave on tape, thus saving you time.

Stop Procrastinating and Start Reporting

A cardinal rule of great journalism: There's never enough time to report the story; never enough time to write it. So don't put off reporting your assignment to the last minute and then complain that you couldn't complete it. That excuse is unacceptable. The news business is about deadline pressure. Try to do as thorough a job as possible within the time limit your editor has set. "Deeply embedded in American journalism is the notion that you do what it takes to get the story. Long hours? No problem. Seven day weeks, broken dinner dates, aborted relationships, missed family commitments? Too bad. The story comes first," explains editor Rem Rieder in the *American Journalism Review*. "An editor, explaining to his wife why he was going to be late—again—exclaimed, 'You don't understand. It's a big story.' To which she replied, 'No, YOU don't understand. It's ALWAYS a big story.'"

Such is the nature of the profession. You might decide you want a saner lifestyle. That's fine. But if you want to compete professionally, start pushing yourself now to learn as much as you can on each story and to try to do the next one better.

A Note on Visual Literacy

To succeed in today's media, you must be visually literate. Writers, reporters, photographers, graphic artists and page designers work together to produce the best, most accurate and visually appealing story packages they can, with photographs, charts and other informational graphics. Because beginning TV or print reporters in small markets are often expected to shoot their own videos or take their own pictures, start becoming visually literate now. Take a class in photography and graphics to learn the basics of composition and design. At the very least, reporters are expected to make photo assignments for their stories, a written form telling the photographer where to go and what to shoot, noting any special situations that would enhance the photograph.

Once on an assignment, you and the photographer should collaborate, helping each other see what might have been missed. Often, art drives story placement, meaning that the quality of the photos or illustrations will help determine whether your story makes Page One or is shunted to the back of the section. Too often, student reporters have no interest in taking on the added responsibility of worrying about the art that goes with a story. They leave the assignments to their editors and make no special effort to help secure the right pictures, graphs and charts. Remember, mentors, journalism professors and internship directors will evaluate you on how well you enhance the product you're producing. Those reporters who think visually and make creative suggestions that improve the story package will receive the highest marks for initiative and enterprise.

I'm a Public Relations Student. Why Should I Care about Reporting?

Good journalists always read news releases, evaluate them for their newsworthiness and follow up on those with merit. A good news release should be as accurate as a news story, short and factual, written well and in AP style. All too often, though, public relations professionals fail because they lack basic skills. The releases they send are useless to journalists, Linda Morton, a public relations professional and researcher, told *Editor & Publisher*.

Morton conducted a study that confirmed what journalists have long known: Press releases are rejected because they lack news, their writers never bother to localize them, they're too long, they contain too much propaganda and too few facts, they arrive late and they are poorly written or written for clients rather than for journalists.

The skills you learn as a journalist are precisely the same skills that will determine your success as a publicist. Journalists depend upon public relations people as important sources for stories. As a beginning journalist on the campus paper, for instance, you should become well acquainted with your school's public relations professionals and ask for releases on a regular basis. From those releases come important news stories; a well-developed public relations source might help you with exclusives or arrange for an interview with a hard-to-reach news maker. Though publicists can be a hindrance, often blocking access to news makers, a publicist you've cultivated as a respected news provider might prove extremely helpful.

Suggested Assignments

1. Visit your campus newspaper office. Meet staff members and ask around for story ideas. Propose three well-focused story ideas you could report and publish.
2. Cover a student government meeting or campus news event or report on a breaking news story. Take notes and collect relevant facts, statistics, anecdotes and quotes. After you're done, present the story's focus to the class and explain, using your notes, what evidence you'll use to support the focus.
3. Research one of your story ideas by getting background on the problem or issue and collecting clips of stories previously written about it.
4. Identify at least three sources for the story you propose and explain what you expect their point of view will be. Then write a series of questions you'd ask of each.

4

Organizing Your Thinking

How do you know when you're done reporting?

1. When you've run out of time.
2. When sources are beginning to say the same things.
3. When you're absolutely certain you understand the problem completely and have spoken to everyone who can help you understand it better.

If you've reached point 3, it's time to think, not write.

Reporters who fail to organize their thinking usually end up with a disorganized, unfocused story. The reason: As we said in Chapter 3, you'll use only about 10 percent of the information you've gathered in reporting. Many reporters believe that when they sit down to write the story, some divine inspiration will guide them. For a lucky few blessed with natural story-telling abilities, writing is effortless and always well done. For just about everyone else, writing without thinking results in a muddled mess. Here's how to avoid that mess and create a well-organized, compelling and easy-to-read finished product.

Finding Your Focus

Throughout the reporting process, you have created, reevaluated and changed your focus repeatedly as the story twisted and turned in different directions. At some point in your reporting, you should have fixed on an angle, approach or theme and discussed it with your editor. Does your editor agree with your angle? If not, better to argue now, before you turn the story in on deadline and precipitate the sort of crisis that is rarely resolved the way a reporter wants it to be. Maybe you're confused or so close to your story that you've forgotten to ask a crucial question. A good editor will help, but you have to ask for help directly.

"Ms. Editor, I have all this information, but I'm not sure what the story's focus is. Can you help me find it?" Your editor should ask you a series of questions that will eventually give you a direction, a sentence that sums up the single most important point you're trying to make. If you can't boil it down to one sentence, you haven't thought hard enough. If you've thought as hard as your brain will allow and you're still unclear, it might mean that you need to do more reporting, that you still don't understand the story. Go back to your sources and ask more questions until the single sentence emerges. Sometimes it's helpful to ask yourself a few obvious questions. "What was the most important or unusual?" "What do I want to say about it?" After you've done that, ask yourself: "Who cares?" and "So what?"

When you and your editor are satisfied with your response, you've found your focus. Now you have to organize the rest of the story.

Good Writing Is Good Thinking

Many reporters refuse to organize stories before they write, preferring to struggle first for the perfect lead and then expecting that "the rest of the story will flow like lava," writes the *Portland Oregonian*'s writing guru Jack Hart in *Editor & Publisher*. These reporters, Hart says, often discover that:

- Writing is agony. For writers who have no guideposts to lead them through confusing material, progress can be painfully slow. Every story degenerates into a stressful series of false starts, detours and wasted time.
- Their stories are repetitious. Because no grand scheme guides the placement of material, the same points show up again and again.
- The good stuff gets cut. Color dropped into a disorganized story as an afterthought is an easy cut for a harried editor.
- Quality trails off after the opening. If you put all your effort into the lead and expect the rest of the story to spew forth from the head of Thor, I can make you a great deal on the Brooklyn Bridge.
- They waste a lot of time and mental resources as they move blocks of copy, shifting material around inside the story. They end up driving themselves—and their editors—crazy.

Hart continues:

> The failure to take time for organizing ends up wasting huge amounts of time in the writing. All those false starts, dead ends and what not. . . . The act of writing down a theme statement and a few main topics imposes on the chaos of detail you often face when reporting ends. It relieves panic because it allows you to ease into the story.

Writing is thinking. That's all there is to it.

Outlines

Spot news stories—also called breaking news—usually follow a standard formula for writing called the inverted pyramid. Using the inverted pyramid formula means organizing your information so that the most important goes first and the least important last. (Think of an upside-down triangle with the broad base at the top and the pointy end at the bottom. The broad base represents the most important information; the pointed end represents the least important.)

If time permits, create an outline before you begin writing. Just as you would never get on the freeway for a cross-country drive without a map, you should never embark on a story without a plan. The outline is the road map you'll consult to figure out the easiest, quickest way to your destination.

The outline for a spot news story contains **some or all** of the following elements. Also included are **suggested** paragraph lengths for each element:

1. **Lead (1 paragraph)**
   - Sums up the focus of your story.
   - Orients readers by telling them something surprising; entices them to continue reading for more details.
   - Answers Who? What? When? Where? Why? How?
2. **Background (1 paragraph)**
   Although not essential in the first paragraph, the information in the background paragraph gives readers what they need to understand the context of the lead. Often, the background paragraph will illuminate the story's impact—the effect that the news, issue, or event will have on your readers.
3. **Cosmic Quote (1 paragraph)**
   The quote must sum up the story's focus, illuminate it, or both.
4. **Reaction and response (1 paragraph)**
   Depending on the lead, you may need a reaction or response from someone accused of wrongdoing.
5. **The body of the story (No specified length)**
   Explain the issues introduced in your lead using parallel construction, facts, quotes, anecdotes and other evidence to support the story's focus.

With your story's focus in mind, you're ready to begin the outline process. On a piece of paper, write the following and answer each question in a few words:

1. Who?
   What?
   When?
   Where?
   Why?
   How?
2. Impact or background? (Some questions you might ask yourself to determine impact include: Who will it help? Hurt? Why is it important?)
3. Reaction? Response?
4. Cosmic quote?
5. Background?

From the answers to those questions, you'll craft the top of the story.

Now go through your notes and identify the facts, figures, quotes and anecdotes you need to support the story's focus, its impact and the reaction it engendered.

How do you decide what goes where in the body of the story? Follow the rules of the inverted pyramid: The most important information is introduced first; the least important goes last.

Remember, too, that though we're providing you with guidelines, your story will dictate what information goes where. Sometimes the cosmic quote will follow the background paragraph; sometimes the reaction will precede the impact. And not all stories contain all these elements (though most do). If you think that reporting the reaction to your story's focus is irrelevant, you may be right. But be prepared to justify to your editor why you failed to include it.

Make sure that you identify the elements you'll need to craft the story before you begin writing. Just as Michelangelo searched the quarries of Carrara for the perfect block of marble before he started chipping away at his sculpture, you, too, should carefully choose the information you'll need before you start shaping your story.

Organizing Follow-Ups

Often you'll follow a routine news story by reporting what's new. Sometimes the follow-up is the next day; sometimes it's months later. Next-day follow-ups are especially important in disaster and fire stories. Readers and viewers want to know why something happened. If a hospital collapses during an earthquake, is the earthquake the reason it collapsed? Ostensibly, yes, but there could be other, more relevant reasons. Did the hospital meet earthquake codes? Had inspectors cited it for code violations in the past? Did hospital officials respond to the citations or ignore them?

If four children die in a fire, you must find out what caused it. Fire officials frequently tell reporters that "the cause of the blaze is under investigation." Keep calling back until you know the cause. Were there smoke detectors? Did they work? Was it faulty wiring? Whose fault was it? An absentee landlord who refused to fix the outlets despite repeated requests from the tenants? Disaster and fire stories are never fully reported until you and your readers know the real reason that the crisis occurred and who's to blame for it.

Before you write, organize the reporting in the same way you organized your spot news story: using the formula we discussed in the previous section. Sometimes you'll follow up news stories that occurred weeks or months ago. Or it might be the next day. Find a fresh angle that focuses on what's happened since you last weighed in on the story and identify a news hook—the reason the issue is in the news now.

Let's look at a *Long Beach Press-Telegram* story about a local vote on same-sex marriage. The story is a follow-up to the previous day's story on the Long

Beach City Council's failure to pass a resolution opposing a proposed federal ban on same-sex marriage. As you read the following excerpt, note what the most recent spot news story might have been and when it might have run. Here it's fairly obvious: the last story obviously ran the day before. In this case, the newspaper found it important to get an explanation in the next day's issue on why the resolution failed. Also, ask yourself why there are so few quotes in the top of the story. And why does the reporter paraphrase so much information?

By Jason Gewirtz

LONG BEACH—An ill man on an airplane in Phoenix may have kept the Long Beach City Council from opposing a proposed federal ban on same-sex marriages. [Lead]

Had she attended an emotional Tuesday council meeting, Councilwoman Jackie Kell would have broken a 4-4 split on a council resolution to oppose the Federal Marriage Amendment. The proposed constitutional amendment would define marriage as a union between a man and a woman. [Impact]

The council's resolution, which needed five votes to pass, failed on the split decision after nearly two hours of impassioned public debate Tuesday on the issue of same-sex marriage. Area pastors largely spoke in favor of the proposed same-sex marriage ban on religious grounds, while gay and lesbian advocates argued on behalf of civil rights and nondiscrimination. [Background]

Kell missed the meeting after being delayed on a return trip from Missouri. A connecting flight she planned to catch in Phoenix was canceled because of a passenger's illness. [More background]

Had she voted, Kell said Wednesday, she "probably" would have supported the resolution sponsored by council members Dan Baker, Bonnie Lowenthal and Tonia Reyes Uranga.

Kell said she supports a "legal, civil commitment for those in the community that desire that." She added that she sees the issue as a state's right to decide.

"I think it tells you basically I probably would have gone with Baker's (position), except I like my verbiage better," she said. [Reaction]

In Kell's absence, the council deadlocked.

The council did, however, endorse wording for a more vague resolution that would support any amendment that protects equal rights and oppose an amendment that denies those rights.

—Long Beach *Press-Telegram*

Organizing Trend Pieces

Even more difficult to organize are trend pieces—enterprise stories that document change over time and put a series of seemingly routine stories or news events in perspective. Trend pieces usually have a news hook, a recent event that makes the story timely. Unlike a spot news story that focuses on a single specific event, issue or problem, a trend piece forces the reporter to investigate myriad events, issues or problems to illuminate for the reader how the seemingly disparate pieces fit together into a coherent story. Look, for example, at the following story "Over the Brink and Into Poverty"; it details an emerging trend of poverty in middle-class suburbia and small-town living as well as traditional impoverished areas of urban America and Appalachia. The story illuminates a larger problem and tells what it means. The story's news hook is the 40th anniversary of President Lyndon Johnson's declaration in 1964 of a War on Poverty across America.

The story's focus is summed up in the first two sentences.

By Alan Johnson, Catherine Candisky and Jonathan Riskind

It hides in plain sight in the hills of Appalachia, the cozy suburbs of central Ohio and the urban streets of Columbus.

Forty years after President Johnson came to southern Ohio to declare War on Poverty, the old enemy is making a comeback. [Lead]

But this is the new poverty.

It's not about those living in shacks or begging on the street, but about people from many walks of life who find themselves, often unexpectedly, struggling to meet their most basic needs.

This new poverty shows its face in Springfield, where a family of four eats popcorn and water for dinner—with peanut butter if they're lucky; in Athens County, where a husband and wife work six jobs between them trying to make ends meet; and in Westerville, where a young mother repeatedly glues her own shoes together so she has enough money to buy new shoes for her two children.

But the most glaring evidence of Ohioans' newfound struggles is the lengthening food lines across the state.

Dispatch reporters and photographers traveled to food lines during one week to learn why this supposed relic of the Great Depression has returned.

In that one week, from April 26 to May 1, the number of Ohioans served by food pantries statewide—more than 150,000—would have filled Ohio Stadium one and a half times. Nearly 2 million pounds of food were distributed—enough to fill 70 tractor-trailers.

The number of people seeking help at food pantries statewide has risen three straight years.

The Ohio Association of Second Harvest Foodbanks, which serves much of Ohio through 3,000 agencies, reported a 44 percent increase in people seeking assistance during the first three months of the year compared with the last three months of 2003. At the same time, the food available at pantries rose 4 percent. [Background]

And now beleaguered families of reserve and National Guard troops who have been stationed for months in Iraq or Afghanistan are showing up in food lines.

Vince Chase of Catholic Social Services of Clark, Champaign and Logan Counties calls Ohio's economic climate "Depression-like," the worst he's experienced in 30 years of helping people in need.

"We're seeing people who never thought they would be in this situation. Half of them are working people who have 10 to 15 to 20 years of work experience but don't have jobs. There are no jobs."

"It shows how fragile things can be for folks. You're cruising along, and an illness, an accident, the loss of a job can throw you into poverty. It doesn't take much for even middle-class people. Before you know it, you don't have anything left." [Cosmic quote]

In relatively affluent Butler County, where unemployment was 4.2 percent in April, President Bush said during a May 4 campaign stop that "the life of the average Ohio citizen is improving." Yet business is booming at The Lord's Cupboard pantry in the county seat of Hamilton, where the number seeking help nearly quadrupled from 2000 to 2004.

Invisible Americans
It's difficult to quantify those who have fallen into economic despair. Once workers lose their jobs and exhaust unemployment benefits, no agency counts them. When people go off welfare, the government doesn't track whether they have become self-sufficient—the mantra of welfare reform.

And nobody knows for certain how many people line up for free food across the United States. The number seeking emergency food nationwide from Catholic Charities USA and its partners has jumped about 20 percent annually in recent years, said Sharon Daly, the charity's vice president of social policy.

A U.S. Conference of Mayors survey of 25 cities in December 2003 found the demand at food pantries rose 17 percent over 2002. And the 2002 figure was 19 percent higher than the year before.

"These folks have become invisible," said Jack Frech, director of the Athens County Department of Job and Family Services. "Yet we all see them, no matter what you do. If you go to a retail store, a nursing home, if you have a child in day care, you're dealing with someone who has trouble feeding themselves.

"These people have done everything society has asked them to do, and they are not seeing the rewards that society promised."

Daily Struggles

Ohio's new poor are not easily categorized.

They are young and out of work, old and struggling with high medical bills, downsized or laid off from manufacturing jobs, grandmothers raising grandchildren, couples working two or more low-wage jobs.

Most never thought they would be poor. Some don't consider themselves poor now, and they aren't compared to many who struggled through the Depression or reside in Third World countries.

Although pantries check income, advocates acknowledge that a few less-deserving people sometimes slip through the food lines. But for the vast majority, setting foot in a food line means overcoming a stigma. They come because they are desperate.

Sheila Miller, who was laid off as a $36,000-a-year supervisor of an assisted-living company, came to a Logan pantry for the first time recently. Her husband works at a Haydenville sawmill, but the couple with two young children is having a hard time.

"It's embarrassing to come here," said Miller, 30. "It makes me feel ignorant—like I'm trash, and I'm not.

"Hopefully, there'll be some things in here my kids will eat," she said after her car was loaded with food.

Ginger Walls' unemployment ran out in February, leaving the single mother of two from Carbon Hill in Hocking County with $500 a month in child support and $359 in food stamps.

"I've got a lot of stuff at the pawn shop, and I borrow from my dad to pay the bills until the child support check comes," she said.

Since being laid off from her $10-an-hour job at Anchor Hocking in Lancaster nearly a year ago, Walls, 32, has been listed with three different temporary services; no one is hiring.

Mark Craig, 38, retired with a disability because of a back injury, relies on a food pantry to feed his wife and three children.

They have a monthly income of $1,993 from Social Security disability and family benefits. That's about $24,000 a year—slightly above the federal poverty level for a family of five.

But after paying the bills, the family has little left for food.

"There's been many times we've had popcorn and water for dinner, or popcorn and peanut butter. That's no joke," said Craig, who gets food from a Springfield pantry.

"Honest to God, I don't know what we'd do without this place."

— *Columbus Dispatch*

Clustering

Clustering—also called brainstorming—is one of the best and easiest tools for organizing trend and news features. Some of you have been doing clustering since your fourth-grade teacher taught it to you; others have never heard of it. Clustering forces reporters to figure out what evidence they need to support their story's focus.

We'll use the previous story as an example to explain to you, step by step, how to do it.

1. **Put away your notes.** This is a thinking exercise.

    Throughout the exercise, resist temptation to refer to your notes. You know a lot more than you think you do. Remember, part of what we're trying to help you develop is confidence.

2. **Cast your story's focus as a single-sentence statement.**

    This may seem simple, but with complicated stories, it might take you as much as an hour to figure out that single sentence. Finding a story's focus takes discipline, hard work and concentration; imagine it as the thread that holds together a diamond necklace. If the thread is flimsy and poorly woven, the necklace will break. If the thread is well-constructed and of high-quality material, it will hold the diamonds in place and allow them to sparkle. The story's focus is the thread that holds your story together. It should be well-woven, sturdy and unobtrusive.

    To assist you in constructing the sturdiest possible focus, we offer a few suggestions. First, cast your story's focus in terms of actors and action. Who's doing what to whom? Use action verbs to craft the focus, not static "to be" verbs or passive voice. A focus statement for the previous story might be this:

    > ACTORS: The number of Ohioans seeking help at food pantries
    > ACTION: Is increasing and causing concern among officials
    > FOCUS STATEMENT: A number of Ohioans from many walks of
    > life are unexpectedly struggling to meet their basic needs and are turn-
    > ing to food pantries to feed themselves and their families.

3. **In the middle of a piece of paper, write down your focus statement and draw a circle around it.** Imagine your circle as a wheel and draw spokes coming out from it.

At the end of each spoke, draw a smaller circle. Each of these circles represents the diamonds you'll string on the thread that is your focus.

In each of the circles, write down one of the many aspects of your story that relates to the focus. Any time you get stuck, analyze your focus statement or a statement you've just written and ask yourself, "So what?" "Who cares?"

Let's refer again to the story about the growing number of people seeking public assistance in Ohio. The study alerts the reporter to a problem. The reporter's job is to tell readers and viewers not only that a problem exists but why it exists and what can be done to help solve it. The reporters interviewed both the officials providing food assistance and the people seeking help.

As you fill in your cluster, do it randomly, drawing as many spokes and circles as you have information to illuminate the focus. Connect the circles that are related. Keep going until you feel certain you've put down on paper every aspect of the story, and you've noted how the various parts of the story relate to one another.

Now you're ready to create your outline.

Before we move to the crucial outline step, let's walk through the process once again, using a different story. We'll start with the idea, create the focus, cluster, and then outline.

The idea: Recently released statistics from the College Board showed that tuition at the nation's public and private colleges and universities continues to rise. By 2005, it had risen to more than $11,000 and $27,000, respectively. At the most exclusive private universities, the College Board estimated, it can cost even more.

At the same time, Congress has cut back sharply on federal grants for students.

The focus: As we discussed with the last story, the writer reports not only the problem but also how the problem affects people. In this case, the reporter must determine what effect the tuition hike and the reduction in government assistance has had on students. After interviewing sources and gathering statistics, the reporter formulated a main point.

ACTORS: Students
ACTION: Seek financial help as college costs soar.

Outlining Trend Stories

Now it's time to create the outline. The cluster provides us with the information we need to construct a solid road map. It consists of

1. The story's lead (1 paragraph)
2. Nut graph/Focus statement; also answers the questions who, what, when, where, why and how. (1 paragraph)
3. News hook (1 paragraph) (Answers: Why is this story in the news today?)
4. Background (1 paragraph)
5. Cosmic quote (1 paragraph)

Those elements constitute the top of your story. The body of your story, the bulk of it, explains and amplifies the top of your story.

The body of your story is usually divided into three parts (though in longer, more complicated pieces, it may stretch to as many as six parts.) Those three parts explain the most important conclusions you have to support your story's focus. You'll then support conclusions with the evidence you've collected in your reporting—the statistics, anecdotes and quotes you have to prove your point.

To determine what those three conclusions are, refer back to your cluster. Though we've noted 15 points, many of the points are related to one another. Arrange the related points into three separate lists. Each of those lists of evidence, when considered as a whole, points to a conclusion. Formulate those three conclusions using the same method we discussed for creating a focus statement: Who are the actors? What action did they take? What happened as a result?

> ACTORS: Colleges and universities
> ACTION: Charge students more.
> POINT 1: Colleges and universities continue to charge students more for tuition.
> ACTORS: Students
> ACTION: Cope.
> POINT 2: Students cope with tuition increases as best they can.
> ACTORS: Politicians
> ACTION: Propose solutions.
> POINT 3: While politicians propose solutions, college officials urge students to keep seeking financial aid.

Now that you have the three major points, fill in the top of the story, piece by piece. Start with the nut graph, or focus, followed by the lead, the cosmic quote, the news hook and the background paragraph. (Turn to your notes for assistance in finding the evidence you need to create these elements.)

NUT GRAPH: Students and parents are approaching the entire college-selection process with a far sterner eye on finances, counselors said. More students are considering state universities, are applying for merit-based scholarships and are working to make ends meet.

LEAD: American students are becoming more careful shoppers when it comes to choosing—and paying for—their college educations.

COSMIC QUOTE: "Spiraling college costs have reached a saturation point in the eyes of many people," says Frank Burnett, the executive director of the National Association of College Admission Counselors.

NEWS HOOK: After decades of soaring tuition costs

BACKGROUND: The financing problem intensified during the 1980s and early 1990s, when college administrators found themselves facing a shrinking market as a result of the birth dearth of the late 1960s and early 1970s—and a potentially sharp decline in revenues.

The hardest part of the job is over. You've identified the major parts of your story. But there's still more thinking to do. Review carefully the three major points. Does each follow logically? If not, recast the parts until they do.

When you're satisfied with the order, go through your notes and identify the relevant anecdotes, statistics and quotes, and mark each with a 1, 2 or 3, depending upon which point the evidence illuminates.

Writing an Organized Story

It's time to write.

First, look at the elements that make up the top of your story. Does one logically follow the next? If not, reorder them until they do. Write the top of your story.

Next, turn to your notes and review all the material marked with a 1. From that material, write the first part.

Repeat the process for part 2 and part 3.

You're done. The story is written without pain, writer's block or loss of hair.

WASHINGTON—American students are becoming more careful shoppers when it comes to choosing—and paying for—their college educations. [Lead]

After decades of soaring tuition costs [News hook] counselors say that students and parents are approaching the entire college-selection process with a far sterner eye on finances.

More students are considering state universities, applying for merit-based scholarships and working to make ends meet. [Nut graph]

"Spiraling college costs have reached a saturation point in the eyes of many people," says Frank Burnett, the executive director of the National Association of College Admission Counselors. [Cosmic quote]

The financing problem intensified during the 1980s and early 1990s, when college administrators found themselves facing a shrinking market as a result of the birth dearth of the late 1960s and early 1970s—and a potentially sharp decline in revenues. [Background]

POINT 1:

Instead of reducing tuition prices, many colleges sought to compete for more students by improving their services—hiring better faculty members, increasing the maintenance of grounds and buildings and expanding student support services, says Arthur Hauptman, a consultant.

As a result, the 1980s saw an explosion in tuition and other charges at the nation's colleges—often several times the economy's overall rate of inflation.

In 1980, for example, the average cost for undergraduate tuition and room and board at the nation's public colleges was

$2,422; for private schools, it was $6,570. Today, those costs are well over $11,000 and $27,000, respectively.

At the most exclusive private universities in the nation, it can cost even more.

Meanwhile, Congress—facing a tight budget at the federal level—has cut back sharply on federal grants, forcing many more students who traditionally have benefited from federal scholarships to rely on student loans instead.

The change has been significant. In 1982, for example, students at 42 of the nation's leading black colleges had amassed about $27 million in student loans; by this year, that number had almost doubled—to $52 million.

POINT 2:
"People looking for financial assistance are no longer the needy poor," Burnett points out. These days, "needy as it relates to higher education can be middle-class people," Burnett said.

The students themselves are very aware of financial pressures. Sonja Benkovich, 20, a student at the University of Virginia, put in more than 60 hours a week this summer at two different jobs, trying to raise $5,000 for next year.

In the past, Benkovich has received part-time jobs through her school's financial aid office. But budget cuts affecting the institution have Benkovich wondering if she will be able to get a similar job during the upcoming academic year.

Ironically, perhaps, the rush toward public universities is coming as some of the most prestigious private schools are beginning to limit the size of their tuition increases, while state schools are increasing their bills.

UC Berkeley will increase its tuition by almost 40 percent starting this autumn, but Stanford University will boost its charges by only 5 percent, its smallest such rise in more than a decade, university officials said.

Berkeley still had a much larger increase in applicants this year than Stanford had. Even with a steep tuition increase, its tuition for California residents is almost $10,000 less than tuition at Stanford.

POINT 3:
Washington politicians are pondering legislative solutions to the problem of rising tuition costs. One proposal includes providing higher cash grants to low-income students and increasing the maximum amount for federally subsidized loans. Another plan would eliminate the financial need requirements for federally subsidized loans.

Meanwhile, Dallas Martin, president of the National Association of Student Aid Administrators, urges students not to be discouraged. "Financial aid," he said, "is still out there."

A Note on Anecdotal and Example Leads

Don't let trend stories with anecdotal leads confuse you. Most follow the same outline format we just discussed, with a slight variation. The writer chooses an anecdote that best sums up the story's focus and uses it to introduce the problem or issue the story then explores.

In the following story, about sex offenders, notice how the writer constructs the anecdote and follows it with the cosmic quote and background.

By Paul Young

The way the landlord acted just didn't seem right. He cooed over an 11-year-old girl's appearance. He was caught eyeing a 12-year-old as she bent over to wash his car. And young children were often seen going in and out of his apartment.

So, just as a precaution, one of his tenants decided to do some investigating of her own, to ensure that her daughters were safe. Her husband described the result.

"My wife came home one day and was out of breath," the husband says. "I asked what was wrong, and she said, 'You won't believe what I found out. He's a sex offender.'" [End of anecdote]

As media continue to focus on recent kidnappings and child murders, more people across the state are flocking to their computers and those of law enforcement to find out whether sex offenders are living in their neighborhoods. [Focus/nut graph]

Millions of people have logged onto a new local site, www.lacounty.info, since its launch about two weeks ago. For the first time, Californians can find out whether sexual predators live in their neighborhood without ever leaving the house. Then, they can go to a designated police or sheriff's station and look up the details in California's Megan's Law database.

Supporters say the database is a safeguard against sex offenders, a useful tool for law enforcement and a boon to society. Critics question the system's effectiveness and say the resulting public reaction may violate a sex offender's Fifth Amendment rights by, in effect, punishing him twice for the same crime.

This year, the community has put the databases to plenty of use. Lacounty.info has had nearly 12 million hits since it was launched Sept. 6. Even before the Web site opened, the Long Beach Police Department saw a nearly 600 percent increase in the use of its sole public Megan's Law computer, located at 333 W. Broadway.

The terminal was used by 126 people this year, compared with 23 people in the same period of 2001. [Background paragraphs]

"Through the years, any time there is a high-profile case— either child molestation or a kidnapping—there is an increase in people going to police stations (to use the terminals)," says Mike Van Winkle, a spokesman for the Department of Justice, which runs the database. [Cosmic quote]

"A number of departments say dozens of people are coming in each day, where before, they only saw a few people a week." [Comment from a public official]

The database stops short of giving offenders' exact addresses, but users can glean plenty of information, such as the block on which a sex offender lives and his (or her) picture, name, criminal history and risk to society.

In a recent search, Elizabeth Guerra, 36, of Long Beach, says she found 44 sex offenders living in her 90807 ZIP code.

She says the idea of using the Megan's law computer had been in the back of her mind since 7-year-old Danielle van Dam of San Diego was murdered by her neighbor, David Westerfield, who lived two doors away. [News hook linked to quote from a local resident]

What moved her to action, however, was the fliers posted on about a dozen trees and poles in her California Heights neighborhood. They read: "ATTENTION PARENTS. SEX OFFENDER WARNING. There are registered sex offenders living in this neighborhood. . . You have a right to know. A message from your concerned neighbors."

Guerra says she appreciates the knowledge she gained about who lives in her neighborhood, but it left her more fearful that her children are at risk. "I used to be outside every day, but it's a little different now," she says.

"I look at everybody who goes by in cars to see if they're looking at my kids funny. I look in (her children's) closet before they go to bed at night. I don't let my kids talk to people they don't know. . . I never let my guard down anymore."

—Long Beach *Press-Telegram*

Suggested Assignments

1. Report on a story idea you've proposed. Following the guidelines discussed in this chapter, create an outline using clustering.
2. Cover a student government meeting or campus news event or report on a breaking news story. Following the guidelines discussed in this chapter, create an outline using clustering.

5

Writing the Story

In the previous chapter, you took apart and rebuilt several stories. Now create your own story. Since we presume you followed the organizing steps outlined in the previous chapter, we can spend considerable time in this chapter teaching you how to improve and fine-tune your writing.

Before you begin, ask yourself a couple of crucial questions: Do I understand what I'm writing about? Can I state it in two sentences or fewer?

If the answer is no, reread Chapter 4. If the answer is yes, ask yourself: Do I know what point I want to make? Can I state it in two sentences or fewer?

If the answer is no, reread Chapter 4. If the answer is yes, you're ready to write.

Follow the outline you created in the previous chapter as you would a road map. If en route, you realize that your outline took you to a dead end, redraw it to reflect a new route. If you find yourself moving around blocks of copy in your story as you write and you're becoming frustrated, you have either a faulty outline or a reporting problem. Either way, stop and spend a few minutes thinking. After you've diagnosed the problem, it becomes much easier to correct it. False hope and pride make writers think they can "write through" disorganized thinking. Without clear thinking, you will never have clear writing.

One last caveat: We assume you know some mechanics. We assume you know basic rules of grammar (the difference between its and it's, for instance) and punctuation (especially how to punctuate a quote). We assume you know to use a computer spell check or a dictionary before you submit a story for editing. We assume you know the difference between first, second and third person and between past, present and future tense. For simplicity's sake, write your stories in third person and stay as much as possible in the past tense, especially when you're attributing quotes. (More on that later.) If these basic style and grammar concepts are foreign to you, consider enrolling in a beginning composition course.

Putting It All Together

If you've thought through your story carefully, your focus is clear and so is your lead. A spot news lead telegraphs the focus and essential news of the story, answering the questions who, what, when, where, why and how. The best lead also answers the question "who cares?" by telling readers what's unusual about this particular story, what makes it different from other stories of its kind. Where possible, leads should focus on people doing things, since readers have a hard time identifying with impersonal institutions and abstract, important issues of the day. If an event is the story's focus, show how the event will affect or has affected people.

The following lead from the *New York Times* is about the signing of a Middle East peace treaty. The writer, Thomas L. Friedman, makes clear that this is not just another treaty signing. He frames the story by focusing not on the treaty but on the people signing it. Through the story's human elements, Friedman is able to communicate the treaty's essential history and meaning and keep the reader's attention focused. As you read the lead, point to the words or phrases that telegraph the story's essential news, its focus and how it differs from other stories of its kind. Also, identify the who, what, when, where, why and how of the story. (In this case, the how signifies how they came to reach the agreement, not how they physically signed the treaty.)

Note, too, the details the writer observes and how he uses those details to advance the story's focus. When he describes Yitzhak Rabin, he says his "face is etched with the memories of every Arab-Israeli war." Not only does he paint a vivid portrait of Rabin's face, he gives the reader background on Rabin's relationship to the peace process. The writer's skill at communicating complicated ideas simply and precisely is also evident in the story's first few words: "In a triumph of hope over history" puts the treaty in its proper historical context.

As you write your stories, strive to achieve the same sort of economy of language. Ruthlessly prune your writing until every word is essential to understanding the story's focus. By carefully outlining your story and attending to each word's importance, you'll avoid repetition, the worst sort of wordiness.

By Thomas L. Friedman

WASHINGTON, Sept. 13 — In a triumph of hope over history, Yitzhak Rabin, the Prime Minister of Israel, and Yasir Arafat, the chairman of the P.L.O., shook hands today on the White House lawn, sealing the first agreement between Jews and Palestinians to end their conflict and share the holy land along the River Jordan that they both call home.

On the sun-splashed South Lawn of the White House, with 3,000 witnesses watching in amazement — including former Presidents Jimmy Carter and George Bush — Foreign Minister Shimon Peres of Israel and Jahmoud Abbas, the foreign policy spokesman for the Palestine Liberation Organization, signed a "Declaration of Principles" on Palestinian self-government in Israeli-occupied Gaza and the West Bank at 11:43 a.m.

Mr. Rabin, whose face is etched with the memories of every Arab-Israeli war, captured in his remarks the exhaustion of all parties with the centuries-old conflict. "We the soldiers who have returned from the battle stained with blood," he said, "we who have fought against you, the Palestinians, we say to you today in a loud and clear voice: 'Enough of blood and tears! Enough!'"

Mr Arafat, relishing his moment of acceptance on the White House lawn, strove to give Mr. Rabin the appropriate response, declaring in Arabic: "Our two peoples are awaiting today this historic hope, and they want to give peace a real chance."

—New York Times

Observe how Friedman translates complicated ideas into simple, plain English. He chooses concrete examples over abstract concepts and paints a picture with words by focusing on the scene's actors and the meaning of what they did that day.

Readers want the news to make sense quickly and easily. Being thorough and complete, though, does not mean dull, wordy, complicated and long. (Friedman's report is far from shallow.) By consistently following a few simple rules of good writing, you can communicate complicated ideas in ways that make sense. In short, you can connect with your readers rather than overwhelm and confuse them.

Show, Don't Tell

We've already discussed the importance of preferring the concrete to the abstract. Now, let's explore another rule: choosing action verbs over dull adjectives and tired clichés. In other words, show, don't tell.

Let's go back to comparing the *New York Times* and the description of the signing of the Middle East peace treaty.

How does the *New York Times* describe the scene? Using active voice and action verbs. Friedman lets the scene's details communicate drama. He shows his readers, he doesn't tell them:

President Clinton, who gracefully shepherded Mr. Arafat and Mr. Rabin through their awkward reconciliation, hailed them both for their "brave gamble that the future can be better than the past."

The agreement, which will eventually allow Palestinians to run their own affairs as Israeli troops pull back within months from the Gaza Strip and Jericho in a first step, was reached during secret negotiations over the past few months between Israelis and Palestinians, under the direction of Mr. Peres and Mr. Abba, through the mediation of Norway.

The documents were signed on the same wooden table on which the Peace Treaty between Egypt and Israel was signed in 1979. That table stood today as a silent memorial to the assassinated Egyptian President Anwar el-Sadat, whose path-breaking visit to Israel in 1977 and subsequent agreements at Camp David brought him denunciations as a traitor by Mr. Arafat but who was now being followed by the Palestinian leader.

But the audience in attendance, and perhaps millions more watching back in the Middle East, seemed less interested in the formal signing than in the visual moment that would somehow make this tentative peace real: the handshake between the two old warriors who personified the conflict between their peoples.

Moments after the documents were signed, Mr. Clinton took Mr. Arafat in his left arm and Mr. Rabin in his right arm and gently coaxed them together, needing to give Mr. Rabin just a little extra nudge in the back. Mr. Arafat reached out his hand first, and then Mr Rabin, after a split second of hesitation and with a wan smile on his face, received Mr. Arafat's hand. The audience let out a simultaneous sigh of relief and a peal of joy, as a misty-eyed Mr. Clinton beamed away.

Two hands that had written the battle orders for so many young men, two fists that had been raised in anger at one another so many times in the past locked together for a fleeting moment of reconciliation.

But much difficult work, and many more compromises, will now have to be performed by these same two men to make it a lasting moment. That reality was underscored by the fact that both Mr. Rabin and Mr. Arafat invoked their peoples' undying attachment to Jerusalem in their respective speeches.

This is far better than using adjectives and clichés to describe the same scene. Instead of showing the action, another, less skilled writer might have used clichés such as "swift pen strokes" to describe the signing, or "under brilliant sunshine" to describe the weather.

In the *New York Times* account, we discover just how significant that small smile was. We understand, without being told, how and why the signing was emotional. Only in the *New York Times* account do we learn that the president of the United States had to literally push Rabin into shaking hands with Arafat. Writing on deadline stories as complicated as these requires considerable historical and political knowledge. Knowledge, combined with keen observational skills and an ability to organize complicated information into clear, focused prose, make a well-written story. Just as Friedman has applied the basic rules of good writing to a spot news story, so should you.

The following excerpt from a *Long Beach Press-Telegram* story is an example of a well-crafted lead. Note that it contains the essential elements we've discussed: It makes a concrete, simple, clear statement conveying the essential news of the story. It includes the five W's, how and who cares in the first few paragraphs. The writer provides a background paragraph when needed. Note the rich details contained in the direct quotes that convey the emotion behind the ruling.

By Wendy Thomas Russell

NORWALK — A successful real-estate agent was sentenced to 15 years to life in prison Friday for killing his wife, the daughter of a late state senator.

Bruce Koklich, 44, pursed his lips and clasped his hands tightly together as Norwalk Superior Court Judge Philip Hickok imposed the sentence mandated for second-degree murder. Hickok also denied a defense motion for a new trial and a request to release Koklich on bail pending his appeal.

Despite repeated claims of his innocence, Koklich was convicted last October of killing Jana Carpenter Koklich, the daughter of Paul Carpenter, whose dying wish was that his son-in-law be charged with murder. [Background]

Jana's body still has not been found, and prosecutors tried the unusual case without a body, murder weapon or motive — facts that now form the basis of Koklich's appeal.

Koklich appeared largely unemotional throughout Friday's hearing, even when his wife's mother and two of her close friends read from passion-filled statements, at times addressing the defendant directly.

"I lost my only child when she was in the prime of her life," said Janie Carpenter, Jana's mother, reading from a prepared statement. "There is a permanent hole in my heart. It will be there for the rest of my life."

Janie Carpenter told the judge how much her daughter had loved Bruce Koklich, and how her heart would have broken if she had known about Bruce's ill intentions toward her.

"Before she died," Carpenter said, "did she realize that her husband was committing the ultimate betrayal?"

—Long Beach *Press-Telegram*

Tips for Writing Effective Leads

1. Use Blind Identification Leads to Streamline Stories   Blind identification leads omit the names of unknown sources and identify them more generally by their age, hometown, title or occupation. In the next two leads, the names of the story's subjects are omitted. Instead, the writers refer to a "champion horseman" or "a screaming 9-year-old girl." The reason: It streamlines the lead, trimming it to the essentials needed to understand the story's focus. If people are not well-known in the community, their names are less important than other more salient facts that identify them: "a champion horseman" or a "screaming 9-year-old girl," for instance.

> Early this morning, five days after the Arlington police say a stranger seized a screaming 9-year-old girl from her bicycle and stuffed her into a black pick-up truck, local officials said that a body recovered on Wednesday night was that of the missing girl.
>
> The Tarrant County Medical Examiner's office today ruled the death of the girl, Amber Hagerman, a homicide.
>
> *—New York Times*

> A champion horseman and son of one of the richest men in the United States was sentenced yesterday in Chicago to almost three years in prison for his role in the killing of a show horse for insurance money.
>
> The defendant, George Lindemann Jr., son of a cellular phone magnate and the operator of a horse farm near Greenwich, Conn., was ordered to report to federal prison within 30 days.
>
> *—New York Times*

Readers recognize well-known community members, so reporters usually name them in the lead. If your college president was sentenced to three years in prison, for example, you would lead the story for your campus newspaper with his name:

> Knowitall University President I.M. Lying was sentenced Tuesday to almost three years in prison for his role in the killing of a show horse for insurance money.

2. Find the News and Focus on It Shoddily crafted leads are cluttered with details that smother the story's focus. Save the details for the rest of the story. For example:

> Roger Carlson, 19, Carol Barnes, 18, and Andrew Grimes, 21, suffered injuries last night when their 1985 Camaro was in a collision with a 1993 Buick Regal driven by Dwight Jones, 27, at the intersection of Addison and Birch streets, when Jones, according to police, failed to stop for a red light and was violating the speed limit.

Compare it with this lead, which focuses on the most important news of the story: who was hurt.

> Three people were injured last night when two cars collided at Addison and Birch streets.

3. Prefer the Specific to the General When reporting on a meeting, for example, the lead should focus on the action taken and explain what will happen as a result. People getting together for a meeting is not news; neither is the fact that they discussed issues or a prominent person spoke. Tell readers how the news will affect them. Give them a reason to care about your story. In the following leads, the reader is left wondering: Who cares?

> The city council met last night in its regular session.
> The city council last night took a vote on the proposed sale of Boyce Park after two hours of discussion.
> State Attorney General Norma Lowe spoke last night in the Shriners' Auditorium.

Rewritten, the leads tell readers what action was taken or what controversial opinion was shared.

> The city council last night voted 6–3 to sell half of Boyce Park to a group of real estate developers who plan to build a condominium complex.
> The death penalty is immoral and ought to be outlawed, State Attorney General Norma Lowe told a room packed with her supporters Tuesday night at a $25-a-plate fundraiser in the Shriners' Auditorium.

4. Be Thorough in Your Presentation of Facts   Answers to all the important questions—who, what, when where, why and how—may not be in every lead. You should either answer them or explain why you can't. Sometimes we must wait until more facts unfold. The cause of air crashes, oil spills or explosive gas leaks may not be known until several days later. For example, you might write, "The cause of the blast is under investigation" or "officials want to see lab results before they announce a cause of death."

5. Identify the Time   When in doubt, put it after the verb.

> After a wild battle that raged through the night and left bodies scattered across the snow-covered plains, President Boris N. Yeltsin said Wednesday that the Russian Army had finally managed to overcome a group of rebels who had been trapped in a village near Kemsi-Yurt.

6. Shorten Titles   Often, your sources will have titles so unwieldy that even they have no idea what they mean. For cases in which titles overwhelm the news, shorten them without diminishing the source's position. Make sure you ask sources whether your abbreviation still adequately reflects their titles. The following lead needs a rewrite:

> Jane Doe, chairwoman/vice president of Knowitall University's division of internal communications and diversity affairs, told a group of students Tuesday that she believes disabled students receive less attention than they deserve.

The title must be shortened and the lead rewritten to reflect the importance of what's being said, rather than who's saying it:

> Disabled students receive less attention than they deserve, the university's administrator in charge of diversity said Tuesday at the first meeting of a group of students and faculty charged with making the campus more wheelchair accessible.

7. Avoid Question Leads   As journalists, we're supposed to answer questions, not ask them.

8. Avoid Quote Leads   An exception sometimes may be made when a speaker is marking a historic occasion or when a quote is so dramatic that it cries out as a lead.

Reading is a disorienting process. It requires people to look at a white piece of paper covered with a bunch of squiggly black marks and make sense of them. Leads that begin with quotes often disorient readers by distracting them unnecessarily.

If you start a story, "Come right in. Let's get going," you invite confusion.

Instead of orienting readers to the focus of your story, that sort of lead forces readers to ask themselves distracting questions: Who's talking? Where are they going? What are they doing? What does this have to do with me?

Orient your reader with answers, not questions.

Clear Writing Reflects Clear Thinking

Students often ask, How do I know what to put in the story and what to leave out? The question answers itself if you've created an outline. Irrelevant information is anything that fails to advance the story's focus. Leave it out. Often, after students have organized their notes, they realize they spent a great deal of time collecting interesting yet irrelevant information and still need to do more reporting to clearly explain a story's focus. The outline finds the story's holes quickly, telling you what you need to find out. It also identifies information potentially useful for a sidebar.

A sidebar to a story explores an issue or idea that, while interesting, fails to fit into the main story because it remains tangential to the focus. Sidebars engage readers by giving them more information if they want it, helping to draw them into the issues of the main story. Decide with your editor at the outline stage what information you want to put into the main story and what you'd like to use in a sidebar.

Micro-Organization

Your outline reflects the story's macro-organization; now let's talk about micro-organization. Each sentence, paragraph and section of your story requires organization, too. Writers who use outlines rarely encounter micro-organizational problems. But nearly all young writers unwilling to invest time in thinking before they write find themselves at some point frantically "dumping the notebook," as it's called, putting their notes into a story without mentally processing them first, moving around sentences and paragraphs without any sense of why they want them to go someplace else.

A few rules of micro-organization bear remembering:

1. Each sentence should contain one central idea.
2. Each sentence should lead logically to the next.
3. When necessary, transitions should ease the reader from one issue to the next and connect the main points of your story. The aim is to move the reader easily from paragraph to paragraph.
4. The top of your story should include the essential information needed to inform the reader of the news and, if necessary, should have a background paragraph, a news hook and a cosmic quote.
5. Put attributions at the end of the sentence, unless who's saying it is more important than what's being said.

Variations on the Inverted Pyramid in News Stories

Today's news writers must become adept at reporting and writing a hybrid of spot news and features called the news feature, news analysis or trend piece. Writing this story well depends on the initiative and enterprise of the reporter in going beyond the day's news events and making sense of them.

In writing and organizing these stories, you must still observe the rules we've already discussed: the top of the story must answer who, what, when, where, why, how and who cares, for example. At the same time, though, news features, news analysis and trend pieces have a news hook, a reason for being in the news, and often a background paragraph to explain the significance or larger historical context of the lead.

The following story analyzes the controversy over the appropriateness of whether religious sloganry should be displayed at public ceremonies, in this case at a college graduation. As you read, try to identify the elements used to construct the top of the story: the news hook, nut graph, background and cosmic quote.

Sometimes reporters put news events or conflicts into context with details and visual writing. Scenes are chosen carefully not only to hook the reader but also to advance the story's focus, to convey essential news and to answer who, what, when, where, why, how and who cares. As you read the following lead, notice how the writer used details to illuminate the story's focus:

By Marlo Jo Fisher

IRVINE—A green stole that some Muslim students plan to wear around their necks at this weekend's University of California, Irvine, graduation ceremonies has become symbolic of the tensions on campus this year between Jewish and Muslim student groups.

At last count, 11 members of UCI's Muslim Student Union were planning to wear stoles bearing religious slogans over their gowns—the same slogans that students say were worn last year at three UC campuses without incident.

This year, however—after incidents that included the mysterious burning down of a cardboard wall erected by pro-Palestinian students and Jewish complaints over anti-Zionist speakers invited by Muslim groups—the words seem to have new meaning.

The controversy began after rumors began circulating on campus that Muslim students planned to wear Hamas armbands to graduation—an allegation that they vigorously deny. Hamas is a pro-Palestinian group that promotes suicide attacks.

Jewish students and outside groups began to vigorously protest to campus officials about the Hamas armbands—reports of which even surfaced Wednesday night on "The O'Reilly Factor," a Fox television show.

A very different truth soon surfaced, though. Although no one was wearing armbands, a handful of Muslim students did plan to wear stoles over their gowns, as do many other graduates who want to commemorate groups they have ties to.

On one side, the stoles say "God, increase my knowledge."

On the other side, they have the word "shahada" written in Arabic.

Jewish students and outside groups that have gotten involved in the controversy, such as the American Jewish Congress, say the wearing of a garment with that word implies approval of terrorism and suicide bombings.

"I am offended by that," said Larry Mahler, president of the UCI chapter of the Jewish fraternity Alpha Epsilon Pi. "What they are doing is ratifying the suicide bombing that killed innocent people."

Muslim students said the word is intended only as a religious statement. According to the U.S. Central Intelligence Agency Web site, shahada may be translated as, "There is no God but God; Muhammad is the Messenger of God."

"It's written in mosques. The Saudi flag has it on it," said Muslim student Aatif Abdul-Qadeer, dispelling the notion that it is a terrorist message.

However, frightened by allegations on "The O'Reilly Factor" that they have links to terrorism, Muslim students mostly laid low Thursday, a day that was marked on campus by final exams and preparations for commencement.

"That was a slanderous statement," Abdul-Qadeer said. "We are being called terrorists when all we are doing is speaking out."

UCI received an onslaught of calls Thursday.

"This has gotten so out of control," said UCI Dean of Students Sally Peterson, who was preparing to meet with another set of students to discuss the issue. "At last count, there were 11 students planning to wear the stoles. . . . Some of the students are not sure if they want to wear them now."

UCI Chancellor Ralph Cicerone issued a letter to the campus on the controversy, reiterating that UCI will not ban the students from wearing the stoles.

"UCI is a public university with people from diverse backgrounds who enjoy the rights and protection of the First Amendment," Cicerone wrote. "Our history includes the free and peaceful expression of political and nonpolitical ideas, no matter how controversial."

UCI professor Mark LeVine, who teaches Middle Eastern history, blamed a lack of critical thinking for the political tensions among students this year.

"There is very little self-criticism among any of the groups, who should be brutally searching for the truth," said LeVine, who is Jewish. "(College is) one of the few times when you have the luxury of thinking things through, but both sides would rather denigrate the other."

LeVine, who teaches a class on Palestine and was in Iraq in March, said he was not disturbed by stoles with the word shahada on them, as long as the people wearing them were not claiming ties to terrorist organizations.

"This is not helping anything and not doing anything to bring peace and justice anywhere," LeVine said.

More than 6,000 students will get degrees in eight separate ceremonies on Saturday and Sunday.

—Orange County Register

NUT GRAPH: A green stole that some Muslim students plan to wear around their necks at this weekend's University of California, Irvine, graduation ceremonies has become symbolic of the tensions on campus this year between Jewish and Muslim student groups.

NEWS HOOK: This year, however—after incidents that included the mysterious burning down of a cardboard wall erected by pro-Palestinian students and Jewish complaints over anti-Zionist speakers invited by Muslim groups—the words seem to have new meaning.

BACKGROUND: The controversy began after rumors began circulating on campus that Muslim students planned to wear Hamas armbands to graduation—an allegation that they vigorously deny. Hamas is a pro-Palestinian group that promotes suicide attacks.

COSMIC QUOTE: "UCI is a public university with people from diverse backgrounds who enjoy the rights and protection of the First Amendment," Cicerone wrote. "Our history includes the free and peaceful expression of political and non-political ideas, no matter how controversial."

On Writing Well

The rules we've discussed thus far apply to any sort of writing, not just journalism. Though stylistic differences exist between journalism and other sorts of writing, certain truths still apply.

Some of those truths include some basic rules.

1. Cut unnecessary fat. "If I had more time," Mark Twain once wrote to a friend, "I would have written you a shorter letter." Twain believed in conveying the greatest meaning with the fewest words, and so should you. Preserve meaning, but prune ruthlessly.

2. Use simple, clear language. Stories lose their punch when they contain vague, mushy words. In photography, the sharper the focus, the better the picture. Writers bring meaning into focus with concrete examples and vivid writing. The following examples show how to sharpen your focus by using specific nouns and active verbs to convey actors and action.

> *Fuzzy*: His head was injured by a blunt instrument.
> *Clear*: An unidentified attacker fractured his skull with a sledge-hammer.
> *Fuzzy*: The chief executive rode down the main thoroughfare.
> *Clear*: Gov. Paulson rode down Spencer Avenue in a convertible BMW.
> *Fuzzy*: Officers removed a gun from his clothing.
> *Clear*: Police took a .32-caliber revolver from his pocket.

3. Say what you mean. This principle is best illustrated by trying to figure out what's wrong with the following example:

> The divers strapped on oxygen tanks, jumped into the water and began searching the swollen river for the body of the lost heiress.

Divers breathe air, not oxygen. When in doubt, look it up.

See what's wrong here:

> The controversy centers around the ongoing battle between the Republicans, who want less government spending, and the Democrats, who want to preserve assistance programs for the poor.

It's not possible to "center around"; the controversy "centers on."

See what's wrong here:

> Over 150 people attended the conference, which drew delegates from as
> far away as Africa and Asia.

"Over" does not mean "more than."
See what's wrong here:

> Hopefully, Charles Whitcomb will remain in prison for the rest of his
> life, said June Thompson, the woman he was convicted of raping.

Unless Whitcomb is serving his sentence "full of hope," the word "hopefully" is misused.

These are only a few of the common mistakes students make because they forget to choose words carefully. To people who love language, glaring mistakes such as those previously mentioned are as offensive as obscenities.

4. Choose active over passive voice.   Wherever possible, replace static "to be" verbs ("there is," "is going," "will have gone," and so on) with action verbs. Be careful not to confuse tense with voice. You may write in active voice using past tense. For example:

> *Passive voice*: The money was owed by him.
> *Active voice*: He owed the money.
> *Passive voice*: There was a lot of money that they said was won by
> the couple in the lottery.
> *Active voice*: The couple won a lot of money in the lottery, they
> said.

5. Craft transitions carefully.   Transitions—a few words or a full sentence— act as a bridge linking related but different ideas. They help readers orient themselves in the story by telling them where they've been and where they're going. The most commonly used transitions are chronological (*now, since, then, a few days later,* and so on) and conjunctions (*and, but, then, however,* and so on).

Instead of crafting appropriate transitions, beginning writers often rely on attributions to move the reader from one thought to the next. Try to avoid misusing attributions as transitions.

6. Replace clichés and adjectives with nouns and action verbs focusing on actors and action.   Over the years, TV news viewers and newspaper readers have come to expect politicians to toss their hats in the ring, prisoners to hear sentences without visible emotion, and state legislatures to work against the clock to pass bills. Any figure of speech that you're used to seeing in print or any word or phrase that springs easily to mind is a cliché. Writers avoid clichés by looking for fresh words and images and recasting clichés to focus on actors and action.

He was caught by the long arm of the law.
Police officers arrested him.

The mayor is a veteran campaigner.
The mayor faces his fifth campaign, the most contentious yet.

Bancroft was an outspoken critic of the school board.
Bancroft often criticized the school board.

The council grappled with the issue for several hours.
Council members discussed the issue for several hours, rarely agreeing.

Police scoured the neighborhood.
Police officers searched the neighborhood.

7. Translate jargon by paraphrasing dull, wordy quotes.   Let's say that test scores at the local high school are way down and you're assigned to find out why.

The principal tells you: "Our challenge is to consider the recent impact of the influx of differently abled and economically challenged students in our district and to launch a course of action exploring the possibility that this recent variation in the student demographic probably influenced the previously unforeseen declivity in academic achievement."

Your challenge: to translate this bureaucratic nonsense into English. This is actually what the principal is saying: A recent, large increase in the number of poor and disabled students coming into the district may have contributed to declining test scores.

8. Use quotes correctly.   Quotes in stories are like exclamation marks at the ends of sentences or punch lines of jokes. They should illuminate, support and surprise.

In a well-organized story, quotes fall into place easily and never require clumsy explanation. Instead of writing:

> "If they had told us ahead of time, we would have stayed home and not wasted all this money," said Rina Fox, referring to the family's recent trip to the Beaver Town amusement park and the fact that they were unable to enter the park because officials failed to publicize the two-day shut down for remodeling.

Set up the quote as you would the punch line to a joke:

> Beaver Town officials ruined the plans of many families—some had come from as far away as Des Moines—by failing to publicize the amusement park's recent two-day shutdown for remodeling. "If they had told us ahead of time, we would have stayed home and not wasted all this money," said Rina Fox, her two disappointed children by her side.

• Try to avoid quoting people who speak in expected clichés or say the obvious, like the coach who tells you, "We won because we played real well."

- Unless you're recreating dialogue, avoid bumping quotes, the practice of following one person's quote with another person's quote. Always use a transition to separate people's dialogue.
- Follow basic rules of usage. This is incorrect: "I couldn't be happier," he grinned. A grin doesn't speak. "I couldn't be happier," he said, grinning. Much better.

   The same holds true for: "I couldn't be happier," he smiled. "I couldn't be happier," he said, smiling, is correct usage.

9. Prefer the concrete to the abstract.   If you must introduce an abstract concept, make sure you explain it with a concrete example. This is especially true of:

- **Numbers:** If you say the county lost $2 billion in a bad investment scheme, tell your readers what that means: "Officials lost $2 billion in a bad investment scheme, enough money to house every homeless family in the county for 25 years."
- **Abstract nouns:** What is a facility? An issue? A problem? They mean different things to different people. If "the facility" is a factory where workers assemble circuit boards, say so.
- **Adjectives:** As Mark Twain once said, "When you catch an adjective, kill it." Adjectives are subjective. You and an Eskimo have different understandings of "cold," just as you and an unemployed single father living on welfare with five kids in a one-bedroom apartment have different understandings of "posh." Stick to factual descriptions based on the details you've gathered in your reporting. Instead of using "cold" to describe the weather, write: "The temperature never rose above freezing Tuesday."

   Instead of using "posh" to describe the accommodations, write: "The delegates, assembled to discuss ways to abolish welfare, will spend the weekend at a five-star hotel with gold-plated sinks, ocean views and a $400-a-day price tag."

On Journalistic Style

Now we move to the specifics of journalistic style. Most journalists work with a basic set of guidelines. As you craft your stories, pay careful attention to the following elements.

1. Attributions

- Any fact or opinion that isn't widely accepted must be attributed to a source. (Examples of widely accepted facts: The earth revolves around the sun, or a week has seven days.)
- Attributions almost always go at the end of the sentence unless who's saying something is more important than what's being said.

- Avoid loaded words. Instead of writing "he admitted," stick to "he said." It conveys less judgment on the writer's part. A well-crafted story lets the facts speak for themselves.
- Never attribute a single quote to more than one person unless people are speaking in unison.
- Cut any unattributed opinion from your story.
- Statistics and numbers should be paraphrased and attributed to their proper source.

2. Tone   Journalists tend to write in the third person and use a conversational tone. Imagine as you write that you're telling the story to someone you know well—your mom or a best friend, for example.

3. Language

Avoid Acronyms   Unless acronyms are well known—CIA or FBI, for example—never use them. Even with CIA or FBI, you must tell the reader what the acronym stands for on first reference. Beginning students writing for the campus paper love to make alphabet soup of their stories. Let's say you're writing about a philosophical change in the Department of English and Comparative Literary Studies curriculum.

A beginning journalist might write:

> The Department of English and Comparative Literary Studies (ECLS) at Knowitall University (KU) will offer fewer courses focusing on white male authors. With the approval of the KU provost, the ECLS department will refocus its curriculum to offer courses featuring women, minority and gay and lesbian writers, which angers many in the more traditional School of the Humanities and Fine Arts (SHFA).
>
> "We think this makes up for years gone by when we didn't offer a single course with a female, minority, gay or lesbian voice," said ECLS department chair Joseph Book. But not all agreed. SHFA officials denounced ECLS professors and accused KU of favoring the department of ECLS over the SHFA.

Simplify the story by deleting the acronyms. On first reference, identify the departments by their correct names. On second reference, refer simply to the English department, the university or the humanities school.

Avoid Sexist and Racist Assumptions   Some commonly misused references to gender include *housewife,* which implies that a woman is married to her house. *Homemaker* more accurately describes a woman who works in the home.

Use of the word *man* to describe an important position—chairman, councilman, congressman—excludes large numbers of women who fill these posts. Change references to make them gender neutral; for example, *chair of the committee, city council member* and *member* of Congress.

Use a person's race, religion or sexual orientation only when relevant to the story—for instance, when describing a fugitive from the law or a controversy that centers on race or gender. If an all-white club denied membership to a black executive, race would likely be an issue discussed in the story. But if a Latino teen was arrested on suspicion of embezzling funds from the campus yearbook account, his race is irrelevant. (You would never write, for instance: "A white teenager was arrested Tuesday for embezzling funds from the campus yearbook account.")

4. Focus on People and Their Stories   Bureaucrats love to speak abstractly. For instance, one might say: "The American people support our plan to save their hard-earned tax dollars by ending federal handouts like welfare and Medicare."

What does that mean? Explain it by focusing on the people most affected: Tell their stories and open the window on their world for your readers or viewers. Find the single mother with three children living in a homeless shelter and show what cutting welfare means to those who depend on it. Or find a senior citizen who forgoes meat to pay for the medicine he needs because the government cut his Medicare benefits.

Use people, anecdotes and quotes to make the facts and figures of your story come alive. Each section of your story should include quotes, anecdotes, examples and statistics to support your focus.

5. The Ending: Crafting the Kicker   Try to end gracefully, usually with a quote. At the very least, avoid ending on an attribution, thus diluting the quote's powerful impact. The following ending to a story about two Los Angeles high school crosstown football rivals leaves the reader with a sense of finality:

> "The Banning coach is sending out a false message about Los Angeles that you can't even attend a football game without being afraid of losing your life," said City Councilman Nate Holden, who represents the Dorsey area. "Banning has nothing to fear but losing the game."

A less skillful writer might have ended the story on an attribution:

> "The Banning coach is sending out a false message about Los Angeles that you can't even attend a football game without being afraid of losing your life. Banning has nothing to fear but losing the game," said City Councilman Nate Holden, who represents the Dorsey area.

Well-told endings are sometimes called "kickers" because they give the reader a little kick or surprise. Save a particularly funny quote or an unexpected detail for the end of your story to leave readers with a sense of finality.

Good Reporting Leads to Good Writing

Editors will judge your story on its reporting as well as its writing. A well-written story will answer readers' or viewers' questions and explain how the problem or controversy affects them. Writers without solid reporting won't have the necessary information to carry out their mandate. As you craft your stories, try to anticipate readers' or viewers' questions. Ask yourself: How much will it cost me? What will I get out of it? How will it affect me? Why should I care?

And of course, never raise questions you fail to answer. The following story, riddled with passive voice, never answers a basic question. Try to figure out what it is; the answer is at the end of the excerpt.

New backyard swimming pools would have to be made child-proof through the use of self-closing fences or special alarms if cities pass stringent regulations adopted last week as part of the Uniform Building Code used throughout the western United States.

The new standards, spurred by the drowning deaths of 350 children nationwide each year, were approved by the International Conference of Building Officials at its annual convention in Denver.

The regulations were urged by building officials from the Southwest and West, including two from Orange County. But they were opposed by other city officials, primarily from colder-climate areas, who argued that pool safety should be the prerogative of local government, not a national standard.

In light of this opposition, the pool-barrier requirement was relegated to the appendix of the 1991 Uniform Building Code, meaning it serves only as a model for cities to pass into law. Had it been included in the body of the code, it probably would have been adopted with other new building regulations.

"I believe those cities that do not have a history (of children drowning) may not be as moved to adopt this amendment," said Tony C'De Baca, Costa Mesa's assistant development services director, who testified in favor of the measure at the conference. "I would hope that all jurisdictions with a preponderance of pools would adopt it for the safety of the children."

In Orange County, 14 children younger than seven have drowned or suffered brain damage after nearly drowning this year. Of those incidents, six drownings and three near-drownings occurred in swimming pools or spas.

According to the national Centers for Disease Control in Atlanta, 40 percent of drownings and near-drownings could be prevented through the use of fences.

For years, pool owners have been required to have fences to prevent neighborhood children from wandering into their yards. But in more than 98 percent of drowning or near-drowning incidents, the child involved lived in or was visiting a home with a pool, according to the U.S. Consumer Product Safety Commission.

The new code would require that all newly constructed pools have a wall or fence at least 4 ft. high to block access from the house to the pool. The gate in the fence would have to be self-latching. If the pool area is bounded on one side by the house, all doors on that side would have to be self-closing, with an alarm system to alert parents if the door is opened.

Pool-safety proponents said the new pool-barrier code is an important first step, but it does not go far enough.

"It's better than what they've got now, which is nothing," said Jim Landis of Newport Beach, who formed the Children's Pool Safety Association after his 18-month-old son almost drowned in December.

Lee Baxter, Western regional director of the Consumer Product Safety Commission, which drafted the original version of the new code, said the measure provides a minimum standard of protection. It should prod local governments to adopt their own ordinances, which may be more stringent, he said.

"This definitely is a major step forward," Baxter said. "I think a lot of jurisdictions that have not been seriously pursuing this issue will do so now."

Landis has devised a pool-safety ordinance, which calls for a 5 ft. fence and would apply retroactively to pools at homes with children under six.

An ordinance similar to the one Landis is proposing went into effect in Phoenix in May. The city has had nine drownings involving children this year, compared to 13 at the same point in 1989, said Division Chief Doug Tucker of the Phoenix Fire Department. The number of near-drownings for the same age group has decreased from 78 to 30, he said.

Tucson began enforcing a pool ordinance in January that is stricter than that adopted by Phoenix but applies only to newly constructed pools. Only one child has drowned this year in the city, compared with eight last year, said J. Randall Ogden, administrative paramedic supervisor for the Tucson Fire Department.

—Orange County Register

(Answer: The story never says how much the new requirements will cost pool owners. Ideally, this information would go in the lead or background paragraph. If the information was unavailable, the reporter should have told readers so.)

The Importance of Accuracy

Your story's reporting will be judged on two criteria: Is it accurate? Is it fair? Accuracy means you got the facts straight and you spelled the names correctly. Anything less than perfect means your sources can and will ask for a correction. Factual errors also leave your publication or TV station open to a libel lawsuit, an expense media owners would rather forego.

Even a few factual errors call into question the veracity of the entire story. In an article for the *Columbia Journalism Review,* author Alicia Mundy described the strategy PR firms use when reporters report stories unflattering to their clients: "Attack any and all flaws in a reporter's story, then use them to discredit the whole piece," Mundy wrote. "(The) philosophy is: If you get (reporters) to back down on the minor details they've screwed up on, they're unlikely to fight you on the major ones."

To ensure that your piece is accurate, double-check every fact you use against your notes. Whenever possible, call back sources to confirm statistics, anecdotes or quotes. Make sure you always ask sources to spell their names and tell you their correct titles, even when it seems obvious.

Rarely read back quotes, though, since it gives the source an opportunity to censor what was said. But it is possible—and desirable—to double-check the correct spelling of names, titles, dates and other facts you use in your story.

In "Getting It Right," from *Editor & Publisher,* journalist Keith Shelton exhorts reporters to "re-adopt Joseph Pulitzer's motto: 'Accuracy, accuracy, accuracy.'" "Accuracy is not all that difficult," he continues. "A set of commandments can go a long way toward correcting the problem." He offers the following ideas:

1. Select sources wisely. It is not acceptable to an editor or news director for a reporter to say, "That's what so-and-so told me." A reporter is responsible for the selection of his or her sources.

2. Verify all key facts. Sometimes a veteran reporter can get all the facts straight on the first run-through, but even the veteran can profit from verification. The accurate reporter does not trust the printed word, the press release or the information chiseled on the side of a building without checking. A printed program often contains errors. Police officers are not hired for their grammar, spelling or geography skills.

   Writing by ear, as some have called it, can be disastrous, such as the writer who wrote of the "bluebonnet plague" in the Middle Ages, the new Italian restaurant serving "link weenies" instead of linguini or the menu writer who noted "chicken Gordon blue" for lunch.

3. Good reporters qualify anything they can't prove. It is "believed to be" the first in history, not "it is the first." A good example is two versions of the same story, one by the Associated Press and one by United Press International.

The UPI version:

"A baby girl died Monday of a bite she suffered Friday from a brown recluse spider."

The AP version:

"A baby girl died Monday of what doctors speculate may have been the reaction to the bite of a brown recluse spider."

The follow-up reported:

"An autopsy report Tuesday said 1-year-old Carolyn Gomez died March 16 of bronchial pneumonia. The autopsy report ruled out any toxic effects from an insect bite."

4. When reporters guess or take chances, they become more likely to make errors. Don't ask other reporters for answers to questions. Reporters most often are poor reference sources. Every news department should have a neon sign saying, "Look it up!"

5. Questions that are pending should not be presented as fact. The school board will consider a budget Tuesday, not the school board will adopt a budget.

6. Be on guard for phony stories. If someone calls in with an obituary, verify it with the funeral home.

7. Persevere. Never give up too soon. Two phone calls do not an effort make. It is amazing how many reporters ignore basic resources: the phone book, city directories, tax rolls, almanacs, "Who's Who," ZIP code directories, atlases.

8. Double-check all information. An illustration: Former professional football running back Chuck Muncie had a brother playing at the same time named Nelson Munsey. Yes, they spelled their last names differently. Names often are not spelled the way they are pronounced. Tad "Schultz," for instance, is spelled Tad Szulc.

A Note about Style

Consistency is a hallmark of journalism. Abbreviations, punctuation, titles and capitalization must be the same throughout the story. To guide the writer in the matter of style and usage, newspapers use stylebooks, generally in conjunction with a primary reference such as *Webster's New World Dictionary of the American Language*. Usage covers everything from ethnic designations, religious references, the use of vulgarity, obscenity or profanity to acronyms. Most newspapers base their guidelines on *The Associated Press Stylebook and Libel Manual,* a reference manual that sets standards of consistency for dates, numbers, titles, addresses, capitalization, abbreviations, acronyms, punctuation, hyphenation, possessives, grammar, spelling and word usage.

Writers are expected to know by memory the stylebook's main elements and to refer to it for more arcane usage. Begin by mastering what beginning reporters most often use incorrectly: dates, numbers, titles, addresses, capitalization, weights and measures, acronyms and geographical locations.

The Art of Self-Editing

When finished writing the story, beginning writers often believe the work before them is a masterpiece. It isn't. You've created just the first draft. You're half finished. Now comes the hard part. If you haven't already, check your ego at the door. You must assess your work critically, dispassionately, as an editor or a reader would, and imagine as you review it that you're reading it for the first time. This is often difficult, especially since you've likely become close to the subject and lack the distance needed to ferret out a story's weaknesses. But remember: Constructive criticism improves the work and has nothing to do with you as a human being or your potential as a writer. For you and your editor, the goal is singular: to create the best possible story in as little time as possible. That means you may get little encouragement from editors more concerned with polishing a diamond in the rough than attending to your feelings. In fact, after a careful editor works over your story, you may decide to pursue a career that involves no writing at all, like dish washing or selling insurance.

Accept from the start that good editors will return your stories filled with demands for revisions and rewrites. If your story lacks those edits, then assume one of three things: (1) you are among the rare and truly gifted, a Mozart of the printed word; (2) your editor is an idiot; (3) you have perfected the art of self-editing.

Self-editing is as much a skill as writing a lead or organizing a story, and you must dedicate yourself to the discipline it requires.

The first draft of your story is rarely your final draft. The first draft gets it down on paper. Now comes the rewrite.

Whenever possible and as time permits, evaluate your own story for editorial soundness. Measure it against the basic guidelines we've outlined in this chapter. The following is a checklist you should use before you submit your story to an editor.

1. **Lead**
   - The lead clearly states the essential news of the story and includes the five W's, how and who cares.
   - A background paragraph provides perspective, when necessary.
2. **Organization**
   - The story has a clear focus.
   - Evidence supporting the focus follows a logical progression.
   - Each sentence relates logically to the next.
   - Readers move easily from paragraph to paragraph.
   - Transitions ease readers from one issue to the next.
3. **Writing**
   - Active voice is used throughout.
   - Simple, clear, precise language is used throughout.
   - Writer shows instead of tells.

- Unnecessary fat is cut.
- Concrete examples explain abstract concepts.
- Dull, wordy quotes are paraphrased.
- Attributions are put at the end or middle of sentences instead of at the beginning.

4. **Reporting**
   - The story accurately describes the event or issue.
   - It quotes correct and appropriate sources.
   - It has no holes and is missing no important information.

5. **It is free from spelling, style and grammar errors.**

Careful editors read a story quickly first for organizational soundness. If structural problems exist, the story usually goes back to the reporter for a major revision. After problems with the lead and organization are solved, editors usually line-edit a story, reviewing the story line by line, noting places where the writer failed to meet expectations on writing, reporting, style, spelling and grammar.

The writer fixes those problems and sends the story back to the editor, who reads it once again, checking for any problems that might have been missed on the previous read-through. The process might be repeated four or five times, depending on the severity of the story's flaws. When it's finished, the story goes to the copydesk, where another editor reviews it, paying special attention to issues of AP style, fairness and accuracy. The writer might once again be expected to revise the story based on the copy editor's suggestions and comments.

That brings us to two important questions many students ask right about now: Why work so hard? Why practice a craft that demands so much? Columbia University Professor of Journalism James Carey answered the question "What's it all for?" in an address made to an incoming class of aspiring journalists (published in the *Columbia Journalism Review*). "The struggle of people against power is the struggle of memory against forgetting," he said. "To make experience memorable so it won't be lost and forgotten is the task of journalism. To be able to do this and to do it well is all that one can ask for in a career."

Suggested Assignments

1. Put the following facts into a news story lead:
   a. An automobile accident at the intersection of Argylle Avenue and Rodemacher Road.
   b. The time was 4:12 p.m.
   c. One car was a 1994 Buick Regal and was driven by Sylvester Colfax, 29, 5329 Elwood Avenue, Clarksville.
   d. The second car was driven by Norma Springston, 43, of 18 Chesterton Drive, Ridgewood. It was a 1988 Volkswagen Rabbit.
   e. Three persons were injured.

f. Alma Fiorello, 34, a passenger in Springston's car, suffered a fractured skull, pelvic injuries, and facial cuts. She was in serious condition at Loman Memorial Hospital.

g. Colfax sustained a broken nose and right arm. He was in fair condition at the same hospital.

h. Eric Colfax, Sylvester's brother, suffered a dislocated shoulder and knee injuries. His condition was good. He is 18 years old.

i. It was raining at the time of the crash.

2. Rewrite the following paragraphs into a news story:

> The Second National Bank was struck by robbers four days ago at 2:10 p.m. One robber held a shotgun on employees and three customers while his two accomplices went behind the tellers' cages and grabbed approximately $30,000 in large bills.
>
> About 10 minutes before the robbery the local police station was ripped by an explosion that blew out all the windows and knocked out all communications lines from the building, including an alarm system to the Second National Bank.
>
> As the robbers were leaving the bank, the apparent leader of the trio ordered everyone to lie on the floor. Then he tossed a bomb into the bank lobby. It shattered desks, blew holes in the wall and broke windows. A woman teller, Agnes Corey, age 41, was cut in the face by flying glass. The robbers escaped.
>
> Today, Sheriff August F. Henshaw, who has held his position for 10 years, announced that an arrest had been made in connection with the robbery. He said that a man named Alex Cody, age 30, had been picked up by State Police in the neighboring city of Westville yesterday.
>
> Sheriff Henshaw was in bed with the flu when the bank robbery occurred. He just got up this morning from his sickbed and said he was still feeling weak.
>
> Henshaw said he will leave for Westville this afternoon to question Cody. According to Henshaw, Cody was arrested and charged with assault after he had allegedly hit a restaurant short-order cook during an argument over the cooking of Cody's hamburger. Henshaw said that Cody denied robbing the Second National, but state police said he matched the description of one of the bandits. Cody was reportedly carrying $3,500 in cash when arrested.
>
> The Second National, which had been boarded up since the robbery, was open for business today. There was the usual number of customers but a much larger number of sightseers. At one point there were so many people in the bank that William Redmond, the bank president, ordered the bank closed at 2 p.m., instead of 3, the usual closing hour.
>
> Sheriff Henshaw also revealed that, according to State Police, Cody was convicted of bank robbery six years ago in Lincoln, Nebraska, and served five years in prison.

3. Write substitutes for the following sentences:

a. Police said Jenkins was prone to violence.

b. Harry Blake, an investment counselor, tossed his hat in the ring for mayor today.

c. A storm lashed the East Coast today, killing three persons and causing an estimated $2 million in property damage.

d. It was an irony of fate that brought Richards out of obscurity.

e. The grandstand was a riot of color.

f. Marilyn Jones became a wealthy woman by burning the candle at both ends when she was young.

g. It was a gala occasion for the Tomkins Knolls Homeowners' Association.

h. Allerton was as pale as a ghost when the night janitor found him hiding in a storeroom.

i. Morgan landed his blows with telling effect.

4. Select a news story of 10 or more paragraphs. Explain in class how the writer maintained continuity. Point out the transitional devices.

5. Replace each of the following words or phrases with a short, plain word or phrase that means the same thing:

immerse	minions of the law
discharged	sickening thud
obese	with bated breath
elongated	soupy fog
weaponry	snare and delusion
altercation	ill-fated ship
incarcerated	sadder but wiser
expounded	the nuptial know
undernourished	groaning board
underprivileged	wrought havoc
taken into custody	supreme sacrifice
made an appearance	Lady Luck

6. Here are the facts for a meeting story. Write it with an eye to news values.

The Craigmont County Board of Supervisors met for six hours last night at its regular time. The body meets every two weeks. Ten of the 13 members were present, making a quorum.

Of the eight items on the agenda, one involved replacing the lights at Henley Stadium, a county-owned facility rented out to local high school and semipro baseball and football teams. The lights are reported to be outdated and have been providing relatively poor illumination for teams at night games. Replacement cost was given by County Administrator Clifford Gaines at $371,000. The cost was approved 8–2. Supervisor Ellen Clayton voted against the replacement, saying, "What I would be in favor of is selling the stadium. Every time there's a game there, a fight breaks out in the stands, and we have a police situation."

The matter of Craigmont General Hospital also came up. The hospital had been scheduled to close down next month. The supervisors had voted to shut it down on recommendation of Gaines, who said its book-keeping procedures were poor, its records were sloppy, and it had trouble hiring nurses at competitive salaries with other hospitals in the area. He said the hospital also was lax in collecting fees and consequently was losing money. The hospital's annual budget is $11.3 million.

General is the only hospital in the county with an alcoholic treatment center. It also treats indigent patients and has a skilled nursing center for comatose patients.

The board's decision Sept. 6 to close the facility drew many objections from county residents. The board received more than 300 letters objecting to the closing. Many other letters went to newspapers. Employees of the hospital also voiced their concern. They said no other hospital in the county, profit or nonprofit, provided some of the care that General does, especially for alcoholics. Dr. Barbara Ollsen, director of the alcohol treatment unit, appeared at the meeting to plead to keep the entire hospital open. Four other doctors, eight nurses, and five business office personnel came with her. Said nurse Jeannine Bellerman, "If you close the hospital you'll be telling the poor of this county there is no room for them in any hospital." Dr. Ollsen said, "I find it hard to believe that you even considered closing General." The hospital was built in 1938. It has 312 beds.

After a two-hour debate and listening to views of the audience, the board by a vote of 6–4 voted to take $12 million out of reserve funds to keep the hospital open for at least one more year. At that time, the whole issue will come before the board again. Meanwhile, General was ordered by the board to get its books and other procedures straightened out. The chief administrator of the hospital, Wilson O'Bannion, was at the meeting. He told the board he had recently fired both the hospital's chief bookkeeper and auditor. He told the board, "You can be assured the hospital will be run on a much more businesslike basis."

Another item of business concerned the imposition of a fee for putting pets out for adoption at the county animal shelter. The policy has been to give impounded cats and dogs free to the public. New owners do pay for rabies and other shots, however.

Dr. Carla Davidson, a veterinarian and director for the shelter, has told the board that the shelter believes those taking pets should share at least part of what it costs to feed the animals prior to adoption. She considers the present shelter budget of $402,000 inadequate in any case and believes free pets put an added burden on it. She recommended a fee of $15 for each pet, plus the cost of medical shots.

The board was divided on the question. Supervisor Emil Jentry said he feared a fee would mean that a lot more dogs and cats would have to be "put to sleep" because people seldom want to pay for mongrels.

"I would hate to see one dog or cat lose its life because somebody didn't have $15 or didn't want to pay it," Jentry said.

He was answered by Supervisor Rhonda Royce. She said, "If someone really sees a dog she wants, I don't think that $15 will stop her. It wouldn't stop me."

Roger Oliphant, chairman of the board of supervisors, said, "There's no question we will lose customers with a fee, but nothing comes free these days. I would be in favor of some kind of fee."

The debate lasted 45 minutes. Three members of the audience opposed fees. One, Mrs. Hilda Morrisen, said, "Would you really deprive a cat or dog a good home over $15?"

The vote to impose a fee was 8–2 in favor. The fee voted for was $7.

The $7 fee came on a motion by Supervisor John Loeb. Sentiment appeared to be running against a $15 fee, and the $7 was offered by Loeb as a compromise.

Reporting Meetings, Speeches and Special Events

Reporters and editors can keep a calendar on certain news happenings, among them meetings, speeches and special events. For each, the reporter cannot be sure whether coverage will produce sheer boredom or front-page news. Even with a prepared agenda, these events can take on a life of their own, often going in a direction not foreseen (or desired) by the participants and the audience. That's why it's a good idea not to predict what you'll find. Although it's true that most meetings and speeches follow a script, deviations are common and often provide the best part of the story. In short, news is simply a reflection of life—anything can happen. Approach any story with an open mind.

Covering Meetings

Meetings are a prime example of expecting the unexpected, especially when personalities and egos clash on issues. What started as a routine city council session can explode into a shouting match among the council members and even the audience. A startling item may emerge in the "new business" portion of the meeting, or the mayor suddenly may announce she's giving up the job. But even if nothing untoward happens, the business of a council, school board or planning commission is of interest to your community and your readers. A council may vote to raise hotel taxes for transients as that body in Irvine, Calif., did. At first blush, this may not seem to be of great interest to residents but the *Irvine World News* pointed out that revenue from the "bed tax" would be used to bring new business to the city, thus broadening the tax base, and to fund cultural programs—clearly of interest to readers.

In a democracy, public bodies are under constant scrutiny by the press and public, as they should be. State open meeting and open records laws help keep officials honest. City councils, boards of supervisors, state legislatures and Congress are conducting public business and spending public money. Even less-visible elected officials like members of the zoning or public utilities commissions take actions vital to the lives of citizens.

The news media are the watchdogs of these agencies. Most people attend meetings only when they are affected by a particular item on the agenda. Otherwise, they depend on the press to keep them informed. Some of these gatherings are boring and virtually newsless. Others may have enough meat for three Page One stories. But the problem is that the reporter often can't estimate the value of the proceedings until she sits through them. What may start out as a routine council session could wind up as a near brawl among members or a blockbuster of a decision that wasn't even on the agenda. There may be charges of dishonesty; a councilman may hurl allegations of rigged bids for a fleet of new police cars. A word of caution: Never leave a meeting before it's over, no matter how late the hour. Some officials will seize on your departure as a golden opportunity to take some dubious and perhaps illegal action or pass verbal judgments on other people in city or county government. It happens.

Agendas are usually mailed or handed out to the public and the media before the meeting. City editors may have them delivered to their desks. But this is no guarantee that the officials will follow the script 100 percent. An eruption may occur during the public discussion period. An agenda item called "new business" may be a sleeper that produces shock waves that will be felt around the city. By all means, however, get a copy of the agenda before covering a meeting so that you can easily follow the proceedings. Get to the council chambers 15 or 20 minutes early to study the agenda and possibly chat with officials on what will come up.

Reporters who have been covering a particular council, commission or agency on a regular basis have an easier time writing a knowledgeable story. They know the background of the issues, the members of the body and the members' backgrounds, as well as the arguments and compromises made around the table. They are able to assign instant value to a subject under debate.

Conventional wisdom holds that the longer a newsperson stays on a particular beat, the greater his capacity to handle the story. However, sometimes he becomes stale and jaded to the point where his copy becomes dull and lifeless. The beginner, on the other hand, is able to bring an enthusiasm and imagination to the assignment that may be lacking in her more experienced but burned-out colleague. Besides, the newcomer can supplement her lack of background by studying old news clips, reading her own paper carefully and talking to officials before and after the meeting to fill in the holes. City and county clerks and city attorneys and city managers are highly useful sources on the mechanics of commission business, the legal ramifications, if any, and the background of the issues.

For the beginner, note taking at a meeting can be made easier by drawing a diagram of the table and identifying each individual sitting around it. If you can arrive a few minutes early, you can get the names from the clerk and make your sketch. You will not need it for long if the meeting becomes a regular assignment, but it certainly helps in those first days when everything is unfamiliar. When a certain supervisor speaks, for example, you will know immediately who he or she is.

Getting the names of audience members who speak out is a bit trickier, but it can be done. You can't run to each speaker for names during the meeting, so take a shortcut. In your notes, identify the persons as "red tie," "blue dress," "gold chain" and so forth. At the end of the meeting, simply go up to the individuals and ask for their names to go along with their quotes. Most will be flattered. Work fast before they get out the door.

If you use a tape recorder, get one with a microphone strong enough to pick up voices at the table and with a counter so that you can quickly go back or forward to review remarks. Recorders are a blessing in staving off writer's cramp or the curse of not being able to read your handwriting. And a tape recorder gives you generally complete sentences in perfect context if you keep it on all during the meeting. But there is a downside. Transcribing your notes from the machine can be too time-consuming for meeting fast-approaching deadlines. This is why many reporters use recorders primarily to search out particular quotes and facts via fast forward and reverse. This is where the counter comes in. Jot down numbers as they relate to speakers. Some officials will allow you to place your recorder at the table for better volume.

The main idea covering a meeting is to understand what is going on. Just as for a breaking story, you can't explain a council motion for the reader unless you yourself comprehend it. You can't interrupt the discussion to ask for an explanation of a certain piece of business, but you can get it cleared up after the meeting or during a break. Don't leave until you understand what's happened. One or two targeted questions may let in the light. Legislative maneuvering and decision making often lose their mystery when closely examined. And if you start on a smaller paper, don't worry that issues will become more complex in a bigger city, county or state. If, for example, you learn on a small daily how a municipal budget is hammered out, presented and resolved in your community, tackling a budget in a metropolitan city will be simple because the mechanics are generally the same. The numbers will be bigger, and there are more departments to consider, but otherwise it's a virtual replay. The same is true of property tax assessments, which work about the same way throughout the land.

In any event, let's say that you are about to write the meeting story. Or will it be more than one story? When a meeting has generated a lot of news, some newspapers will publish a main story, perhaps on Page One, and then sort out the rest of the stuff in smaller "sidebar" stories. Don't count on this, however. If there is a tight paper, which means a smaller-than-usual newshole, you may have to compress everything in a single piece. In this case, good news judgment and a sense of organization are crucial.

Basically, the news value determines what goes on top and what ends up at the bottom of the story—or remains in your notes. For instance, the relative value of a city council's actions depends on such factors as how many people in the community are affected, how much money is being spent or whether the city is taking a significant new direction.

Be wary of being carried away by a loud and angry delegation that creates a stir in the chambers but is concerned about a matter that is of minor interest to the community at large—such as infrequent trash pickups in a certain neighborhood. The protest may be worth mentioning only if placed in proper perspective. The major development of the evening may be a motion that sailed through without a single objection or murmur from the audience. This could mean that the council members or supervisors could have hashed out their arguments at a secret, pre-public session or the issue may have been thoroughly chewed over at previous meetings.

Closed-door, or "executive," sessions are the bane of the news media and the public. In some localities, the practice is endemic. Fortunately, almost all states have open meetings laws, which severely restrict the conditions under which a public body can meet in private, which many of them love to do. Newspaper and broadcast managers and reporters should invoke the law quickly—before or during the meeting if there is knowledge of it. If there isn't, word of these clandestine sessions usually leaks out, and the media may then take legal action, which can prevent the body from doing it again. Public business should be conducted publicly. The exceptions in the open meetings laws are usually limited to personnel matters, such as hiring a city manager, or sessions with attorneys involving lawsuits against a city or county, particularly when a settlement is involved.

Such journalistic organizations as the Society of Professional Journalists and First Amendment watchdog groups in California, Texas and other states will back up reporters locked out of meetings, often going to court to gain their admittance. But it helps enormously if you have your own copy of the open meeting and open records statutes that you can wave in front of a secrecy-inclined council or commission.

Strong quotes, color, humor and human interest can be employed to dress up a meeting story. News writing should be interesting as well as informative, and a funny or outrageous remark can turn an otherwise drab article into one with zest and high readability. Just be certain that you are quoting accurately and that your idea of color is not too far away from that of your readers.

Your final product should be a story that highlights the news, reads coherently and takes advantage of whatever elements there are to glue the reader to her seat.

Arthur Gelb, former deputy managing editor of the *New York Times,* has this advice for reporters covering meetings:

> Tell the reader all you know. You can't play games with him. If a program is announced in the story tell what the chances of its success are. Plug every hole. A good reporter keeps ahead of his reader because he is aware of what the reader will ask. He never frustrates the reader. The writer must answer all the questions that are likely to be asked. If a law is passed, how will it affect the man on the street, the homeowner, etc.? How will the law be implemented and who will do it?

Finding answers to these questions need not be confined to the participants at a meeting. You are free to garner additional information from any source you choose. Thus, reporters, after a meeting, often work the phones to get explanations and reactions from outside sources. Say you've covered a board of education meeting replete with complex and/or controversial segments relating to school financing, classroom overcrowding and extending the school day by two hours. To supplement what you gathered at the meeting, it might be a good idea to talk to school principals and teachers, the state education department and parents. Such information can round out the story, giving it more body and credibility. Your readers are obviously better served.

The following is a meeting story that gets right to the point in the lead, follows up with details and contains pertinent quotes. Best of all, it explains the issues.

By Jason Gewirtz, Staff Writer

LONG BEACH—Hearing impassioned pleas from medical marijuana patients and advocates, the City Council on Tuesday asked the Police Department to change a policy that essentially requires officers who see marijuana to arrest patients first and ask questions later.

The council asked the police to return by Sept. 14 with a proposed new policy to eliminate what several residents said was unfair and inhumane treatment of medical marijuana patients.

The city's police policy calls for officers who come across someone with marijuana to seize any evidence and arrest or cite the person as appropriate. Medical marijuana patients can then prove their cases in court.

Proposition 215, passed by voters in 1996, makes it legal for patients to possess or cultivate marijuana for medical use.

"We have not been following the law," said Councilman Dan Baker, who called for the review with Councilman Val Lerch.

Since 2000, five medical marijuana patients have been arrested in Long Beach.

Baker and Lerch called for the review after the council's Public Safety Advisory Commission asked the council to get involved. The advisory board heard months of testimony from residents who said the police policy was at odds with the state law.

Council members heard emotional testimony from residents, including several who have been arrested for possession or cultivation.

David Zink, the first Long Beach medical marijuana patient to be arrested after Prop 215 took effect, said he was not satisfied with the time frame for the new review. Zink's case for possession and cultivation was eventually dismissed. But, he said, he spent about $15,000 in legal fees.

"I feel like this is another delay," he said. "They've had eight years to come up with a reasonable policy."

Michael Barbee, who helped the San Diego City Council recently change that city's similar police policy, said Long Beach needed to follow suit. After studying the issue, San Diego settled on a policy to require identification cards for residents taking marijuana for medical purposes.

"We have police officers making medical decisions," Barbee said of Long Beach's policy.

But police officials said that changing the policy isn't as easy as it might appear.

Deputy Chief Robert Luna said the department would need to consult with the Los Angeles district attorney's office as well as the Long Beach city attorney and prosecutor to account for any liability a policy change could bring.

In addition, he said, marijuana use has been the cause of property crimes, violent crime and gang activity, making it difficult for officers to differentiate between who has the right to use marijuana legally. Although there have been five arrests for medical marijuana since 2000, he said, there have been about 5,000 other marijuana-related arrests over the same period.

"The police officer on the street is dealing with a lot of serious issues," he said.

The request for a new policy passed on an 8–0 vote with Lerch abstaining.

Lerch, whose wife suffers from multiple sclerosis, said he was too emotionally attached to the issue to vote with an open mind.

"My wife will probably not use marijuana," he said. "But damn it, she should have the right to do so."

—Long Beach Press-Telegram

The Speech Story

In this public relations age, there is often little suspense in a speech for the reporter. Advance copies of the text are frequently available to the media before the event, particularly when the speaker is prominent in government, industry, the military and the professions. Frequently, the news media receive copies hours in advance. The reporter need just follow the script and make notes only when the speaker veers away from it–as can easily happen. Swift-moving events might force a last minute change. A politician, for example, may alter his remarks in an evening speech because of charges an opponent made earlier.

And not all speakers have prepared texts. Some are so polished that they don't need a text, relying on repetition or their ability to ad lib. This is often true of celebrities. Talk show host Larry King, a much sought after speaker by groups around the country, relies on a set speech, which always seems to go over well with an audience. After all, conventioneers in Buffalo didn't hear his same spiel in St. Louis a week earlier. And most likely, Buffalo newspaper readers didn't, either.

Reporters on the campaign trail sometimes don't even take notes, so familiar are they with the candidate's boilerplate speech they have heard a dozen or more times before. It's only when the politico departs from her worn text—perhaps due to a sudden development in the campaign—that the press perks up. The frequent speeches of President George W. Bush offer an example. Prior to the Sept. 11, 2001, bombing of the World Trade Center, Bush made few public speeches and held few news conferences. But, in furtherance of the war on terrorism, he has appeared before many groups and often his remarks land on the front page, so important is the issue. The same is true of his public castigations of Saddam Hussein.

An instance when a prepared speech was relegated to the back burner occurred in the California gubernatorial race between incumbent Gray Davis and his Republican challenger, Bill Simon. Under media questioning, Simon admitted he erred when he earlier had accused Davis of taking an illegal campaign contribution. In print and on the air, that became the story.

Whether the speech is new or old, there are ways a reporter can make coverage easier. Not everything said must be written down, taped or noted in your laptop computer. Most of the jokes or anecdotes speakers frequently use to warm up the audience can be safely skipped. The same goes for unrelated digressions, other persons' quotes and tributes to his hosts and the community. This is mostly fluff and need not take up space in your story.

As in all reporting, the main thing to look for is news. What does the speaker say that is new, startling, provocative or controversial? Does he hit any hot buttons? In an otherwise routine speech, the late President Lyndon B. Johnson announced near the end that he would not run for another term. Of course, that was an easy one for the media.

In most cases, a wise reporter has done her homework by obtaining background on the issues to be discussed so that she will know when the speaker makes news, which can come anywhere in the talk. Research the newspaper library for background.

When an advance copy of a speech is handed out, it may contain a release date at the top. The speaker doesn't want his words in the newspapers or on the air before he utters them. Or there may be a strategic reason for the date. This is called an embargo. If no release time is stated, newspapers often will print the story before the speech and note that it was taken from an advance copy.

If the address is made in a large, crowded hall or hotel dining room, try to get as close as you can to the podium. This not only helps you hear better but also enables you to dash up to the platform for any questions before the speaker gets away. It's not uncommon for a speaker to rush from the dais to catch a plane for her next engagement. Ask any questions that enable you to write a clear, understandable story. Speakers don't always make perfect sense. There may have been inconsistencies. You might want her to respond to statements made by a political opponent or, say, a doctor who happens to disagree with her opinions as an MD. Then there is the individual who garbles the language of his speech, and you have to ask him to fill in that blank spot in your notes. Advice: If you rely on a tape recorder, get a good one with a counter to enable you to rewind or fast forward to a particular quote whose number you have scribbled down.

Use the best cassettes available. Replaying a speech or interview can sometimes be frustrating because of background noises or a slurred voice. Top-rated equipment won't solve all these problems, but it will help considerably.

In the following story, the lead is likely to capture reader interest because it hits on a vital current issue in the nation and, of course, because of the prominence of the speaker.

Notice how the writer leads off with a solid statement supported by a direct quote. Observe as well how the story shifts smoothly to include background and the comments of others on the subject.

By Jennifer Peter

Cardinal Bernard Law told parishioners Sunday that the sexual-abuse scandal was a "wake-up call" for the Catholic Church and that "immediate and decisive changes" were required to stem a crisis that "some have likened . . . to Sept. 11."

Law, who has been at the center of much of the growing criticism over the church's handling of sexually abusive priests, appeared in public for the first time since Easter as he and other U.S. cardinals prepared for a rare meeting this week at the Vatican.

The Vatican needs to understand that the abuse scandal is "a very serious issue undermining the mission of the church," he said. "Some have likened the situation . . . to last year's Sept. 11 tragedy, a crisis which shocks the heart and soul and which must spark immediate and decisive changes to prevent possible recurrence."

Cardinal Theodore McCarrick of Washington, D.C., spoke on television about his hopes for a meeting in Rome. He said it should give Pope John Paul II the chance to convey his concern for the victims, his disappointment in letting down faithful Catholics, and his pain over the tarnishing of the church's image and its good works.

When they meet with the pope and other Vatican officials Tuesday and Wednesday, the cardinals will be looking for guidance and backing on a wide range of issues, including whether the church should ever consider reassigning sex offenders and creating a policy of reporting abuse claims to police.

McCarrick said Sunday on "Meet the Press" that he supports creating a uniform policy for handling sex-abuse allegations in all U.S. Catholic dioceses.

The latest sexual abuse controversy began in January, when published reports disclosed that Law and other church leaders had reassigned a priest accused of pedophilia. The now-defrocked priest, John Geoghan, was convicted this year of fondling a boy at a swimming pool and has been accused of molesting dozens of others.

Law, on Sunday, acknowledged criticism of his dealing with priests accused of sexual abuse, at least two of whom were moved from parish to parish despite the allegations.

"Despite the anger and broken trust that many feel toward me, and despite perceptions that next week is simply a gathering of aged conservative cardinals and Vatican officials," Law said, "please know that as long as I am in position to do so, I will work tirelessly to address this crisis and to underscore its severity."

Law's remarks were met with applause inside the Cathedral of the Holy Cross, but outside about three dozen protestors continued to call for his resignation. Sunday afternoon, he stepped into a plane bound for Rome.

Cardinal William Keeler of Baltimore asked his parishioners to help make church officials aware of allegations of wrongdoing by priests. "We are committed to vigilance with your assistance," he said. "If you are aware of instances of wrongdoing, please let us know."

—Associated Press

Writing the Speech Story

Observe in the preceding story how the writer judiciously used direct quotes with strong impact. Sometimes you can lead with a strong quote, but more often, as in this article, the main thrust of what the speaker said makes up the lead with perhaps a part of it in quotation marks.

A speech is written like any other news story. The most important thing the speaker said goes at the top, followed by supporting paragraphs. The lead should have the power to pull the reader into the story. This dull, flat-footed beginning is too bland to generate any interest:

> Ellsworth Haines, president of the ABX Corp., spoke at the Rotary
> Club yesterday on the business climate in the state. A better approach
> would be "The state's business climate is on the upswing, Ellsworth
> Haines, president of the ABX Corp., told a Rotary Club audience yes-
> terday."

The story also must provide a good mix of direct and indirect quotes, making use of the former when the words carry a solid punch. Keep building on the lead. If the opening paragraph cannot be supported in the body of the story, you have chosen the wrong lead. During the course of a 45-minute speech, the speaker may toss out one sentence that may be a shocker. But if there is no further reference to it, it would be pointless—and journalistically unsound—to base the story on a one-liner. Perhaps it can be worked into the piece without playing it out of proportion to its value. Or you can buttonhole the speaker later to see whether he wants to elaborate on his cryptic reference.

Rallies and Demonstrations

In today's climate of confrontation on political and social issues, special interest groups can whip up a demonstration or rally within hours. Most rallies are peaceful, but some are shattered by steamy rhetoric and violence. Outrage at the verdict freeing police officers accused of beating black motorist Rodney King led to the explosive Los Angeles riots of 1992. However, in either case, the reporter's skill and judgment are critical.

It is also not uncommon for demonstration leaders to attempt to manipulate the media to draw attention to their cause. Some groups have become so adept at this that they are familiar with newspaper and broadcast deadlines and stage their protests or promotions accordingly. For TV, they bring eye-catching signs or perhaps wear bizarre costumes to ensure their getting on the 6 o'clock news.

Covering these events calls for level-headed thinking and sound news judgments. There may be much "sound and fury" but little in the way of news value. Speaker after speaker may essentially say the same thing, much of which was heard at previous rallies. The reporter must winnow out the reiterations while evaluating the significance of the gathering—whether the issue be a labor dispute, the environment, race, politics, censorship or the protest of a group of homeowners opposed to the construction of a prison in their community.

It should be pointed out here, however, that some demonstrations or rallies are confined to such unemotional causes as blood donations to the Red Cross and raising money to send the school band on a trip.

In the more volatile assemblages, noise and shouting may create an air of excitement, but when it's all over, there may be little to write about. Some protest gatherings, of course, become highly newsworthy. Nuclear freeze movements, farm labor boycott demonstrations and anti- and pro-abortion gatherings often carry deep implications and are deserving of close media attention. As this was written, rallies on both sides of the Israeli-Palestinian conflict are taking place in the United States and Europe, as are gatherings over the war in Iraq. In California, Gov. Arnold Schwarzenegger has been met in his state travels by turnouts of teachers and nurses angry over his budget plans.

In the fall of 1995, hundreds of students at the nine University of California campuses held rallies to protest the Board of Regents' decision to end affirmative action at the schools. Not only was this a hot state issue, it reached across the nation and into the halls of Congress. For many newspapers it was a Page One story—and still is.

Thus, the reporter's job is to take a hard look at the event and attempt to determine its real impact and news value. Soaking up background material on the rally issue from the newspaper library is a big help in sorting out facts.

Crowd size alone is not always an indicator of a demonstration's importance. Many people attend rallies just to gawk and couldn't care less about the issue. Yet rally organizers in statements to the media may lump several hundred onlookers with partisan members simply to inflate the attendance in hopes of getting in the paper or on the air.

But to enhance the credibility of your story, you should attempt to ascertain the size of the crowd. You can make your own estimate by circulating among the people or looking down at them from a height, say a hill or fifth-story window. Confirm or negate your guess by interviewing the organizers and police officers or other officials at the scene for their figures. Remember, rally leaders tend to exaggerate the turnout, which must be taken into account.

At one mammoth rally, the size of the gathering became a story in itself. In October 1995 thousands of African-American men poured into Washington, D.C., for what was called the Million Man March, organized by Louis Farrakhan, leader of the Nation of Islam, as a means of forging black pride and self-reliance. The National Park Service estimated the throng at 400,000, which was duly reported along with Farrakhan's contention that a million or more men were there. This provided a "follow" story in which Farrakhan announced he would sue the park service over its numbers. Subsequently, ABC News hired an independent professor of mathematics and his researchers who, from looking at helicopter photos and loading data into a computer, came up with a probable count of 800,000 but said the figure could have been a million or more. But, in any case, crowd counting is not an exact science, a fact that readers understand.

Perhaps the reporter's most difficult obligation is to remain neutral and objective despite her own biases. This is necessary for both the reporter's and the newspaper's credibility. Emotions may rage, but someone must remain above the battle to report events clearly and dispassionately. Advocates are a minority among readers, most of whom seek straight information, not partisan viewpoints. They want the facts presented fairly and accurately so that they can make up their own minds.

Here are guidelines for covering rallies and demonstrations:

1. Fix the scene in your mind before plunging into reporting the action. Crowd size, types of people, noises and banners all lend color to the story.
2. Seek out leaders for the name of the organization, its goals, its size of membership and an estimate of the attendance. The latter should be confirmed or balanced from estimates by police and others. Make your own assessment, too.
3. Don't blow up the story merely because of bombast hurled from the speakers' platform. Concentrate more on the speeches that marshal facts and figures and present a clear plan of action. Back in your office you can check the paper's library or make a few well-placed phone calls to determine the accuracy of assertions made by the organizers.
4. Supply background on the organization and the issues in your story to make it more understandable for the reader.

The following story involves a demonstration about one of the critical problems of the day. In this instance, the writer took a narrative approach to the subject, which can be an effective way to reach the reader. There is a lot of color and human interest, but notice also the factual background material on gang violence.

By Geoffrey Mohan

None stands much taller than 5 feet, but mustered together, two dozen strong, these mothers form a determined picket line at the crossroads of youth and violent death.

They come to 1st and Clarence streets in Boyle Heights every Friday night because some of those who have died here in the latest gang war hot zone have barely crossed from childhood into adolescence.

Gangs have long fought their turf battles here and at nearby intersections of the Pico-Aliso housing projects. Their members, and bystanders, fall in numbers that vary from year to year. This year's tally of five—four during the summer alone—is unusually high for Pico-Aliso, police say.

But if the story can be told in numbers, they are 13 and 14, for the youngest victims, who fell on consecutive days in early June.

Their passing was largely unheralded, in contrast to the hue and cry that attended the shooting death of 3-year-old Stephanie Kuhen, a passenger in a car riddled by gang members' bullets after it turned down a dead-end street in Cypress Park on Sept. 17.

In a city seemingly inured to curbside violence, the mothers of Pico-Aliso have emerged as a reminder that every mother's worst nightmare is to see her child on either side of a gun; every mother's child is mourned.

In recent months, the mothers of Pico-Aliso—known formally as the Comite Pro Paz en el Barrio (Committee for Peace in the Neighborhood)—have confronted violence in their neighborhood with tactics that are more perilous and passionate.

In one instance, the mothers formed a human wall between taunting rivals after a funeral for the last of five young men slain this summer. On another occasion, a gang member threatened one of the mothers with a gun.

And still they come.

On any given Friday, the mothers display a banner that says "Raza, Que Pasa?" a weighted phrase for which the closest English evocation was singer Marvin Gaye's exasperated cry of "What's Going On?"

The answer is implied in the candle-lit faces of the mothers. There are too many of us dying.

"There was always an intention to confront the violence," said Leonardo Vilchis, a community organizer from Dolores Mission Roman Catholic parish, where the mothers' group is based. "But we couldn't come as outsiders. We had to approach it with love. 'It's because we love you that we want you to stop shooting.' If the gang members know the mothers and the mothers know the gang members, it's hard to shoot."

The logic has held through many a violent session.

The committee began holding "love marches" and peace barbecues in the projects during a violent period in 1991. But their actions were never confined to holding—or wringing—hands. They aimed a maternal wrath at police, whom they accused of brutality, and even the Jesuit hierarchy, over keeping Father Greg Boyle, a leader in the fight against violence, at Dolores Mission.

Clad in a Bruce Springsteen T-shirt with faded letters that proclaimed "The Boss," Natividad Lopez urged the mothers to defy and embrace the gang members who routinely shoot at one another across the crowded space of these public housing areas east of Downtown.

"We've always had marches, because the situation is so desperate with all the shooting," Lopez said. "As mothers, we can cross into different neighborhoods and they don't ask us, 'Why are you in this neighborhood?'"

The 40-year-old Salvadoran was among the mothers attending the July funeral of the latest victim of gang violence when they were all put to a test.

Members of the Cuatro Flats gang walked provocatively down Gless Street, the turf of TMC (The Mob Crew), to a funeral mass in Dolores Mission Church. By the time it was over, rival gangs lined the street, Lopez said.

"They got out of their cars with pistols!" said Lopez, still awed by the memory.

The women promptly surrounded the Cuatro Flats members and began walking them home, at times shoving and holding them back when they surged toward their taunters.

"We made a wall of just women," Lopez said. "There were some women grabbing as many as two kids. At first we were afraid but we prayed for the power and we felt it."

Father Boyle, who said the Mass, was startled to see the reaction of the gang to its rough maternal escort.

"You could tell they actually liked being held back," Boyle said. "They were physically and lovingly held back."

"The mothers' action may have been the most affection some of those gang members ever felt," Boyle noted. It also gave the mothers an added measure of confidence in their unique power. Simply put, it's hard to shoot someone's mother.

"We're part of everyone, because what we are about is that all of them live," Lopez said.

—Los Angeles Times

In contrast, this AP rally story is told in a straightforward manner with a traditional news lead. Which style you use usually depends on the nature of the story but sometimes on deadline pressures. Wire services work on a 24-hour deadline, and colorful writing must often give way to speed.

By Steve Elliott

CARLOTTA—More than 2,000 demonstrators rallied at a Pacific Lumber Co. mill yesterday near this Humboldt County town to protest plans to log the Headwaters Forest, the last stand of old-growth redwoods still in private hands.

More than 120 of the demonstrators were arrested when they crossed into Pacific Lumber Co. property, said Ingrid Hanson, spokeswoman for the Humboldt County Sheriff's office.

Pacific Lumber owns the forest—about 20 miles southeast of Eureka—and a number of adjoining plots; together they make up the largest virgin-redwood forest in the world. The approximately 5,000 acres of towering trees provide shelter for several endangered species, including the marbled murrelet and northern spotless owl, and rivers in the area are home to the rare coho salmon.

The rally was billed as the start of a long period of civil disobedience against the giant lumber company. The atmosphere was festive with drums beating, jugglers performing and music blaring. Towering piles of logs and finished lumber two- and three-stories tall formed a backdrop for a stage set up near the mill.

Pacific Lumber had a special salvage exemption issued by the state Department of Forestry that permits logging of fallen, dead or dying trees on the contested land once the nesting season ended yesterday.

U.S. District Judge Maxine Chesney issued a temporary restraining order through next Friday prohibiting the removal of downed trees in response to a request for an injunction by the Environmental Protection Information Center in Garberville.

The dead and fallen trees must be left where they are, to form new soil and provide nutrients for the next generation of forest, said center spokeswoman Cecelia Lanman.

She insisted that demonstrators were not out to cost the area jobs. "We're here in solidarity with them," she said. "We feel if we can work with them we will have a healthy forest that will be here for generations to come."

Also yesterday, the state Senate overwhelmingly approved a bill by Assemblyman Byron Sher, D-Stanford, that would direct the state Resources Agency to begin negotiations with Pacific Lumber to buy the Headwaters Forest.

At the camp, the rally—and the arrests—were carefully orchestrated through negotiations between leaders of the demonstration and law enforcement and Pacific Lumber.

—Associated Press

Public Hearings

America's democratic system provides for public hearings on a number of federal, state and local issues and problems. The gatherings often give citizens a greater opportunity to vent their views and grievances than, say, regular meetings of the city council, county board of supervisors and other public or private bodies. This is because the express purpose of the hearing is to listen to the public on the matter at hand. Whereas a city council might set aside only a half-hour for audience participation at its meeting, the public hearing is devoted solely to sampling public opinion. Ideally, officials listen to the speakers and take their views into account when the issue comes to a final vote before a public body.

The U.S. Senate, the House of Representatives and state legislative and administrative agencies hold similar hearings. Often, the latter go on the road to hear grassroots views in towns and cities across the country. Those going up to the microphone may be experts in a particular field, spokespersons for trade, business or professional groups or ordinary folk airing their gripes and concerns. This is one example of citizens speaking their minds.

By James W. Crawley, Staff Writer

No one inside the auditorium of Tierrasanta Elementary School last night could hear the roar of a jet fighter flying overhead.

Surely not over the din of unanswered questions from about 100 area residents mostly unhappy with plans to bring Marine Corps jets and helicopters to Miramar Naval Air Station in coming years.

Worries about noise fueled most of the comments made by residents at a hearing examining the environmental impacts of the Marines taking over Miramar during the next four years.

"It's going to be good-bye tourism, good-bye the environment," said Margaret Stevens, a La Jolla resident complaining about the plans to bring about 286 aircraft—eight helicopter squadrons and 11 jet fighter-bomber units—to Miramar.

A draft environmental report, released last month, stated that noise levels would increase in some neighborhoods.

Sorrento Valley noise levels will increase because plans call for helicopters to be located at the west end of Miramar's runways. Mira Mesa will be adversely affected because more Marine jets will use a northern departure route over the neighborhood.

The Marines also plan to start flying as early as 7 a.m., 30 minutes earlier than Navy pilots. Most flights would end by 11 p.m., the report stated.

The report also mentions the destruction of some vernal pools because of additional construction and plans to explode World War II explosives found on the former Camp Elliott, which is now East Miramar.

The thump-thump-thump of helicopters above their neighborhood was the greatest complaint voiced by speakers.

"They make one hell of a lot of noise," complained Stevens.

Interrupted sleep and disrupted conversations were repeated worries from more than a dozen speakers.

One former Navy pilot, F.R. Fleming, chastised Marine aviators for deviating from flight paths.

"The Marines are not following course rules," said Fleming, using aviator's slang.

Many at the hearing complained that they were getting few or no answers from military officials. And, many added, few people knew of the public hearings or the report.

"This hasn't gotten around to a lot of people," said Mira Mesa resident Mark Kornheiser, referring to the environmental report.

He urged a 45-day extension of the comment period during which federal officials will receive public statements.

"The answer is to delay this," he added. "We need some real facts."

"The Marine officers present last night were there to listen, not answer questions," said Lt. Col. George Martin, who is in charge of moving the Marines to Miramar.

But before the hearing, Martin said Marines would like to make some changes to flight paths around Miramar.

Commercial and general aviation flight corridors "lock us in," said Martin. "We think it's advantageous to move those corridors."

—San Diego Union-Tribune

In the preceding piece, the reporter highlighted the residents' concern over the Marine flights while supplying enough background to make the story understandable. In short, he put it in context.

Quotes always enliven a public hearing article. Attaching names to the quotes can be difficult, especially in a crowded room. Some speakers will announce their names; others won't unless the moderator requires identification before allowing statements. Often, you must weave your way through the audience to buttonhole speakers. Be sure to get the names spelled right.

Awards and Installations

Compared with some other stories, covering dinners and ceremonies involving awards and installations is not the most exciting kind of journalism, barring, perhaps, the awarding of the Nobel Prize or other nationally and internationally recognized honors.

However, to a community newspaper, the prize won by a Cub Scout den or Jennifer Chan's being named valedictorian of her high school class may be more important to readers than the Nobel. Similarly, the elections of officers at the Chamber of Commerce, Kiwanis Club or the local chapter of the National Organization of Women (NOW) are read avidly, and editors know it. Even metro dailies are aware of the interest in hometown news and feed it to readers in the main paper and in zoned editions for various sections of the community.

These stories require care and close attention. Getting names right is an absolute must. Such news is of interest not only to the award winners and their families but also to friends, relatives, neighbors and members of the particular organization. Misspelling a name can generate irate letters and phone calls—even canceled subscriptions.

Much of this kind of news arrives at the newspaper in mailed or faxed press releases, making, in some cases, attendance at the meeting or ceremony unnecessary. But if the event is big enough and/or boasts a speaker, a paper will usually staff it.

The attending reporter must be sure to get a correct list of names—at least those he intends using in the story. If a list is not available, it may be necessary to get the names from the awardees or elected officers.

As with other types of stories, there may be more there than meets the eye. When covering an awards presentation, look for possible angles. Perhaps a winner is a Vietnamese refugee who ten years ago arrived in the United States penniless and unable to speak or write English. There you have the ingredients for a good human interest element to weave into the story. Maybe it will be the story!

A group of immigrants being sworn in as new citizens is a perfect situation for human interest and drama. You can make it a cut-and-dried piece about 150 people becoming Americans and the usual congratulations from the presiding judge, or it can be developed into a heartwarming, positive narrative in which the experiences of three or four of the group are given prominence in the overall story. The trick? There is no trick. You have to dig for this kind of material. Move around. Talk to the newly minted citizens themselves, their friends and relatives and anyone else who knows them.

In both election and award events, there is often a number of names. Not only is a president elected by a club but also a vice president or two, secretary-treasurer and sergeant at arms plus a board of directors.

Don't clutter the lead with a lot of names. In most cases, the president occupies the lead, like this:

> Richard R. Colwell, president of Datacycle, a local microchip manufacturing firm, was elected president of the Business Round Table Club yesterday.
>
> He pledged to expand the club's current internship program for high school and college students and to work toward establishing an overseas exchange arrangement with foreign businessmen and women.
>
> Other officers elected were Cheryl Ames, vice president; Roger Braden, second vice president; Vito Torrentino, secretary-treasurer, and George Portis, program chairman.

If a speaker at an installation delivers newsworthy remarks, you can lead off with them and work the elections in later. The lead and second paragraph might read:

> Congresswoman Della Morrison told the Downtown Association yesterday she was optimistic that Winfield would qualify for Federal disaster relief in the wake of last month's tornado that devastated a 14-block area.
>
> Speaking at the association's annual Civic Awards day, Morrison said she had been informed by the White House that the president was prepared to sign the relief order.

The awards themselves could go down in the story since what the speaker said was more important to the community at large. Still, the awardees are of interest to many readers. Be sure all are listed, particularly in smaller communities. However, space limitations may dictate that recipients of smaller prizes are bunched in a paragraph or two, often in small type. A number of newspapers have introduced "Neighbors" or other community-focused sections in which news of this kind is featured. The *San Francisco Independent,* a triweekly, has enjoyed great success by virtually devoting the entire paper to neighborhood items that the city's dailies generally overlook. The next story appeared in the daily Long Beach (Calif.) *Press-Telegram*'s "Neighbors" supplement:

> By coincidence, the Veterans of Foreign Wars Post 3173 at Anaheim and the American Legion's 29th district had banquets the same night—to honor law enforcement officers who distinguished themselves in the line of duty.
>
> Gustavo De La Torre, a 43-year veteran with the Orange County Sheriff's Department, received the Gold Medal Award commemorating the late FBI director J. Edgar Hoover.

De La Torre recently saved two victims of separate accidents by administering cardiopulmonary resuscitation. Recently, the deputy persuaded a distraught youth not to take his own life as he had threatened.

The American Legion honored Investigator Stuart R. Benicky with the Award for Valor for distracting a fugitive who was pointing a gun at Benicky's partner. The suspect then fired at Benicky, who traded shots before arresting the wanted man.

Sgt. William Francis received the Award of Courage for helping quell a disturbance at the Orange County Jail a year ago, when inmates went on a rampage with makeshift weapons and set several fires.

Deputy Francis was stabbed in the back during the fracas but refused medical care until the riot was controlled.

Deputy Don Heffern received a Certificate of Commendation for a series of patrol arrests and observations leading to solution of crimes. He also provided information leading to the arrest of a bank robber.

—Long Beach *Press-Telegram*

Writing the Obituary

There are two main things to remember about obituaries: They have a high readership and they must be pinpoint accurate. Even a wrong middle initial can bring a barrage of complaints. For loved ones, the obit is the final tribute to the departed and they want it right. You may find that typing out an obituary for an ordinary citizen is a dull chore that keeps you from going after that Pulitzer-possible story, but the person's relatives and friends will be examining it the next day with a critical eye.

Who gets an obit? On small dailies and weeklies virtually any death in the community will rate a story, be he or she bank president or mail carrier. Metropolitan papers and the wire services work on a different standard. Because there are so many deaths per week or month, usually only the more prominent local, national or international figures will rate an obit. The relatives of others may buy a paid obituary in a newspaper's classified advertising section. Because this is not an editorial function, the account may be written by a funeral home or the bereaved, sometimes with the help of the ad department. Editors with a limited obit "hole" also have to make room for the passing of national and international luminaries that come over on the wires.

Don't take "prominent" too literally. Yes, a community's movers and shakers are likely to dominate the obit page, but a third-grade teacher who has won the admiration of generations of pupils also is a candidate for an obit.

Gathering information for an obit may be harder than writing it. Getting facts and background on the deceased from grieving family members sometimes calls for a great deal of tact. Although a death is a matter of public record and thus can be published with or without relatives' cooperation, some kin may refuse to talk about it, particularly to a reporter. One approach is to suggest to a wife or husband that the departed's friends, acquaintances or business associates would want to be informed of the death and to attend the funeral. Again, be circumspect.

Of course, the newspaper's library will likely have clips on well-known individuals, who may have held public office, won awards, engaged in an act of heroism—or have a police record. There also are numerous other biographical references such as "Who's Who," the Internet and "Current Biography." Other sources include old friends, colleagues, employers and employees. However, they may have hazy memories as to dates and events; if so, their information must be verified.

Remember that an obit is a news story and should be handled that way. The standard format is a lead that tells who, what and when. But don't leave it at that. Whatever the person did or accomplished in life, no matter how humble, should be part of the opening sentence. Here are typical leads:

> Gerald R. Mumford, president of First Technologies and a longtime arts patron, died at his home yesterday following a brief illness. He was 79.

> Amanda Logan, 62, founder of the Chatworth Nursery School and an authority on child development, died suddenly Tuesday while visiting friends in St. Paul.

> Major Gen. Richard Rollins U.S.Army (Ret.) who commanded troops in Vietnam and the Gulf War, died of a heart attack yesterday at Georgetown University Hospital. He was 74.

Avoid leads like this, which might be taken from the telephone directory:

> Rolf Berglund, 51, of 576 Blaney Ave., died following a stroke yesterday.

Instead, try it this way:

> Rolf Berglund, a tool and die maker here for 28 years, died early yesterday from injuries received in an auto accident last month.

In the standard obit, the second paragraph may describe the place and cause of death while building on the highlights of the person's life. The rest of the obituary includes birthplace, schooling, career highlights and memberships. In some cases, remembrances from relatives and friends may be included. The final paragraph usually is devoted to funeral or memorial information, if any.

Examine this typical obit for style:

> Barry Tembey, who won gold and silver medals in speed skating at the 1969 Olympics in Japan, died yesterday from injuries suffered in an auto accident. He was 72.

Tembey, who died at Northwestern University Hospital in Chicago, went on after the Olympics to win several awards in international competition. He also conducted a skating school in his hometown of Racine, Wis., and served two terms in the state legislature.

The accident occurred outside of Winnetka, Ill., as he was en route to visit his son at the University of Illinois. Police said a tractor-trailer jackknifed on the highway and toppled on Tembey's car.

Tembey graduated from the University of Wisconsin, where he honed his skills as a skater. He also played varsity baseball as a shortstop.

He is survived by his wife, Vivian, his father, Alfred, of Racine, and two sons, Richard and Lawrence. Funeral services were pending.

Here also is an Associated Press lead and following graph for an obituary of a well-known figure:

LOS ANGELES—Ruth Handler, who created Barbie, the world's most popular doll and an American icon that helped shape girls' dreams while infuriating feminists, has died. She was 85.

Handler, who also co-founded the Mattel toy company, died at Century City Hospital on Saturday morning, Elliot Handler, her husband, said.

Some newspapers today are drawing away from the obit's standard format in favor of a more narrative account with heavy emphasis on color and human interest. The traditional lead is passed up for a story-telling opening with the facts of the death buried in the fifth or sixth paragraph. This is an example:

By Robin Hinch

There was no question who ran Lucky's Nursery in Garden Grove. It was Lucky. And that wasn't "Mr. Lucky."

It was Lucille "Lucky" Ragsdale, who for 45 years cared for her business as a mother hovers over her first-born child.

Even her husband, George, didn't make major decisions, "I'd better go tell the boss," he'd tell a salesman before clinching a deal.

Lucky was never overbearing about it. But she knew what she wanted. And how she wanted it.

When a shipment of plants arrived at the nursery, her eyes narrowed as she inspected each sprig. One wilted leaf or bud and back it went. No discussion.

It was a small place—just an acre on Westminster Boulevard east of Brookhurst—but it was home, literally and figuratively. The family's modest house was right there on the property. Lucky could run home to make a quick dinner, all the while watching out for customers. If she had to desert the meal and let it burn, so be it.

And so it was that she ran her business until she had a stroke three years ago—open 9 a.m. to 5 p.m., seven days a week, closed only on Christmas and Thanksgiving. If gardeners needed supplies early in the morning, they banged on her door at 7 a.m.

If you look carefully, you may still find traces of soil under her fingernails. Lucky was 80 when she died Wednesday.

She was born Lucille Fairchild in Garden Grove, and was always proud of being a Garden Grove native. . .

You could always find her in her little smock apron smudged with potting soil, front pockets sagging with pruning shears, keys and her stash of Kleenex, slogging down the muddy aisles, making sure everything was properly watered and pruned.

Family vacations were out of the question. Lucky wouldn't leave the nursery. If she *had* to be gone, George or one of their daughters had to stay behind to mind the store. And even then, Lucky would call daily to check in.

A tiny woman at 5-foot-3, she was proud of her physical strength. No customer—not even a burly man—was allowed to load a 100-pound bag of fertilizer into a car. Lucky heaved it in there like it was nothing. . .

—The *Orange County Register*

A prime example of this kind of obit appeared for weeks in the *New York Times* following the Sept. 11 World Trade Center attack. The *Times* published on one page short biographies of the victims. Here is one lead:

Vincent Morello
One weekend every summer, the commissioner of the Male Bonding Association would lead eight buddies to the Hamptons—but what happened there remained a mystery. His rules: No guy could call his wife. No guy could *mention* his wife. If a wife asked what the husbands did, the guy had to reply, "I can't tell you. . ."

Of course, color and human interest can be woven into any obit—if the ingredients are there. This might require some digging on your part to lift the story from the mundane to the striking.

Follow this checklist in all obits:

1. Make double sure that names are spelled correctly.

2. If there is doubt about facts, go back to the source or check it through reference sources such as the phone book, an encyclopedia, almanac or city directory. Never guess about the facts.

3. Never publish an obit volunteered over the phone without calling back the family or other reliable source to determine whether a death did occur. Pranksters with a sick turn of mind have made false calls to newspapers and broadcast stations about a demise.

4. Get the time and place of the funeral correctly. Friends and relatives depend on your information.

5. Be tactful and considerate when attempting to glean information from the deceased person's family.

Suggested Assignments

1. Check the campus and local papers for upcoming speeches. Dig up background on the speaker and cover his or her speech; try first to get an advance copy of the text. Write the speech, using the most newsworthy lead you can find.

2. Sometimes advance notice is given of a rally or demonstration. If so, cover and write it.

3. Seek out a public hearing by a local, state or federal body and cover it. Hearings by a citizens group is also a possibility. Acquire as much background on the subject as you can before going to the gathering.

4. By calling various campus and local organizations, you may find some that have recently elected new officers. Take the information on the phone and ask the group to send you a list. Do a story.

5. Clip three speech and three public hearing stories from newspapers. Analyze in class how each succeeded or failed in capturing the news value, how each is organized and whether or not the writers made good use of quotes and color.

6. Clip two demonstration stories from any newspaper and discuss in class these points:
   a. Are the leads justified by the facts?
   b. Are the stories fair to both sides (or all sides) in terms of space and emphasis?
   c. Is sound use made of color and action without sensationalizing the stories?
   d. Are the positions of the stories in the paper appropriate in terms of page or location above or below the fold?

7. Write a story from the text of the speech below. The speaker is Walter F. Mondale, former U.S. ambassador to Japan and former vice president of the United States. He addressed the World Affairs Council at a noon luncheon in 1994 at the Biltmore Hotel, Los Angeles, on the topic "America and Japan—Building an Asia-Pacific Community."

> I have been in my job now for almost one year. I have had several first impressions. First, I'm quite impressed by the public approval of my appointment. A Republican friend of mine told me if he had known President Clinton was going to send me out of the country, he would

have voted for him. Another unexpected pleasure of this job is that when I arrived in Tokyo, I thought the phone wasn't working. The best part of this job is that when they're awake in Washington, I'm asleep. Even better, when I'm awake, they're asleep. So, I've got my own little job, and I do it my way. It's a great joy.

It's refreshing to start a new public career at my young age. I was very honored to accept this appointment. I have been in public life for a long time. With every year, I have become more convinced that the future of this world is heavily involved in how well Japan and the United States understand each other and cooperate. If we're able to understand, work together, and cooperate across the board, practically every significant problem that confronts mankind can be handled or handled better at least than we're handling the problems now. But if we, through some kind of foolishness, consult our darker side and permit the relationship to deteriorate, to rupture, I think the consequences for society and the world are such that we simply can't let this happen.

In a sense, I took this job for my grandchildren and yours. We are talking about what kind of a world they're going to inherit. I think as we moved toward the West Coast I have to say less and less about the Pacific and the Asian basin. You have a much more direct and personal stake. All you have to do is look out your window and know that you're on the Pacific. But I still think we have a job ahead of us in teaching Americans to understand the profound nature and significance of the U.S.-Asian relationship and to become part of the U.S.-Japan involvement.

Number one, the economics of this region are providing basic economic growth into the next century as far as the eye can see. With that rising economic strength will come growing political and strategic influence. Already 40% of our trade is in the Asian Pacific region, and by the year 2000 the size of the trade in Asia will be double that of what we have in Europe. I saw a figure the other day that Singapore, little Singapore, imports more American products than does Italy or Spain. Malaysia imports more American goods than Russia does.

The magnitude and dynamism of the growth and the economic vibrancy of that area are some of the most profound phenomena of our times. We simply must be a part of it in every possible way. Last July in his speech at a university, the president laid out his vision of a new Pacific community based on shared strengths, shared prosperity, and a shared commitment to democratic values. The three pillars are mutually reinforcing. Security is essential for economic development. Economic progress promotes democratic change. Prosperous democracies make for peaceful neighbors.

The U.S.-Japan relationship is the bedrock of the Pacific community. Only if our two countries work together economically, strategically and on global issues can the promise of this region be fulfilled. Only if this community flourishes can the prosperity and security of Japan and America be assured. In pursuing these objectives, I see three major challenges facing the region. In my lifetime, the three wars all started there, and thousands of American lives were lost trying to restore and maintain stability in that region. Thanks in large part to American sacrifice, to our continuing presence of our security forces, and our involvement, Asia today is happily free of significant military conflicts.

Democracy is spreading, and the standard of living is rapidly rising. The fact is that only a continuing American military presence centered on the UN-U.S.-Japan Security Treaty and supplemented by other alliances can maintain regional stability for the foreseeable future. Why do the U.S. forces have to be there? I think it's very important that we get this clear. The United States plays a role that no other country can play there. We are accepted as an honest broker, and our military presence is welcomed by all members of the Asian Pacific community, with the possible exception of North Korea, and I'm not even sure about that.

Because of lingering suspicions based on historical animosities, no other country plays the role the United States now plays there. In East Asia there is no framework such as NATO or any other institutions found in Europe to manage such problems. Therefore, the United States must continue to lead there in ensuring stability. Others must help out. But even there, I'm happy to say, we're making progress. The heart of our presence in Asia is to be found in Japan, and in our bases there we have roughly 47,000 military personnel in all the services. Without those bases found throughout Japan, it would be impossible for us to meet our treaty responsibilities.

Under the agreement, the government of Japan is now assuming half the cost of our forces there—some $4 billion or 10% of their defense budget. It is one of the best bargains the American taxpayer has because it would cost far more to bring those forces home. It's a good bargain for Japan. It's an indispensable contribution to stability in the region.

Another challenge for the Pacific community is to advance the opportunities for prosperity. Free flow of trade and commerce among nations is a critical element in improving regional and global prosperity. As the major economic powers in the region, the U.S. and Japan must take the lead in securing the prosperity of this community into the next century. The U.S. will continue its role as the engine of growth. We will keep our markets open. We will provide investment capital. We will export innovative, high quality, competitively priced goods and services.

Japan, for its part, will continue to be the major source of economic assistance and direct investment and the major provider of economic products. These are important contributions, but I don't think they are enough. If we are going to take full advantage of the opportunities for growth and prosperity, Japan must open its economy more completely to the region and to the world.

In the postwar period, Japan has been among the greatest beneficiaries of the open trading systems of the world. She has taken full advantage of free access to the American and other markets to expand exports and build her economy into the second largest in the world. But Japan has not fully reciprocated in opening her markets to foreign goods, services and investments. Japan, for example, absorbs far fewer manufactured imports relative to the size of her economy than any other industrialized nation.

Japan also takes in very little of the world's foreign direct investment. Japan faces a similar challenge to these sectoral issues at the macroeconomic level. We have been urging Japan to stimulate her economy—not just the United States, but the G-7, all the major central bankers. What the world now needs from Japan is a sustained period of domestic demand-led growth that will increase imports and bring a substantial reduction in the enormous Japanese account surplus. The surplus now stands at about $130 billion and is a global problem hindering the efforts of other countries to expand their economies and increase employment.

It is an invitation to protectionism around the world. This past weekend, Mickey Kantor (U.S. chief trade negotiator) and other negotiating officials were meeting with MIRI Minister Hashimoto and Foreign Minister Kono to try to move forward on the so-called Framework Accords that call for the opening of certain areas that we established as priority areas for progress.

One area is in government procurement that deals with medical equipment and telecommunications. Another is in insurance and the third is in auto and auto parts sectors. We have reached several important agreements in the past year, one on construction, one on cellular phones, another on property rights. But we have yet to reach agreement on any of those priority issues under the framework. I think we're getting close on insurance. Some progress was made on government procurement, but we have two or three weeks when we have to redouble our efforts to get agreements in these crucial areas.

As we face deadlines under our trade laws, we hope that we can make the necessary progress. This is important for Japan itself. As many Japanese are pointing out, it is in Japan's own national interest to embrace market opening reforms. They would strengthen their domestic economy, improve living standards by expanding consumer choice, and lower the high prices that currently prevail in China.

Before I close, I would like to make one final point. One of the things that struck me in my new duties is the way crime and violence have started to cut across the American message and image. Shortly before I arrived, a young Japanese student was killed in Louisiana. He was out with friends on Halloween, and he didn't hear the command and didn't give the right answer and was shot and he died. Two Japanese students were also killed in a parking lot shortly after I arrived in Los Angeles. The impact on Japan was one that ought to sober all of us.

The fact itself was horrible enough. Young Japanese love this country and want to come here. There are some 50,000 of them studying in the United States. I met with several young students just after they returned. They were all scared. They are afraid for their lives. They wonder what is going on in this country, whether it is falling apart. This is unknown in Japan. They don't have guns available the way we do. It reminds me of my young years in politics when our nation discriminated and still had official laws that separated blacks from whites in schools and transportation. Every time the United States wanted to push a point to the rest of the world, our failure to deal effectively with this moral disgrace of discrimination undermined the capacity of the United States to lead.

I believe we are getting to the point where violence, the availability and use of guns, and the inability of people to feel secure in the streets are starting to have some impact on the American message. When those two men were killed, first of all I apologized. The tragedy here is that it looks like everybody is getting shot in America when, in fact, most people live wonderful, safe lives. It distorts. The mail I got from people in the United States said, "Mr. Mondale, where have you been living?" They challenged that. I think we cannot think any longer that this is just a domestic issue. It is an international issue as well and we have to get control of it.

8. Pick out a standard obit from a newspaper about a local figure. Do some interviews and research to rewrite the story with more human interest and color.

7

The Reporter and the Law

The United States has the freest press system in the world. Yet this freedom, guaranteed by the First Amendment to the Constitution, does not give the news media immunity from the laws of the land.

In recent years, a growing number of journalists and their newspapers have learned this the hard way through lawsuits for libel and invasion of privacy that have cost defendants up to $10 million or more. Win or lose, the mere cost of fighting such a suit is enormously expensive and can put some small newspapers out of business.

In addition, there are legal hazards for journalists such as contempt citations, gag rules, closed court proceedings and denial of access to public meetings and records.

In recent years, the number of libel trials won by the media has increased, according to the Libel Defense Resource Center, a media-funded organization. Still, the Center noted, awards to news organizations averaged more than $1 million, compared with less than $500,000 in the late 1980s. "Libel awards averaging in excess of $1 million are a chilling phenomenon," said LDRC general counsel Henry Kaufman.

What Is Libel?

Libel is damage to one's good name and reputation. Words, pictures or cartoons that hold a person up to public ridicule, contempt, disgrace or shame are libelous *per se,* that is, on their face. When injurious words are spoken during a public address or broadcast, they are called *slander.*

All 50 states have libel laws that are similar in wording. Libel actions also can be brought in federal court when the plaintiff, the one filing the suit, and the defendant(s) live in different states.

Most libel cases arise from stories involving alleged crime, dishonesty, shady dealing, corruption or immoral conduct—behavior that is likely (1) to defame an individual and to cause him or her to suffer professionally or in business and/or (2) to subject the person to the contempt or ridicule of friends, associates and the public at large. Accusing a doctor of filing a false Medicare claim is an example of injury to his professional reputation. To say that a police official took bribes is to invite a libel suit. A school teacher charged in a story with molesting children is another possible plaintiff.

The *Detroit News* and the *Detroit Free Press* were sued by the owners of a commercial skating rink over stories of gang-related shootings near the rink. The court complaint claimed the articles were defamatory, falsely portraying the facility as an unsafe place to patronize. An appellate court ruled in favor of the newspapers and said the stories were fair reporting. More of this defense in a moment.

Usually when a libel suit is filed, the defendants named will include the offending publication, the reporter(s) who covered and wrote the story and possibly the source of the information. Editors also may be listed as defendants for having edited the story and allowing the disputed material to be published.

There are, of course, defenses to libel. The most effective in all courts is provable truth. The plaintiff has the burden of convincing a judge or jury she was libeled. If the defendant can prove that the newspaper story was substantially correct, the libel is not likely to stand up. However, quoting a source correctly is not a strong enough defense. Hard evidence that the plaintiff stole money, cheated on his income tax or didn't pay court-ordered child support for five years will usually carry the day for the party sued. That's why investigative reporters look for the "paper trail," documents that clearly show wrongdoing. Getting such evidence often requires hard work, long hours and patience.

"Follow the money," advises *Boston Phoenix* reporter Al Giordano. "The dollars politicians take in, through campaign contributions, and the dollars they dole out, through government budgets and tax loopholes, have made for a revolving door of legalized bribery."

A second defense against libel is *privilege*. The law gives news media the privilege of reporting the actions of judicial, legislative and other public proceedings without running the risk of libel. Certain proceedings such as court trials have *absolute privilege*. This means that while covering a trial you can quote lawyers and witnesses under oath—no matter how damaging their words—with total immunity from a libel suit. Similarly, remarks made on the floor of Congress or state legislatures can be published freely without threat of libel.

In the case of a trial, however, be careful of writing what you hear in the corridors during a recess or lunch break from attorneys, witnesses or anyone connected to the case. Your immunity to libel stops when the judge bangs down her gavel, ending the court session.

There is also a gray area of *qualified privilege,* where reporters also must be careful. It's all right to report the arrest of someone on a drunk driving charge, if the facts are accurate. But press conferences and interviews with police officers or a district attorney carry some risk. Consider carefully what you write and, if unsure, discuss the matter with your editor or the paper's attorney. A cop may say things that would indicate that a suspect can expect a conviction and a life sentence. It may turn out that she is simply questioned and released without even a charge placed against her. You should be especially careful about copying material from police log books because they do not offer absolute privilege—and sometimes contain misinformation.

A third libel defense is *fair comment*. This is a legal concept that gives the press the right to comment on affairs of public interest. A sportswriter may comment with impunity on the sloppy ball handling of a third baseman. A theater critic is allowed to pan the actors performance in a play or the play itself. The same right is extended to political columnists, editorial writers and other journalists who deal in commentary. The comments, however, must be based on facts, free from ulterior motives, and an honest expression of the writer's opinion.

In a New York case, the court summed up fair comment this way:

> Everyone has the right to comments on matters of public interest and concern, provided they do so fairly and with an honest purpose. Such comments or criticisms are not libelous, however severe in their terms, unless they are written maliciously. Thus it has been held that books, prints, pictures and statuary publicly exhibited and the architecture of public buildings, and actors and exhibitors are all the legitimate subjects of newspapers' criticism, and such criticism fairly and honestly made is not libelous, however strong the terms of censure may be. (*Hoeppner v. Dunkirk Pr. Co.,* 254 N.Y. 95)

Now a warning: The private lives of baseball players, film stars, politicians and other celebrities do not offer a shelter from libel, as some supermarket tabloids have learned in recent years. Among the plaintiffs have been actress Carol Burnett, the late comedian Rodney Dangerfield, entertainer Michael Jackson and actor Clint Eastwood. These well-known individuals sued and won libel or privacy cases against the publications. In a press conference statement after his victory against the *National Enquirer,* superstar Eastwood said about the *Enquirer*: "When you trash people with a lie, that's not fair." The tabloid published a story, reputedly based on an interview with Eastwood, that portrayed him as a heavy drinker, who mistreated women and was indifferent to the raising of his daughter. Eastwood claimed the interview never took place.

"Know what not to investigate," Al Giordano advises further. "Good political reporters have better things to do than invade people's privacy. Leave sexual practices, with or without benefit of clergy, or whether someone 'inhaled' to the pseudo-journalists. And leave family members alone. Loss of privacy keeps too many good people out of politics, leaving us with a class of pols who have led boring, unadventurous lives."

The sensational tabloids attract more libel suits because they take more risks. But the mainstream press has fought its share of libel suits, including the *Wall Street Journal, Washington Post, Miami Herald* and several other papers. Such newspapers may not delve into the bedroom antics of Hollywood celebrities, but they, too, take risks, although usually of a different kind. Watergate was a risk. After all, the *Washington Post* was probing the role of the president of the United States in this investigation. Often when a newspaper seeks to uncover corruption, big names are involved. That's why editors constantly demand that reporters diligently check and double-check facts, rumors and allegations. Ben Bradlee, the famed former editor of the *Washington Post,* insisted that Bob Woodward and Carl Bernstein, the young reporters who broke the Watergate burglary story, have at least two sources for every significant development they wrote about.

Although libel is an ever-present danger for the press, a landmark case, *New York Times v. Sullivan* in 1964 dramatically changed the libel law in the United States, creating a strong bulwark against a defamation charge.

In this instance, the Supreme Court reversed a $500,000 libel judgment against the *New York Times* and four black ministers for an advertisement condemning police actions against Montgomery, Alabama, college students seeking financial support for the late civil rights leader Dr. Martin Luther King, Jr. The high court ruled unanimously that public figures cannot sue for libel unless it can be proven that a statement was printed or broadcast with the knowledge that it was false or with reckless disregard for the truth (in other words, if a reporter, knowing that something is false, goes ahead and writes it anyway). This is a tough nut for a plaintiff's lawyer to crack since it often means getting into the mind of the writer to show harmful intent.

The decision made it much harder for prominent persons to sue the media, but libel suits are not filed only by persons in the limelight. The Sullivan decision does not apply to ordinary people who feel themselves victims of damaging statements. The janitor who is reported as having caused an apartment house fire by his careless dumping of oily rags could file a $10 million damage suit against a newspaper as easily as the governor of the state—more easily, since a governor seldom wants the publicity the suit would bring and would likely lose in court because he is a public figure.

The former girlfriend of one-time Atlanta Hawks basketball star Dominique Wilkins sued both Wilkins and the *Atlanta Journal-Constitution* for his remarks printed in the paper, which allegedly "dissed" her. But a Georgia state court threw out the $5 million suit and declared that freedom of speech gave Wilkins the right to express an opinion, unflattering though it may be. Although the girlfriend lost, it was not because she was a public figure. She was not, her dating Wilkins notwithstanding. In another nightmare for the press, Richard Jewell has settled several lawsuits against the media and is pursuing others following his release as a suspect in the Atlanta Olympics bombing. Jewell, a security guard at Atlanta's Olympic Centennial Park, was the subject of huge media coverage after police detained him in the bombing. At a Florida program of the Society of Professional Journalists titled "Privacy: Whose Life Is It, Anyway?" Jewell's attorney, Lin Wood, blasted the media for their portrayal of her client, naming in particular the *Atlanta Journal-Constitution,* one of the defendants in Jewell's suits. The newspaper, which refused to settle, maintained that its stories were based on information from authorities. Wood, who opined that the Jewell case may not have taught the media to be more careful, compared the reporting on Jewell to the Monica Lewinsky sex scandal involving former president Bill Clinton. "Look what happened to [her]," Wood said. "Look how much incredible information was put out by the reputable members of the press— the semen-stained dress, the Secret Service agent watching them do something—

reputable journalists who were dead wrong on key facts that got tremendous national play." At the same forum, Kathy Pellagrino, legal counsel for the Ft. Lauderdale *Sun-Sentinel,* countered that the U.S. media system works. Aggrieved parties of media attention have access to the courts, she said. She added that the public is not aware of the mass of material newspapers decide not to publish for fear of damaging someone and exposing themselves to litigation.

Editors and lawyers agree that the best defense of all against defamation suits is careful reporting. Libel actions resulting from malicious intent by the reporter are extremely rare. Normally, the writer has no personal interest in the story. Thus, most libel cases stem from sloppy reporting—plain carelessness in gathering facts. The reporter accepted information on its face value without checking it out. An anonymous tip on the phone or a letter from an informant, even if signed, is just the beginning of investigative reporting, not a signal to rush to the computer.

A number of libel suits originate in police reporting, where caution should be the watchword. Under our legal system, a person is innocent until proven guilty. An individual arrested or taken in for police questioning is a *suspect,* not a felon. The story must make this clear. Additionally, great care must be taken to *attribute* statements to authorities when describing someone as dishonest, violent or in any way linked to a crime or misdeed. Let the detective say that Harry Jones was arrested while carrying a bag of cocaine and a .32-caliber pistol. Cultivate terms like *allege* and *suspected* when writing the story. The following story exemplifies this kind of protection against libel. (The italic type in the example is ours.)

A 31-year-old Los Alamitos computer programmer was arrested on murder charges Monday after a police dispatcher took the man's call for help, then held the phone while the man allegedly shot his mother, according to Sgt. Rick Hobbs.

Hobbs said McCormick called police around 5:30 p.m. Monday seeking assistance at his mother's house at 6540 Grand Maman St., Cypress.

"During the conversation, he (McCormick) left the phone for a few minutes, then the dispatcher heard a gunshot in the background," *Hobbs said.*

When the police arrived moments later, they found Cloud on a patio behind the home, dead from a gunshot wound to the head," Hobbs said.

Police found a 12-gauge shotgun at the scene and arrested McCormick, Hobbs said.

Hobbs said Cloud apparently arrived at the house while McCormick was talking to the dispatcher.

Hobbs said two shots were fired, one near a garage, the other in the patio area of the condominium.

> "We're still investigating the motives," *Hobbs said.* "Apparently there were some bad feelings between Cloud, Zoe and Zoe's son."
>
> McCormick, who is employed by Jaycox Disposal Co. in Anaheim, is being held at Cypress City Jail without bail.
>
> —Long Beach *Press-Telegram*

Richard R. Cardwell, general counsel to the Hoosier Press Association, outlined the thought process he uses in determining whether certain material should be published.

1. Is the material defamatory of an identifiable individual, or small ascertainable group?
   a. If it is not defamatory, print it.
   b. If it is defamatory, then . . .
2. Is the material privileged?
   a. If it is privileged, print it.
   b. If it is not privileged, then . . .
3. Is the material probably true?
   a. If it is probably true, print it.
   b. If it is not probably true, don't print it.

Editors regularly make decisions to print stories even though they risk a libel suit. Because something is true doesn't mean a person who imagines herself aggrieved will not sue. But if newspapers spiked every story over which there might be a libel suit, a lot of news would never reach readers. The *New York Times* was sued by the former chief medical examiner of New York City for its reports about his being fired for allegedly falsifying autopsies. *Times* editors no doubt believed the story was legitimate news, even though it might trigger a lawsuit.

To protect themselves, newspapers retain lawyers who are experts in libel. Most papers also carry extensive libel insurance against a day when a judgment might go against them.

Reporters should not take too much comfort in the fact that they are backed by libel lawyers and an insurance policy. When a journalist gets his employer enmeshed in a court case, he runs the danger of sullying his reputation and the credibility of the news organization. On the other hand, reporters, editors and publishers have stuck by a challenged story, won the case and actually enhanced their reputations. Still, the best route is to avoid libel suits by being a careful, conscientious reporter. There are few things more important to an individual than his or her reputation and good name. Careless wording in a crime story can ruin one's standing in society, even when later corrections are made. Of course, a reporter's account is often only as reliable as his sources. A case in point involves a story about a missing child in Miami that got national play. An Associated Press lead states: "Child-welfare workers were unaware that a woman given custody of a 5-year-old girl whose disappearance went undetected for more than a year had a criminal record and used 20 different names in 20 years, officials said." The sourcing is reinforced in the second paragraph, which reads: "A records (agate) check showed Gwendolyn Graham served time in a Tennessee prison for food-stamp fraud, served five years probation for bad checks in Miami-Dade County and had been diagnosed with mental illness. . . ." If you are going to write such things about anyone, make very sure that the information is attributed to official sources. This in itself won't prevent anyone from filing a libel suit, but your chance of winning the case is greatly improved with strong attribution.

Criminal Libel

Actions between private parties come under civil law by which most libel cases are tried. Libel, however, can become a criminal offense when it causes a breach of the peace. The news media are rarely subjected to such charges, but a district attorney could move against a newspaper for violation of a criminal libel statute. In many other countries, criminal libel is used as a government weapon for stifling media that happen to disagree with official policy. In a dictatorship, criminal libel can be what the dictator decides it is.

An example of criminal libel in the United States would be a story that falsely stated that the city's water supply was contaminated, thereby creating a panic. Law books in various states also include malicious maligning of public officials as grounds for criminal libel.

Invasion of Privacy

Libel has deep roots in English common law, but privacy is a twentieth-century phenomenon, an outgrowth of mass media. To this day, few states have privacy laws, although suits can be brought under common law.

When the courts have dealt with privacy, they have defined it as the right of seclusion as to one's name or representation of himself. In plain language, this means the right to be left alone while maintaining one's social, political and occupational rights. Any violation of this privilege is deemed an invasion of privacy and may be actionable.

But who enjoys the right of privacy? The courts have held that the privilege does not exist where a person has become so prominent that she is recognized wherever she goes. A famed actress entering a nightclub with an escort is fair game for the bevy of photographers waiting to shoot celebrities. But what if this same actress is sunbathing in the nude on her private patio and a helicopter with a cameraman swoops low and a picture is snapped? The photo in a tabloid could very well end up as evidence in an invasion of privacy trial. The courts have deemed that even public figures are entitled to privacy in their own homes.

Actor Alec Baldwin apparently felt so strongly about this that he slugged a freelance photographer who took pictures of Baldwin and his then-wife, actress Kim

Basinger, as they were entering the house with their newborn child. Baldwin was charged with assault.

On the other hand, Princess Diana was dogged by photographers wherever she went in public, and paparazzi were following her when she died in a Paris auto crash.

One thing is clear. There is generally no privacy in the dissemination of news. Persons involved in accidents, assaults, robberies and riots normally cannot claim interference with their privacy if their names and/or faces are published in a newspaper. The courts have taken the position that news is public property and journalists are merely doing their job when they interview and photograph individuals as part of news coverage.

Again, however, it is wise to differentiate between what is legitimate news and what is not. Sometimes the issue is whether a person agrees to have his or her picture taken and be interviewed. Let's take a situation in which a reporter and photographer converge on a neighborhood where a child has been kidnapped. Some neighbors talk freely about the crime, but one woman firmly states that she doesn't want to discuss it and, above all, "No pictures!" The photographer shoots one on the sly anyway, and it's published. Grounds for a privacy suit? Very likely. Moreover, if the cameraman is on her property without permission, a trespassing complaint may ensue. More about trespassing later.

Paul P. Ashley, former president of the Washington State Bar Association, told a group of Associated Press editors: "The essence of the wrong [in terms of privacy] will be found in crudity, in ruthless exploitation of the woes or other personal affairs of private individuals, who have done nothing noteworthy and have not by design or misadventure been involved in an event which tosses them into an area subject to public gaze."

Particular cases are often cited as examples of suits for invasion of privacy. Several years ago, a 12-year-old mother gave birth in a hospital. The story was published, prompting her and her husband to sue for privacy invasion, charging that the publicity brought them "extreme embarrassment, humiliation, mental agony, wounded feelings and loss of privacy." The court turned down the suit, declaring, "It is rather unusual for a 12-year-old girl to give birth to a child. It is a biological occurrence which would naturally excite public interest."

But a former prostitute who had been tried and acquitted for murder, and then was married and living a respectable life for many years, won her case after her name and picture had been used in an advertisement. The court ruled that although a statement in the ad noted that the story was taken from real incidents in her life, her privacy nevertheless was violated because she had a right to pursue and obtain happiness.

What many lawyers and judges regard as a major Supreme Court decision involved an illustrated *Life* magazine article. *Life* reviewed a play entitled "The Desperate Hours," based on a true-life episode in which a married couple had been held hostage in their home by thugs. For art, the magazine posed actors in the actual house in which the crime had taken place. The family sued for invasion of privacy and won in a lower court.

In reversing that decision, the Supreme Court held that the constitutional guarantee of a free press applies to alleged invasion of privacy if a report involves newsworthy incidents. Finding that the article was "basically truthful," the justices said:

> The line between the informing and the entertaining is too elusive for the protection [of freedom of the press]. Erroneous statements are no less inevitable in such case than in the case of comment upon public affairs, and in both, if innocent or merely negligent, it must be protected if the freedoms of expression are to have the "breathing space" that they need to survive.
>
> We create grave risk of serious impairment of the indispensable nature of a free press in a free society if we saddle the press with the impossible burden of verifying to a certainty the facts associated in a news article, a person's name, picture or portrait, particularly as related to non-defamatory matter. (*Time, Inc. v. Hill,* 385 U.S. 374, 17 L.Ed. 2nd, 456, 85 S. Ct. 534 [1967])

Newspapers are vulnerable to privacy suits even when they don't mention the plaintiff's name in a story. A rape victim sued the *Fort Worth* (Texas*) Star-Telegram* for privacy invasion, contending that its article about the crime included details that identified her in the community, although her name did not appear. A judge barred the paper from printing her name despite the editor's assurance that the *Star-Telegram* had no intention of revealing her identity, which was brought out when her assailant went on trial.

Contempt

Kathy George, a reporter for the *Seattle Post-Intelligencer,* was cited for contempt by a Superior Court judge after she refused to answer questions concerning her story about a domestic violence case heard by the same judge. The paper's attorney saved her from going to jail by phoning the state Supreme Court's commissioner, who granted a stay until the *Post-Intelligencer* could appeal.

Earlier, an Idaho newswoman was jailed and fined for declining to identify a confidential source for her story about a divorced mother accused of abducting her child.

The two were among several journalists in the last 25 years who have been threatened with jail or actually incarcerated for refusing under oath to disclose the source of their information or defying some other order of the court.

The press has several privileges in this country, but defying the law is not one of them. The courts have the power to cite and punish anyone for contempt. A reporter may be held in contempt if a judge decides he is interfering with the administration of justice. Usually this means that the judge agrees with a defense attorney that a suspect cannot get a fair trial unless the reporter's information is made available. Such a drastic legal recourse pits a judge's interpretation of the law against the newsperson's traditional obligation to the confidentiality of sources who have requested anonymity.

For various reasons, some sources will not talk to a reporter unless they are assured that the information will not be attributed to them. A "whistle blower" may fear being fired from her job by confiding that her company regularly violates environmental regulations. Some underworld sources risk being killed for even talking to a reporter.

A journalist does not have to accept unattributed information, but if he does, he is ethically bound to honor the agreement to keep his confidant's name a secret. The unwritten rule in journalism is that you do not "burn" a source. In addition to the moral obligation of the writer to keep his word, he knows that he will not be trusted again if he breaks his promise. His colleagues, also, will likely scorn him as well because his transgression reflects on the profession as a whole.

In investigative reporting particularly, there comes a time when a reporter and her newspaper must make an important decision: to accept the information with a promise to protect the identity of the informant or not to take it with that condition. More and more, editors are insisting that reporters come to them for permission on this issue. An editor looks at the bigger picture. Is the story worth all this hush-hush? What problems will an agreement bring down the road? A public relations man sued the *Minneapolis Star Tribune* because it named him as a source for a political revelation—and he won.

A reporter should be aware that he risks going to jail if he refuses a judge's demand to hand over the name of his confidential source. The late Bill Farr, then with the *Los Angeles Herald Examiner,* spent 42 days behind bars because he would not disclose his source for a story in connection with the Charles Manson murder case.

Experienced members of the Investigative Reporters and Editors organization advise journalists to first determine whether the source has strong objections to going public with her information. There have been occasions when the informant has been persuaded to allow her name to be used in the story after first objecting. If the person remains adamant about anonymity, it is suggested that she be asked whether she would be willing to come forward if the reporter is threatened with jail for not revealing her name.

When a reporter receives a legal order to surrender the name of a confidant, the stage is set for a clash between the First Amendment, which guarantees press freedom, and the Sixth Amendment, which guarantees the right to a fair trial. In this face-off, the media have one big ace in the hole: the shield law. Many states have laws on the books protecting news gatherers from forced disclosure of information. The rationale behind these statutes is that journalists should be free to obtain information and make editorial decisions on what to publish without unnecessary interference. The wording of the shield laws varies—some states have stronger protection of journalists than others. But even the tougher laws are not absolute. Generally, in criminal cases, attorneys can challenge the shield by affirming that the facts sought are necessary for a client's case and are not obtainable elsewhere. There also may be a determination as to whether the information is confidential or nonconfidential, whether it was published or unpublished, or whether the reporter gained it while gathering news during working hours or just happened to be an eyewitness to an event.

An Arizona appeals court interpreted the state's shield law as being limited to covering only persons who gather and write news on a regular basis, thus eliminating from protection a book author who had sought to keep his unpublished manuscript, files and notes from public view. Still, in states with sturdy shield laws, a number of judges have decided in favor of maintaining confidentiality.

Nevertheless, judges and lawyers tend to maintain that the Sixth Amendment is more sacred than the First. They want the news media to tone down their pretrial and trial coverage to ensure that defendants get a fair trial. Lawyers often insist that the identity of a reporter's secret source is necessary to ensure that fair trial.

There are other things on their wish list. Many judges and attorneys, both prosecution and defense, want to impose restrictions on the reporting of suspects' confessions, prosecutors' statements and the accused's previous police record so that potential jurors will not be influenced in the case by what they read in the newspapers or heard on TV and radio. With the swift development of interactive telecommunications, news is now also obtainable on the Internet.

Several years ago, an American Bar Association committee recommended restrictions on news given to reporters by the prosecuting attorney, defense counsel and police officers before and during a trial. The so-called Reardon Report was opposed by editors, reporters and publishers, who considered it an effort to manage the news. But the report remains very much on the minds of many in the legal profession. During the O.J. Simpson double-murder trial in Los Angeles, which caught the attention of the world, Superior Court Judge Lance Ito imposed a number of restrictions on media coverage, even deciding which reporters would be allowed into the small courtroom each day. Interviews with attorneys in the corridor during a trial recess were forbidden, as were still and televised pictures. Two reporters came close to being held in contempt for refusing to reveal their sources for trial reports, and two others were ordered out of the courtroom for such offenses as chewing gum and whispering. The trial, however, was televised with a pool camera, a privilege that Ito later indicated he regretted allowing, blaming it for helping to create a "circus" atmosphere around the trial. It's significant that a judge prohibited televised coverage in a high-profile murder trial following Simpson's acquittal (the Menendez brothers charged with slaying their parents). The term "circus trial" is tossed around a lot by press critics. Actually, as in the O.J. Simpson trial, the circus is created not by the media but by hordes of T-shirt vendors, crackpots and just plain curious onlookers who bunch outside the courtroom.

One journalistic objection to attempts to force the revelation of confidential sources lies in a belief that district attorneys and defense lawyers frequently want the press to do their job—tracking down people who can help one side or the other. Editors and reporters point out that the attorneys, particularly prosecutors, have investigative staffs to ferret out what they need. In the Simpson trial, both sides used investigators to good advantage.

Journalists should not be naive about a source's motivation for telling what she knows. Certainly, there are high-minded individuals who act in the public interest when, for example, they blow the whistle on an employer dumping toxic waste into a waterway. But there also are tipsters whose motives are not so pure. They want to get revenge or settle a score with someone. Perhaps your informant was passed over for promotion and is seething with hatred of his boss. Don't let this stop you from collecting all the information you can get. It's not your job to delve into the reasons for his coming forward or to make moral judgments. However, it is your job to check and double-check the person's story. In short, take nothing at face value. Thorough digging may save you and your paper later grief. Again, look for documentation, which usually carries more weight than what someone tells you. And, incidentally, tape your interviews. The tapes are your backup if the informant recants.

Don Harrison, former managing editor of the *Philadelphia Daily News,* observed that "People with personal axes to grind are a good first line of offense, but it's poor journalism to just go with what they tell you."

The Problem of Access

Virtually every day reporters are being barred from covering court proceedings, city council and school board meetings, legislative committee hearings and other official gatherings. The barrier also exists in connection with access to records. This goes on even in states that have open meetings and records laws.

A judge, at the request of a defense lawyer, can keep the press out of a preliminary hearing in a criminal case. The city council or school board can meet in an "executive session," closed to the media, to discuss "personnel" matters exempted from the open meetings law. Some public bodies resort to such tricks as meeting in members' offices—or in their homes to avoid press scrutiny. A number of boards of regents of state universities gather privately to discuss institutional business.

Whether it's to gain access to meetings or records, many newspaper and wire service reporters keep demanding openness by government. Frequently, newspapers go to court to achieve that objective. The San Jose (Calif.) *Mercury News* sued the city of Oakland and Alameda County for the release of documents they allegedly used to lead taxpayers to believe they would not be hit financially by the return of the Raiders football team from Los Angeles to Oakland. The complaint accused officials of giving the records to outside consultants as a ruse to duck public scrutiny. The *Los Angeles Times* sued the City Council to open its unauthorized secret meetings, a problem faced by the media—and the public—all over the country.

Louis D. Boccardi, former president and chief executive officer of the Associated Press, told a Society of Professional Journalists' conference, "Some battles are fought with a certain finality to them and, indeed, that does characterize some of the specific cases on which we go to war. But in a broader sense, this fight against secrecy, against the closing of the public process from public scrutiny, this fight is one that simply does not end."

On the federal level, the press is aided by the Freedom of Information Act (FOIA) and the Privacy Act, which maintain that all federal agency records are available to any person—with some exceptions. Moreover, "federal agency" does not include Congress, U.S. courts, the General Accounting Office and other bodies. Also exempted is information deemed vital to the nation's defense and foreign policy.

The act does not include state and local governments, but they have open meetings and records laws, which serve the same purpose.

Numerous journalists have obtained previously sealed documents through FOIA requests, enabling them to write revealing stories in the public interest. But it's not always an automatic process. Agencies that don't want records exposed find ways to stall the requests by taking an inordinate amount of time to produce them or through other means. Before the FOIA was reformed by Congress in 1986, several agencies sought to delay or make it impossible for some news organizations to obtain documents by charging copying fees, sometimes running into thousands of dollars.

Even with the loosening of the FOIA, government agencies still find reasons to withhold records. Former AP correspondent Terry Anderson learned this when he tried vainly to pry documents from the State Department relating to his seven-year captivity by terrorists in Lebanon. Anderson, who needed the material for a book he was writing about his experience, commented bitterly in a speech that efforts to get information about his captors and American agents were blocked by 11 federal agencies, including the CIA.

Another problem for the media is the acquisition of court documents. The *Riverside* (Calif.) *Press-Enterprise* lost a bid to see preliminary transcripts in a widely publicized trial of a male nurse charged in the deaths of 12 hospital patients. A state appeals court ruled that the news media have no right to view such transcripts when subsequent publicity might jeopardize the defendant's right to a fair trial. In Los Angeles, the *Los Angeles Times,* Associated Press and the *Daily Journal* challenged the judge's withholding of certain motions and transcripts in the shoplifting trial of actress Winona Ryder. Judge Elden S. Fox declared from the bench that the "pervasive nature of the media coverage creates a substantial probability that the interests of the accused in a fair trial will be prejudiced if the records are disclosed." *Times* attorney Al Wickers, who filed legal action to overturn Fox's ruling, was quoted in the *Times* as saying about the judge's position, "It unfortunately sets up the possibilities that any celebrity trial could be subject to a different standard in access than trials involving other citizens."

But there are victories. Media lobbying was mainly responsible for the legislature altering a 105-year-old California law permitting closed preliminary hearings. Today, hearings must be open unless a judge makes a finding that excluding the public is absolutely necessary to ensure the defendant's right to a fair trial.

In day-to-day skirmishes with courts, however, media often lose even when they win. By the time a judge's closure order is argued and perhaps appealed, the hearing is over and no longer has news value. The only solace is that the publicity-shy courts may be more lenient the next time.

Newspapers have argued there is no hard-and-fast evidence that potential jurors are influenced by what they may read about criminal cases and that they usually forget the story anyway. Still, it's well to remember that defying a closure order can bring a contempt citation from the bench. Reporters who have tried to crash secret hearings have been escorted out by bailiffs.

Gag Orders

The First Amendment stops a judge or anyone else from determining what a newspaper may or may not print. But a judge can make news coverage very difficult by barring lawyers in a court case from speaking to the media. It's called a gag order. The rationale for its issuance is to assure a defendant a fair trial, untainted by publicity.

The device also is used by mayors, police chiefs, governors and a host of other officials. Underlings are ordered not to talk to reporters about a particular matter in the news. Occasionally, the order is a standing one for any kind of contact with journalists. The former mayor of Milwaukee once forbade his staff members to have any contact with any representative of the *Milwaukee Journal,* so angry was he at the paper.

Fortunately for the press and the public, such commands are less than airtight. Usually someone will leak information—on a not-for-attribution basis—to a reporter. That's why it's a good idea to try to build reliable contacts within a public agency. When a judge or district attorney puts a lid on a story, a court clerk or deputy district attorney could be your roadway to breaking through the gag.

The official imposing the gag may not care about adverse media reaction to the order, but staffers with ambitions for higher office are generally not keen on an adversarial relationship with journalists. Under the rules of the game, information obtained in violation of a gag order can be printed, no matter how much a judge or mayor may grind his teeth over the leak. When a newspaper attributes a disclosure to a "White House source," "city hall insider," or "senior official," someone could well have talked out of turn. Of course, she could be fired for such indiscretion, but she is aware of the risks and has her own reasons for disobeying a gag order.

Another celebrity murder trial in which a gag order was imposed occurred in Los Angeles when actor Robert Blake was accused of fatally shooting his wife. A judge slapped a gag order on both the prosecution and defense, but plenty of news got out through various channels. In one instance, Blake, who in 2005 was acquitted, made a preliminary court appearance with a dramatic personal plea for bail.

His statements before a judge were privileged, gag or no gag, and made for a major follow story. Also, reporters can go beyond "officers of the court" for information and do—friends of Blake or his wife, people who worked on movie sets with him, and so on. In short, gag orders do not stop the presses in this country.

Pre-Trial Publicity

Criminal defense lawyers in cases in high media interest cases sometimes ask a judge for a "change of venue"—moving a trial to another city. They argue that so much publicity has surrounded their client that a fair trial is impossible in the jurisdiction in which the crime occurred. Choosing an impartial jury would be impossible or, at least, highly unlikely, they add. Most such requests are denied, but occasionally an attorney wins the argument. This happened in the recent case of a San Francisco couple, both lawyers, whose pit bull fatally bit a woman who lived in the same apartment house as the defendants. The trial was moved to Los Angeles but the change didn't help the accused. A jury convicted the wife of murder (later reduced to manslaughter) and the husband of a lesser charge.

Although the San Francisco case was an exception, lawyers seeking a venue change are more likely to succeed in small towns, where almost everyone is familiar with a major crime and many may know the person(s) charged, perhaps as relatives or close friends. In big cities, competition drives the coverage. Even if newspaper editors know they are overplaying a story, the fact that other media, especially television, are flogging it impels them to continue putting it on Page One. There's little the individual reporter can do to moderate the process except to do a conscientious job of reporting the story fairly and accurately.

Trespassing

News reporters sometimes tread where the public fears to go. Legally, "No Trespassing" signs apply to everyone, but sometimes, in the rush of newsgathering, reporters knowingly or unknowingly cross onto private property.

Some 400 demonstrators against a nuclear power plant broke down a fence on a pasture owned by an Oklahoma utility company. Several reporters followed the protestors onto the private land and took notes and pictures of the melee between police and the antinuclear group. Several demonstrators and eight reporters were arrested for trespassing. The former were freed, but the reporters were convicted of the charge. The Oklahoma courts held to the theory of total landowner privacy and said the company had the right to demand the arrest of anyone who trespassed.

In their appeal to the Supreme Court, the reporters argued that once the crowd had spilled onto the company's land it no longer had privacy. The high court refused to review the convictions.

More heartening to the media was a later Supreme Court decision that upheld a California law requiring owners of shopping centers to permit some political speech on their premises. Yet reporters interviewing shoppers at such centers are subject to ejection, depending on the policy of the mall owner.

The Reporters Committee for Freedom of the Press (RCFP) believes there is a strong First Amendment argument that reporters and photographers cannot be convicted of criminal trespass when they follow news events into private, nonresidential land. Writing in *Editor & Publisher* magazine, Jack Landau, attorney-reporter and former executive director of RCFP, stated, "As long as reporters go along only as passive observers and do not damage the property or interfere with its use, they would seem to have a strong right to cover such events as political demonstrations, picketing and major fire and police department actions which occur on private property."

Landau noted that, despite the Oklahoma decision, the Supreme Court and other courts have been cutting down the privacy rights of landowners, at least in regard to fields, pastures and other lands not closely connected to a residence.

Whatever the rulings on a particular trespass, it is unlikely that reporters, in the heat of a story, will stop in their tracks if demonstrations or other breaking news events flow over to private property. Competition, if nothing else, keeps them going. Besides, not every such incursion will lead to an arrest. Shopping malls and other businesses are private property, but during the 2002 sniper shootings in the Washington, D.C., area, reporters chased after police in those places, which were crime scenes. However, attempting to interview shoppers at such locations, say for a story on a political campaign, might well get you ushered out by the management.

In some kinds of stories, flouting a trespass sign can lead to serious trouble. For instance, sneaking at night onto the grounds of a chemical company to check out a tip that the firm is polluting a stream could not be supported by the excuse that you were merely caught up in the excitement of a spot news story. The prosecution could assume your foray was planned and proceed accordingly in court. And although a manufacturing firm might overlook a trespass in the case of a horde of journalists pursuing a hot news story, it would likely take a harsher view of a single reporter climbing over a fence at night to investigate alleged wrongdoing.

The most spectacular example in recent times of a reporter's being where she was not supposed to be occurred in connection with the 1995 bombing of the Alfred P. Murrah Federal Building in Oklahoma City, which cost 169 lives.

Brenda Moore, a news editor for the *Chickasha* (Okla.) *Daily Express,* donned emergency rescue gear and joined regular rescue workers in crossing into the wreckage while the rest of the media core were kept behind police lines. She got an exclusive first-person story, but at some cost. Members of the county rescue team were outraged, her superiors reprimanded her and other journalists scorned her for her ruse, although some probably wished they had thought of the idea.

In a public statement, Moore said: "I had to get in, to get a picture as a reporter and a citizen. Stress and a need for the story spurred my article. I was overwhelmed and lacked focus. I mourn for my poor judgment and will use this as a learning experience. But I didn't do anybody any harm."

A federal building is public property. But police have the right to bar the press from disaster scenes at their discretion. Moore's action posed legal and ethical issues. She could have been arrested, and the local district attorney considered that move. And although initiative and aggressiveness are generally considered good journalistic traits, a reporter who is deemed to have taken unfair advantages over her colleagues to get a story can expect sharp professional criticism.

Search and Seizure

A new kind of security is being practiced in many newsrooms around the country. Reporters and editors for newspapers and broadcast stations are concealing or destroying notes, photos and outtakes. The reason: Police may come in with a subpoena or search warrant and seize them.

The right of authorities to conduct such searches was upheld in a 1978 Supreme Court decision in the case of *Zurcher v. Stanford Daily.*

Seven years earlier, demonstrators stormed into Stanford University Hospital and were driven out by police, some of whom were hurt by the protestors. The *Stanford Daily,* a campus newspaper, published photos of the altercation taken by its photographer. The county district attorney obtained a search warrant for the paper's office, which was probed by officers for prints and negatives.

A lower court upheld the *Daily*'s claim that the search violated its First Amendment rights, a ruling that was reversed by the Supreme Court. The high court decided that neither the First nor Fifth amendments prevented the right to issue a search warrant to obtain criminal evidence.

In 1980, however, Congress passed and President Jimmy Carter signed a bill that forbids federal, state and local law enforcement agencies from carrying out surprise newsroom searches unless there are "exceptional circumstances" to permit them.

Nevertheless, the threat of such searches remains. Several newspapers and broadcast outlets have instructed their staffers on how to behave in such occurrences. Usually, employees are advised not to interfere with the police and, at the same time, not to do anything to aid them. One May afternoon in 2002, investigators from the Los Angeles district attorney's office swooped down on the *Metropolitan News-Enterprise,* a small legal-affairs newspaper, shutting it down for three hours and sending reporters and editors into the street. Armed with a warrant, they were searching for an ad in connection with a corruption probe. A *Los Angeles Times* editorial termed the raid an "outrage," comparing it to "countries where newspapers either toe the government line or find their offices padlocked and their reporters jailed." Yes, it can happen here.

A year earlier, a perceived assault on the media of a different kind occurred. Louis D. Boccardi, the former AP president, lodged a protest with Attorney General John Ashcroft after the Justice Department subpoenaed AP reporter John Solomon's home telephone records in connection with an investigation of Senator Robert Torricelli (D-N.J.). The subpoenas were believed to be a means of determining how Solomon learned about wiretaps on Torricelli's telephone. In his letter to Ashcroft, Boccardi termed the subpoena "an extraordinary strike against the press." Another critic, Johan P. Fritz, director of the International Press Institute, observed, "In seeking retribution for information provided the media, the government is hindering the flow of that information and journalists will find it increasingly difficult to find people willing to speak on matters of import."

A further insurance against seizure adopted by some news organizations is to destroy or hide notes, audiotapes, and outtakes to prevent their being seized. The problem with this is that a reporter's notes or tapes may be his only means of defending himself and the paper against a libel suit because they back up his story.

The adversarial relationship between law enforcement and the media on search and seizure, disclosure, and other First Amendment issues continues. The media will win some and lose some. The problem in winning is that often the news value of the story diminishes as the issue is fought in the courts. The bright side is that in a democracy like ours these questions can be debated or submitted to the courts. In many other countries, the response from authorities to the press's assertion of its rights is to shut down newspapers and put editors and reporters in jail—or to murder them.

Suggested Assignments

1. Interview two local judges, two lawyers with criminal trial experience, the president of the local bar association, a newspaper editor and a newspaper court reporter. Based on their comments, write a feature on the issue of free press–fair trial. Try to find a recent court proceeding that will serve as a peg for the story.

2. You are a general-assignment reporter for a daily newspaper. You receive a tip from a disgruntled man that his employer, a large interstate trucking firm, is engaged in coast-to-coast hauling of computer hardware and software and airplane parts for illegal shipment to Iran. You learn that the FBI is conducting an investigation of the company but has not released any information to the media. Agents will not talk to you about the alleged shipments. Your investigation indicates that the man's information is well grounded. You write an exclusive story, which is published.

    The attorney for the United States obtains a subpoena, and you are put on the witness stand under oath. The prosecutor, who has obtained indictments against officials of the trucking firm, asks you to reveal your confidential source, and the judge backs her up. Earlier, you learned that your informant himself was involved in the illicit trading and lied to you about it.

    State your response to the prosecutor's demand and the reasons behind your response. Remember, you can be jailed for contempt for refusing to reveal your source. There are no right or wrong decisions here. Your score on the assignment depends mainly on your grasp of the issue.

3. Check the meeting habits of the local city council, planning commission, school board or other public bodies. Do they hold open meetings in conformance with the state's open meeting law? If not, why not? Write a story after interviewing the officials themselves, the city attorney, the editor of your local newspaper and any others involved.

8

Inside the Newsroom

Don't believe what you see on TV and in the movies. The media have made famous a journalism that no longer exists, one that used to take place in a chaotic newsroom with a hard-drinking city editor barking orders at tough-as-nails reporters who would dash from crisis to crisis, elbowing out the competition in pursuit of hot stories. Today, most of America's large dailies look a lot more like insurance companies than the decrepit, tobacco-stained hovels in *The Front Page*. Reporters and editors dress better, drink less and work more than their latter-day counterparts, thanks to considerable changes in the business of journalism over the last several decades.

The rules are different than they were 30 years ago, when newspapers had a "raw, heartfelt sense of belonging to a cause," as publisher Jim McClatchy of the McClatchy Newspaper family put it, when reporters felt duty-bound to comfort the afflicted and afflict the comfortable, to shine bright lights in dark places. But the old style of journalism has proven problematic in the 21st century, a time when nearly all large dailies and TV news stations are part of companies traded on Wall Street. The business of quality journalism, as it had been practiced in the past, runs counter to every common sense notion in American capitalism and the Editor Inc. mentality it bred. The conflict, inefficiency and freewheeling spending of the old days often produced the sort of creativity that won newspaper wars—and left American cities with nearly 1,500 daily monopolies. A seismic shift has taken place, prompted by technological, economic, competitive and cultural changes that have transformed journalism: nearly all of the country's largest dailies have switched from private or family-owned to publicly traded, providing an enormous financial windfall to investors and forcing cultural revolutions in newsrooms nationwide.

Today's corporate owners are far more focused on economic performance than on journalism, and news has increasingly become an instrument to lure advertisers and charge them ever-higher rates, while cutting news gathering staffs so that margins can "increase, increase, increase," says Gilbert Cranberg, who along with Randall Bezanson and John Soloski wrote *Taking Stock: Journalism and the Publicly Traded Newspaper Company* (Blackwell Publishing). The authors point out that publicly traded newspapers, at their worst, draw energy "entirely [from] the financial market's greedy expectations [becoming] indifferent to news and ultimately to the fundamental purposes served by news and the press."

As publicly traded companies have gobbled up family-owned newspapers, several important changes have occurred: Many of the worst family-owned newspapers have improved dramatically, but many of the country's best newspapers have worsened under corporate ownership. Experts predict the situation will deteriorate even more as media companies merge to form ever-bigger conglomerates, shifting power from journalists to publishers and CEOs, who have made once fearsome editors middle managers in a vast corporate chain.

In fact, ownership is the central question facing journalism in the 21st century. No publicly traded company has unraveled the Gordian knot of the newspaper business: How to make enough money to satisfy Wall Street, while producing journalism that serves the public interest.

Publicly traded newspapers must produce a hefty profit quarterly to appeal to investors buying stock. But newspaper profits tend to be cyclical, depending on the state of the economy. To understand how that works, you have to understand the economics of newspapers: The largest share of newspaper revenues comes from advertising. In fat economic times, businesses spend a lot on advertising. When the dot.com craze hit the nation, for example, advertising dollars flowed like beer at a frat party. But when dot.com went dot.bomb, advertising dollars dried up—and so did newspaper revenues. Newsprint prices—one of the largest costs for a newspaper—are also cyclical, making it difficult to assure investors of ever-increasing profits.

Labor costs—the other large expense for owners—tend to increase, regardless of the amount of revenues coming in. Media barons have decided the only way to assure ever-growing revenues is to cut labor and newsgathering expenses and divert cash into buying more and more media properties; hence, the media merger mania of the last decade. But buying more and more properties requires lots of cash or large loans, putting pressure on publicly traded companies to spend an ever-increasing share of its profits on more newspapers and television stations rather than on reporters, editors and newsgathering. "A company our size either has to grow or die," says David Zeeck, editor of the *Tacoma Tribune,* part of the McClatchy chain. You either need to be a lion or a gazelle. You're either gonna be eaten or [be] an eater. We want to be an eater."

The pressure to expand has had a significant impact in the newsroom: Instead of powering the engine that pulls the train, reporters and editors huddle in the caboose, while men in pinstripes and women in pearls passionately plot strategies to take market share from radio, television, talk shows and the Internet. Instead of focusing on stories that comfort the afflicted and afflict the comfortable, reporters are being asked to produce journalism that won't jeopardize local economic interests, to do more features, consumer, sports and entertainment news, and fewer hard-hitting investigations that hold the titans of business and government accountable. Most significant, managers are driving out newsroom guilds that protect journalists' salaries and rights, allowing them to cut staff positions and to demand more from the reporters and editors.

The push for profits—and the petering passion for old-style journalism—became more and more apparent in the late 1980s and early 1990s, as corporate executives looked for ways to squeeze higher profits out of their properties to see their profit margins fatten. Newsroom veterans of the 1970s who remember the heady days of Watergate and the reporting that held even a President accountable for his misdeeds are now feeling pressured to produce more with less support and fewer resources. For young people coming into the business, the pressure is less onerous, since none has first-hand knowledge of what the veterans recall as the Golden Age of Journalism.

Who Does What in the Newsroom?

Traditionally, on major dailies the managing editor oversaw the day-to-day operations of the paper, calling news meetings in the morning and afternoon during which the editors of the paper's various sections—news, features, sports, business, state, national—discussed the stories that would appear in the next day's edition. The paper's editor was rarely involved in these meetings but instead busied herself with the paper's vision, working with the publisher to ensure editorial quality and profitability. The managing editor and the assistant managing editors were responsible for making routine news decisions about coverage and story placement in the paper. Section editors made assignments and had assistant editors to help oversee a staff of reporters to cover various beats, or areas of expertise, like courts, cops, education, transportation, city hall, state legislature, county government and so on. On smaller and medium-sized papers the person who oversaw local reporters had the title of metropolitan, or city, editor.

Traditionally, young reporters landed a general-assignment job, which meant they did whatever the more experienced reporters didn't want to do, like interviewing farmers with Liza Minelli–looking potatoes, chasing fire trucks and tracking the police scanner. The assignments were drawn to ensure that the most important institutions of government were covered and veteran reporters spent most of their time going to meetings and interviewing bureaucrats, politicians and law enforcement officials. In the late 1980s, though, the economic environment of the newspaper business started to change.

The 1970s and early 1980s brought an explosion in monopoly newspaper markets; even in bad years, newspapers outperformed other industries by three and four times. The late James Batten, chairman of Knight Ridder newspapers, was fond of telling the story about an acquaintance who went into newspaper publishing because he could make money "even if he was brain-dead." Just as monopoly newspapers were becoming the norm, fewer people were choosing to read papers at all, prompting Batten and other corporate newspaper executives to rethink traditional attitudes toward readers. Widespread demographic change in America's large cities prompted editors to reevaluate the way they covered the news. Middle-class people, fleeing cities and moving to the suburbs, left behind the poor and large numbers of immigrants, who were not traditional newspaper readers. Meanwhile, suburban dailies began encircling many large urban papers, siphoning off the affluent readers they needed to attract advertisers. Even though newspaper profit margins continued to outperform other industries by more than double, owners wanted to protect the profits they were used to enjoying. Many responded by becoming regional rather than urban papers, moving resources to the suburbs and changing the old city desk into the metropolitan section.

In early 1990, the *Orange County Register* in Orange County, California, became one of the first in the country to experiment with newsroom reorganization, a strategy widely copied by other newspapers. Instead of focusing coverage on institutions, bureaucracies and meetings, top editors reorganized the newsroom staff and assigned reporters and editors to topic teams, placing an even greater burden on journalists to practice enterprise and in-depth reporting. The business editor became the topic editor for money. There were topic editors for features, entertainment and sports, for cops, courts and social issues, for science and government. Within those groups, for example, were assistant topic editors for politics and government, for cities and for food, fashion and shopping. The staff of eight general-assignment reporters was winnowed to four and assigned to the SWAT team, a group capable of doing big stories and investigations.

Editors hoped the reorganization would help break down traditional barriers between sections, improve overall coverage and ensure flexibility on breaking news. No independent assessment has been made to determine the success of the reorganization, but other newspapers, looking for ways to fight declining revenues, began moving to the team approach as well. Consequently, the nation's newsrooms vary widely in how they're organized, though many still retain the more traditional structure.

The Bureaus

Most large newspapers have bureaus, some in foreign countries, state capitals and Washington, D.C. But most common are rural and suburban, city hall, county government, cop and courthouse bureaus. Bureau reporters are expected to pitch and pursue story ideas constantly and to make decisions about what does and doesn't get covered on their beat or topic. A court reporter, for example, may have to pick one of six trials going on simultaneously or try to duck in and out of several trials on any given day. Traditional police reporters might occupy the pressroom at police headquarters and monitor the scanner and decide which crime and mayhem stories have the most news value and thus deserve coverage.

The Copydesk

At most newspapers, the copydesk editors edit stories for style, accuracy, spelling and grammar and write headlines. On larger papers, various editorial departments — news, sports, features, for example — have their own copydesks, although the trend is toward a universal desk that handles all sorts of stories.

Copy editors go to work on a story after the assigning editor has edited it and the reporter has made any necessary changes. The copy editor makes changes, too, and, depending on the individual newspaper's policy, will discuss those changes with the reporter. The copy editor writes cutlines for photos, charts and graphs, headlines, decks and informational boxes.

Copyediting is a highly skilled, high-precision job that requires an obsession with details. When hiring copy editors, news executives look for a driven journalist, "an educated person, one who takes two courses in Latin American political history—or Shakespeare or mathematics—when only one is required," said one senior news executive. Some papers are experimenting with eliminating the copydesk altogether. At the *Wichita Eagle,* shock reverberated through the newsroom in 1995 when the paper did away with its copydesk. Copy editors, assigned to reporting teams, write stories; reporters write their own headlines. At the same time, the paper underwent a newsroom reorganization, grouping journalists into teams and eliminating middle-management positions.

The Editors

In traditional newsrooms, the managing editor reports to the editor, executive editor or even the publisher of the paper. In addition to day-to-day news coverage, the managing editor usually oversees the paper's various editorial divisions and hiring and firing. Depending on a publication's size, the managing editor may also get involved in page makeup and assignments such as an investigation into the misuse of funds intended to pay for poverty programs or increasing violence at a state prison. At the *San Francisco Examiner,* for example, the managing editor played a key role in dispatching a team of seven reporters and photographers for an in-depth report on social and economic conditions in Latin America.

The news editor directs the copydesk and dummies the pages, often working with the managing editor on page makeup. Page design—the graphic treatment of stories and art—has become increasingly important, thanks to the influence of television. In order to compete with the myriad information sources now available to news consumers, editors realize that they must work to make newspapers as attractive as possible. For reporters and editors, it means becoming well versed in page design, graphics and the use of color.

The number of editors at a newspaper depends on its size. Dailies of more than 100,000 circulation may have editors responsible for real estate, the arts, travel, fashion, food, gardening and home repair, among other areas. Nearly all newspapers have an editor for the editorial and opinion pages. On larger dailies, a separate staff sometimes puts out the Sunday paper or weekend papers. And most have a separate graphics department, charged with creating the most attractive design, photographs and art for the paper.

Reporters, editors, photographers, graphic designers and artists work together to present the best package of stories possible. Reporters assist graphic artists and photographers, routinely making photo assignments and discussing what would best illustrate the story's focus and why.

Other Departments

The publisher is the paper's top manager and often its owner. If a large corporation owns the paper, the publisher represents the owner's interests and ensures the business's profitability. The owner's or publisher's opinion on the news of the day is usually echoed by the editorial page editor in editorials and on the op-ed page (opposite the editorial). It is common for the editorial page editor to report directly to the publisher, not the paper's editor. Publishers work with general managers, who oversee the paper's business operations, circulation, production, promotion and advertising. The general manager and the publisher set the editorial department's budget, usually with the guidance of the paper's editor or managing editor.

The Separation of Church and State

The business side brings in the money; the journalists spend it. A tradition evolved in journalism that kept the two sides distant. The journalists often thought of the business executives as money-grubbing and themselves as idealists charged with serving the public interest.

But due to the recent economic changes we've already discussed, the wall that used to separate the two sides is coming down. Publishers can and do exert considerable influence on coverage indirectly by pressuring the editorial side to keep budgets lean and journalists productive.

And, in the interest of improving the bottom line, some newspapers are encouraging contact between editorial and advertising as a way to tap into readers' likes and dislikes, to give readers more of what they want and less of what editors believe citizens must know to act responsibly in a democracy. Senior executives say surveys show that readers want more consumer and lifestyle news, more of the sorts of stories advertisers prefer. In Boca Raton, Florida, the *News* was redesigned with the aim of attracting young professionals without alienating older, wealthier readers. Editors transformed the paper with splashy color, bold graphics and few jumps, prompting one media critic to call it "a shopper's guide masquerading as a newspaper."

In the early 1990s, Knight Ridder newspapers, the country's second-largest chain, initiated a project of sweeping change. Nearly all the company's newspapers "undertook major projects of changing the way they put the paper together," Bill Baker, then the company's vice president for news, told *Advertising Age*. News coverage changed to emphasize topics readers deemed important, including more local and lifestyle news. At the *Post-Tribune* in Gary, Indiana, editor William W. Sutton Jr. restructured the newsroom and eliminated meeting coverage in favor of "reader-focused stories," he says. After some readers complained, the paper reinstated some meeting stories, "but in a different context. It's news and information that can help make their life easier, that can give them control." The newsroom underwent a culture change, he says. "I tell readers, 'I'm the editor of your newspaper. Tell me what you want in your newspaper and we'll do our best to please as many of you as we can.'"

The trend toward allowing economics to interfere with news decisions can take its toll on coverage. "In the quest for higher profits, we end up putting a lot of energy into corporate (garbage) that doesn't seem to serve any purpose," says *Philadelphia Inquirer* reporter Michael Sokolove. "The paper's journalistic visionaries are usually, or often, so involved in some huge initiative from corporate headquarters—and these initiatives keep on coming. So instead of putting all their energy and talent into great journalism, they're writing reports or attending meetings. If they're involved in all that, even if for good reason, the leadership they can devote to journalism is diffused. And that has an impact on the quality of the paper."

Editors and reporters "are being asked to do more with less, absolutely, no question about it," says former *Philadelphia Inquirer* editor Maxwell E.P. King. "Newspaper people are workaholics. They'll work like hell if you create an environment in which they feel reasonably sure they can do their best work. We have to choose not to do some things. We put less emphasis on process news and on incremental news developments."

Financial matters do distract top editors, King says, but not just at the *Inquirer.* "It's happening at almost any newspaper company I'm aware of," he says. "There's no way out of it."

The role of the editor has changed with the advent of corporate journalism, says former Knight Ridder editor John Carroll, now editor of the *Los Angeles Times.* "The values of American corporate life—to the exclusion of nearly all other values, such as community service, spirited journalism—take precedence. Editors are more in line with business values and are less and less independent arbiters of right and wrong in their communities."

A Note About Newsrooms

Most of the general discussion we've had has been just that, generalizations about how journalists operate in today's major metropolitan newsrooms. Remember, though, the operation of a small- to medium-size daily or a weekly or a biweekly may differ considerably. Each paper will operate differently depending on the needs of the community and the owner it serves.

Is it an urban daily? A suburban weekly? In a competitive or monopoly market? Is its circulation a few thousand? Or 500,000? Before you apply for a job, inquire after an internship, send a press release, pitch a story, research the newspaper or TV station as you would a story by looking for key sources and the most up-to-date information about how the newsroom operates.

Suggested Assignments

1. Visit a local newspaper for a tour of the plant. (Newspapers will generally arrange tours for journalism classes if given proper notification.)
2. Interview the mayor, city council member, police chief or city manager on a current issue involving his or her job. Write a story as a feature unless the

interview produces hard news for which a straight news story would be more appropriate.

3. Accompany a police, city hall or county seat beat reporter on his or her rounds. Write an account of what you learn.

4. Your community has been hit in recent weeks by 15 fires of unknown origin. List 10 questions you would ask a detective who had just arrested three men and a woman on arson-for-hire charges.

5. Select three newspapers and critique them for general content, writing style, makeup, graphics, the editorial page and local, state, national and foreign coverage.

9

Ethics and Accuracy

Patricia Bowman accused William Kennedy Smith, nephew of the late President John F. Kennedy, of raping her. He was acquitted of the charge in a massively covered trial.

Although newspapers usually do not identify rape victims, Bowman's name became internationally known, first through publication in a London newspaper, then in a supermarket tabloid in the United States, followed by an NBC News report. Her name eventually appeared in the *New York Times* in August and in several other mainstream newspapers. It was a chain reaction.

In a first-person article in the Associated Press Managing Editors magazine, *APME News,* Bowman said she was "assaulted again" by the media seeking her out.

"I heard car doors slamming outside my home," she wrote. "The doorbell rang. The telephone rang. My daughter and my life were under siege. By that night there were satellite trucks outside my home. . . . I realized with horror that if the media had found me, so could the man who raped me. The second victimization—the second rape—had begun."

Bowman went on to ask why she had been selected for exposure while other rape victims were not.

"The media have the power to educate and inform," she noted. "The release of my name did nothing to educate, or to help anyone form an opinion."

She was "selected" because of the prominence of the accused and the growing fascination with tabloid journalism and its competitive frenzy.

Many journalists agree with Bowman, and many more agonize over such ethical questions. There is hardly a conference of editors or reporters where there is not at least one panel discussion of ethical concerns and what to do about them. The Society of Professional Journalists (SPJ) has adopted a code of ethics (see end of this chapter) to guide journalists, and the Associated Press Managing Editors (APME) is developing one at this writing. Several newspapers have posted their own rules for ethical behavior, which are strictly enforced. Some papers also employ ombudsmen, special staffers who represent readers with complaints about editorial content but are independent of the news department and even the publisher. They probe the reasons for an erroneous claim or one in which the ethics have been questioned, and they publish a column on their findings, often with their personal opinion, which may find a reporter or editor at fault. For that reason, ombudsmen are not among the more popular of colleagues.

And you may have noticed in your local newspaper a "correction" box to right errors. Make no mistake, the high-flying journalism of the 1920s, '30s, '40s and '50s, with its roughshod reporting with little concern for ethics, is gone. Newspapers, faced with fierce competition from other media and declining circulation, are not about to lose more readers by flouting ethical standards—standards that they themselves set. In addition, most of the entry-level hires are graduates of journalism schools whose curricula include courses in ethics.

But because journalism is neither an exact science nor an ideal profession, lapses in ethics and accuracy occur. Here are the main issues facing the media in the first decade of the 21st century.

Conflict of Interest

Both a reporter who moonlights as a public relations writer for a political candidate and a business writer who receives "insider" trading information for his own gain are clearly acting unethically and are likely to be fired if their activities become known to their bosses. Likewise, a reporter who accepts a bribe for writing a favorable story about someone or some organization faces dismissal.

A female sportswriter for a Southern California weekly paper told the authors that the father of a high school volleyball player offered the reporter $50 if she would give his daughter a prominent mention in a game story. The offer was refused with a polite explanation to dad as to why his payment was unacceptable.

Sandy Nelson, a copy editor at the Tacoma (Wash.) *News Tribune,* sued the paper to get back her former job as a reporter. She was transferred because management objected to her public activism on behalf of various causes, including anti-homosexual discrimination. The company took the position that her involvement in these activities presented a conflict of interest with her duties as a reporter and cast doubt on the credibility of the newspaper itself. Nelson maintained that she didn't cover the issues she supports and had always been strictly objective in her reporting. Further, she insisted that she is entitled to a private life on her own time. The case went all the way up to the U.S. Supreme Court, which ruled in favor of the newspaper.

The *Hollywood Reporter,* an entertainment trade tabloid, fired reporter Donna Balancia after she filed a lawsuit against a major talent agency and other defendants, claiming that her idea for a TV series was stolen for a similar show featured on ABC-TV. According to Balancia, who sought at least $750,000 in damages, her boss told her she was embarrassing the newspaper. She asserted the *Reporter* had no policy banning staff members from working on outside projects and that there was no conflict of interest because she did not cover TV.

One factor, which may have played a role here, is that editors also worry about the perception that a conflict exists, although there may not be an actual one.

In Seattle, it was the newspaper itself that was the center of an ethical controversy. The *Seattle Times* drew criticism from a segment of readers and raised concerns among its own staff members when it donated $40,000 in advertising space to the promoters of a new baseball stadium. Those who opposed the project thought the *Times* had stepped over an ethical line and said so publicly. Publisher Frank Blethen justified the free ads as benefiting the city as a whole, saying: "When we put on our corporate hat, we have to ask ourselves are we doing our fair share for the community. The real question was, as a major corporation and employer, 'Did we feel a need to participate in this?' The answer is 'yes.'"

The lesson from all of this is to think long and hard before you commit your-self to an activity that could create a conflict of interest—or the perception of one. You may not only be risking your job but your entire career. Reporters tainted with this stigma have a tough, if not impossible, time finding another position in jour-nalism.

Falsifying news is another way to wind up permanently stigmatized. *Washington Post* reporter Janet Cooke won a Pulitzer Prize (in 1980) for a chilling series about an 8-year-old heroin addict who was regularly shot up by his mother's boyfriend. The stories later were found to be faked from start to finish. The boy did not exist. Cooke was fired and the prize returned. That ended her career, at least on mainstream newspapers.

More recently, major ethics scandals have hit the nation's two top national newspapers, *USA Today* and the *New York Times*. In 2004, reporter Jack Kelley re-signed after an internal investigation found "strong evidence that he had fabricated substantial portions of at least eight news stories, lifted nearly two dozen quotes or other material from competing publications, lied in speeches he gave for the news-paper and conspired to mislead those investigating his work."

In the spring of 2003, the *New York Times* reporter Jayson Blair, a 27-year-old African-American reporter, was forced to resign after it was discovered he had made dozens of fraudulent errors in stories. A team of ten *Times* editors, reporters and researchers discovered a slew of errors in stories run under Blair's byline between October 2002 and April 2003. The corrections for incorrect whereabouts, denied reports, factual errors and plagiarism ran almost two pages in one issue of the newspaper.

What is worse, Blair's *Times* editors should have suspected that something was wrong with some of his stories. The paper had failed to track his expense reports and to oversee his travel. The paper acted only after the editor of the *San Antonio Express-News* asked the *Times* to investigate a story by Blair about the family of a missing soldier. The story was almost identical to one the *Express-News* had run. Blair resigned when he couldn't provide evidence he had ever traveled to Texas to cover the story.

The Blair incident raised another disturbing question. Were *Times* editors too willing to overlook misrepresentation by a promising young African-American writer? The *Times,* along with most U.S. newspapers, has a hard time attracting and keeping African-American reporters in their newsrooms, despite exhaustive re-cruiting efforts. Blair, like Cooke, was African-American, and relatively green when hired. Whatever one might think of this issue, however, the chief victim was not the *Times*. The chief victim was Blair, a reporter who lost his career and livelihood over errors he should have known eventually would be discovered. Ethical lapses such as Blair's compromise the integrity of all American journalism.

If your heart is really set on an outside activity that creates a real or possible conflict of interest, there are ways to go around the problem to preserve your reputation and livelihood. You can resign or, better yet, request a leave of absence until your outside objectives have been met. Some newspapers will permit a reporter to switch beats or assignments if a conflict arises. An education reporter obviously cannot continue in that role if her husband is elected to the school board—nor should she want to. But moving to sports, entertainment or city hall would eliminate any suspicions. Incidentally, media supervisors take a very dim view of a staff member running for public office during her employment. The above-mentioned education reporter or any writer in a similar situation may be quintessentially ethical, but editors worry about the *perception* of unethical behavior even when it's nonexistent.

A last word: If there are published guidelines on your paper governing conflict of interest, read them carefully and then read them again. If there is no such document, consult with your editors for guidance or a straight yes or no answer on a questionable activity.

The Objective Writer

Pay no attention to cynics who say there is no such thing as objectivity among journalists. These pontificators assert that reporters and editors come into the profession the products of their upbringing, social and economic status, education, religion, ethnic makeup and personal biases, which are bound to affect their views of the news. "Objectivity is a myth," is their familiar cry.

It's no myth (although myths can be true). Objective writing is a staple of American journalism, and it's practiced across the country every day. Critics are correct in saying that journalists may be shaped by their backgrounds, as are most people. They don't come from Mars. But what is overlooked is that they are trained—in journalism schools and on the job—to submerge their personal feelings in the interests of giving the public straight, unadorned facts, which is what most readers want and expect. They can find opinions in the editorials, personal columns and the op-ed pages. The doubters of objectivity also don't seem to realize that reporters have no personal stake or interest in the great majority of the stories they cover. So why would they want to put a particular spin on them? What's uppermost in the writer's mind is turning out a good story that beats the deadline.

It was noted previously that journalism is not a perfected field. A few reporters, alas, do have an ax to grind and will slant a story either by commission or omission. Maybe the ax is ground by the publisher or other executive, and the writer produces what he imagines the brass wants. This is rare, however. Most publishers maintain a hands-off policy regarding the news side, concerning themselves more with the business end of the paper. In recent years, however, as advertising and circulation have declined (although profits remain healthy), some front-office executives of major newspaper chains have made it clear to local editors and publishers that they expect the newsroom to be among the departments contributing positively to the bottom line. This has led to staff and other budget cuts on some newspapers. But the economics of publishing are cyclical. As this is written, advertising revenue is slowly increasing in various markets. Budgets have shrunk even more in television news, with some networks and local stations reducing hard news reporting in favor of talking heads that are cheaper to air. Overseas reporting by the major networks is minimal compared to their former efforts.

Let's say, though, that it's the reporter alone who allows his biases, prejudices or viewpoint to slip into the story. Editors are good at spotting such lapses in objectivity and are likely to bring the writer up short—if not fire him. In the final analysis, objectivity is simply fairness. Writers should present both sides—or five sides—of a controversial issue. Someone accused in a lawsuit of wrongdoing should be called for a response she might want to make. A company charged by federal authorities with selling a defective product is entitled to a phone call for a statement.

Test this thesis for yourself. Examine five or six newspapers for fairness and objectivity in news stories. We think you will find that the papers lean toward the Associated Press style of reporting: straight down the middle with no coloration. The exception, of course, is feature stories in which creativity, humor, offbeat leads and narrative are acceptable. But even with this latitude, objectivity can be maintained. Actually, there is a growing tendency for news stories to be given a feature treatment as a means of drawing the reader.

Of the two following stories, the first demonstrates a straightaway presentation of information and the second the application of a feature mode to what is essentially also a news account.

By Jolayne Houtz

A year-old program that recruits young, mostly minority college graduates to teach in the Seattle School District is in danger of folding after this school year because of money and staffing problems.

Teach for America, a national teacher-internship program, brought 17 new teachers to Seattle schools when the district agreed to give the program a try.

Both the district and the interns benefit from the arrangement. The college graduates, recruited nationally and sent to districts across the country, make a two-year commitment to teach in urban schools. At the end, they can qualify for teaching certificates—a short-cut route to teaching that eliminates the need for a teaching degree.

And the district gets help meeting one of its key goals—to increase the number of teachers of color in the schools.

But Seattle's program is running into several problems this year, including:

- Lack of private funds to sustain operations. Teach for America tries to raise as much as 70 percent of its operating costs from private donations. But in Seattle, the program has only raised enough from companies such as IBM to cover one-fourth of its costs, said Lori Hidek, a Teach for America member overseeing the Seattle program this year.

- Lack of openings for new members in Seattle schools. This year, the program planned to bring in a new group of Teach for America recruits, but because the district had budget problems that forced teacher layoffs last spring, the district and Teach for America agreed to hold off this year.

- A reassessment at Teach for America's national office in New York City about its mission. Teach for America is trying to refocus its efforts on districts with a shortage of teachers, said communications director Christine Thelmo. That's not the case in Seattle.

The decision on whether to keep the program going will be made by Feb. 1 after looking at whether the district will have teacher openings for new recruits next year, Hidek said.

"I know there's definitely a desire on the part of the district to keep us around in terms of the quality of the teachers we're bringing in as well as helping them with the diversity issues," she said.

District and state evaluations of the program have been "overwhelmingly positive," Hidek said.

Of the original 17 Teach for America members here, 15 are still in Seattle middle and high schools this year. Thirteen of them are people of color, Hidek said.

The district's goal is to have a workforce that reflects the city's ethnicity—now about 28% minority, said Richard Cruz, the district's human relations director. The district's teaching corps is about 23% minority.

"That's very difficult to get to in the absence of special programs like this," Cruz said. In the past three years, 6% of teachers earning certification through traditional Washington colleges and universities have been minorities, he said.

Teach for America grew out of a Princeton University student's senior thesis in 1989 about how to get diverse, recent college graduates without teaching backgrounds to fill jobs in school districts with a shortage of qualified teachers in math, science and language arts.

—Seattle Times

By Jocelyn Allison

MARION—As communities throughout Ohio struggle to stay viable in a global economy, several years of economic development have helped keep Marion in the race.

Located about 60 miles from Ashland along U.S. 23, this community of about 35,000 people has undergone a painful transition over the years from a heavy equipment manufacturer to one of light manufacturing, distribution and assembly.

"We're still undergoing that metamorphosis from 'that's what we were' to 'what are we going to be,'" said David Claborn, president of the Greater Marion Community Area New Development Organization Inc., or CAN DO!, Marion's nonprofit economic development organization.

Marion's story isn't all that different from Ashland's, or from many other small cities in Ohio. As the need for the city's products diminished—or manufacturers found they could make it cheaper elsewhere—the factories closed and the community found itself in crisis.

In the late 1990s, the last of the big union plants, Marion Power Shovel Company, closed its doors for good after the company was purchased by a competitor. At one time, it had employed more than 2,500 people.

"We're almost a microcosm for the industrial Midwest," said Claborn. "All these things that define the vestiges of the rust belt were here, as they were in many other places."

Some of the town's staples have survived, such as the dryer manufacturer Whirlpool Inc.—now the town's largest employer with about 2,800 people—and salty snack-maker Wyandot Inc. For the most part, however, Marion has had to diversify to stay afloat.

Nick Chilton, president and chief executive officer of Wyandot Inc., is one of several in the community who believe recent industrial growth has helped balance out the community and make it less susceptible to the ups and downs of the economy.

"We're in a nice position to weather those kinds of storms," he said.

Sometimes it's serendipity

While local business people first formed Marion CAN DO! in 1993, the organization's most notable accomplishment didn't come until the arrival of its current president, Claborn, in 1997.

At the time, LTV Steel, then the third largest steel-maker in the U.S., was considering Marion as a place to locate its new $66-million steel tube production facility. To win the project, Claborn and other local officials threw together a last-minute deal that involved creating from scratch a 431-acre Dual Rail Industrial Park at the northwest corner of the city two miles from the U.S. 23 interchange.

In addition to being surrounded by the necessary infrastructure, the plot of unused land was crossed by two rail lines, CSX and Norfolk Southern, offering companies the unique option of competing rail service. CAN DO! pooled funds from the city, its own reserves and the state to come up with the $1.2 million necessary to purchase the land, 47 acres of which it gave to LTV at no cost.

"Sometimes it's serendipity," said Claborn. "This was the trigger to getting a lot of other companies (to locate here)."

A few years after the plant's completion, however, LTV went bankrupt. The contents of the Marion facility were up for auction when Canadian steel producer Dofasco Inc. decided instead to purchase the whole plant. The operation now employs about 121 people and is planning to add 30 to 35 jobs over the next two months, according to a company official.

Now the park is home to three other companies, including two Honda suppliers that support the Honda operation in Marysville about 30 miles away. Marion Industries Inc. makes brakes for Honda and U.S. Yachiyo Inc. makes plastic fuel tanks.

Along with a fourth occupant, Japanese parts refurbishing plant Sakamura USA Inc., employment at the industrial park should be more than 500 in the next couple months, said Claborn.

The cost of new jobs

Development also has sprouted at Marion's Airport Industrial Park just east of the city, where Silverline Windows Products built a plant in 2002. Marion's second-largest industrial employer, the vinyl window manufacturer employs about 730 people.

Starting wages at the plant, however, run about $7.25, according to Claborn. Most workers are earning about $9 or $10 with longevity, he said.

While Claborn and others tout the company as a success, Marion City Councilman Michael Thomas believes it represents the decline of manufacturing in the city—and country. When the Silverline project was pending a few years ago, Thomas, president of the Mid-Ohio AFL-CIO central body, tried to pass a living-wage issue.

If the city was going to give Silverline tax abatements, argued Thomas, the company needed to pay at least $9.04, plus health-care coverage so its workers could support themselves and their families without relying on public money to subsidize their expenses. Council voted down the issue 5–4.

Thomas sees the Silverline project as a disturbing trend in the kinds of jobs economic development is attracting to the city — lower-paying ones. But he's not necessarily against tax abatements.

"Just make sure the money you're paying out is for jobs that people can survive on," he said.

For some people, Claborn argued, Silverline is a good opportunity.

"For folks who have worked maybe a series of retail jobs or in a bar or waitressing that didn't have benefits, this is a step up," said Claborn.

Silverline could open the door for those who wish to work their way up Marion's manufacturing food chain, he said.

Local real estate developer Ted Graham believes that food chain is a healthy one. Graham, whose Marion Industrial Center comprises 317 acres of industrial acreage in four Marion area locations, believes the town is in "definite expansion mode."

Along with finding new tenants for the former Marion Power Shovel buildings, Graham has transformed a former World War II-era government supply depot southeast of the airport park into a center for light manufacturing, assembly and distribution.

While turnover is high, Graham historically has kept occupancy levels at more than 95 percent.

Graham estimated a town Marion's size will see companies leave two to three times a year, but continued local economic development efforts help the city at least break even.

"You never have zero unemployment," said Graham. "You're always going to be in transition."

Tough road ahead

In fact, Marion may be facing its toughest year yet, according to Mayor Jack Kellogg. Last year's income tax revenues came in flat for the first time in several years and the city was forced to make cuts — including layoffs in its police and fire departments — in order to balance its 2005 budget.

Since 1992, city income tax revenue had grown from $6 million to $12 million while the collection rate remained the same. This year, however, promises to be another flat year for returns, said Kellogg.

"Right at this moment I don't see any increases coming," he said.

Marion CAN DO! also cut staff in order to trim its $250,000 budget to about $149,000 for 2005. Both the county and city cut back economic development funding, but the bulk of those cuts resulted from a drop in private contributions from local businesses.

Claborn attributed that drop to overall belt-tightening among many companies, but also to a general attitude of complacency. He's working to ramp up marketing efforts for CAN DO!, and not just within industry. He's hitting up doctors, too, and calling their contributions "practice insurance."

"They aren't going to have a town to practice in if we don't have an economic development side," said Claborn.

Kellogg feels the same way, despite the financial storm clouds ahead.

"When your city's down, economic development is the most important tool you have," he said.

Graham used an image from one of Marion's formative industries—railroading—to describe the future of the city's economic development. Giving up now, he said, would be "like uncoupling the car from the train."

"That locomotive eventually is going to leave you," he said.

—*Ashland* (Ohio) *Times-Gazette*

Gifts and Favors

The practice of news sources bestowing gifts and favors on reporters is far less of a problem than it was 30 or 40 years ago, but it still goes on. One reason that most sources have opted out of the practice is that they know reporters today have much higher ethical standards and that most newspapers have strict rules against employees accepting such offerings.

Taking presents, complimentary tickets, free plane trips or hotel discounts—"freebies"—compromises a journalist, no matter how well-intentioned the giver. The issue is simple: An ethical reporter does not accept anything of value from a source.

At one time, reporters covering major league baseball teams had their road expenses paid by the club. No longer. Many newspapers pay the traveling costs of sportswriters, travel writers and others on out-of-town assignments. Acceptance by reporters of sizable gifts always has cast doubt on their integrity, but today the practice is cast in a particularly bad light. So bad, in fact, that pocketing such largess can cost a journalist his or her job.

The *St. Petersburg* (Fla.) *Times* is an example of newspapers with a posted ban on gifts and favors. Unacceptable are free tickets for movies and other entertainments and even courtesy lunches or dinners for reporters covering speeches and press conferences. Other papers have rules barring any gift valued at over $2.

However, many individual newspersons and their newspapers do not feel that an occasional free lunch or hors d'oeuvres at a press conference presents a danger to their reputations. It's quite common for host sources to provide lunches or dinners at some news events, and reporters would argue they cannot be bought with a complimentary meal or drink. Nor, they add, would a sensible source or his public relations representative expect to get favored treatment for such hospitality. Some organizations, like the Los Angeles World Affairs Council, give reporters covering their dinner speakers a special media rate or else provide nondinner seating for those who prefer to take their notes without food.

Expensive gifts are another matter. Acceptance of a TV set, new car, computer, or spring wardrobe would not be approved by any respectable newspaper. The same goes for such goodies as Hawaiian vacations, season tickets to the local NFL team's home games and even restaurant meals. If it's necessary or desirable to meet for an interview in a restaurant, either pick up both checks or go dutch. Most newspapers provide expense accounts—within reason. As for the above-mentioned gifts, just say, "Thanks but no thanks."

Who Do You Want to Be?

Whether to accept a free trip to Hawaii or a case of French champagne from a source is not a difficult ethical decision. Company rules and ethical codes notwithstanding, your own common sense should tell you to refuse them.

Other ethical issues, however, are not as clear-cut and stir debate in the public and among journalists themselves. One of the thorniest is assuming a different identity to get a story. Over the years, reporters have masqueraded as homeless bums to report skid row conditions, as ward attendants to uncover mistreatment in hospitals and nursing homes and as high school students to bare dope peddling on campus. *Chicago Sun-Times* reporters once operated a real bar—equipped with a hidden camera—to get the goods on burglars who fence their loot. The journalists posed as fences, buying thousands of dollars worth of stolen merchandise at the Mirage bar.

More recently, the Food Lion supermarket chain won a whopping $5.5 million damage award against ABC's "Prime Time Live" for the TV show's use of hidden cameras to expose the chain's alleged unsanitary handling of meat products sold to the public. The interesting—and for the media, chilling—aspect of the case is that Food Lion did not challenge the accuracy of ABC's report but concentrated its lawsuit on the fact that the show's reporters obtained jobs at one store with the sole purpose of spying on its meat practices with the use of cameras concealed in wigs. The award was substantially reduced on appeal.

The Mirage setup and other journalistic ruses to gather information have drawn plaudits—mostly from other (but by no means all) journalists—and stinging criticism. Those opposed to such practices say that it's not a journalist's job or responsibility to play private detective. That's work for the police, they contend. Some media people worry that their profession, which is not held in very high regard anyway, suffers even more from such stunts. It demeans their standing, they insist.

Defenders of the "I spy" investigative technique reply that there are situations in which the only way to gather information about wrongdoing is by this method. They point out that nursing homes and hospitals where patients are mistreated and lying in filthy beds don't invite the press to witness this spectacle and don't send out press releases on their mismanagement. Likewise, school principals, if they know about drug traffic on campus, don't broadcast the fact. Most of all, newspapers and reporters who use these means to gain access declare that their efforts are in the public interest.

Good arguments can be made for this position. Journalism awards have been won on the basis of this kind of reporting, although some judges shy away from bestowing honors on exposés achieved by sneaking in.

But can the arguments hold up when a reporter, pressed by time and the desire for a scoop, lies on the telephone about who he is to garner a story? The phone is a perfect instrument for fudging your identity. You can be anyone you want to be, and it has not been uncommon for some reporters to pretend on the phone to be police officers, social workers, bail bondsmen and others. Most journalists regard this as a sleazy and unethical way to get information—often from a grieving relative or friend—and shun its use. And you can imagine what the general public thinks about it.

Actually, people are more likely to talk to a bona fide reporter than the tricksters may imagine. Whether on the phone or face to face with a source, if a journalist properly identifies herself, is polite and conducts herself in a professional manner, she more often receives cooperation than a rebuff. Certainly there are individuals who won't speak to reporters for one reason or another, but that's their right. The president of the United States and other officials hold news conferences, but there is nothing in the Constitution that says they have to.

If you strike out with a source, it doesn't mean you're stymied. Seek out other sources who will talk, and from them get the names of others who might do the same. Keep asking questions until you get printable answers.

Anonymous Sources

Putting anonymous sources in a story is a trade-off. A source may offer information only if his name is not revealed. The reporter may choose not to accept the material with this restriction, but if she does, she is ethically bound to keep her word.

Is the widespread use of anonymous sources an ethical problem? This is true only if the source is made up—not a real person.

Almost any journalist would rather have her sources identified. Actual names give the story more credibility. Readers may be suspicious of such phrases as "According to a White House spokesman. . ." "A source close to the governor said yesterday. . ." or "A company official denied yesterday that it defrauded stockholders."

These faceless individuals usually have their reasons for keeping their names out of the paper. The president may be launching a "trial balloon" through a top aide to see how high it flies—that is, to test public reaction to a new idea. The spokesperson could be the secretary of state. If the idea flops, neither the president nor the secretary wants to be publicly attached to it. If it soars, the president may make a full-scale announcement, taking credit for the proposal.

On a lower level, reporters frequently deal with local officials or minor functionaries in government who approach journalists on a confidential basis because their jobs or careers may be at stake as a result of their revelations. Often they will call a reporter they know and can trust with information of city hall thievery, unauthorized junkets or a lucrative sewer contract going to the brother-in-law of the city council president. A reporter who spurns a tip of this kind because the source won't allow his name to be printed may be passing up a blockbuster story that the competition will jump at.

The journalist normally cannot afford to be judgmental about why a tipster is handing over information that could send someone to jail or ruin a career. A reporter, who acts in the public interest, should be primarily concerned with the truth of the revelation, not the motive behind it. Often, this means seeking confirmation or verification from other sources. Sometimes it's better to sit on a story for a day or two in order to get it right—and to preserve your job.

The Associated Press, like the newspapers it serves, would rather have named sources than secret ones, but strict rules apply when there is no alternative to anonymity. The AP's rules on material from anonymous sources are

- Fact only—no opinion.
- Fact critical to the story.
- Fact unattainable in any other fashion.
- Fact verified wherever possible by a second source.

"Whenever possible, we've tried to include as much information as we can about who those sources are or at least what their positions are relative in the investigation," said AP managing editor Darrell Christian.

Incidentally, AP's second-source effort was mandatory in the Watergate investigation by reporters Bob Woodward and Carl Bernstein. Then–*Washington Post* executive editor Ben Bradlee insisted that they find another source for each of their exclusive tips. Despite AP's admonition, opinions do find their way into news stories. An example has been the speculation over whether terror chief Osama bin Laden is alive or dead. By the time you read this the issue may be resolved one way or another. But various persons, some in government, others not, have, in response to reporters' questions, made educated guesses as to his status. And politicians routinely offer opinions on legislation and other matters. However, a story containing only opinions is not likely to travel beyond the editor's desk.

Source Relationships

Conflicts of interest, gifts and favors are easy to deal with compared with the cozy relationship that can develop between reporter and source. In this situation, there is usually no blatant ethical malfeasance. The source, says a member of the city council or school board president, is not offering anything of value, only friendliness. And that's the problem.

Reporters who cover beats or otherwise spend a lot of time with particular officials find that it's easy to develop a warm relationship with them. They may get on a first-name basis with their sources to the point of entertaining each other at their homes. This can—and does—happen at the highest levels of journalism. Washington correspondents are invited to many parties of government officials, and the favor is returned. On the city side, police reporters have been known to socialize with off-duty cops. Sportswriters do the same with coaches and players. These contacts can lead to good stories.

James C. Warren, Washington bureau chief for the *Chicago Tribune,* recalled that when he was first assigned to Washington, D.C., he wrote about "the fawning over White House staffers at a Christmas party where journalists lined up dutifully for 20 or 30 minutes before they got to the head of the line and met the president and the first lady. Then it was on to ample free food and booze and schmoozing with the folks many routinely cover." A number of Washington journalists feed off this proximity to political power, and especially if assigned for long stints covering the capital, can forget that their chief allegiance is to their readers. They become Washington Beltway insiders who rarely if at all visit their paper's newsrooms.

Of course there is nothing wrong with having cordial relations with people you cover on a day-to-day basis, but the danger is in getting too close to the sources. The day may come when the school superintendent, police captain, mayor or star quarterback gets into trouble. It's not easy to write a damaging story about someone with whom you have partied and truly like. The superintendent might be charged with embezzling school funds, the captain with taking a bribe. Your editor is not interested in your feelings about the individual. She wants a straight, objective story—and so do your readers.

Is the answer, then, to shun all social contact with news subjects? Not necessarily, as long as you clearly understand the different roles each play. A little socializing when others are present is harmless and may even result in hearing a juicy lead or two. Attending a city hall office party, for example, would hardly compromise a reporter's ethical values. But being invited to a restaurant by the city manager who pays the check is another matter.

A casual source proved to be the undoing of Bob Greene, a popular syndicated columnist for the *Chicago Tribune.* Greene was forced to resign in 2002 when it was revealed that 14 years earlier he had had a sexual encounter with a high school girl who had come to the office to interview him for her school paper. The newspaper took the position that despite the time lapse and the fact that the girl was at the age of consent, Greene had committed a serious ethical violation. Not all journalists concurred. Although some believed Greene had used bad judgment, they felt the punishment was too harsh, noting that more than one of their colleagues had made a similar misstep. But Dave Astor of *Editor & Publisher* magazine wrote that Greene deserved his fate. ". . . Greene's status as a famous columnist helped bring this situation about—meaning he abused that status," he declared.

Aim for Accuracy

Accuracy in reporting is not hard to achieve; it just takes a little longer. For many readers, accuracy is bound up with ethics. Certain errors appear suspiciously deliberate because they give the piece a particular twist. They may even interfere with the paper's editorial policy.

The truth about mistakes is much less sinister. Most are caused by careless reporting or editing, laziness and putting speed over accuracy. The reason accuracy is so stressed in journalism schools and in the newsroom is because a newspaper's credibility depends on it, as does a reporter's.

On occasion, an incorrect story stems from incorrect information fed to a reporter either intentionally or inadvertently. The paper will still be blamed, although many newspapers now run a next-day correction box that puts the blame where it belongs—either in-house or outside.

There are safety valves to avoid errors. One is to take careful notes and to ask sources to explain anything you don't understand. There are very few dumb questions in journalism. Here are other precautions:

- Check and double-check dubious information with other sources or documents. Use your newspaper's library and public records.
- Make sure you get the right spelling of names, particularly on the telephone. Ask, "Is it C as in Charlie?" It's a good idea to spell a name back to the source for a double check. Confirm names with the telephone or city directory when in doubt.
- Read your copy very closely before turning it in. Many mistakes can be caught by careful self-editing.
- Never guess. You may think something is obvious and be wrong.

The late Professor Curtis D. MacDougall of Northwestern University wrote in his textbook, *Interpretive Reporting:* "The newspaper has no reason for not being 100 percent accurate in by far the majority of stories it publishes. Thus, one of the first lessons the beginning reporter must learn is how to avoid making mistakes. . . . Lucky is the cub who starts his/her reporting career under an editor who 'raises the roof' whenever he detects a misspelled word or incorrect middle initial in a piece of copy."

Accuracy is not only a matter of misspelling names or garbling facts. It also can occur in commission and omission. It may be factually correct to report that "More than 200 Pine Grove homeowners piled into the City Council chambers last night to protest the city's decision to take down gates at the entrances to their subdivision." But if the story does not note that the residents were notified six months earlier that the gates would be removed because they violated a county ordinance, it would not be fully accurate.

By the same token, it's certainly okay to report that a speaker attacked his political opponent for not having his official residence in the district where he is running for state senator—if it's also brought out that the rival previously admitted the charge and has purchased a house in the district.

In short, being accurate means being fair. This story illustrates how balance was achieved in writing about a situation where there clearly was more than one point of view:

By Catherine Bowman

Nearly 90 senior citizens are being evicted from their San Francisco home because an out-of-state corporation plans to renovate the building and raise the rents.

Residents at Victorian Manor in the Western Addition were told earlier this month that they must move by Feb. 1. Social workers say the building is the only large board-and-care facility in the city that accepts low-income people who are in wheelchairs or use a cane or walker to get around.

News of the pending closure prompted a meeting Wednesday of social workers, city officials and other advocates for the elderly. They say there are not enough beds in San Francisco for elderly people on fixed incomes, meaning many Victorian Manor residents may have to leave the city.

"We think it's outrageous that an organization like this should care so little about the occupants that it gives them such short notice," said Sid Wolinsky, director of litigation for Disability Rights Advocates in Oakland. "It's a tremendous shock to people who have followed a little routine in a little room to suddenly be uprooted to a new environment. . . . There's no way to overstate the emotional trauma."

For the past five years, Victorian Manor was managed by Cedar Village, Inc. in Hayward. Orrin Grover, an attorney for Cedar Village, said the building fell into foreclosure about a year ago when its owner, a Bay Area woman named Fil Runez, ran into financial trouble.

Grover said the building then wound up in the hands of the financial institution Bankers Trust, which turned over day-to-day management responsibilities to a group called Emeritus Corp. in Seattle last month.

Larry Claunch, vice president of operations for Emeritus, said the Feb. 1 deadline for residents to move is not firm. No one will be forced to leave, he said, until an appropriate place is found.

"We're going to work with each and every resident," Claunch said. "This is not something that has to happen overnight."

Claunch said the company will spend about $2 million to renovate the facility, a process expected to take about six months. Along with private bathrooms and improvements to the floors, kitchen and other areas, Emeritus plans to build two penthouses.

About half the residents now pay less than $700 a month; fees for other clients are based on a sliding scale, depending on income, up to $2,400 a month. After the renovations, there will be about a dozen low-income beds, but most residents will pay between $1,500 and $3,000 a month, Claunch said.

Claunch said the steeper rents are necessary to keep the facility open. Under the previous management, he said, Victorian Manor was losing money.

"If it's losing money, it wasn't going to be there anyway," he said. "Instead of shutting down . . . we're making it a nicer place."

Grover, however, said the business is "marginally profitable" and had turned the corner.

"If they say they are going to make it a nicer place, they're wrong," he said. "They're taking the housing for which there is the greatest need—the people at the lowest end of the economic scale—and they're going to make a rich hoity-toity place."

The eviction letters, which arrived during the holiday season, have created confusion among the residents. Emeritus officials say they wanted to give people as much notice as possible, but critics say they are being insensitive.

"Very few people know what the whole thing is about," said resident Edwin Davidson, 78. "I don't like it at all. There's so much strain on us."

Davidson has lived in San Francisco since the 1950s and gets by on government assistance and a small union pension. He pays about $750 a month and cannot afford to pay any more.

"I'm comfortable here," he said. "I'm used to San Francisco. I know every street and every corner."

Emeritus said it is working with local agencies to find appropriate new homes. Current residents have the first option of moving back, assuming they do not need a higher level of care than what Emeritus will provide.

Some residents say they do not mind leaving.

"I'm 82," said Gertrude Leonard. "When you get that old, it don't matter where I go as long as I go somewhere."

Both sides say the problem at Victorian Manor underscores a larger crisis: how to care for an aging population at a time when government resources are shrinking.

"We have to make some better plans for the (low-income elderly) in need of board and care in the city," said Mary Emma Dean, who heads the city's geriatric mental health program. "This may be our wake-up call."

—San Francisco Chronicle

It should be obvious that in a story of this complexity the reporter must touch all bases—getting different viewpoints for fairness and balance. Note also how the article is enhanced by good quotes from residents, the new owners and social workers. Issues may be important, but they can lose impact if they're dully presented.

Codes of Ethics

Earlier in this chapter, journalistic codes of ethics were discussed. It should also be mentioned that a number of editors and reporters don't believe in them. It's not that they're unethical but that they feel a set of rules or guidelines places restrictions on them despite the fact that, unlike ethical codes for doctors or lawyers, they can bring no sanctions from a body like a medical review board or bar association. American journalists are not licensed.

Some critics of ethics codes fear they may give government ideas about shackling the press in some way and furnish lawyers ammunition for libel suits. The latter concern is not entirely groundless. Attorneys representing libel plaintiffs have pointed to a newspaper's written ethical standards to bolster their argument that they were violated, thus damaging their clients.

Still, in the newspaper business, interest in codes of ethics appears to be growing along with criticism of the press. To burnish their image newspapers are looking at themselves more intensely than ever before. Ombudsmen, in-house media critics, op-ed pages and other means are being used to open the newspaper to the public. Some papers have gone so far as to invite local citizens to sit in on editors' news meetings. Tapping "focus groups" for their likes and dislikes about a newspaper is quite common.

Newspapers' concern about their image is well-founded. In a survey a few years ago by the Washington, D.C.–based Times Mirror Center for the People and the Press, public respondents thought reporters' ethics were about the same as those of public officials. The bad news in this finding is that, when asked to rate the honesty and ethical standards of Washington public officials, more than three-quarters of the public ranked them as low or very low. The sort of good news is that when members of Congress were asked to judge reporters, 63 percent said they were about as ethical as public office holders in the matter of conflicts of interest. But 25 percent said reporters were less ethical than public officials.

The news got a little better when local politicians were polled on the same issue. More than three-quarters of them believed the press was about as ethical as they were, which some journalists would consider a dubious compliment.

Newspapers fared better in the survey than reporters. The public graded its local daily newspaper higher than the major national newspapers such as the *New York Times, Washington Post* and *Los Angeles Times*. More than half the respondents gave the daily paper with which they were most familiar an A rating (58 percent) or a B (38 percent), but only 30 percent gave the major papers similar grades. Of course, it can be assumed they were much more familiar with their local paper than the national dailies.

A more recent poll by the National Constitution Center gave journalists and their employers nothing to cheer about. When 1,520 adults were asked to pick whom they would choose to most protect constitutional rights and freedoms, the press ranked dead last behind "ordinary citizens," "the government and the courts," and "civil-liberties groups." Ordinary citizens snagged 35% of the vote while the media got 8%. Moreover, 43% of the respondents believed society has "gone too far in expanding freedom of the press." But it's also true that the public doesn't like bad news, which the media deliver as part of their job. From dislike to blame is an easy step for many people. They blame the press for bad news for want of a better scapegoat, not bothering to reason that journalists are not responsible for terror attacks, sniper killings, West Nile fever and train wrecks. That some media practitioners, notably in television, egregiously sensationalize and distort some news events, probably contributes to the press's bad ratings, but they are outweighed by the number of reporters and editors who, day after day, produce responsible, accurate and ethical journalism.

Dealing with ethical questions is almost a daily occurrence on newspapers. A typical case was reported in the Associated Press Managing Editors (APME) magazine by Louise Seals, managing editor of the *Richmond* (Va.) *Times-Dispatch*. A weekend news anchor for a local TV station was arrested on a misdemeanor charge of soliciting sex from an undercover officer of the same gender in the restroom of a public park. The question was whether to report it in the paper.

On the side of disclosure, Seals said, were the facts that the anchor was a public figure and well-known and that families frequent the park. The arguments for not publishing, she continued, were that the paper rarely reports sexual solicitation charges, similar police undercover operations have sometimes amounted to entrapment and, if the arrest went to trial, the charge would likely be plea-bargained down to disorderly conduct. Said Seals:

> Does something about the anchor's public persona make sexual practices an issue? In this case, no. Only when someone claims to be a role model or arbiter of moral rectitude do we print such arrests. Now the toughest questions: Does the anchor meet the exceptions to reporting misdemeanor arrests on charges involving sex — high public officials, major public figures or persons in high positions of public trust? Is the weekend anchor the same as the main news anchor?

The paper decided to wait until the case went to trial, but a competing TV station broke the story, forcing the *Times-Dispatch* to print it — but only as a four-paragraph piece, the same length, said Seals, the paper would have published if the paper had broken it. When the matter did go to trial, the newspaper reported it.

Seals recalled that some readers protested that journalists were "protecting their own" by not publishing the story when the anchor was first arrested.

Both newspaper management and staff continue to be aware they are under a constant spotlight regarding ethics. Such awareness led to the code of ethics of the Society of Professional Journalists (SPJ) listed below. The code was first adopted in 1926, revised in 1973 and again in 1984, 1987 and 1996.

The Society of Professional Journalists believes the duty of journalists is to serve the truth.

We believe the agencies of mass communication are carriers of public discussion and information, acting on their Constitutional mandate and freedom to learn and report the facts.

We believe in public enlightenment as the forerunner of justice, and in our Constitutional role to seek the truth as part of the public's right to know the truth.

We believe these responsibilities carry obligations that require journalists to perform with intelligence, objectivity, accuracy and fairness.

To these ends, we declare acceptance of the standards of practice here set forth:

- RESPONSIBILITY: The public's right to know of events of public importance and interest is the overriding mission of the mass media. The purpose of distributing the news and enlightened opinion is to serve the general welfare. Journalists who use their professional status as representatives of the public for selfish or other unworthy motives violate a high trust.

- FREEDOM OF THE PRESS: Freedom of the Press is to be guarded as an inalienable right of people in a free society. It carries with it the freedom and responsibility to discuss, question, and challenge actions and utterances of our government and of our public and private institutions. Journalists uphold the right to speak unpopular opinions and the privilege to agree with the majority.

- ETHICS: Journalists must be free of obligations to any interest other than the public's right to know the truth.

  1. Gifts, favors, free travel, special treatment or privileges can compromise the integrity of journalists and their employers. Nothing of value should be accepted.

  2. Secondary employment, political involvement, holding public office and service in community organizations should be avoided if it compromises the integrity of journalists and their employers. Journalists and their employers should conduct their personal lives in a manner which protects them from conflict of interest, real or apparent. Their responsibilities to the public are paramount. That is the nature of their profession.

  3. So-called news communications from private sources should not be published or broadcast without substantiation of their claims to news value.

  4. Journalists will seek news that serves the public interest, despite the obstacle. They will make constant efforts to assure that the public's business is conducted

in public and that public records are open to public inspection.

5. Journalists acknowledge the newsman's ethic of protecting confidential sources of information.
6. Plagiarism is dishonest and unacceptable.

- ACCURACY AND OBJECTIVITY: Good faith with the public is the foundation of all worthy journalism.

1. Truth is our ultimate goal.
2. Objectivity in reporting the news is another goal which serves as the mark of an experienced professional. It is the standard of performance toward which we strive.
3. There is no excuse for inaccuracies or lack of thoroughness.
4. Newspaper headlines should be fully warranted by the contents of the articles they accompany. Photographs and telecasts should give an accurate picture of an event and not highlight a minor incident out of context.
5. Sound practice makes clear distinction between news reports and expressions of opinion. News reports should be free of opinion or bias and represent all sides of an issue.
6. Partisanship in editorial comment which knowingly departs from the truth violates the spirit of American journalism.
7. Journalists recognize their responsibility for offering informed analysis, comment, and editorial opinion on public events and issues. They accept the obligation to present such material by individuals whose competence, experience and judgment qualify them for it.
8. Special articles or presentations devoted to advocacy or the writer's own conclusions and interpretations should be labeled as such.

- FAIR PLAY: Journalists at all times will show respect for the dignity, privacy, rights, and well-being of people encountered in the course of gathering and presenting news.

1. The news media should not communicate unofficial charges affecting reputation or moral character without giving the accused a chance to reply.
2. The news media must guard against invading a person's right to privacy.
3. The media should not pander to morbid curiosity about details of vice and crime.
4. It is the duty of the news media to make prompt and complete correction of their errors.

5. Journalists should be accountable to the public for
    their reports and the public should be encouraged to
    voice its grievances against the media. Open dialogue
    with our readers, viewers, and listeners should be fos-
    tered.

-   PLEDGE: Journalists should actively censure and try to pre-
    vent violations of these standards, and they should en-
    courage their observance by all newspeople. Adherence to
    this code of ethics is intended to preserve the bond of mu-
    tual trust and respect between American journalists and the
    American public.

A footnote can be added to number 5 under Fair Play. As already noted, several
newspapers, notably those in the Knight Ridder chain, are engaging in "public
journalism," in which the papers become involved in issues and problems in their
communities by helping to organize discussion groups and task forces to deal with
them. These publications have gone from their traditional role of observer and
chronicler to becoming participants in the day-to-day life of their communities. But,
as previously discussed, public journalism does not sit well with some journalists,
who believe it compromises their objectivity and blurs the newspaper's role of reporting the news, not making it.

10

Covering Cops, Courts and the Criminal Justice System

There seems to be no end to high-profile arrests and trials that capture public attention with a major assist from the media. In recent years, we have witnessed the Oklahoma bombing trial of Timothy McVeigh; the conviction of Michael Skakel, a nephew of the late Robert Kennedy, for the bludgeon murder of a neighbor; the guilty plea of John Walker Lindh, the so-called American Taliban for his alleged tie to a terrorist group, as well as cases of business tycoons such as Sam Waskal, who was arrested on insider-trading charges for which he pleaded guilty. In these stories, as well as in the hundreds of lesser-known criminal cases, reporters follow well-worn legal procedures from arrest to trial to possible appeal.

The Arrest Process

Before there is a criminal court proceeding, there is a crime and an alleged criminal. Under our justice system, an accused person is assumed to be innocent until proven guilty. The reporter must take great care not to convict anyone in print. This is not only a matter of responsible reporting but can be a fail-safe method to avoid a libel suit. Until there is a guilty verdict by a judge or jury, you are writing about a suspect or an accused person.

An arrest of a suspect can be made in three ways:

1. A police officer makes an arrest on the basis of a warrant issued by a judge, often on the basis of a grand jury indictment.

2. The officer who sees a crime committed, or has reason to believe one was committed, seizes the suspect.

3. A private citizen can make an arrest under certain conditions, although this is not common.

In all states, crimes are either felonies or misdemeanors. A felony or high crime is the more serious, calling for prison and/or a fine upon conviction. There also may be a lengthy probation period imposed after time served. Misdemeanors, which are usually heard in municipal or lower justice courts, may also result in a fine and incarceration on conviction, although the sentence is likely to be served in a county jail rather than a state prison. In many jurisdictions, the line between a felony and a misdemeanor in a theft case depends on the value of the missing item. A stolen radio costing $59 may fall into the misdemeanor category because the law states that for a felony to be committed the value of the property must be at least $100. In certain assault cases, the district attorney might decide whether to prosecute the accused on a felony or misdemeanor charge, depending on the circumstances. For example, a judge agreed with the district attorney that actress Winona Ryder should be tried on felony charges of second-degree burglary, grand theft and other charges for allegedly shoplifting merchandise from Saks Fifth Avenue in Beverly Hills. In some instances, shoplifting can be a misdemeanor.

In today's crime-ridden cities, the felony/misdemeanor distinction is blurred in certain instances. California, for example, has a "three strikes" law by which a criminal with a prior conviction record could be sent to prison for life for merely stealing a six-pack of beer from a convenience store. Previous convictions are also taken into consideration by other states in filing charges. Moreover, the $59 radio could be the centerpiece of a felony charge if it was taken in a burglary involving breaking and entering of a building.

Crimes fall into these main categories:

1. Crimes against the person
2. Crimes against property
3. Crimes against the public peace
4. Crimes against public health and safety
5. Crimes against the government
6. Crimes against morality and decency

Crimes against the person include murder, rape, robbery, assault, kidnapping and voluntary and involuntary manslaughter. First-degree murder in all states is the killing of someone with premeditation or "lying in wait." Second-degree murder is usually described in the statute books as taking a human life without plan—as in a rage—but, nevertheless, having an intent to kill. A jury could vote a conviction on one or the other if a judge so instructs it. First-degree murder carries a harsher sentence that could include the death penalty in several states. In a first-degree murder conviction in many jurisdictions, a jury will vote on the death penalty after rendering a guilty verdict. A judge can sustain or overturn the jury's penalty decision.

Crimes against property include burglary, arson, trespass, larceny, embezzlement, forgery, receiving stolen property, malicious mischief, fraud and passing bad checks.

Crimes against the public peace may involve rioting, fighting or drunkenness, improper behavior, disturbing the peace (such as a loud party), parading without a permit and other violations found in various state law books.

In recent years, protection of the environment has made crimes against public health and safety an important newspaper story. Corporations and individuals convicted of polluting lakes, streams, coastlines and areas near dwellings have been fined, jailed or both. Also in this grouping are violations involving obstructing roadways, removing or tampering with stop signs and allowing rotting garbage or dead animals to remain on one's premises. In some instances, authorities may remove children from a home considered filthy and unsanitary, and their parents may be charged.

The most serious crime against the government is treason, which, upon conviction, is punishable by long prison terms or, in wartime, execution. Other crimes in this category are sedition (seldom invoked), perjury (lying under oath), bribery of a public official, counterfeiting (a federal crime when it's money) and smuggling, to name the more common ones.

The federal government has its own criminal statutes and law enforcement agencies, including the FBI, Secret Service, Drug Enforcement Administration, Customs Service, the Internal Revenue Service, Postal Inspection Department and others. Since the 9/11 terror incident, a new Department of Homeland Security was formed with the stated purpose of combatting terrorism more effectively.

A crime committed on federal property would probably be tried in federal court. Often, however, federal and state crime statutes overlap, as in the case of bank robbery. It is fairly common for a U.S. district attorney, the federal equivalent of a state district attorney, to let a bank holdup suspect be tried for the offense in a state court. If he is convicted, the feds will likely drop their charges. Car theft also may involve both state and federal crimes. If a stolen vehicle is driven across state lines, it is a federal offense.

Among the crimes against morality and decency are prostitution, incest, bigamy, adultery (seldom invoked), obscenity and blasphemy, which is the denigration or ridiculing of God or religion. The application of these laws, many of them more than 100 years old, depends on the state or community and the personal view of prosecutors. A charge of blasphemy, for example, rarely reaches a courtroom. Also, these laws continue to evolve with societal attitudes and mores. For example, prior to June 2003, five states had laws prohibiting gay sodomy. The U.S. Supreme Court ruled that those state statutes, although rarely enforced, violated privacy when applied to private consensual sex between adults.

As noted earlier, arrests can be made by a peace officer on her own information and belief or with a warrant. A warrant is issued by a judge upon the recommendation of the district attorney or by a grand jury voting a true bill. This means that the jury believes that the evidence presented by the prosecution is sufficient to remand the case for trial. A grand jury, which may consist of as many as 25 persons, does not determine guilt or innocence. That is for the trial or petit jury to decide. Even when a district attorney asks a judge for a warrant without a grand jury recommendation, he will seek a grand jury indictment.

Grand jury deliberations are closed to all but the prosecution and witnesses. Its finding is submitted to a judge, sometimes sealed, making it hard for the media to learn the outcome. Although the media are not allowed inside the grand jury room, it's sometimes possible, by stationing yourself outside the room, to get a hint, clue or outright information on what happened inside by interviewing lawyers during breaks.

The Arrest

In a bona fide arrest, the accused is first booked at a police or sheriff's station. In covering crime stories, make sure you make a distinction between a booking and someone merely being brought in for questioning. The difference is important. A person being interrogated may be totally innocent of any crime and have voluntarily come to the station. She may merely be a witness or have other information useful to the police. Booking is a formal process and indicates that the individual is under arrest. The suspect is fingerprinted and surrenders his pocket possessions, and his name, address and physical description are noted on a special form. Most likely he will also pose for a "mug" shot. He is then put behind bars unless bail is provided to set him free. In serious felonies, prosecutors usually ask for very high bail to ensure the accused's safekeeping. Bail requests of $500,000 to $2 million are not uncommon, but a judge rules on the amount after hearing arguments from the district attorney and the defense lawyer.

Bail is money or property offered to guarantee the suspect's appearance in court. If he fails to show up for a hearing, the bail may be forfeited. Since big bail money is beyond the reach of most defendants, professional bail bondsmen put up the amount for a sizable fee. An accused person with a home, a family, a job, no crime record and deep roots in the community may get off with light bail or may be freed on his "own recognizance," meaning no bail at all. However, in many states, courts do not permit bail on a murder charge.

Reporters covering the police or court beat often find bail bondsmen good sources of information to fill out an arrest story. Some will tip off the pressroom to the arrest of a prominent individual. Here is an arrest story:

By Kevin Mayhood and Evan Goodenow

Police raided four convenience stores and homes yesterday and arrested 31 men accused of taking part in a national theft ring involving inner-city convenience stores.

Four store owners have been charged with federal crimes, including interstate transport of stolen property and conspiring to launder money. The others, store employees, are charged with state violations of receiving stolen property.

Authorities said the defendants encouraged others to steal baby formula and health and beauty aids from other stores and then bought the goods from the shoplifters at a fraction of the selling price. The merchandise was then taken to a warehouse on Phillipi Road where it was repackaged and sold at markets here and in Los Angeles and Florida.

The ring brought infant formula stolen from Raleigh, N.C., and Pompano Beach, Fla., and sold it in stores here, authorities said.

After two years of investigating, police and agents from 13 local and federal law-enforcement offices began raids at 2 p.m. yesterday.

Inside stores along E. Main Street, deputies, FBI agents and Columbus police officers searched the aisles and questioned employees while bewildered customers were turned away.

A federal indictment unsealed yesterday said illegal buying and selling took place at Champion Market on E. Whittier Street; Alhadid Market on Cleveland Avenue; and Long & 20th Carryout on E. Long Street.

Ahmad S. Alamansour, 30, of 7487 Brandshire Lane in Dublin, is charged with 14 counts of interstate transportation of stolen property and money-laundering offenses. If convicted, he faces up to 55 years in prison.

Khalil T. Alhawawreh, 42, of 175 Mithoff St., and his son, Faud K. Alhawawreh, 19, of the same address, are charged with a total of three counts of interstate transport of stolen property.

Khaled M. Abdel Jabbar, 47, of 3865 Heatherglen Dr., is charged with two counts of interstate transport of stolen property.

In addition to the arrests, the U.S. attorney's office is seeking $708,907 through a forfeiture proceeding. Authorities say that's the amount of money sent out of state to those who shipped stolen merchandise to the defendants in Columbus.

—*The Columbus* (Ohio) *Dispatch*

Because police stories are among the most vulnerable to libel suits, the writer wisely attributed most of the facts to the police, or in this case, "authorities." This is always a good idea when arrests are made and charges filed. Strictly local city or county arrest stories usually attribute the facts to city police or to county sheriff's deputies.

And, in reporting an arrest and booking, make every effort to round out the story. Don't rely solely on the police log, which gives only a skeleton version of the event. Talk to the arresting officers, the district attorney, an assistant or a press liaison person. Look up witnesses and talk to the suspect if that's possible. Once out on bail, some suspects will grant interviews and even hold press conferences to get their side across. Some reporters have gained jail interviews, a tough, but not impossible, task.

Now let's look at how a grand jury story was handled.

By Sandra Chereb

RENO—Two men suspected of trying to blow up the Internal Revenue Service office building here with a 100-pound bomb were indicted Wednesday by a federal grand jury.

Joseph Bailie, 40, and Ellis Hurst, 52, each were charged with conspiracy to destroy or damage a government building, attempted destruction of a government building and use of an explosive device while committing a violent crime.

They face 50 years in prison if convicted on all counts stemming from the Dec. 18 incident, Assistant U.S. Attorney Ron Rachow said.

Both are scheduled to enter pleas during their arraignment this morning before U.S. Magistrate Phyllis Halsey Atkins.

The bomb, contained in a 30-gallon white plastic drum wired to a red hand truck, was packed with 100 pounds of ammonium nitrate and fuel oil—the same explosive mixture used to blow up the federal building in Oklahoma City in April, killing 169 people. That bomb weighed nearly 5,000 pounds.

The bomb in Reno was found in a side parking lot by an IRS employee arriving for work around 7:15 a.m.

Agents with the U.S. Bureau of Alcohol, Tobacco and Firearms and the FBI said a fuse had been lit, but the explosion failed because a blasting cap was not strong enough to detonate it.

Bob Stewart, resident agent in charge of the ATF office in Reno, said if the bomb had exploded, it would have caused significant damage to the building and possibly killed anyone in the vicinity.

Bomb experts stabilized the device, then took it to the desert east of Reno and destroyed it.

Co-workers of the suspects said Bailie often boasted that he refused to pay taxes.

The two men recently worked forklifts at a building materials business in Gardnerville, 50 miles south of Reno.

A criminal complaint filed earlier said Bailie enlisted Hurst to help him with the plan and borrowed Hurst's pickup to transport the bomb on Dec. 17.

When federal agents closed in on Hurst, he blew the whistle on Bailie.

"Hurst related both he and Bailie had difficulties with the Internal Revenue Service in the past," the complaint said.

The complaint said the men had tried to detonate the bomb the previous day, a Sunday, when the building was empty.

ATF agent Richard Stoltz wrote in the complaint: "Bailie took the device, wheeled it over and placed it behind an IRS vehicle. Hurst further related that Bailie ignited the fuse and then as the two drove away, they heard a pop."

—Associated Press

The story is made more readable by its strong use of detail—the bomb's components, the specific charges against the two men, how the bomb was housed, how it was moved, where it was found and who found it. And obviously the reporter did more than just read from an FBI report. She interviewed enforcement officers and co-workers of the suspects as well. The result is a tightly written, well-honed article, another example of layering a story to give the reader as complete a picture as possible within the restrictions of a deadline. Since this is more than a one-day story, more details will appear in "follow" stories as the case develops.

Trial Coverage

Covering court proceedings—from preliminary hearing to trial—gives you a front-row seat at one of the most exciting shows in town. Not every day in court will be rewarding, but over a period of time you are bound to witness human drama of a kind that's often better than movie versions of the legal system at work.

Procedures in a criminal trial are virtually the same for state and federal courts since our system of justice derives from English common law and practice.

In both federal and state courts there is a flood of opportunity for dramatic news stories. You will see defendants and witnesses lay their emotions bare, with prosecutors and defense lawyers trying to out-duel each other, often in spectacular fashion. The O.J. Simpson and Michael Skakel murder trials frequently made the front pages and led evening news broadcasts, but they were only two of hundreds of trials that have captured reader attention in Page One stories. And frequently, a trial of an obscure defendant can produce drama or surprises that make for vivid reading.

One fact about trial reporting is that you don't have to hype the story to make it interesting. Simply telling what happened is sufficient, in many instances, to rivet readers.

First, let's examine what precedes a criminal trial. Following the arrest and indictment, the defendant faces a preliminary hearing at which he is advised of the charge or charges against him and asked by the judge whether he has an attorney. If not, and he cannot (probably) afford one, a public defender will be appointed to represent him. If he is accompanied by a defense lawyer, the latter may move to have the charges dismissed for lack of evidence. A judge may actually hear witnesses to determine whether the case should go to trial. Usually, motions for dismissal fail.

Next comes an arraignment, during which the accused enters a guilty or innocent plea. If he pleads guilty, the judge will set a date for sentencing. Meanwhile, he will get a report from the probation department to guide him in sentencing. If the plea is innocent, a trial date will be set.

A defendant has a constitutional right to a jury trial but may waive it in favor of having his fate decided by the judge. In a jury criminal trial, the first step is the selection of 12 jurors from a large panel of men and women summoned to jury duty, usually from voter registration lists.

Picking a jury may take several days. Both the defense and the prosecution seek jurors they believe will support their case and thus question them closely to detect a bias or probe their occupations and background for information that could offer a clue as to how they will vote in the jury room. A female panelist whose 7-year-old son was killed by a hit-and-run motorist would surely be dismissed by the lawyer for a person charged with vehicular homicide. Potential jurors whose spouses or other relatives are law enforcement officers are also likely to be challenged by the defense.

From the larger panel sitting in another room, prospective jurors are called by a kind of lottery system into the jury box, where they are questioned by both sides. Each side is entitled to a limited number of challenges of two kinds: peremptory and for cause. In the first, a defense attorney or prosecutor may dismiss a juror without giving a reason. Challenges for cause are unlimited if the judge agrees with the reason for dismissal.

Jury selection may not be the most interesting part of a criminal proceeding, although it can produce stories and should be watched closely. Questions posed by attorneys for both sides can indicate trial strategy, and jurors themselves may provide copy by their replies. In big cases, defense lawyers with affluent clients have hired jury-picking specialists who examine the background of prospective jurors to form a psychological profile of each one. This process is made easier by the issuance of lengthy questionnaires filled out by panelists in major cases, as happened in the O.J. Simpson trial and that of Robert Blake. Despite the personal information a potential juror may supply on the questionnaire, lawyers will admit that it's not a foolproof gauge of how the juror might be leaning. Questions involve family background, economic status, education, religion and social and professional affiliations. Of course, jurors are expected to enter a trial with an open mind and to reach a verdict only after hearing all the evidence. But, in an imperfect world, that is not something that can be counted on. In this major trial, jury selection made for an absorbing story:

By Linda Deutsch

John Z. De Lorean's prosecutor, frustrated by mounting dismissals of jury candidates for bias against the defendant in the cocaine-trafficking trial, said Thursday the panelists are being "mousetrapped" by De Lorean's clever lawyers.

"In a case that's been as heavily publicized as this, of course people have formed opinions," Assistant U.S. Attorney James Walsh said outside court.

But he said they should not be systematically ousted for those opinions.

"The kind of juror you want is someone with something between their ears," he said. "And those jurors have opinions. The question is can they set those opinions aside?"

Walsh, breaking his long silence about commenting on the case, said he felt the jury selection was going "slowly" and suggested it will be more protracted than it needs to be.

"It only took seven days to create the world," he said. "It shouldn't take several months to pick a jury."

De Lorean, 59, is charged with conspiring to distribute $24 million worth of cocaine.

An exasperated Walsh expressed frustration Thursday at being unable to combat the probing questions being asked by De Lorean's attorneys, Howard Weitzman and Donald Re—questions which have led many prospects to declare they thought De Lorean was "probably guilty" of trafficking in cocaine.

"People want to be fair and honest," he said. ". . . They're not legal scholars. They're ordinary Joes, working stiffs, housewives. And they're being mousetrapped. Howard and Don are very clever questioners."

"I don't know how to deal with it," Walsh said during the hallway conversation. "I'm trying to structure my questions so the jurors will be saying what they mean."

Meanwhile, U.S. District Judge Robert Takasugi obviously was disturbed by the candidates' unwillingness to presume De Lorean innocent unless proven guilty—a basic premise of law.

Several panelists said they could not find him innocent unless he proved his innocence to them.

De Lorean, seated at the counsel table, appeared unperturbed by the repeated declarations that he is guilty.

Takasugi began lecturing the prospects on the law of presumption of innocence. He also took over some of the questioning from attorneys and told jurors sternly: "Publicity certainly is not evidence."

Walsh said the lengthy quizzing by attorneys—which has stretched as long as one hour for each panelist since it began Tuesday—is almost unprecedented in federal court.

"This is extraordinary," said Walsh. "You usually don't get into this kind of searching inquiry. This is the first time I've done it."

Normally, federal judges do all questioning, with attorneys submitting their questions to the judge in writing.

At Thursday's court session, the first three candidates questioned were accepted tentatively after they said they could put aside opinions and judge the case on the evidence.

Those passed on the publicity issue will face more questioning later on nonpublicity issues such as their attitude toward drugs, crime and the judicial system.

Weitzman's questioning of one woman prospective juror became so antagonistic at one point that the woman complained, "I know you're upset with me and I don't know why."

The woman apparently contradicted some things she had said on the written questionnaire given to all prospective jurors in the case. "Why are you being less than truthful when this man is on trial for serious criminal charges?" asked Weitzman.

"With all these questions," said the woman, "I don't know anymore what I wrote down."

She promised to "do my utmost to be as honest as I can be," and was tentatively accepted.

—Associated Press

After the jury is chosen, the trial begins with an opening statement by the prosecutor, who tells the jury what he will establish in due course. The prosecutor also may attempt to sway the jury with an unfriendly description of the defendant's character and motives. The defense lawyer also is entitled to an opening statement but may defer it until the prosecution's case has been presented.

According to law, nothing that a lawyer says during a trial is to be considered evidence by the jury. Thus, lawyers' remarks should not be confused with evidence in writing the story, although they sometimes make for dramatic quotes.

The prosecutor, who is the district attorney or an assistant district attorney (in federal court trials, a U.S. attorney), begins her case by calling witnesses for direct examination. When she is finished with her witness, the defense attorney is entitled to cross-examine him in an effort to repair any damage to his client and possibly cast doubt on the witness's veracity. Cross-examinations are often sharp and heated; they may be the lead of your story. Both the prosecution and defense tend to portray their witnesses as the embodiment of truth and their opponents as people who don't know what the word means.

Expert witnesses (doctors, engineers, psychologists and handwriting specialists, for example) are treated differently. Their truthfulness is not an issue, but their opinions or findings will be challenged—sometimes by other experts. Some of the best courtroom duels are between an expert and a lawyer who has done his homework on the witness's area of expertise. He may throw enough doubt on the expert's testimony to virtually nullify it.

The O.J. Simpson trial is a classic example. The defense heaped so much doubt on the prosecution's scientific witnesses, particularly over blood samples, that the attack was regarded as a significant factor in the verdict to acquit Simpson.

Most trial witnesses tend to be truthful—to the best of their ability—on the stand. To lie is to invite a perjury charge, which could lead to prison. You will, however, hear "I don't remember" frequently from witnesses asked to recall events of several months or even years ago. Certain witnesses spark skepticism among lawyers with this reply, but there is little the lawyers can do about it. But if a witness pleads a faulty memory in nine out of 10 questions, it should probably be mentioned in your story.

There may be trial maneuvers and testimony you don't understand. Wait until a recess or the lunch break to buttonhole the prosecutor or defense attorney for an explanation. Never try to write something about which you are not clear.

Be careful, though, of what you quote from your corridor interviews with attorneys or witnesses. Lawyers' statements and witness testimony in court are privileged and thus libel-proof. But the privilege does not extend to statements made outside the courtroom. Under no circumstances should you publish any witness's comments that might influence the jury if seen. That kind of journalism is apt to net you a judicial contempt citation and perhaps jail time. Getting background information from a witness is fine. Persuading the individual to expand her testimony or offer a personal opinion about the case for publication is dangerous in the extreme.

Interviewing jurors during a trial is strictly forbidden, and no experienced journalist would attempt it. Judges try to insulate jurors as much as possible, admonishing them not to discuss the case with anyone, read about it in a newspaper or watch TV reports on it. In a high-profile trial, the judge may sequester the jury, putting it up in a hotel under the watchful eye of bailiffs for the duration of the trial, as happened in the Simpson case. Still, as in the Simpson trial, when jurors complain to the court about their living conditions or contend they can no longer stand the isolation from their families, it becomes legitimate news.

Generally, when a trial is over jurors become fair sources for comment although a judge may advise them that they are not obligated to talk to the media and even urge them not to. But there are exceptions. A judge charged four *Philadelphia Inquirer* reporters with contempt for disobeying her order not to interview *former* jurors in a major New Jersey murder trial that ended in a hung jury. *Editor & Publisher* magazine quoted attorney Amy B. Ginensky, representing one of the reporters, as saying the order ". . . could be very damaging to efforts to let the public know about the process that jurors go through." Lucy Dalglish, executive director of the Reporters Committee for Freedom of the Press, pointed out that the ruling not only departed from the usual practice of judges to merely frown on the practice of interviewing former jurors but was unfair in that it barred the press from talking to the ex-jury members but did not restrict the latter from speaking with the public at large.

Does trial reporting seem like an interesting way to make a living? It can be, but first listen to Linda Deutsch, special correspondent for the Associated Press, who is considered the dean of American trial reporters, having covered virtually every major trial in the last 20 years, including the O.J. Simpson and Manson murder cases. Says Deutsch:

> Unlike general assignment reporting in which journalists immerse themselves in many stories, each for a very short time, trial reporting is an intense experience which requires patience, expertise, a long attention span and the ability to sit for prolonged periods.

Each trial can seem like a mini-lifetime, and high profile trials, which can last as long as a year, can try anyone's patience.

A reporter assigned to a high profile trial must be dedicated to maintaining strict objectivity in spite of a clamor of opinions bombarding the case. It's important to remember that people's lives—or at least their livelihood—are at stake in almost every trial, and it's up to the jury or judge—not a reporter—to decide the outcome. Those in front of the bar have a vested interest in the proceedings. But the reporter in the courtroom gallery is a disinterested observer, there to deliver an account of what happened.

The reporter should have no stake in the outcome and should remember that readers, viewers and listeners are perfectly capable of reaching their own conclusions if given an unbiased account of both sides in any case. If you have opinions, keep them to yourself. No one is asking you to decide the case.

In reporting the facts, try not to get too bogged down in jargon. It has become trendy for trial reporters to have law degrees. But it's unnecessary and sometimes interferes with the journalist's ability to report from the perspective of a lay person. If only lawyers can understand the story, it's of little value to the general public. Keep it simple, straightforward and colorful. The law can be very exciting if reported properly.

There is one trial you probably won't be allowed to cover: juvenile court. Most states keep the proceedings private unless, as has happened quite frequently in many jurisdictions, the crime is so heinous that prosecutors recommend that the juvenile be tried as an adult and the judge agrees. This has happened quite frequently in recent years, notably in school-shooting cases.

Writing the Trial Story

In daily trial coverage, whatever is most newsworthy belongs at the top of your story. The longer you sit through a trial, the easier it will become to fashion a lead because you become familiar with the cast of characters, the main issues and previous testimony. At the beginning, you will have to go with jury choosing and opening statements. From then on, witnesses usually shape your story.

Don't feel you have to write about testimony in sequence. Direct examination of a DA's "friendly" witness may not amount to much and would form the lead if that's all you have. But if the same day brings a withering cross-examination that all but destroys the witness's statements, that is probably the crux of your piece.

In any event, the trial story must have a logical, coherent order. If there are several witnesses in the same day, they should be presented in order of their importance to the case; some should be given several paragraphs and others one, two or none. Rapid deadline writing may force the elimination of testimony by minor witnesses.

Some background should be included in every story, even in trials running for weeks. Some courtroom addicts will read the paper every day for an account of the trial, but many readers come in late or follow the trial sporadically and should be given a modicum of background. Generally, background requires only a couple of paragraphs, giving the date and particulars of the crime and perhaps a brief reference to important earlier testimony. Background also can be slipped into the article at an appropriate place to avoid shattering its continuity or to highlight a marked conflict in testimony from two different witnesses.

The accused taking the stand is always an opportunity for a dramatic story, but you may not get the chance to write it. Under law, the defendant is not required to testify, although some choose to do so. It's permissible to question a defense attorney in advance to learn whether she plans to put her client in the witness chair.

Drama, emotion and color also have a legitimate place in the trial story if they are not overblown or sensationalized. Mawkish, superheated accounts of trials were popular in the 1920s and 1930s but are out of place today. Even so, nervous or calm witnesses, sarcastic attorneys, stern or whimsical judges and physical descriptions of witnesses, including their dress, can enliven a story. What a witness is wearing, his evasiveness, the number of spectators and their audible reaction to testimony supply more grist. Think of the whole spectacle as a stage and witnesses and lawyers as actors—as they often appear to be. Make the reader feel that he or she was there.

Examine this trial story as a guidepost:

FALL RIVER, Mass.—A young mother spent six grueling hours on the witness stand, admitting she lied to welfare workers, denying she plans to sell her story, and calmly standing by her testimony that she was raped and jeered by strange men in a New Bedford bar.

The 22-year-old woman remained calm yesterday despite intense cross-examination by three different defense attorneys, displaying the same composure she showed them when she first took the stand Friday.

Six men are charged with aggravated rape in the case, in which the woman alleges she had gone into Big Dan's tavern in nearby New Bedford last March 6 to buy a pack of cigarettes and was repeatedly raped on a pool table while onlookers cheered.

Daniel Silva and Joseph Vieira, both 27, are being tried in an afternoon trial. Victor Raposo, John Cordeiro, Virgilio Medeiros and Joseph Medeiros (no relation), all 24, are being tried in a separate morning session.

The trials were split to avoid the use of possibly incriminating statements by some defendants against co-defendants in the same trial. The setup means that defense lawyers' questions often overlap.

The woman, the mother of two, has testified that two men actually committed the alleged rapes. Defense attorney Kenneth Sullivan pointed out yesterday that she originally told police she stopped counting after being raped by six men.

Sullivan asked whether she had a better recollection of the facts the night of the rape.

"They're clearer now than they were then," she said in a low monotone.

She quietly denied a statement by defense lawyer David Waxler, representing Vieira, that she told a rape counselor police were prosecuting the wrong men in the case.

And, she said, her $10 million civil suit against the bar owners was not a matter of money.

"I'm suing them for the principle that they were wrong," she replied.

The woman's testimony was first challenged by two attorneys who claimed her story had undergone a "dramatic switch" from what she had said in pretrial interviews with attorneys. Two asked Judge William Young to declare a mistrial.

"She's cast the defendant in a totally different role than he's been in previous testimony," said Edward Harrington, representing Silva. Harrington said the change "caused irreparable damage" to his case.

The woman has testified she went into Big Dan's to buy a pack of cigarettes and that she stayed for one drink and conversation with a woman who was with two men playing pool.

When she got up to leave, she said, she was grabbed from behind and dragged to the pool table where two men took turns raping her, then one of them and another man tried to force her to perform oral sex.

Under yesterday's cross-examination, she admitted she delivered drinks to two of the defendants while they played pool. She identified the two as Raposo and Cordeiro, pointing them out in the courtroom.

—Associated Press

The story makes clear that hyped-up writing is unnecessary for a compelling trial report. Often—and certainly in this case—the testimony provides enough drama for readability. The use of quotes here also enhances the story. Good note taking is important in trial coverage since most judges will bar tape recorders. (M.L. Stein can attest to this from experience. A bailiff spotted him with an audio tape recorder at a major civil trial, with the result that he was summoned to the judge's chambers for a lecture on why he could not use the device in the courtroom. It was disruptive, the judge said.)

For those who easily fall victim to writer's cramp or have a problem reading their own scribbling, there is another way. Court reporters—the men and women who machine record almost every word of a trial—will sell the media transcripts of their recordings, albeit at a high price per page. The question is, can you get the pages in time to make your deadline? Most reporters don't need the full day's transcript, only certain testimony. This, of course, saves time.

While the Jury Is Out

After the prosecution has presented its case, the defense may ask the judge to dismiss the charges on the basis of insufficient evidence. If this is refused—as it usually is—the defense has its day, which consists of presenting its witnesses, who also are subject to cross-examination. Remember, the defendant cannot be compelled to testify.

When the defense is completed, both sides deliver final statements—their last chance to sway the jury. The prosecutor speaks last. The judge then instructs the jury on the law and the various verdicts it can bring in. Then the jury retires to the jury room for its deliberations, accompanied by one or more bailiffs.

The jury room is sacrosanct; no one is allowed in except the jurors, who choose a foreman or forewoman. Bailiffs guard the door and lead the jurors to and from meals in a prolonged session.

It's unwise to speculate in print on how the jury will vote or how long it will take to reach a verdict. Even lawyers can be very wrong in predicting an outcome. The Simpson trial ran almost a year, and the jury took less than four hours to arrive at its decision! In the East Coast trial of Ira Einhorn, a man accused of murdering his girlfriend, the jury found him guilty after deliberating less than three hours. Incidentally, Einhorn was a fugitive for 21 years before this second trial. Previously, he had been found guilty in absentia. There is no statute of limitations for a murder charge.

In a major trial, newspapers keep the story alive by various means when the jury is out. The length of time the jury takes may in itself be significant, indicating that it is probably deeply divided or that it finds the evidence enormously complex. Jurors also may ask the judge for permission to review particular testimony or physical evidence. What they seek might tip off their thinking, but again, don't break a leg jumping at conclusions. Approach such a lead cautiously. Juries are unpredictable. This lead would play it safe yet pique reader interest:

> The jury in the Bart Simpson malicious mischief trial asked Judge Stanley Perkins yesterday for a rereading of a letter sent to Simpson's parents by the principal of his school.

The best story, of course, is when the jury comes in with a verdict or to report that it is deadlocked, which is called a hung jury. If it's the first announcement of a deadlock, some judges will send jurors back for further discussion. If a judge is convinced the split cannot be resolved, he will declare a mistrial. Whether the case is retried is up to the district attorney. Retrials are quite common, but they rarely command the same media attention as the first one.

If a jury finds the defendant not guilty, he can walk freely out of the courtroom unless he is facing other charges. If the verdict is guilty, the judge will set a date for sentencing. The court also has the discretion of allowing the defendant to remain free on bail or revoke bail and remand him immediately to jail. A defense attorney will routinely ask that her client continue on bail pending the outcome of an appeal, which can take a year or more. If it's a murder conviction, the lawyer is usually wasting her breath.

Verdict stories are generally written in a straightaway fashion unless there is a violent outbreak in the courtroom over the announcement or the defendant, whether guilty or innocent, faints or reacts in some other dramatic way. The following piece is fairly standard:

By Stuart Pfeifer

NEWPORT BEACH—Five animal-rights activists were convicted Wednesday of misdemeanor charges for unlawfully entering UC Irvine Chancellor Laurel Wilkening's office last spring to question the university's animal-testing practices.

A Harbor Municipal Court jury convicted the activists under a law that makes it unlawful to commit an act likely to interfere with business on a state campus.

Judge Frances Munoz sentenced activists Crescent Velluci, Sheila Laracy, Gina Lynn and Richard McLellan to 50 hours of community service and ordered them to pay $750 fines. Sentencing for the remaining activist, Robin Schroader, was delayed until Jan. 31.

District Attorney Elizabeth Otter said she was disappointed that Munoz did not place the activists on probation, which could have provided for stiffer penalties in the event of another illegal protest. "I don't have a problem with their cause," Otter said. "I have a problem with the way they are going about it."

Velluci said the protesters plan to appeal the convictions.

—*Orange County Register*

In the next sentencing story, note how the reporter has interviewed both the prosecution and defense lawyers for their reaction. There also is sufficient background to make the article understandable for almost any reader.

By Vicki Allen

UKIAH—A high school honor student who was described by teachers as exceptionally bright and thoughtful will begin serving four months in the county jail Friday for vehicular manslaughter.

Originally charged with murder in the alcohol-related, fatal head-on auto accident, Douglas Bennett—who became 18 on Dec. 9—was told by a Superior Court Judge that with credit for good work at school he could be free in three months.

Mendocino County District Attorney Vivian Rackauckas had sought to have Bennett sentenced to the California Youth Authority for a minimum of 16 months, but a teacher, school counselor, an employer and family friends said Bennett was "already punishing himself."

Under the judge's order, Bennett will be allowed to attend regular classes at Ukiah High School, located across the street from the county rehabilitation center, where the youth will serve his sentence. Bennett has maintained a 3.7 grade point average while playing on the basketball team. He is scheduled to graduate in June.

"Some days the system works and some days it doesn't. I don't feel it worked well today," said the district attorney.

"This is a day when the system did work," said defense attorney Richard Petersen. "This sentence will assure that Doug Bennett will go on with his good life and will still show kids who drink that there are serious consequences."

Bennett, who was sentenced in an open juvenile court hearing, also was ordered to pay restitution, including unpaid medical bills to the victim's family, to participate in a counseling program and to refrain from using alcohol and drugs while on probation. Probation will be scheduled following the completion of his sentence.

The Bennett case has been a community controversy since he was charged with murder in the Oct. 23 death of Linda Opager, 26, of St. Paul, Minn., in a head-on collision on a curve of a Ukiah street.

Hall, a retired Contra Costa County Superior Court Judge, dismissed the murder charge, but convicted Bennett Jan. 26 of vehicular manslaughter with gross negligence and felony drunk driving.

Tests showed that two hours after the accident, Bennett had a blood alcohol level of 0.09 percent, just below the 0.10 percent level which state law has set for intoxication.

Opager, the mother of a 5-year-old daughter, had a blood alcohol level of 0.11, court records reported. Her husband, the only passenger in her car, was seriously injured.

When Rackauckas filed the murder charge, many parents, teachers and teenagers condemned drunken driving but urged leniency for Bennett because of his clean record.

Bennett, sentenced as a juvenile because he was 17 at the time of the accident, testified Monday for the first time in the proceedings. In a serious, quiet voice, he said he was willing to be punished but "I don't feel there is much need for rehabilitation.

"I've realized the mistake. Hopefully, other people can see what happened and learn from my mistake.

"It's hard to feel any worse than I feel. There's really nothing more that can happen to change the way I feel."

Brad Opager, who returned to Minnesota after the accident, issued a statement for the probation report in which he expressed no bitterness or anger.

"I don't know if he is like me, but if he were me, the pain of living with the fact that I had killed someone would be the worst punishment."

—Sacramento Bee

The above story obviously lends itself to a human interest treatment. Criminal cases often have emotional underpinnings with which readers can identify. To bring them out in a story not only makes it more appealing but also serves an educational purpose. Drunk driving by teenagers, as depicted in the story, is more than just a statistic or a problem that is generally deplored. It was a real tragedy that involved real people.

Some criminal cases achieve high-profile status because of the identity of the suspect, not the heinousness of the crime. Such was the case in the arrest of actress Winona Ryder for alleged shoplifting from Saks in Beverly Hills, and the 10-day jail sentence in Miami of Noelle Bush for violating the terms of her court-ordered drug rehabilitation program. Bush attained a kind of celebrity status by being the daughter of Gov. Jeb Bush of Florida and the niece of President George W. Bush. Celebrity crime stories should be reported with the same sense of responsibility and accuracy as with any other defendant. Famous or not, each individual deserves a fair shake in your article. The supermarket tabloids will likely blow up such stories but should not be used as a model. A popular phrase these days is "media frenzy," which critics apply to almost any crime story that draws a large contingent of press and broadcast journalists. The 2005 child molestation trial of pop star Michael Jackson is just one of the recent examples of this type of coverage. However, a careful examination of such coverage usually finds that the "frenzy" comes in the form of TV reporters chasing news sources at the scene, shoving microphones in their faces for a quick sound bite. Print reporters are more likely to operate in a calmer manner, attempting to get enough information to put together a readable and informative story. They need more than sound bites for the process.

Civil Court Reporting

At first glance, civil cases may not pack the journalistic appeal of the criminal courts, but don't be fooled. Many civil cases have far more significance for the reader and are given more space by editors. The stream of cases involving damages for personal injury; antitrust violations; tobacco effects; product failure; wrongful firing; sex, race and age discrimination and/or harassment; breach of contract and other grounds frequently generate big news. In recent years, hundreds of thousands of persons may be plaintiffs in a sense through so-called class action suits against corporations over faulty automobiles, dangerous pesticides or, as was adjudicated recently, allegedly flawed breast implants. One civil trial involving monopoly charges against Microsoft made headlines almost every day it ran.

Libel, once a relatively rare lawsuit, is now flourishing, causing newspapers and other media to carry millions of dollars in libel insurance. Defamation actions by such luminaries as Clint Eastwood and Carol Burnett against supermarket tabloids are featured by mainstream newspapers because entertainers make news. Industrial shareholders are affected when companies are charged with antitrust offenses. Pesticide suits involve the food we eat. In short, scores of civil cases impact on our daily lives.

Criminal defendants are entitled by law to a speedy trial, but this is not so in civil courtrooms. Today, these courts are clogged with a massive backload of civil cases, some of which will not come to trial for years. There are not enough judges and not enough time to handle them. Readers may be startled to read about the beginning of a trial in which the original complaint was filed six years before. Such a common delay often leads to an out-of-court settlement because the parties believe it's cheaper than prolonged litigation. And some plaintiffs feel they may not live long enough to see their case tried. Settlements, too, are news, although in some cases the terms may not be disclosed by either party.

A newspaper's decision to cover a civil proceeding (it can't begin to cover them all, even in its own area) often depends on the prominence of the parties involved, if and how it may affect readers, and the novelty of the case. Oddball suits crop up frequently in the courts, although judges will dismiss complaints they deem "frivolous." To pass judicial muster, a civil damage suit must present reasonable evidence in the complaint that the plaintiff is likely to have suffered damage inflicted by the defendant.

A number of civil suits are against government agencies, which also can sue private citizens, an income tax delinquency suit being one example. Income tax evasion, however, can result in a criminal charge. The suit covered in the following story is based on an alleged breach of civil rights.

By Edgar Sanchez

Racial tension and intolerance in the Sacramento County Sheriff's Department has prompted a bigoted graffiti, the brutal beating of a Latino inmate and the use of a racial slur by a former jail commander to describe an African American female deputy, according to testimony Friday in U.S. District Court.

The revelations came on the second day of testimony by peace officers in the trial of former Deputy Linda Anthony, who claims she was forced to quit because hostility, discrimination and harassment directed at women and African Americans, such as herself, made work conditions unbearable.

Attorney Nancy Sheehan, representing the Sheriff's Department, has denied that Anthony's civil rights were violated. She said "rule breakers" can exist in any large organization but that racist behavior is prohibited and that conditions have improved significantly under Sheriff Glen Craig.

"I can tell you that I have never seen any outward evidence of racism within the department," Sgt. John McGuinness, sheriff's spokesman, said Friday in a telephone interview. "That doesn't mean that out of 1,600 people, we don't employ some racists. But any outward manifestation of that racism would absolutely not be tolerated."

The most stunning testimony Friday came from Sheriff's Capt. Edward F. Doonan, former commander of the main jail, who said he personally used a racial epithet out of frustration when a review panel of 10 white sergeants refused to recommend the promotion of an African American deputy.

Doonan said he went before the panel in a failed bid to win its endorsement for Deputy Betty Williams, who he believed had demonstrated skills necessary to become a sergeant. Many panelists disagreed, stating flatly that Williams did not deserve promotion, he said.

Doonan, exasperated at the time, said he told review panelists that they didn't understand.

"Then I said the department has been using Betty as our house nigger and we take her off the shelf when we feel like it and put her into (stressful) situations and then put her back on the shelf until we need her again," he said.

Doonan, now commander of the south patrol division, said he made the statement sometime between April 1990 and March 1993 when he was the jail commander.

Under questioning in federal court Friday, Doonan said he believed the department is supposed to reward employees such as Williams who display skill in tough situations. "I felt this group of sergeants didn't understand that," he testified.

Outside court, plaintiff's attorney John F. Whitfield Jr. said Doonan's use of the highly offensive racial term neatly summarized the attitude of the Sheriff's Department.

"They used black folks when they needed them—and when they didn't, they put them on the shelves," he said, noting Williams remains a deputy after 20 years with the department.

But Whitfield said he is convinced that Doonan is not a racist.

Doonan also testified Friday about bigoted graffiti that allegedly was spotted inside a staff bathroom at the jail.

Doonan said he was notified once that "racially motivated graffiti" existed in the restroom. He directed maintenance workers to paint over it but never saw the graffiti himself, he said.

Defense attorney Sheehan contended Wednesday in her opening statement to the 10-member jury that Anthony took a series of unrelated events and "put them in a basket and spun a lawsuit out of them."

A run-in between Anthony and a jail cook in February 1993 that had nothing to do with race or gender triggered the chain of events that led to the lawsuit, according to Sheehan.

Anthony served as deputy from 1988 to 1993, most of that time in the main jail in one capacity or another.

In other testimony Friday, Anastasia Davis, an African American terminated before she could complete probation as a deputy trainee, said she witnessed racial intolerance at the Sheriff's Academy and at two jails where she worked briefly.

Even more horrifying, she said, was having to witness the brutal beating of a Latino inmate by deputies angered when the man spit on the window of a holding cell after he was denied permission to use a telephone. The victim required hospital treatment, Davis said.

Anthony is seeking unspecified damages in the civil rights trial, which is expected to take about two months.

—Sacramento Bee

Observe that the ingredients of a criminal trial are also in the *Bee*'s civil case story: strong testimony, vivid quotes, background information and attribution. This trial occurred three years after the suit was filed, in keeping with case backlog. Thus, when reporting civil trials, soak up the history of the complaint from the newspaper's databank. Trials are always easier to cover when you are armed with plenty of background.

Newspapers learn about civil suit filings by checking the court clerk's office (the complaint becomes a public record) and from tips from lawyers, the plaintiff herself or other sources, known and anonymous. Keep in mind that the legal document called a complaint is not evidence, merely an allegation or allegations. A defendant named in the suit must respond to it or lose by default. A defense lawyer may ask for a dismissal, and if that fails, the case will go to trial. In civil cases, depositions are first taken from both parties.

In a deposition, the plaintiff and defendant, under oath, are questioned by lawyers, usually in an attorney's office. Often, the depositions are brought out during the trial to refresh a witness's memory or to challenge her veracity. Normally, deposition transcripts are not handed to the press but may be revealed—at least in part—through leaks. Prior to his civil trial, alleged snippets from O.J. Simpson's deposition were on the airwaves that same night.

Here is a spot-news story updating readers on the latest details of a civil suit filed against a local township government in Ohio. The story illustrates how general-assignment reporters must be prepared to handle stories involving legal details in their everyday reporting and to make sure all sides of the story are fairly covered.

By Darcie Loreno

SULLIVAN TWP.—The Sullivan Township trustees' attorney says it appears more than $50,000 in billings for emergency squad runs was misdirected by its former volunteer fire service, the latest volley in a civil lawsuit.

At a Tuesday meeting, Trustee Douglas Campbell read from a confidential summary written by the board's attorney, Assistant County Prosecutor Paul O'Reilly, which said the squad-run billings were generated and sent to "entities set up by others" instead of the township as per Ohio Revised Code without trustee authorization since as early as 2001 and during the time Sullivan Volunteer Fire and EMS Inc. (SVFE) provided the township's fire protection and emergency services.

Further, it alleged "probably in 2002" individual members of the department began receiving money for "reimbursements" or compensation also without board authorization, tentatively totaling $39,637.

The allegations are connected with a civil court case that began when SVFE, which now operates out of Lodi, filed a lawsuit against the township board last June after trustees voided a two-year contract with the group in January. The trustees then formed the Sullivan Volunteer Fire Department to replace SVFE.

SVFE alleged trustees breached the contract owing $80,000 it should have paid for the contracted time and said they refused to return items SVFE owned. Counterclaims include SVFE violating the Open Meetings Act and refusing to return equipment and protective clothing purchased with grant money.

Since then, trustees have hired a private detective to look into financial records and approved at least $6,000 toward court costs. The trustees have rejected a settlement offered by SVFE.

"We felt they (township residents) needed an update on what was going on," said Campbell, the board's spokesman, in explaining the decision to share the confidential memo at Tuesday's meeting.

O'Reilly's memo was based on information from depositions and investigations conducted as part of the case. He could not comment on the information contained in the summary.

"Everything is very preliminary at this point and we are at the early stages of discovery," he said.

In regards to the allegations, SVFE's attorney, Timothy Potts, said "there was a levy that includes language to reimburse emergency and fire personnel."

"The facts are what is being gathered through everything which will be presented at the trial," he said. "My client and I are not choosing to try this case until it comes to the jury in the jury box."

The mediation sessions took place in March, but no settlement was reached. At least 10 people, some former and current fire department members and former trustee Michael Canfield, were subpoenaed by O'Reilly for depositions. Canfield and former clerk Roberta Penn were allowed to reschedule by Common Please Judge Deborah Woodward. Others gave depositions last week.

Those subpoenas also sought information connected with a list of several persons and entities including Former Fire Chief Stephen Neff, Sullivan EMS and Continuing Education, Sullivan Township and SVFE, Inc.

Court records show O'Reilly also subpoenaed eight banks for depositions. Those include two Ashland Bank One locations, two Ashland National City Bank branches, Wellington First Merit, Farmers Savings and Fifth Third Banks and Spencer Farmers Savings Bank, according to court documents. Hale & Associates, the department's former billing company, also was subpoenaed.

The subpoenas sought any information on the names listed and on accounts made under them in the past few years. O'Reilly said the banks "have all complied with the subpoena or are in the process of complying" with the exception of Fifth Third Bank.

Transcripts of last week's depositions should be available in about a week, O'Reilly said.

The civil trial, originally scheduled May 10, was continued April 11 by Woodward after O'Reilly requested at least a 90-day delay.

According to court documents, reasons for requesting a continuance include that money and assets being sought "are in the hands of others, only some of whom are named as parties to this action." Motion documents further claimed through "investigation and discovery," SVFE and certain officers or agents or SVFE "had purposefully and knowingly deceived the defendant and formed a secret, shadow government behind the backs of the defendants" to divert ambulance and EMS service run proceeds into "secret bank accounts."

At Tuesday's meeting, trustees hired a CPA to examine the alleged reimbursements and assist in the investigation. They also hired a file clerk to continue with the organization of township records.

—*Ashland* (Ohio) *Times-Gazette*

Although a civil complaint is only an accusation that must be proved in court, fairness dictates that the reporter should attempt to get a response from the other side. In this complicated story the reporter took the time to seek out the SVFE attorney for his comment, and succeeded in getting him to say something in response, although he declined to try the case by responding to all of the township's allegations.

In this kind of story, a general response works well. In covering such cases, don't report a point-by-point response to each allegation (some complaints have 10 or 15); otherwise you may give the impression that you're trying the case in the paper. A general denial or refutation of the main charge in the complaint by the defendant or his lawyer is sufficient. The issue will be decided by a judge or jury on the basis of evidence in court. That's the time to detail the arguments of both sides.

Probate Court

Probate court may not sound like an exciting assignment, but don't be deceived. Real-life dramas are often played out in this arena, which does furnish a number of stories, several of Page One caliber.

Originally, the term "probate" meant the act or process of proving the validity of a will. Today, its usage is more general, covering a number of legal matters.

The jurisdiction of a probate court, which is part of the state court system, extends over wills, the administration of estates, guardianship of minors and incompetents, conservatorships, trusts and money accounts held for minors.

Estate guardianship involves individuals who die without leaving a will (intestate) and those who do leave a will (testate). Minors' accounts refer to funds left to minors through gifts, inheritances or other means.

Sound like dull stuff? Some of it is, but don't write off these proceedings. Wills and inheritances have produced bitter family squabbles that have made news across the country—especially when a lot of money has been involved. Usually, the larger the will, bequest or inheritance, the better the story is.

But there can be twists in this scenario. It's also a story when a reputed millionaire dies and it's learned that he was penniless or when a small-town school teacher, who lived frugally, leaves $10 million to her favorite charity and $50 to her surviving sister.

In the matter of guardianships and conservatorships, probate judges may determine the need for and the qualifications of a guardian or conservator for a minor or someone mentally unfit to handle his affairs. Most of the time the probate process goes on smoothly, but occasionally there is family warfare over the choice. "An example of this kind of court battle occurred in the 1990s when, before her death in 1993, the late tobacco heiress Doris Duke made her butler, Bernard Lafferty, a substantial beneficiary. The family challenged the changes, and the eventual court settlement removed Lafferty from his position of trust.

Wills are filed with the county clerk and are public documents. However, don't bank on getting a detailed account of bequests made by reading the will. The wording of wills is commonly generalized with such terms as "all my property," "community property," "share and share alike" and "distribution of my estate."

If a will is not contested, the will itself is the story. Digging is required to discover the dollar amount of any bequests and specific properties. Sources include lawyers, family members, friends and anyone else who might be privy to the information. If a will is challenged in probate court, its details will likely be unfolded there. A tip: In seeking the nitty-gritty of a will, you should contact the relative who feels she didn't get her fair share. This probate case garnered a lot of media attention:

By Torri Minton

The value of Jerry Garcia's estate is less than the nearly $88 million in claims filed against the late Grateful Dead guitarist, probate lawyers said Monday.

"If all these claims were collected as filed, it would bankrupt the estate, I suspect," said Max Gutierrez, who is representing Garcia's widow, Deborah Koons Garcia.

Garcia, 58, died of heart failure last August while at a San Geronimo Valley drug treatment facility.

Gutierrez and other lawyers appearing in Marin County Superior Court Monday said that royalties from Garcia's music and from merchandise based on his artwork, among other things, could add substantially to the estate.

The two biggest claims against Garcia's estate are over the loss of anticipated profits from the sale of merchandise based on his art.

Garcia's personal manager, Vincent DiBiase, said he was supposed to take over management of the musician's art business. He claims in court documents that he will lose $15 million in profits on watches and jewelry that were to feature Garcia's designs.

Art agent Nora Sage of Bend, Ore., wants $12 million, saying Garcia's representatives are blocking her from selling scarves, suspenders, cummerbunds, vests and other items based on Garcia's art. Sage said in her claim that Garcia furnished her business, The Art Peddler, with about 180 works of art to sell and reproduce.

More than 20 claims were filed, including those by a former wife, a former girlfriend, and bank that holds a home mortgage.

The estate's executor will decide whether to accept or reject the claims. Anyone whose claim is rejected has three months to file a lawsuit.

Garcia's will left most of his estate to his wife, four daughters and his brother.

Last Thursday was the deadline for filing claims against Garcia's estate.

—*San Francisco Chronicle*

The old adage that names make news applies here, although a probate story without celebrities but with unusual elements still makes good copy. In the Garcia story, the focus on detail gives it an extra lift, as does the inherent conflict.

Suggested Assignments

1. Go to your local police station, introduce yourself and cover the story of an arrest and booking. A local reporter may help you get the story.
2. If there is a local criminal trial under way, get over to the courthouse and cover it for a day or at least for a morning or afternoon session.
3. Pick out a civil trial that looks interesting and cover it.
4. Interview the district attorney, private trial lawyers, public defenders, and judges on the court system in your area. Are the courts overloaded? Are there enough judges? Is the district attorney satisfied with police investigations? Write an analytical piece with an attention-getting lead—unless you uncover something strikingly wrong. Then shoot for a straight investigative story.
5. Arrange to visit the pressroom in the criminal courts building or county courthouse and discuss with beat reporters the demands of their job.
6. Do the same for the police beat.
7. Interview lawyers, judges, news people and perhaps past or current defendants on the issue of cameras in the courtroom, which some state and local judges allow while others do not. Cameras are not permitted in federal courts, a factor that should be in the article you will write on the basis of your research. Be sure that the piece has a clear focus and angle.

11

The Feature Story

Feature writing can be a creative outlet for reporters who feel constricted by the standard structure of the straight news story. And there never have been more opportunities for feature writing as newspapers strive to win readers with magazine-type journalism. Even hard news stories are often written in a narrative style with the human interest element uppermost. Going beyond the front page, papers in recent years have blossomed forth with revamped sections on life and style, travel, food, automobiles and entertainment. Even the business and real estate sections contain bright, readable stories plugged with human interest.

In most cases, getting that first newspaper job depends primarily on the applicant's skill at covering and writing nuts-and-bolts news about such subjects as the police, city hall, the courts and neighborhood doings. But the reporter with a deft touch for features will be even more valued. Successful careers have been built on the ability to write lively features laced with humor, human interest, color, drama, pathos and irony. Some well-known syndicated columnists first caught an editor's eye as reporters because of their skill at feature writing. They include Dave Barry, Ellen Goodman, Christopher Matthews, David Broder, Jimmy Breslin, and Georgie Anne Geyer.

The skilled writer bent on specializing in features can achieve this goal usually by first proving herself on general assignment, where opportunities to write this kind of story frequently occur.

What Is a Feature?

The feature story has undergone several changes in American newspapers. The various kinds of features are discussed in this chapter, but its basic component has remained pretty much the same: a combination of circumstances and individuals that put it outside the straight news story. The feature can focus on the funny side of life, the tragic, the strange, the ironic, the bizarre or the maudlin. It can entertain readers or fill them with joy, sadness and wonder. It can also explain and interpret in addition to helping readers with their money, homes or health. Sometimes, it can sort out the complexities of politics and world affairs in a way that a straight news story cannot. It can illuminate a reader's life. Above all, it contains human interest that reaches the reader where he lives. Human interest is at the core of all features. You are writing about what people think about, worry about, are curious about and talk about.

An important fact to remember is that the ingredients for a feature must be present before you can write it. If a school board holds a routine meeting on routine business, there probably aren't the makings of a feature. The same would be true of a standard speech or press conference. In these circumstances it's a waste of precious deadline time to wrack your brain trying to come up with an offbeat lead followed by scintillating prose. On the other hand, if that city council meeting is enlivened by an irate citizen hauling in a pail of garbage to highlight her protest about lax trash collection, the story could take a different turn. This would be a newsfeature, which is discussed later in more detail. In one community, a disgruntled citizen showed up at the county tax collector's office with $3,000 in pennies to pay off his delinquent tax bill.

The right stuff for many features usually is available when human beings are behaving in a way that departs from the norm, when fate deals a curious hand, when events don't happen the way they usually do. Other features need no special twist— profiles of people who lead interesting lives, situations in which an individual, family or community overcome great obstacles to achieve a goal, or a traditional event like Thanksgiving that takes on a new meaning for someone. Whatever the feature, it should hit a responsive nerve in the reader, causing him to be awestruck, repelled, angry, fascinated, stimulated, delighted, enlightened, encouraged or just plain impressed—by your presentation.

In today's worrisome world, newspapers are aware that not all features must make a point. They can just plain be fun to read, or cause one to take time to reflect on life.

In the following story about a small village in Ashland County, Ohio, the reporter does an effective job of weaving direct quotes from villagers into the rich, detailed description of small-town life. Note, too, how the reporter draws the reader into the story with the description of people gathering for a group picture, something nearly everyone has had experience with in their lifetimes. Another effective technique in longer stories such as these are subheads to help break up the gray of news type and keep the reader moving forward. By story's end, the reporter, through effective writing techniques and story organization, has helped explain how life in this small town, like thousands of others in America, is far from mundane to its residents.

By Jocelyn Allison

SAVANNAH—It's early evening and about 30 townspeople are gathered around a truck in the center of town carrying the county's bicentennial ball, ready to kick off a weekend of activities honoring the state's 200th birthday.

With big smiles, they crowd in for the camera, calling out to each other:

"Little guys down in front!"

"Come here and get in the picture."

"If you come, you've got to be in the picture."

The camera snaps and they disperse, onto the business of the evening—planting a Buckeye tree in Academy Park to commemorate Ohio's heritage. The closeness of the moment, however, persists throughout the evening as they move on to share a meal and, later, a laugh as they watch their neighbors tell jokes and sing songs in a variety show in the town hall.

The next day's lineup includes a pancake breakfast, craft show, car show, chicken barbecue and square dance. A community church service and "singspiration" finish out the weekend's events.

A few days later at a village council meeting, council members talk over the success of the bicentennial celebration, which was put on in conjunction with Bailey Lakes and Clear Creek Township Aug. 8-10.

"Town hall was just full Friday night," says longtime council member Dean Hunt. "It was a blast. People that missed it don't know what they missed."

Longtime council member Sarah McBride comments on the variety of activities for all ages, and talks about how the weekend brought back residents to the village who had moved away years ago.

"There was a lot of love flowing," she says later. "Everybody just came together and had a good time, young and old alike."

A village resident for 36 years, McBride said she and her late husband, Robert, moved to Savannah after living in Elyria because they missed the small-town atmosphere this quaint community in the northern part of Ashland County provides.

"You can't explain what life in a small town is like in words," she says.

Getting involved
A sense of civic duty and desire to volunteer have kept McBride—and many others—active in the village for years.

The community spirit of the village was put to use in recent years to build a new fire station for the Savannah Volunteer Fire Company. Completed in December 1999, the entire brick and steel structure was built from the ground up with the handiwork of volunteers, and was funded through loans from dozens of people in the community.

"That was a real community project," said fire chief Jim Dinsmore.

Residents had come together a few years earlier in 1993 to build the bandstand/gazebo at the park. Some pounded nails, while others did their part by providing meals for the volunteers, McBride said. "We were even out there one time when it was snowing, eating a hot potluck meal," said McBride. "It just made people feel good."

With the fire company, Savannah Lions Club, Clear Creek Historical Society, Village Council and three churches in town, there is no shortage of volunteer opportunities in the village, McBride said.

But, according to McBride and others, there may be a shortage soon of volunteers.

"The younger generation doesn't seem to have that desire," said McBride. "Very few of them are interested in the organizations."

Dinsmore said it's sometimes hard to get people who didn't grow up in the village involved in the community.

"They don't have a good idea of how small communities work," he said. "They just kind of stay to themselves, like they did in a big city."

Nevertheless, Dinsmore said he feels much of the town's appeal lies in the fact it still is very much a grassroots community.

"It feels good to go up and talk to these young kids and know who their parents are," he said. "They have an interest in the community, too."

Young people are around in greater numbers these days, according to Dinsmore and other longtime residents. Youngsters can be seen riding their bikes yards from the lumbering tractor-trailers that frequently pass through town at most times of the day and evening.

Children play ball and swing at Academy Park late into the evening, sometimes to the dismay of nearby residents who are disturbed by the noise as late as 11:15 p.m.—causing Village Council to change park hours to 9 p.m. recently.

But, Mayor Tom Kruse said, the park is a "blessing" to the village and adds life to a downtown that is devoid of the businesses that once lined its main thoroughfare.

Linda's Country Cooking across the street from the park also serves as a meeting place, Kruse said, as does the post office catty-corner from the restaurant and the ball fields off Ohio 545.

According to part-time employee Pat Osborne, the post office is a social hub for many longtime residents who come there not only for their mail, but to hear what's new in each others' lives and around town.

"Sometimes they'll stand out there and talk for an hour," she said.

Maintaining the village

Upkeep of the park is a prime topic of conversation at many Village Council meetings, as is recent progress on the installation of a boardwalk at the lagoon and an upcoming housing development in the area of Hickey Street.

A huge step in the progress of the village, according to Kruse, was getting the village hooked up to water and sewer. According to Liston, who is on the water board, the village switched from drilled wells to become part of the Rural Lorain Water Authority in October 1980. By January 1987, the village had its sewer system hooked up.

Besides dealing with infrastructure concerns, most of council members' time is occupied addressing the everyday problems of the village—barking dogs, junk vehicles, property line disputes, children causing trouble, unkempt yards and abandoned homes.

The mayor serves as a sounding board for many of those concerns, usually coming to council meetings with a laundry list of residents' complaints.

"He wears many hats," McBride said of Kruse, who is a resource conservation teacher at the Career Center. "He runs the village and also has to be the cop and the mediator."

One recurring hassle for the village is the traffic on its major thoroughfare, U.S. 250. Village Council pays off-duty Sheriff's deputies to patrol the area in an effort to slow the steady stream of tractor-trailers and summer vacationers heading north.

Council president Gary Liston said traffic along the route has increased considerably from when he was growing up in town.

"It used to be nice and quiet and peaceful," he said. "Now there's about three times the truck traffic."

While much of the traffic is just passers-through now, Savannah was at one time a thriving town, a center of commerce for the northern part of the county, according to many residents.

"It was the center of the universe up there at one time," said Kruse. "You name it, they had it."

A rich history

Originally part of Richland County, Kruse said, Savannah had hoped to be named the county seat when boundaries for a new county were drawn. The proposal was sent to the state legislature three times, but in 1846 Ashland was chosen instead, he said.

"Savannah was known as an education town much as Ashland is known for the university now," he said.

Founded in 1856 at a time when there were no public schools in Ohio, the academy thrived in the center of town until its closure in 1917. Savannah High School opened a year later, and Savannah students eventually were consolidated into the Crestview school district.

Remnants of the village's rich history are visible throughout the town, and preservation of the past is important to many of the town's residents.

A well-known book "Old Keys" by Rae Bailey outlines the history of the village and surrounding Clear Creek Township in great detail, and is considered the authority on the area's roots. The book, however, is hard to come by these days, according to Liston, who paid $65 for his copy.

"Now you can't touch them for less than $150," said Liston, "if they know what they have."

It seems as though many of the residents of Savannah—especially the longtime ones—do know what they have.

As McBride said: "I wouldn't change this small-town living for any metropolitan area."

—*Ashland* (Ohio) *Times-Gazette*

The above story illustrates many of the characteristics of the feature in terms of its lead and style, which is maintained throughout the article. In writing features, the inverted pyramid format so familiar in the news story can be tossed out the window, along with a formal presentation of facts. The facts, however, must remain. Feature writing is not fiction despite the wide latitude that can be taken in approaching it.

In other words, a feature need not pack the five W's—who, what, when, where and why—into the lead. Many feature leads can be in a narrative or story-telling vein. They can be amusing, shocking, anecdotal or interrogatory. There is no single way to handle a feature as long as it's written in acceptable, grammatical English. The point is to make it interesting.

The narrative lead could take this teaser form:

> Harold Pines made his usual weekly trip to the unemployment office yesterday to collect his usual unemployment check.

Or this one:

> The sight of a ballpoint pen sends shudders through the staff of the Huntington Library's new conservation center.

The first lead could usher in a feature about a man who, because of a computer error, is given a check for $1.6 million instead of the $260 amount he normally receives.

The second lead was used for a story by the author about the techniques used to preserve rare books and documents in one of the nation's famous private libraries. Ballpoint pens are not normally permitted in the archives because the ink may smear valuable documents, staff persons said in the course of an interview. The pen angle was picked for the lead, but there were several other things that came out in researching the story that could just as well have served as the lead. Feature writing allows you a variety of choices. This is the way the full story emerged:

By M.L. Stein

The sight of a ballpoint pen sends shudders through the staff of the Huntington Library's new conservation center.

"You're one of the very few people we've allowed in here with a ballpoint," assistant administrator Christy Hedges told a recent visitor.

Her nervousness was understandable. On a work table at her elbow was Henry Thoreau's original manuscript of "The Maine Woods," including unpublished material. Nearby was a bound copy of Susan B. Anthony's first speech for women's suffrage in 1854 (later, as she gained poise at the lectern, she abandoned notes and spoke extemporaneously).

On another table a few feet away, conservation technician Ronald Tank was delicately finishing a repair job on a 1589 document attached to the Great Seal of Queen Elizabeth I.

Priceless, all of them, according to Hedges.

"Ballpoint smears," she explained. "Also, we wash some parchments in water. If ballpoint ink accidentally got on one, it would run during the washing."

Preserving rare manuscripts, books, prints, photographs and maps are routine tasks at the recently completed $750,000 conservation wing of the library building.

The center is named after R. Stanton Avery, who provided the construction money. The Andrew Mellon Foundation pledged $450,000 for support activities, including a training program in the most advanced conservation practices, and the U.S. Department of Education kicked in $648,051 for equipment and supplies.

"We expect to become one of the leading conservation centers in the world," said Suzanne W. Hull, director of Huntington's administration and public service.

The endowments are appreciated but Huntington officials are quick to point out that preserving historical treasures has been going on there since the institution was founded in 1919. Last year alone, according to head librarian Daniel Woodward, more than 20,000 fragile manuscripts dating from the 10th century were conserved or repaired and thousands of photographic prints and negatives placed in protective containers.

Among the priceless materials saved were Benjamin Franklin's "Autobiography" in his own handwriting, a letter written by George

Washington, a Gutenberg Bible and irreplaceable early photos of the American West.

For the 12-person staff, conservation is a process involving both techniques used for years at the Huntington and inventive ideas developed on the spot to deal with a particular problem.

A recent example was the first Queen Elizabeth's wooden seal, which arrived at the library split into two parts. Tank, a Huntington conservator for 30 years, drilled three tiny holes into the pieces, slipped steel pins into them, poured hot wax into the holes and then held the parts together by hand until the wax hardened.

The seal, which bears an excellent carved likeness of her majesty, reveals no trace of repair on one side and only a slight discoloration on the other.

Tank noted, however, that ancient paper, particularly vellum, provides the staff's toughest challenge.

"Vellum usually comes in too fragile to preserve in its present state," Tank explained. "We can't work it or use the heat so we usually back it with Japanese tissue and flour-and-water paste."

The paper preservation workshop, which handles about 8,000 documents a year, also contains a specially designed table for gently stretching vellum that has been folded for years in tight creases. There is also an icebox-like chamber, designed by Tank, for killing mold in old books by means of chemicals and a hot lamp.

Tank, a soft-spoken man who comes to work in a jacket and tie, emphasized that every procedure must be reversible so conservators 50 to 150 years from now can patch up any damage or wear. These future experts, Tank predicted, will probably have a more difficult job with paper preservation, especially the late-19th–20th century variety.

"There are fewer problems with old paper than the modern kind," he explained. "For one thing, they didn't use ballpoint pens in the 15th and 16th centuries and the paper was rag instead of today's wood pulp, which is not as strong."

The chief current task for Tank and his assistant, Carol Verheyen, a recent UC Santa Cruz art graduate, is the salvaging of a remarkable collection of 350,000 items from the Stowe family that lived in England from 1570 to 1883. The papers detail everyday living as evidenced by bills, diaries, love letters, wills, recipes, contracted dowries and marriages, ledgers and correspondence baring conflicts between parents and children.

"The Gutenberg Bible is one of our showcases, which thousands come to see, but it has no research value," Woodward said. "But the Stowe papers are a gold mine for scholars."

More than 1,400 scholars from throughout the world come annually to use the research resources at the Huntington Library.

Many of them pore through books refurbished in the conservation center's bindery run by Rudolph Acosta, a 10-year Huntington veteran who handles the volumes as if they were precious stones.

Probably More Valuable

Most of the books he and his staff handle are probably more valuable than gems. A visitor found Acosta, a slight, shy man, gently turning over a 4-by-6-inch bound manuscript of Charlotte Brontë's poem, "We Wove a Web in Childhood."

"This is a hard one to fix," he said. "It's so small."

Another miniature book on his table was a copy of the Magna Charta in Latin. Beside it rested a normal-size volume of Thomas Brooks' "Precious Remedies Against Satan's Devices or Salve for Believers and Unbelievers Sores" published in 1656. Both needed mending.

The objective with any book, said Acosta, is to preserve the original binding, rather than replace it.

If the binding is missing or too deteriorated, rebinding is done in the style of the original, Acosta said. Boxes or slipcases are made for books whose bindings are of historical interest.

Acosta's assistant, Leonid Gurvits, who came here from Russia 2 1/2 years ago, is amazed at the lavish use of leather binding in the United States.

"In Russia, leather-bound books are made only for special foreign visitors as gifts," said Gurvits, who worked in a bindery at the University of Kiev and descends from a long line of bookbinders.

The Huntington sends out a few books to commercial bookbinders but Acosta makes it clear they are very carefully selected.

"Ninety percent of the binderies do a bad job," he said. "An awful lot of damage can be done by using the wrong glue, wrong sewing and wrong leaf repair. Most binderies use plastic glue instead of animal glue and it won't last."

Work Can Be Undone

Like Tank, Acosta fixes rare books so the work can be undone by future binders.

In some cases, he said, he is able to save the original spine and reapply it to a newly bound book.

Hedges, who had been listening to Acosta, said, "Actually, not all of our preservation work is as dramatic as you find in the paper conservation room and bindery. Much of our preservation depends on keeping the library temperature at 65 degrees and storing paper in acid-free folders. We want scholars working here to be warm and content but if it becomes a question of warm scholars or damaged books, I'm afraid the scholars will have to endure a little discomfort."

Other environmental controls, she said, include anti-insect fumigation of books, monitoring ultraviolet light, which can fade and embrittle items, and maintaining humidity at 50%.

In addition, researchers are forbidden to bring in inks, food, metal paper clips or anything else that might harm materials.

The rules also apply to the center's photo department, headed by Bob Schlosser, a former theatrical photographer whose job at the Huntington involves historical sleuthing.

With a 2 1/2-hour exposure, using X-ray photography, ancient paper can be dated by the film revealing the maker's distinctive logo—in one case it was a hand topped by a star. Thus, he explained, scholars can determine the approximate date of a document by matching it to the paper maker's time.

Schlosser and his staff also examine paintings with an infrared viewer, producing some interesting results.

"Did you know," he asked, "that Gainsborough had started another portrait under 'Blue Boy' (one of the Huntington Art Gallery's most prized possessions)? We discovered a head and shoulders under the picture. The man apparently just used the same canvass for 'Blue Boy.'"

The Huntington's photo library, which is housed in the new wing, contains 180,000 prints and negatives, mostly of California and the West. A recent acquisition is dozens of copies of pictures taken by Jack London. Most are home shots but London, photo librarian Brita Mack said, worked as a photographer as well as a reporter covering the Russian-Japanese War in 1904.

The photo library includes a large number of glass negative plates. To avoid the possibility of breakage, staffers are making work prints and film negatives from the plates. Another conservation measure is identifying nitrate negatives, which are flammable, and properly storing or copying them.

Among the photographers represented in the collection are Edward Curtis, C.E. Watkins and Edward Weston.

Trained Volunteers

The professional conservation staff at the Huntington is assisted by 15 to 20 volunteers, who have been trained in rebacking cloth and leather books, repairing various materials and doing minor paper restoration. One of their current projects is fixing up old Polk city directories which, according to Hedges, are frequently sought by scholars investigating early 20th-century America.

"The volunteers love the work," Hedges continues. "Since we are a small staff, they are a big help."

Her praise was echoed by her boss, Woodward, who added: "We try to keep up with what's going on but there is lots of work here. We could use 200 people."

It's unlikely he is exaggerating. The Huntington Library, a private, nonprofit institution, holds 51/2 million manuscripts, 320,500 rare books and 239,000 reference volumes concentrated in British and American history and literature.

But Woodward noted the conservation staff keeps up to date on preservation techniques by traveling to libraries throughout the world and studying their methods. Tank, for example, has visited a number of libraries in England and Italy to exchange ideas.

Nevertheless, Woodward said, the Huntington takes a cautious approach to any new restoration technology, no matter where it originates.

"It's easy to err in this work," he said. "New processes aren't always the best. Once Scotch tape was considered the greatest thing to come along in preservation work. It was used by the National Archives until it was learned that it turns yellow and leaves stains on paper. It also deteriorates. We must always guard against any process that may be irreversible."

That's why, he pointed out, old-fashioned animal hide glue and flour-and-water paste are still the favored adhesives at the Huntington Center.

—Los Angeles Times

The story sought to bring out that vast, important institutions like the Huntington Library are, in the last analysis, staffed by men and women who take pride in their work. The same treatment could be applied to the telephone company or a major hospital. The more human interest you can inject into a feature, the more readable it will be. The best story is one that unfolds without evident strain—that tells itself. The use of a lot of adjectives and artificial hoopla has never enhanced a feature story.

The more features you write, the more polished you will become with them. Although, as said, you can't make up events or people in a feature, reading fiction helps by giving you a sense of style and use of narrative, which is simply a story-telling technique. You probably first became acquainted with it in kindergarten during the story hour.

Features that tug at people's emotions without being maudlin are popular newspaper fare. This one is typical.

By Jarred Opatz

Jerry Seiter, Ashland YMCA director, has kind of taken a special interest in one of the Y's preschool kids—4-year-old Brandon Deibler.

That's because Brandon has hypoplastic left heart syndrome, a condition Seiter's son, Ben, had.

Since his son's 1994 death at 6 years old, Seiter said technology in treating the rare condition really has progressed and patients with it are living longer.

"He's healthier than Ben was at his age," Seiter said about Brandon. "He's doing extremely well.

"For the most part, he's healthy and able to come to school and be with other kids and have fun," added Seiter, who said if you didn't know Brandon had the condition, you never could tell from watching him at the Y's preschool.

This fall, Brandon is scheduled for the third of three surgeries he needs to treat hypoplastic left heart syndrome, where the left side of the heart—including the aorta, aortic valve, left ventricle and mitral valve—is underdeveloped at birth.

"My heart is broken," is the way Brandon describes it. That's the way his doctors and parents—Tod and Melanie Deibler—have explained it to him.

His grandmother, Carol Deibler, will be having a fund-raiser for him at the Osborn Elementary Craft show April 16 where 40 percent of her Tupperware sales will go to her grandson.

The condition is fatal unless treated days after birth with the first of three surgeries or with a transplant. When he was 11 days old, Brandon had his first surgery. At 8 months old, he had his second. The third needs to be done between 2 and 5 years old. Like the first two, the third will be at the Cleveland Clinic.

According to the Pediheart Organization Web site, patients who get through all three stages, which about 70 percent do, rarely have to be on medications, almost always enjoy normal growth and development and hardly have any trouble with exercise or other limitations.

When his son had the surgeries, Seiter said they were experimental.

"I feel like Ben was a forerunner who has helped kids like Brandon do better," Seiter said.

Brandon has had few problems throughout his ordeal.

Other than getting tired sooner and bruising easier than most kids when he's running around, playing with his 7-year-old brother, Evan, at their rural Ashland home or doing gymnastics at the Y, Brandon pretty much has developed like other kids his age.

However, playing contact sports is unlikely for him.

Being in the hospital for many months after his first two surgeries delayed some things for Brandon, such as walking and talking.

"He only started talking about a year and a half ago," his mother said. Then with a laugh, she added: "Once he started, he never stopped. He had a lot of things bottled up."

Besides being talkative, Brandon also loves working with letters and numbers, his mother added. He likes to spell words with his magnetic letters, page through calendars and memorize license plate numbers.

His favorite month and number?

"Sept. 15," he says without hesitation—his birthday.

She even printed up pages of all the months so she could make him his own calendar for his room where he can cross out each day. He also has curtains with each state's license plate design on it, as well as some real license plates in his room, which also is filled with posters and other things of two of his favorite TV characters—Bob the Builder and Elmo.

"He's such a smart little boy," Seiter said. "One day he was on my lap reading a book to the other kids in his preschool and he was putting the kids' names in his class in place of the names in the book."

Many of the same tendencies Brandon has, his son had, Seiter said. He also said Brandon is very relational like Ben was, making new friends with pretty much everyone he meets with a friendly, outgoing personality.

"I tend to think that's because of the long stays at the hospital dealing with doctors and nurses a lot," Seiter said.

After the upcoming surgery, Brandon will be in the hospital a minimum of two weeks, his parents said.

While his mother said many of their medical bills for Brandon are paid by the Bureau for Children with Medical Handicaps, their expenses add up with traveling and staying in Cleveland for not only Brandon's operations, but also his many doctor visits there.

People and local businesses have helped them in the past with those things as well as with clothes and toys for their two boys which the parents have been very appreciative of, especially the first hectic year with the two heart surgeries, Melanie said.

Seiter and his wife, Sue, who have three grown daughters, have talked to Brandon's parents, as well as other parents over the years, about raising a child with hypoplastic left heart syndrome, which he added is a condition that affects about only one in every 300,000 newborns.

"The Cleveland Clinic still calls us and asks us to talk to parents," Seiter said. "I've told Brandon's mom they have come a long way. They didn't know much in 1987 when Ben was born. They understand better what's going on now."

Getting to know Brandon has brought back a lot of the good memories he and his family had with Ben, Seiter said.

"I'm just so thankful Brandon's doing so well," Seiter said.

—Ashland (Ohio) *Times-Gazette*

Now let's examine the types of feature stories more fully.

The News Feature

The news feature is now a staple of most American newspapers for two principal reasons: to provide readers with a greater mix of stories and writing style and to explain more fully the workings of an increasingly complex society. You might call it a news story with trimmings. The news feature concerns itself with current events but is given a different treatment. An auto accident can be written as a routine occurrence, but a next-day story may delve into the sorrow of a family of one of the victims—perhaps a promising musician, who was killed at 21 by a hit-and-run motorist.

News features make the paper more interesting while giving reporters the opportunity to impress editors with their writing and information-gathering skills. Try these guidelines for writing a news feature:

- In the news-gathering process, look for elements that take the story out of the cut-and-dried. Sometimes the elements will be staring you in the face, sometimes not.
- Ask questions about what you don't see on the surface.
- Use quotes that have impact.
- If the proper ingredients are there, put your literary skills to work to make the story absorbing as well as informational.
- Don't overwrite. If your story can be told effectively in 20 paragraphs, don't bloat it to 50. Padding shows, and editors can spot it.
- Don't forget humor if there is a funny angle.

It also helps if you thoroughly read your own paper and others on a regular basis. Newsmagazines such as *Time, Newsweek* and *U.S. News & World Report* supply further background, as will books on current issues and modern history. Being well-informed enables you to grasp the significance of a story more quickly. A knowledge of the development and treatments of AIDS, for instance, is virtually a must in order to write an intelligent piece about this dreaded disease in connection with a move to establish an AIDS hospice in your community.

Notice how this story turns what could have been written as a standard disaster story into one that gives a deeper understanding of the tragedy.

By Krishnan Guruswamy

DABWALI, India—The party started at 11 a.m., and what a party it was.

Some 1,000 people gathered under the corrugated metal roof with plywood-and-polyester walls, sitting on steel chairs with plastic seats. Tea was served in ceramic cups and saucers and children sang patriotic songs in Hindi.

It was the annual cultural show of the Dayanand Arya Vedic school, a middle-class private school where children of the region's richer farmers and its poorer functionaries mingled.

Like most schools in India, Dayanand Arya Vedic puts on a year-end party to celebrate its students' creativity. Everyone who was anyone in Dabwali, a farming town of 50,000 in a northwest region known as the granary of India, had been invited to Saturday's show.

One of them was Jaimani Goel, the editor of a local weekly newspaper. He got there about noon and was greeted by the school's principal.

Goel was ushered to the second row and began chatting with friends. Around him, parents cheered their sons and daughters as they sang, danced and acted on stage.

Just before 2 p.m., principal Preeti Kamra finished her speech, listing the school's achievements during 1995. There was loud applause.

Then a young boy appeared on the stage to announce the next act, a song-and-dance by a group of children. Members of the audience sipped their tea and sat back for the show.

It never happened.

"I heard this huge commotion about 25 rows behind me," Goel said in an interview at his home Sunday.

In the middle of that commotion sat Suman Devi. Her five-year-old son, Deepak, was part of the next act, and she was waiting for him to come on.

"I saw flames leaping from the exit about 10 feet away," said Devi, 30.

That doorway was the only one. The 30-yard-by-30-yard structure, normally used for weddings, has no walls. But school officials had spruced it up, erecting plywood sides and draping them with polyester sheets.

Hundreds of children, parents, teachers and officials stood up and tried to push their way toward the door.

"Fire! Fire! Run! Run!" they screamed.

Everything was on fire—the plywood walls, the white-and-pink polyester sheets that covered them, people's clothes, the chairs, even the tin from the roof was melting and falling in hot drops.

Initial reports said the fire was started by a short circuit in the lighting system.

"I was propelled toward the exit and I fell outside," said Goel, whose acrylic suit melted and stuck to his body. He suffered minor burns.

Of the hundreds who didn't make it through the door, most were women and children who could not push their way through the surging crowd.

Many were crushed and asphyxiated in the stampede. Others burned to death when their clothes caught fire or flaming debris fell on them.

Outside the structure, there was another crush—this time for the opening in the 10-foot brick wall that surrounded the tent.

There were only two openings in the wall—one was locked and the other, to the right after exiting the tent, was too small to accommodate the crowds.

Those who made it through fled into the surrounding streets and fields. Those who couldn't tried to smash through the wall with pickaxes and iron rods to open more escape routes.

By 2:05 p.m., when the first fire truck arrived, almost 300 people were dead and 100 more were fatally injured. Some 250 others had severe burns. Officials said Sunday they expected the death toll to climb.

Devi, whose little Deepak had been waiting backstage for his big performance, went back to look for him. She saw the scorched masses of human flesh. She saw the charred bones. But she didn't see Deepak.

"I have been searching for him all night and morning," she said Sunday. "All I can do is to pray to God to restore little Deepak to me."

—Associated Press

Note also how the writer used quotes and detail to bring the story closer to American readers, most of whom are familiar with school pageants involving parents, children and school officials.

Features That Explain

A feature need not be hooked to a breaking story like the India fire. It can explain and interpret an ongoing process affecting people's lives. A long-stalled road-building project might call for an article that explains the holdup—or foul-up. A prolonged budget battle in Congress or the state legislature would be made clearer by a story that examines the issues and personalities that account for the deadlock. A plan to convert local schools to a 12-month schedule cries out for background on the necessity for the change. Many of these stories can be produced free of the deadline pressure that hangs over a straight news story.

Subjects such as health, business, entertainment, welfare, homelessness, missing children and religion also lend themselves to explanatory features. *Time* published an excellent feature concerning the efforts to legalize marijuana and those who oppose the idea. The in-depth story explored the issue from various angles: political, medical and law enforcement. A reader, who had only a hazy idea of the question, would be greatly enlightened.

Here is a feature that touches on an important health matter for women.

By Beth Francis

Toni Harris knows the truth as she trembles with sobs.

Her dangling silver earrings brush against her shoulder-length dark hair as her shaky hand reaches up with a tissue to wipe away her tears.

The 37-year-old Fort Meyers woman knows she waited too long to get her Pap smear.

She made excuses for more than eight years not to go—too busy, too young to really have a problem, too turned off by the idea of the embarrassing and uncomfortable exam.

"I figured as long as I didn't catch any diseases and I kept myself clean, I was O.K.," she says. "That's how a lot of women I know feel."

Harris even put off going to the doctor last year when she began bleeding heavily after intercourse. After more than four months of this, she finally went to see Fort Myers gynecologist Debra Skinner.

When Skinner spread open Harris' vagina with a speculum and looked at the small-framed woman's cervix, she was horrified.

Cancer was everywhere.

What women don't know about Pap smears can hurt them.

Despite the promise of the Pap test to prevent cervical cancer from ever forming by detecting it before it happens, 13,500 women got cervical cancer in the United States last year and 4,400 died of it.

One of the reasons Harris didn't go for the tests was because she never understood how important they were. She thought Pap smears were used to find infections or venereal diseases. She never realized that the main reason for yearly Pap smears was to detect early changes in cells that might indicate pre-cancer. When pre-cancer is found, the cervix can be treated before cancer develops and before a woman's life is at stake.

"When I was growing up all this stuff was kept in the closet," she says. "My mother is Roman Catholic and she didn't talk about these things."

Lee County obstetrician/gynecologist Lawrence Antonucci shakes his head when he hears about cases like Harris'. Theoretically, cervical cancer should never happen, he says. The disease is thought to be completely preventable if every woman had regular Pap smears. "The Pap smear is the single most important preventive care measure developed for women in the last 40 years," he says. "It has saved countless numbers of lives."

The Papanicolaou test was developed in the early 1940s by George Papanicolaou.

Since then, the death rate for cancer of the cervix and uterus has decreased by more than 70 percent, according to the American Cancer Society.

But cervical cancer is on the rise—especially in younger women—largely because of the emerging epidemic of human papillomavirus infection in the United States. Certain strains of HPV—also known as genital warts—are culprits in causing cervical cancer, Antonucci says. Women can protect themselves, though. The main thing is to go for Pap smears and know the steps to take to get the most accurate result possible.

"I know it's not something women exactly look forward to," says Lee County obstetrician/gynecologist Marilyn Young. "But there are a lot of things in life you do that you don't particularly like doing.

"The problem is, women put their health last," she says. "The children are first and the husband is next—if he'll cooperate. And if finances are low, the woman is even less likely to get care."

Sounds familiar to Debbie Walker. The 40-year-old Fort Myers health care worker understands the barriers women face when getting Pap smears.

"I made all kinds of excuses—I don't have time, I don't have the money. Then, all of a sudden, I was afraid."

Walker got scared when she found out her younger sister had cervical cancer.

"I was shaking. Something just told me I needed to go. I knew I had waited too long."

She was right.

A few days after she went in to be examined, her doctor, Young, called to say her Pap smear was abnormal. A sample of Walker's cervical tissue showed she had a serious case of pre-cancer, so Young performed a cone biopsy, in which one cone-shaped piece is cut out of the woman's cervix in hopes of removing all of the cancer.

But another Pap smear three months later still was abnormal, so Walker ended up having a hysterectomy. She was lucky the cancer hadn't spread beyond her female organs.

"If I had waited much longer the result could have been devastating," she says.

No guarantees.

But there are times when even regular Pap smears and pelvic examinations aren't enough. A woman can be betrayed by her Pap smear, even though new laws are making that less likely.

The test is only about 85 percent accurate. Sometimes the sample of cells collected by the doctor isn't adequate. Other times, cell changes are missed by the technician reading the smear.

Complicating that, doctors are beginning to believe some cancers are simply faster-growing than originally thought. Even if a woman's Pap smear is performed and read correctly every year, there is a chance she could develop the cancer between tests.

Marilyn Pye knows that all too well. The 32-year-old Lee County native has gone for annual Pap smears since she was 17. And they always were normal.

Three years ago, though, her phone rang surprising her with the news that her Pap smear was abnormal. Still, she didn't worry. She thought it was a fluke.

She went in for the procedure gynecologists perform to make a definite diagnosis, called colposcopy. Colposcopy involves putting a solution on the cervix that exposes suspicious cells as white patches. Pye's gynecologist, Philip Waterman, opened her vagina with a speculum and viewed her cervix with a special microscope called a colposcope. Tissue biopsies were taken from suspicious areas for examination in a laboratory.

The next time the phone rang, Pye—a teacher's aide at Suncoast Elementary School in North Fort Myers and the mother of two girls—got the news she had the most severe stage of pre-cancer.

"When you hear the big 'C' word, all of a sudden, you find yourself scared half to death," she says. Waterman performed a vaginal hysterectomy on Pye. Having her organs removed through her vagina meant she didn't have a scar on her abdomen and her recovery was quicker.

"Dr. Waterman said he didn't think the Paps had missed the cancer before; he just thought this was a fast-growing cancer," she says. "I'm just glad we caught it before it spread any farther."

Theoretically, cervical cancers can take up to 10 years to progress from the earliest cellular changes to a fully developed case of cancer, says Fort Myers pathologist Mary Blue. That's why yearly Pap tests are so important, she says. Because the Pap test isn't 100 percent effective, if it misses pre-cancerous changes one year, chances are it will pick them up the next.

— *Fort Myers* (Fla.) *News-Press*

Francis' article gains much through her interviews with cancer victims. They provide gripping human interest along with the plain-spoken messages from the doctors on prevention. Finding interview subjects for a story like this is not always easy, given its nature. It can be done, however. Probably the author got leads on some individuals from friends or friends of friends. Because of the sanctity of the doctor-patient relationship, a doctor will not automatically give you the names of her patients, but she might take your name and phone number and give them to a particular patient, who may agree to be interviewed if she realizes, as in this case, that an account of her experience would be a public service. The same technique can work for many stories involving hard-to-get interviews. Be politely persistent until the names come forth. "Working the phone" can be a drawn-out chore but it's a necessary one.

Sidebars

Often feature stories are handled as "sidebars" to the main story, feature or not. The sidebar can run on Page One or the "jump" page, where the story continues inside. The sidebar saves the writer the problem of trying to cram everything into one story and running the risk of losing continuity — along with the reader's attention. The sidebar is shorter than the primary story and usually focuses on one aspect of it. A major news or feature article can have as many as 10 or 15 sidebars. Sometimes the sidebar is simply statistical or biographical. The previous piece on the India fire, for example, included a sidebar on demographic and geographic data for the country. The above-mentioned *Time* story on marijuana included a long sidebar on the physical effects of the drug, confirming some general beliefs and dismissing or diluting others on the basis of research findings.

A full-blown news story on, say, the Middle East or Afghanistan is likely to carry with it one or more sidebars with a human interest base. Perhaps a village is singled out for an in-depth look at how its people look at high-level negotiations that will determine their fate and that of their children. A *Los Angeles Times* sidebar on the movement of U.S. troops in Afghanistan dealt with some Special Forces soldiers dressing as natives to blend in with the populace while guarding Afghan officials. The Army later halted the practice.

The Short Feature

Many editors like a short feature, sometimes called a "brevity," to brighten a page. Short means short and that's not as easy as you might think. There's an old newspaper story of a reporter who tells his editor he will write a long story about an event because there isn't time to write a short one. He meant that it's sometimes tougher to write a four- or five-paragraph story that amuses, delights, or stuns the reader than it would be to string the material out for 25 or 30 paragraphs.

The short feature is usually in a light vein, like this one:

> Township officials in Franklin, N.J., said Tuesday they will hire their own psychiatrist to refute the claims of a policeman who said he wasn't napping on the job—just lulled into a trance by passing traffic.
>
> "Maybe we should just call this the zombie factor," said Township Administrator John Lovell, who described Patrolman Robert Lenart's alibi as "preposterous" and "almost comical." Lenart, 29, was suspended without pay for four months after the council found him guilty of sleeping on duty.
>
> Lenart denied he was asleep. His lawyer, Robert Blackman, said he planned to present testimony by psychiatrist Seymour Kuvin, a noted expert on "highway hypnosis."

Or this one:

> More than a month after Valentine's Day, Loretta Grady's room is filled with the sound of "Let Me Call You Sweetheart," and she's getting showered with attention.
>
> But the 89-year-old convalescent-home resident of West Hartford, Conn., is not being wooed by an admirer. It's a battery-operated greeting card that fell behind a dresser in the wall on Feb. 15. Grady doesn't mind the incessant, tinkling tune—she is slightly deaf—and so, fortunately, is Edna York, Grady's 81-year-old roommate at St. Mary's Home. But the nurses can hear it. So can Grady and York's relatives.
>
> "They have taken the drawers out and done everything that is reasonable to see if they can find it. But none of them has had any success," Grady said. Her niece, Joan Pilz, bought the card for $1.89 and is amused that its battery has long outlived its 48-hour guarantee. Grady said it's "fortunate I can't hear it. I like the song, but I think it would get on my nerves if I listened to it all the time."

The brief feature can come from the police blotter, the courthouse, a Salvation Army Santa Claus or class registration week. Often the idea is to look for the quirky element that immediately suggests a short, funny or offbeat piece. Keep your sentences and paragraphs short, too.

Developing Features

Not all stories have to come from standard sources. The aggressive, innovative reporter develops her own stories. Beneath routine city hall, school, police or legislative activities is a bonanza of untapped material needing only two things to bring them out: an unfettered mind and solid digging.

Much news is served up to newspapers via press releases (handouts) or is picked up on beats through tips, scheduled interviews and regular meetings of official bodies like the city council or school board. But newspapers from time to time will offer readers a news feature based on a reporter's or editor's idea. The *Orange County Register* once ran a full-page feature on whales, dolphins and sea lions, pegged on the fact that it was the whale-watching season in California. Probably, someone on the *Register* wondered out loud how much readers knew about the big mammals and suggested a story to fill them in on their size, habits and where best they can be located. The piece was lavishly illustrated with pictures and drawings and contained a sidebar on where to buy whale-watching tickets, how to reach an "InfoLine" to listen to killer whales and a whale-sighting hotline. Of course, the fact that Orange County has a long stretch of coastline added to reader interest. *The New York Post,* a tabloid whose main content is hard news, carried a light feature on a reporter's trek through the city's theme restaurants such as the Hard Rock Cafe to check out their merchandise. Again, somebody had an inspiration.

If you have an idea for an off-the-beaten-track feature, don't hesitate to spring it on an editor. Better yet, submit three or four ideas on the chance that he'll like at least one of them. To our knowledge, no one ever got fired on a newspaper for enterprise. On the contrary, such aggressiveness has led to raises, bonuses and promotions.

Personality Profile

The personality profile reaches into almost every section of the newspaper. We can read profiles about figures in entertainment, sports, business, politics, education, diplomacy and law enforcement. These articles tap what is believed to be a deep reader interest in the people making news. The zooming popularity of magazines like *People, Parade* and *Vanity Fair* make this apparent.

It's not enough that prominent persons are reported on in their fields of endeavor. The public also is hungry for information on how and where they live, work and play and what they think about their jobs, relationships and perhaps the general state of society. There is a curiosity about their marriages, divorces, breakups, clothes and food preferences and almost anything else surrounding their lives. When home-stylist Martha Stewart was being investigated for alleged insider trading, the media blossomed forth with several sidebar features on her background and lifestyle and whether the probe was affecting sales of her products. It wasn't, but the stock in her company had dropped in price.

The skilled writer weaves a word picture (accompanied by a real one) to make the person come alive. A well-written profile puts the reader as close to the subject as the reporter has been.

Most personality profiles hang on a news peg. An actress shines in a new TV series, a dark horse political candidate suddenly captures the voters' attention, a businessman saves a company from bankruptcy through his brilliant wheeling and dealing, a new presidential appointee becomes a media darling. All graduate to instant newsmakers, and the public wants to know more about them. When hard-driving Lee Iacocca saved the Chrysler Corporation from virtual extinction and elevated it to prosperity, he was swamped with requests for interviews. The same happened to an obscure FBI agent, Coleen Rowley, after she blew the whistle on the agency's alleged failure to investigate certain suspects prior to the September 11, 2001, World Trade Center attacks. She became a hot story.

But the essence of the profile is not what the person does. It is the individual who must stand out in the story. The person's occupation plays a secondary role—a backdrop to the personality factor. This means a strong emphasis on physical description, apparel worn, mannerisms, quirks, views, romances (in some cases), likes, dislikes and lots of quotes. The setting of the home or office where the interview takes place can be described in some detail since it is often linked to the subject's personality. If the interview is over lunch—as many are—the kind of food ordered by the individual and the attention paid to her by the restaurant staff and other diners can be grist for the story.

Any action that occurs during the interview can be woven into the story—such as the person playing with his dog, showing off his jade collection or filling and refilling his pipe. A *Wall Street Journal* reporter once interviewed a real estate tycoon who had no intention of letting the conversation interfere with his deal making. Periodically, the phone at his desk would ring, and he would negotiate or consummate transactions in rapid-fire order. The writer, instead of being annoyed at these interruptions, inserted them into his story as a means of demonstrating the man's dynamic personality. A journalist could not have hoped for a better break during an interview.

Many reporters find it expedient to allow a little ice-breaking time before plunging into the interview. This permits the person to feel more at ease with the interviewer and perhaps shed her nervousness. So, instead of immediately firing questions, it's a good idea to first engage in a bit of small talk. You might admire a picture on the wall or comment on a desk ornament.

It's also wise to begin with the easy questions. An opening query of a deeply personal nature might generate hostility from the subject. John Fried, a noted science writer and editor, told a journalism class: "If you want an interview to end in 45 seconds, start out by asking someone about an accusation made against him."

If you save the tough questions for later, the person might respond amiably since you have given him ample opportunity to put his best foot forward. Don't hesitate to toss out the hard questions. Soft, platitudinous queries generate boring profiles. Depending on the person being interviewed, intimate or sensitive matters must sometimes be brought up. You most likely would not ask your friends how much money they have in the bank or about their battle with alcoholism, but if such information is germane to your story, by all means ask it. Remember, the person agreed to the interview and probably expects questions on unpleasant aspects of his life.

The following do's and don'ts are offered for a successful interview.

Do:

- Make an appointment. Very few news makers appreciate reporters popping in unexpectedly.
- Attend to your homework. Get biographical facts on your target. Newspaper library clips and standard reference sources like *Who's Who* should be tapped.
- Have five or six prepared questions to lead off the interview.
- Ask direct, straightforward questions and keep them as short as possible. Avoid two- or three-part questions.
- Use follow-up questions to clarify answers or obtain needed expansion of a point.
- Keep the interviewee on track. If the subject's wandering contributes nothing to the article, gently but firmly bring the discussion back to the main idea.
- Probe for anecdotes that lend color and variety to the story.
- Be observant about your surroundings. Make notes about that African mask on the wall or exercise bike in the den.
- Use an audio tape recorder—with the person's permission.
- Get the correct spelling of names and the right dates.
- Ask for the subject's business and home phone numbers. If he is leaving immediately on a trip, ask where he can be reached. Questions frequently arise during writing, making it necessary to get back to the source.

Don't:

- Be late for the interview. This could get things off to a bad start.
- Be sloppily dressed or even too casually attired, even if the interviewee is prone to jeans and a sweatshirt at home. This is a business appointment.
- Express your personal opinions or argue with the subject. This is unprofessional, and readers are not looking for your views. An interview is not a debate.
- Use the source's first name unless he insists.
- Violate any agreement for off-the-record statements.
- Agree to let the person see your disk or hard copy before publication. You might, however, check with him—by phone—on the accuracy of pure facts. Otherwise, your editor is the only one who has a right to read your copy.

In writing the profile, the rules are about the same as for any feature—chiefly, that there are no rules beyond correct grammar, syntax, spelling, punctuation and, of course, accuracy and attribution. The story should establish early, however, that it is primarily a personality feature, not a piece about show business, sports or politics. It's important to set the tone of the article immediately so that the reader has an inkling of what she is getting into. An anecdotal or narrative lead can serve this purpose.

Here is one example:

By Gary Krino

Ruben Alvarez Jr. reaches into his back pocket, pulls out his wallet and retrieves a time-worn card that ties a big part of his life into a neat 2-by-4-inch package.

The card reads "Ruben Alvarez is a member of the Boys Club of Santa Ana." The expiration date is 12-31-68. But as far as Alvarez is concerned the card is as good as it was the day he set foot in what is now the Boys & Girls Club of Santa Ana.

Today, 27 years later, he's director of operations and one of the guiding forces at the club, an organization that has helped shape his life and become an integral part of it.

"When I was a kid," Alvarez says, "respect was built in. Today, we've got to earn it." And he has.

As Alvarez chats in his small office near the front of the club, a hulk ambles up to the front desk and tries to skate by without showing his membership card.

"Hey," Alvarez says, "membership has its privileges." The transgressor looks a little surprised, but there's no back-talk.

"If I can carry my card this long," Alvarez says, "he can carry his. He just lives next door. He'll be back." Five minutes later, with a membership card, he is.

"Respect" is a word that Alvarez uses frequently. It's sprinkled through his conversation like a fine seasoning. It's that special ingredient that he says makes the club work in a West Highland Street neighborhood that sometimes seems to be adrift in uncertainty and tension.

Some 26,000 children and youth live there, according to the 1990 U.S. Census. That gives it the highest density of youth in California and the second-highest in the United States. And some of those kids are gang members.

Alvarez's position at the club is largely administrative. But his ability to help guide the club's 2,000 members away from the streets and into this safe haven is what makes him a force in the community.

"When I'm out recruiting (kids for the club) or whenever the conversation calls for it, I tell them I was a member of the club and grew up in the neighborhood," says Alvarez, 35. "Here's my card. Where's yours? Look what it's done for me."

The Scene

It's a typical afternoon at the club. Younger kids file past the front desk in an orderly fashion, showing their membership cards and then bursting into the spacious game room. Pool, video games, big-screen TV, Chinese Checkers, Bottle Tops, Guess Who? and Battleship. Spanish and English ricochet off the walls like the billiards bouncing around the bumper pool tables.

Out back, on a large grassy field, guys and girls go nose-to-giggle in a flag football game that makes you forget the Rams and Raiders bailed out and left town.

Over in the crafts shop, Gus Chavez, a part-time employee and volunteer, cuts pumpkin shapes from a flat sheet of wood, mesmerizing a dozen delighted kids who will sand and paint them.

Later in the day, older kids show up to shoot hoops in the club gym, lift weights, pop billiards around the table, socialize and act cool.

People get along with each other, which sometimes does not happen in the streets.

"There are 20 identified gangs within a square mile of the (club) building," says Alvarez, a rather slight, unassuming man. "But nobody claims their gang affiliation when they're at the club."

"Respect" is the key word in the juggling act the club performs when rival gang members (or anyone else) show up.

"Kids who might not get along with each other two blocks from the club get along here," Alvarez says. "They may not hang together and they may not speak to one another, but it works.

"They tend to ignore each other. The club is neutral turf and has been since its inception."

The Kid

Alvarez didn't know the club from Anaheim Stadium when a buddy, Mark Taffola, "dragged me over here on our bikes one day," Alvarez recalls. "I was 8 and had never been here and thought it was great."

Sal Rubino was executive director of the club when Alvarez first showed up. "I spotted him early on," Rubino says. "He was a take-over kind of kid. He knew where he wanted to go and how to get there."

One place Alvarez wanted to go was to the head of the class as student body president at Lathrop Intermediate School. "I wanted to do things that were not normal for Mexican-American kids in my neighborhood," Alvarez says. "We were riding our bikes, hanging out and some of the kids were getting into trouble. I didn't want that."

When word got out that Alvarez was running for student body president, the staff helped him make campaign signs and gave him moral support. Alvarez won.

When it came time for high school, Alvarez opted for Saddle-back High over neighborhood Santa Ana High. "At the time, Saddleback had a higher percentage of kids going to college. I wanted that atmosphere and my parents steered me that way." (Today, Alvarez tells the kids it's not so important where they go to school. What's important is that they finish.)

At Saddleback, then primarily Anglo, Alvarez became the first Mexican-American elected student body president.

After graduation, he enrolled at California State University, Fullerton, and completed a degree in political science.

The Face Down

As executive director of the club, John Brewster is Alvarez's boss.

"Ruben's no bruiser," Brewster says. "But fear is not one of the things that motivates him. If Ruben was afraid of people or situations he would not work here. And Ruben has been in some situations. In one case, a kid stuck a 9mm gun in his face and threatened to shoot him."

Alvarez says the kid was drunk and distraught over personal problems. "He brandished the gun to show he had authority and power. Instant respect.

"I'd known him since he was a little kid. I told him to put the gun away, get out. He did, and I called the police.

"This is one of the things we try to nip in the bud. We try to show kids there are other ways to get attention."

Being confronted by a kid with a gun might be enough to make some reconsider their career choice. But that's not Alvarez's style.

"I've trained myself to be an optimist, to look on the good side so I can put things into perspective and look at the bigger picture," he says. "Then things don't look so bad."

The Kids

Luis Acosta, 13, a seventh-grader at Lathrop, is no pool shark. He leans across the table, steadies the cue, pops the shot and scratches. He gives a so-what shrug, puts down the cue and kicks back to chat about "Mr. Alvarez."

"Sometimes he's like a second father to the kids," says Luis, who was 7 when he joined the club.

"He can be strict and likes for kids to go by the rules. It's to respect the club. He likes them to treat the club like it was their home. He doesn't get mad. He just lets them know that's how it is."

Karina Martinez, 19, was one of the first girls to join the club when it merged with the Girl's Club of Santa Ana in 1990. She's a freshman at Rancho Santiago College and works at the club part-time. In 1994, she was named the club's Youth of the Year.

"Ruben Alvarez? He's a very cool guy," Karina says, taking a break between checking kids in and selling snacks in the club's snack bar. "Kids wonder why he gets to boss them around. They wonder how he got here, what it took to get here, and why he wants to be here. He's an example to the kids and gets them asking questions themselves that they might not have asked if he wasn't here."

The (Latch) Key

Just across from the club is the Pio Pico Elementary School, with its 860 kindergarten through fifth-grade students. The school has "partnered" with the club for a variety of educational and recreational programs, and Alvarez is the club's liaison.

Before Alvarez came on board, parents were hesitant to send their children to the club after school—and that included working parents who sent their children home with no supervision, principal Judith Magsaysay says. Now Alvarez and the club have all but eliminated the latchkey problem in the neighborhood, she says. "He drops by our PTA meeting to tell people what's going on (at the club) so they can send their kids over after school." Alvarez is bilingual, which helps build trust among parents who don't speak English, Magsaysay says.

The Family

In conversations with Alvarez, his associates and club kids, the word "respect" weaves through the talk like a golden thread that binds Alvarez's story into the tapestry of caring and positive action that it is.

The respect was born at home.

Alvarez's parents, Isabel and Ruben Alvarez Sr., still live in the comfortably modest stucco Santa Ana bungalow where Alvarez was raised.

Framed family pictures dot the mantel and side tables. A wedding portrait of Alvarez and his bride, Linda, sits on an antique highchair in the dining area. (The couple has two children, Risa Linda, 3, and Ruben Reynaldo III, 2).

"We always taught our children respect for people," says Isabel Alvarez, who was born in Mexico and came to this country at 18, when she married. (Besides Ruben, Isabel and Ruben Sr. are parents to Diana, 34; Cindy, 28; and Arthur, 25; all of Santa Ana.)

"Ruben and Arthur used to read lots of management books," Isabel Alvarez says. "You can read all you want, I told them. But respect is what you have to do. We always respected our children. That's one way to teach them."

The young Alvarez substituted thinking power for muscle power with his friends.

"Ruben wasn't very stout when he was a kid," says Ruben Alvarez Sr., a retired truck driver. "He wanted to show the big guys that muscle wasn't the way to respond to things in the neighborhood. He wanted to respond with brain power. It was his way of fitting in."

Isabel Alvarez, who assembles artificial heart valves at Baxter Health Care Corp. in Irvine, stayed at home when her children were young, providing guidance and a loving hand.

"It wasn't a big sacrifice (as it can be now)," she says. "Dad made enough money for us and I felt it was my part of the job. I was born in Mexico. There, the men work and the moms stay home with the kids. It's the traditional family way."

Although Alvarez works long days, he follows an updated version of his mother and father's traditional parenting philosophy, with one catch. Quality time is substituted for long hours at home.

Alvarez wakes the kids in the morning and prepares them for the day at a sister-in-law's house. In the evening, he's home by 7, which leaves a couple of hours of time with Risa Linda and Ruben Reynaldo.

"We purchased an annual pass to Disneyland and in the summer we make a point to take the kids to the park once a week," Alvarez says. But even at the Happiest Place on Earth, Alvarez is seeking ways to improve the club.

"I try to teach the kids colors (See? What color is that?) and to count (How many people are over there?)" he says. "On the other hand, I'm system-analyzing Disneyland, how they operate, and how we might apply it to the club."

The Guv and the Dreamer

Alvarez has always been a goal-setter. Early on, he announced to Rubino he wanted to be governor of California.

"He was probably about 15 or 16," Rubino says. "I thought it was a great goal and ambition. He knew he was going somewhere, even if it wasn't Sacramento. I think it's best for the city of Santa Ana that he hasn't pursued that goal."

Back at the club, Alvarez doesn't seem a bit surprised when someone asks, "Still want to be governor, Ruben?"

"Sure," he says, stroking his moustache and laughing. "Forty years from now when I grow up."

—Orange County Register

In some ways, the story draws a picture of Alvarez through his comments, one reason a generous use of quotes is desirable in a profile. Notice also the continuity from paragraph to paragraph. The key to this is picking up the idea from the preceding paragraph and slipping it into the new one. One paragraph in the Alvarez story ends with the sentence, "He knew where he wanted to go and how to get there." The first sentence in the following paragraph reads, "One place Alvarez wanted to go was to the head of the class as student body president at Lathrop Intermediate School."

In addition, the writer drew Alvarez closer to the reader by asking others for their impressions of the man. Call on friends, business associates, current or ex-spouses, enemies and anyone else who can offer a perspective on your subject.

The story also demonstrates that your profile need not be of a big-time celebrity. Readers of both metropolitan and community newspapers welcome insights into the work and lives of local people doing interesting things and making a difference.

In selecting a celebrity for a profile, a little research will help you decide whether she will hold and keep the reader's attention. In the case of a talk show host, for example, a couple of hours of viewing the performer should give you a good idea of whether or not to call for an interview. If someone is not a performer but has audience appeal anyway—a prominent author could qualify—contacting a press agent or others who know the individual can result in clues. And, of course, much depends on whether she is hot at the moment, that is, in the news. What to avoid is the possibility of setting up a meeting with a profile subject who turns out to be stiff, withdrawn and prone to answer questions with a yes or no.

In the following story, the selection process worked just fine.

By Jeannine Stein

When the applause from the studio audience finally dies down, Susan Powter gets some congratulations from the man upstairs. It's not God, exactly, but Executive Producer Woody Fraser, whose voice comes through Powter's tiny earphone.

"Thank you, Woody, thank you very much," she says into her body mike, although it looks as if she is speaking to no one.

Beaming, she turns to her staff and squeals, "My daddy says I did a good job!"

"God," she adds at a normal octave, "I've just gone back 25 years."

Even a professional motivator appreciates a little boost once in awhile.

If you don't know the 36-year-old woman about to launch the "Susan Powter Show," then you haven't been channel surfing. Her "Stop the Insanity" is the tsunami of infomercials. Men who push products by torching car hoods or baking cream puffs in hot-air ovens are ripples by comparison.

She's that wild woman with the spiky platinum buzz cut who jumps around yelling, "Fat makes you fat!" or "You've gotta, you've gotta breathe and you've gotta move!" Then, the next minute, she's the girlfriend who makes the raw confession that she once wanted to kill her ex-husband and stresses that she's "passionate, not angry."

Using straightforward information on food and exercise—info, she admits, that isn't original—she propels her followers, mostly women, into health, self-esteem and empowerment. Don't want those eight glasses of water a day? Don't want to munch on carrot sticks? Don't want to take an aerobics class from a perky Barbie doll in a thong leotard? Fine. Neither does she.

Those who have heard her story and believed have snatched up her $79.80 infomercial package—including audio tapes, a video, a fat caliper and various guidebooks—to the tune of more than $50 million.

The phenom has become the stuff of *People* magazine stories. Anyone vaguely familiar with Powter probably knows this much: She's a former Texas homemaker whose white-picket-fence life exploded when her husband left her to raise two young children on her own. She ate herself into a 260-pound stupor before she "figured it out." That is, she discovered that low-fat foods and a basic exercise program were her salvation.

But her story doesn't end minus 133 pounds later. There was a stint as a topless dancer, the time she was kept by a married man, the tummy tuck, the exercise studio, seminars, books, videos, the infomercial, a second marriage, the brother who blabbed to the tabloids that she never was that fat (she maintains she was).

"My husband said to me the other night, we're lying in bed and he's flicking through the channels, and he said, 'God, they'd give anyone a damn talk show these days!' And I said, 'Thank you. Thank you, honey, I appreciate it.' Actually, he said 'any moron.'"

So here she is, in her partially furnished office in the Santa Monica studios where the show is taped before an audience. Sitting behind a rustic, dark-wood desk decorated with a neo-romantic lamp, Powter exhibits the same unfettered energy as she does on television. She goes from zero to 60 in 1.3 seconds and seldom brakes.

"I came out of the womb with energy," she says.

She gestures with hands that end in fake coral-colored nails, her words tumbling out in great, long rushes. When Powter gets angry—er, passionate—the tendons in her neck stand out. Pushing out so much verbiage at once often results in incomplete sentences, even words.

"What I always do when I start explaining what the show is," she says, "is tell them what it isn't. There will be no tabloid issues at all. There is no exploiting people at all. And there's no yelling and screaming and fighting and if that doesn't fly on TV, it ain't gonna fly."

She's banking that American women are tired of watching people with over-teased hair blather about their addictions to phone sex. Her show will be celeb-free and low on experts. "Oh, please. We've been hearing from experts for years and it hasn't done us a damn bit of good. Women are experts. I want to talk to a woman who's gone through it."

"A million issues, a bazillion. Funny? I'm going to a construction site—this is the truth—and I'm getting up on the beam with the guys and I want to see what the hell they're whistling at. I've got the hat, the lunch box—I'm telling you. I'm doing it. I'm so afraid of heights you don't know. Faaaabulous shows. I don't know why anyone didn't think of this before."

Executive producer Fraser, a veteran of the "Home Show" and "Good Morning America," calls Powter "lightning in a bottle" and adds, "I've put a lot of people in that host seat, and she's the fastest study."

As someone who already has been a target of a "Saturday Night Live" sketch, featuring Kristie Alley in a blonde fright wig, is the hyperbolic Powter in danger of becoming a parody of herself?

"If we get successful in eight or nine years down the line, great," Fraser says with a chuckle. "But you know, she's going to have to fight that fight, and as long as she remains interested in helping people change their lives, then she will not become a caricature of her life."

That life now involves shuttling between Dallas and Los Angeles with her family, sons Damien, 11, and Kiel, 10, from her first marriage, and husband Lincoln Apeland. They recently bought a home in Pacific Palisades.

When in Texas, they share a duplex with her ex-husband and his wife so their kids can see both parents. She turned a bad divorce into a livable situation—look for it as a show topic.

And six years into husband No. 2, marriage still baffles her.

"I don't understand marriage," she says. "I'm not sure I'm very good at it. . . . I'm learning how to be married and it's very hard for me. I'm not that good at it, and he knows it. I mean, I don't scream 'wifey-poo' whatever that means. He's got his own thing, he's a musician, he does his own thing, I do my own thing. I'm not sure that I've decided on it yet. I'm not sure it's my thing."

Work is definitely her thing. But juggling a family, workouts and a TV show isn't enough for Powter. She has written another book, this one titled, "Food." It will have her trademark no-nonsense information about nutrition and diet, plus low-fat recipes.

"I've been working on this for eight months every day from 5:30 in the morning," she says. "Every day. I love this book. I love it! I can't tell you how excited I am. Fabulous. 'Food' by Susan Powter. That's the title. 'Food' by Susan Powter. I'm very excited.

"I interviewed . . . I can't even tell you. I mean, books. You don't know. Interviews? You don't know. Researching and doing and going and talking to dairy farmers and everything. The FDA. We've got it all here. We took all the mishegosh, the muck, that everybody is confu—I mean HDL, LDL, cholesterol, saturated fat, oil, good, bad, boil, fry, what do we do with this? I broke it down."

That ability to relate the basics to her audience has given Powter staying power, says Dr. David Heber, chief of clinical nutrition at the UCLA School of Medicine.

"Her greatest asset is that people can connect with her, and think that's an important part of the therapy of obesity—there are both psychological and physical aspects," he says. "She is honest and upfront in that she does not claim to be a scientific expert. She's taking bites and pieces from scientific literature and paraphrasing it correctly."

Indeed, because her program is grounded in common sense, Powter has not drawn the criticism heaped on some weight-loss gurus.

"Swear to God, you'll understand everything when you read this book, I'm telling you, you're going to love it," she says, slapping the stack of "Food" pages next to her laptop. "And then you make your own decisions because it's your decision with your body. Have you ever seen cuter kids than this in your life? I just wanted to ask you," she says, suddenly grabbing a picture of her sons.

"In your life have you ever seen cuter kids than this? Now they're 10 and 11; they were like, 5 and 6 here. But have you ever? I mean, c'mon. They're very cute kids."

This is the Susan Powter viewers will get beginning Monday (5 p.m. on KCAL) in their living rooms—the Susan Powter who will talk about anything from her kids to her failed marriage to her obesity.

Because the time when she was too fat and unhealthy to play in the park with her kids is still very real in her mind. So is the memory of being too broke to pay the electric bill. She taps into the past and her emotions easily, as if they sit in a shallow well.

When she brings up her problems, women listen. They understand the pain of being left for another woman, of hurting so much that they stuff themselves, and hurt more and stuff more.

Powter might not be where she is without Rusty Robertson, the manager-publicist who took on the struggling aerobics-studio owner back in Dallas. The two are practically joined at the hip, businesswise and emotionally. They even have the same rapid-fire patter.

"I'm the planner of the future for us, and Susan makes the best of where we are," says Robertson, a former actress.

She recalls their first meeting. "(Susan) walked in, bald, in a black leather jacket, looking great. She sat right in front of my desk and said, "I've got this program and I'm saving people's lives. . . . Susan had literally been living below the poverty level. . . . This is a woman who truly lived on nothing. That's why I respect Susan more than any other woman in the world, including my mother."

With Robertson tending the big picture, Powter can work on the here and now.

"There's a balance now that I think a lot about," Powter says. "I have a friend staying with me for a week and . . . I spent the afternoon shopping with her, and that was hard for me and I told her that. I realized that I'd become very selfish with my time, which made me think—is that good, is that bad, is that right? I don't know.

"Basically I don't ever want to stop working on stuff. The day I stop working I'm going to be 10 feet under. . . . The day that it's all OK is the day I want to have a Mack truck hit me. I mean, it's not OK. It never will be all OK. I never want it to be all OK. I want all of it, everything.

"The other day I went for a walk and I just said, 'Wow, I love this and I want everything and I'll take the good and the bad, you know?' Who the hell knows who I was talking to. I was probably talking to a ficus bush. But I mean it. I want . . . I want . . . I'm willing to take the responsibility. I will work on the bad. I'll work toward the good, but I want it all, I just . . . c'mon, 'cause I like it."

—Los Angeles Times

Commenting on the preparation for her article, Stein said:

To prepare for my interview with fitness guru Susan Powter, I compiled all the stories on her I could find, from magazines to newspapers. I also read her autobiography, "Stop the Insanity." Since I was familiar with her infomercial, I didn't feel I needed to view that again.

When profiling a celebrity, I find it especially important to do as much background research as possible before sitting down to talk.

Often, these people have been interviewed to death, asked every question imaginable and tend to go on what I call "autopilot," or give the same responses they've given hundreds of times before without even thinking.

By being prepared, I could steer the interview away from things that had been covered before and get some fresh material. It's inevitable that you're going to go over some familiar ground, but at least you can use that as a springboard for new topics.

In preparing a feature, always look for the little things—gestures, quirks, and so on—that bring the subject to life, as in this excerpt from a *Time* piece on Pulitzer Prize-winning novelist Michael Chabon:

Chabon runs his fingers through his unkempt hair and looks up at the ceiling. He's one of those radiant-child adults, the kind you can imagine as the dreamy fourth-grader he must once have been. . .Chabon answers questions, the dog barks, Waldman (Chabon's wife) picks a piece of fluff off her husband's face, Sophie's school calls with the news that Sophie just threw up. . . The interview took place at Chabon's Berkeley, Calif., home. A subject's home is usually an excellent place for interviews because it's where he is most likely to be his natural self.

Lifestyle Features

As noted earlier, features can appear in almost any section of the paper, but probably more of them show up in lifestyle sections adopted by many newspapers, particularly the metros. This section has, in most cases, replaced the traditional "women's page," although news and features primarily directed at women continue to dominate many of the lifestyle sections, which go by such names as "Living," "Life & Style," "Style," "Accent" and "Lifestyles."

These pages reflect a changing America. Former taboos against publishing articles about such matters as sex, divorce, drug use, alternative lifestyles, race and unwed mothers have all but disappeared. And stories involving education, housing, welfare and working women are written today with far more depth than was seen in the press of 50 years ago.

Still, lifestyle sections allow room for lighter stuff, either locally written or in syndicated columns and free-lance submissions. Stories about coping with Christmas shopping, "quality time" with children, dealing with a grumpy boss, fitness programs and apartment hunting are common fare. But lifestyle content, whether light or serious, has one element in common: Most stories deliver useful information to help people understand our society, open new vistas and provide insight into how things are. Lifestyle writers try to lock in on what touches their readers' lives and to reveal what's happening in readers' communities that they will not find in the main news section. This article, appearing in the *Orange County Register* on Father's Day, provides information for readers on parenting through the eyes of experts on the issue and parents themselves.

By Cheryl Rosenberg Neubert

Dan Hazard left his corporate job six years ago to spend more time with his only child, Brittany.

He was there to walk her to school when she was still young enough to occasionally need a hand to hold along the way.

He joins her on the father-daughter activities through the local YMCA. He cheers her at her soccer games.

And now that she's 13, he has pored over books to help him prepare for those often-tumultuous teenage years.

Hazard, 50, who has a business with his wife at their Huntington Beach home, has been a willing and avid participant in raising his daughter. His involvement will pay enormous dividends throughout her life, experts say.

"There's an awful lot of cultural belief that fathers are second-class citizens," said Joe Kelly, who founded the national advocacy nonprofit Dads and Daughters. "We're not more important than moms, or less. We're different."

A father's impact and the role he plays are far more important than one might think.

Fathers are cited more than mothers in issues such as psychological maladjustment, substance abuse, depression and behavioral problems, according to research done by Ronald Rohner, director of the Center for the Study of Parental Acceptance and Rejection in the School of Family Studies at the University of Connecticut, and his colleague Robert Veneziano. They also found that a father's love helps prevent the development of these problems and can contribute to a child's good physical health.

This influence is equally vital for daughters and sons, although how each are affected differs.

When it comes to girls, Dad is clearly the first man in her life.

"A daughter looks to her father, and there she sees the standard of what it means to be a man," Kelly said. "Girls are hammered thousands of times a day with outrageous messages that boil down to 'how you look is more important than how you are.' They think so much is based on whether or not a man notices them.

"I can be the most important force in her life to tell her that is a lie. What I value is what you have to say, what you do, what you think, your spunk, your soul, your heart. That's what's important. We can show that about all women," Kelly said.

Girls notice the relationship their father has with their mother—even in families where the father lives outside the home. They see how their father talks about women, how he treats them, and that's her foundation for her future relationships.

The father's job is to show her the way.

"A lot of us don't expect ourselves to be involved parents," Kelly said. "I think it's changing with younger fathers, but it's not changing fast enough. . . . We grow up with the idea that we are supposed to be providers. We have too narrow a definition of provider. We reduce it to the wallet. We have to provide time, strength, masculinity."

Hazard counts his father-daughter activities, including camping trips with the group from the YMCA, as among his favorite times. He does not want to forget a moment of the time he's spent with Brittany. He also wants to leave her a legacy, something for her to revisit over the years.

Since she was born, Hazard has kept a journal of Brittany's life. It is a book in progress in which Brittany is the main character. He has recorded the ordinary, everyday details along with the bigger moments of her childhood. He got the idea from his great-grandfather's diary of his daily life as a beat cop in Providence, R.I., in the 1800s.

"It's a story of her," Hazard said. "It's a family heirloom to pass on to generations to come, something so special and unique that few children ever receive this kind of gift from their parents. When she's older, and she's a mother, she can look back and see life was good."

The Boys

Being a good father isn't important just to those with daughters. The father-son relationship also is critical.

"What your son gets is an emotional foundation that very few men have," said Dr. Stephan Poulter, a licensed clinical psychologist in West Los Angeles and author of "Father Your Son: How to Become the Father You've Always Wanted to Be." "It's like giving your son gold bricks. He gets emotionally fluent. He becomes comfortable with showing love, hopeful, generous and compassionate."

Poulter has seen the results of what happens when there is no father or strong positive male influence in a boy's life.

"So many times, the guys I would see for violent crimes were always fatherless sons," Poulter said. "And I mean always in the true sense of the word. A lot of men don't think they matter, but fathers matter to their sons."

He is not saying that all fatherless sons become criminals. It's just the criminals he's seen all have that element in common. That the father matters is a powerful idea that can help change a father's behavior.

"You're going to act differently," Poulter said. "You're going to take into consideration his feelings, your time commitment to him, your job."

The job as father begins the second the child is born. An emotional connection to the father helps with the development of cognitive and motor skills. It also helps with the child's ability to bond and attach to others.

But the crucial time is the teenage years. That's when the father teaches the son limits and rules. He shows him, literally, how to be a man.

Dave Wilcox, 36, of Yorba Linda, is trying to set that groundwork with his three children. He has two boys—Brandon, 14, and Richie, 7—and a 15-year-old daughter, Stephanie.

Two weeks ago, Wilcox took Richie on their first father-son fishing trip.

"We're so active with sports and school and church, a lot of times you wake up and realize you haven't had a real conversation with the kids," Wilcox said. "I always make it a point to take the sons and daughter away separately. It's kind of a bonding time.

"We had a lot of laughs. I could just see the look on his face. He hugged me a little tighter at night in the tent, stuff he wouldn't ordinarily do. The next few days after we got back, he wanted me in bed with him. So I'd lie there 10 minutes, then say good night. It brings them closer. Otherwise, you could really get lost in the shuffle."

Men who aren't heavily involved in their son's lives at the beginning can still repair any damage.

"It's never too late," Poulter said. "And that's the truth. All men crave their father's approval. If you don't know what to do, give your son approval. It's like watering a plant. They're going to thrive. Don't blame him. Understand him. That takes time. At the end of the day, give him your time."

There was a time when Dad was, simply, the guy who came home from work. Raising the family fell on the shoulders of the mother. Dad was a peripheral figure, meting out discipline and perhaps tossing around the ol' pigskin on the weekend.

Now the role of the father has taken on an increased, if not equal, responsibility—and not just because men are becoming more enlightened.

"The reason men are having to do more is that the extended families have broken down," said Michael Gurian, author of "What Could He Be Thinking, How a Man's Mind Really Works."

"This stuff was done by the aunties and grandmas and grandpas. Social technologies were taught by extended families. Now, Dad and Mom have to do more."

That's a job Don Dormeyer, 58, of Orange took seriously, even before it was fashionable. He and his wife, Mary, raised a daughter, Kelly, 30, and a 27-year-old son, Darin. His goal was to prepare them for life by giving them the basics—honesty, responsibility, curiosity and self-esteem.

"They have to be equipped with the basic judgment, attitude, respect and desire to learn," Dormeyer said. "That's parenting in my opinion."

—Orange County Register

Notice that the article focuses on one father-daughter relationship, then goes on to quote experts in father-daughter and father-son relationships. The writer organizes her story to talk first about fathers and daughters, and then writes about fathers and sons. The editor uses a subhead, "boys," to help the reader make the transition. Note, too, how the focus may be on specific relationships, but the comments from experts are interwoven into the story to provide authority. The result is a story to which all fathers, daughters and sons, of all races and nationalities, can relate.

Writing a Column

College journalists often vie for the position of columnist on campus newspapers. Actually, their time would be better spent covering standard news events. Editors hiring entry-level reporters are usually little impressed by one's credentials as a college columnist, preferring instead graduates who have demonstrated they can cover basic news stories and cover them well. Most of today's newspaper columnists are former reporters who proved their writing ability on general assignment, the route that is usually followed for that goal. Newspaper job-seekers can make the best use of their time by covering hard news for the campus paper or being hired as a stringer by a local daily or weekly.

Still, being a columnist is not an impossible dream after you have gained reporting experience. Columns decorate virtually all newspapers and have a strong following. Editors are always interested in bright new writers with new ideas and a unique style.

But don't wait to be "discovered." If, after your stint in the newsroom, you want a crack at a column, display your talents by writing five or six sample columns and showing them to an editor who can make the decision. Steer away from copycat columns or style. Come up with a different viewpoint, a different approach. It helps your chances if you've been turning out feature stories that have been favorably received by editors and readers. Convincing editors that you have a deep interest in pets, TV, health care, politics, finance or some other subject will strengthen your hand, everything else being equal. On smaller papers, editors generally prefer columns that dwell on the community rather than the writer's view on national issues. Always keep in mind that a column should not mirror a standard news story or feature. It must have a personal point of view or bite, which can be expressed humorously—like Dave Barry and Art Buchwald—or acidly, like Bill O'Reilly and Jimmy Breslin.

Persistence pays off for achieving any change of assignment on a newspaper. So keep blowing your own horn until somebody hears it—if not on your current job, then on another newspaper. Remember, most of today's famous columnists started in the newsroom: Dave Barry, Mike Barnacle, Ellen Goodman, Robert D. Novak, Thomas Friedman, Chris Matthews, Molly Ivins, Tony Kornheiser and many others.

Suggested Assignments

1. Clip three different types of feature stories from newspapers and write a 300-word analysis of how they succeed or fail in their apparent objectives.
2. Dig up material for an enterprise feature out of the news mainstream that you believe is still of concern or interest to readers.
3. Gather material and write an explanatory feature on fund-raising at your institution and how it affects curriculum, laboratory equipment and faculty hiring.
4. Select someone on your campus or in your community for a personal profile. Research as much material as you can about the individual and call for an interview.
5. Write a feature from the following facts:
   a. WWCT-FM is a radio station in Peoria, Illinois.
   b. Thomas Cahill is sales manager for Bill Clasen Ford in Morton, Illinois.
   c. Rick Lewis, of Peoria, is an unemployed sheet metal worker, age 38.
   d. WWCT-FM sponsored a contest for listeners. Listeners sent their names in on a postcard, and the station held a drawing, picking a name.
   e. The prize was an Aurora automobile. It is a sports car made in Canada. It cost $58,000 at the dealer's.
   f. Lewis won the car. During the contest, the auto was held at Bill Clasen Ford. The contest was five months ago.
   g. Lewis did not pick up the car right away. He said the radio station told him he could delay paying taxes on it for a year if he waited until after Dec. 31 to pick up the car.
   h. The station gave Lewis a brochure on the car and a certificate saying he was its legal owner.
   i. Monday, Lewis got some bad news. The Ford agency called and wanted to know when he planned to pick up the car. Cahill told Lewis there was a $37-a-day storage fee on the vehicle, and storage charges now amounted to $5,558.
   j. Lewis has filed a complaint with the Illinois Attorney General's office against the Clasen agency. He seeks possession of the car. He says he is an innocent third party. He says further that the storage fees are a matter between WWCT-FM and the Clasen agency.
   k. Lewis, who said, "I wish I had never entered that contest," got more bad news yesterday (Wednesday). He was told by Cahill that he will owe about

$1,800 in state and local sales taxes on the car—due whenever he takes possession.

l.   Lewis said in the interview, "Nobody ever told me about any storage fee. Anyway, I'm broke and can't pay it."

m. Lewis said Cahill told him the car was taking up a stall, where a mechanic could be working at the rate of $65 an hour. Cahill confirmed this to you.

n.   Lewis, who has yet to step into the car, was further told by Cahill that he cannot take out the car until the storage fee is paid.

o.   The Aurora is a handmade car.

p.   Lewis currently drives a 1988 Plymouth with a bad engine and tires that need replacing.

12

Specialized Reporting

Although there is little chance that your entry-level job will be that of a specialist, specialized journalism is becoming increasingly important to the media and is a goal of many journalists. The complexities of reporting on a myriad of subjects demand reporters with a solid understanding of a particular field, the ability to explain it to the ordinary reader and an instant knowledge of where to get specific information. A survey by Scripps-Howard Newspapers found that editors of medium- and large-sized papers seek applicants with journalism skills, a broad background in the liberal arts and also training in accounting, computer science and marketing.

Many journalism graduates—some with professional experience—enroll for a master's degree in whatever subject in which they want to specialize, such as science, politics, health care or law. In the latter area, some journalists finish law school with the idea of writing exclusively in that area. However, as a journalism undergraduate, you can better equip yourself for specialization by taking a second major or a minor in the subject of your choice.

Specialists in politics, law, the arts, international affairs, environment and medicine, among other topics, are generally found on the larger newspapers, those with staffs—and budgets—ample enough to afford them. Still, the smaller newspapers are good places to prepare yourself for specialization. You may be hired as a generalist for a paper that prints a number of stories in special fields such as science and education. Most of these articles are generated by the wire services, but some may have to be locally written. If you have an interest in a particular subject, volunteer to take it on. When you are ready for metropolitan or wire-service journalism, you can safely tell the hiring editor you are qualified to handle a subject. Much of the craft of journalism is learned on the job, and that's what you'll be doing. We know a polished political writer who achieved that status by pleading to be assigned to any political story that the then-main political specialist couldn't handle because he was out of town on a more important story. When the latter retired, our friend stepped easily and fully prepared into the slot.

The trend toward specialization submerges the time-honored notion that a reporter should be able to cover any kind of story. It's a romantic idea that is still around.

General-assignment reporters may be called upon to cover a variety of stories ranging from ribbon-cutting to a crack cocaine bust to an environmental scandal. But as the world becomes more complicated, it can no longer be completely explained by straight reporting. Some stories need more background, explanation and interpretation to make them understandable. Science and medicine, for example, are advancing so rapidly that only expert writers can keep abreast of developments and distill them for lay readers. The corporate scandals of 2002, which became a Page One story as top executives were arrested, required skilled, knowledgeable reporting with sufficient background.

Their expertise must, of course, be accompanied by the ability to communicate their knowledge in clear language. Given the choice between a PhD in biochemistry who cannot write very well and a reporter without such a degree but with the drive to collect the right information and the ability to convey it lucidly, the editor will pick the latter. For journalists, what's the good of knowledge if it can't be related simply and clearly?

Fortunately, a number of newspapers and magazines and a few TV stations have reporters with great expertise in certain areas and the competency to communicate it. Those who come immediately to mind include Lawrence Altman of the *New York Times,* a medical writer who has an MD degree; religion reporter Larry Stammer of the *Los Angeles Times,* whose work has been praised by clergy; award-winning science writer David Perlman of the *San Francisco Chronicle*; and Jane Bryant Quinn, *Newsweek* magazine's highly regarded business columnist. These journalists and other experts like them spent years developing their specialties after first proving themselves as first-rate general reporters.

There isn't space enough in this book to discuss every specialization in detail, but let's examine some of the more traditional ones.

Science and Medicine

It wasn't until the then-Soviet Union launched the space satellite Sputnik in 1957 that the American news media got serious about adding science writers to their staffs. It was a wake-up call not only for the U.S. government and the American scientific community but also newspapers, magazines and broadcasters. Previously, only the wire services and a few leading newspapers like the *New York Times* and the *Washington Post* boasted science writers. Sputnik created an awareness throughout the nation that the world was entering a new age. For the media it meant that readers and viewers, fascinated by the space breakthrough, wanted it explained to them. And it was, by a growing corps of journalists who entered the realm of specialized reporting not only of space rockets but also of the world of science itself. These men and women combine a deep comprehension of their subject with the knack of being able to write about it in clear English. Their questions at press conferences with scientists are knowledgeable and incisive. In fact, some become irritated at these gatherings when a general-assignment reporter tosses what they consider a "primer" query at the news source.

The best of these science and medical reporters are respected by scientists and doctors. Dr. John E. Cleaver, a University of California physicist who discovered the inherent cause of a rare form of skin cancer, credited a story by David Perlman as giving him the idea for the research.

The science or medical writer (on smaller newspapers, one person may cover both) keeps one eye on the uninformed lay reader and the other on the scientific establishment, which is quick to complain about erroneous reporting. There is a fine line here. Reporters cannot oversimplify esoteric research, but neither can they entirely couch it in scientific terminology. They must also keep in mind that scientific and medical discoveries can affect the lives of millions of people but that such news can be misunderstood or misinterpreted by readers eager for the "silver bullet" that will cure cancer, heart disease or whatever ails them. So science and medical writers must be careful to clearly point out, for example, that an experiment, although promising, was conducted with mice, not humans, and that it is only a first step in a process that might take years. Many years of research were expended before the announcement of an effective polio vaccine. Even when experimental treatments are conducted on human beings, it may be months or years before the application receives approval by the Food and Drug Administration for general use.

The School of Health at the University of California, Berkeley, offers these pointers to readers of its *University of California, Berkeley Wellness Letter,* but the advice makes sense for medical writers as well:

- Don't jump to conclusions. A single study is no reason for changing your health habits. Distinguish between an interesting finding and a broad-based public health recommendation.
- Always look for context. A good reporter—and a responsible scientist— will always place findings in the context of other research. Yet the typical news report seldom alludes to other scientific work.
- If it was an animal study or some other kind of lab study, be cautious about generalizing. Years ago, lab studies suggested that saccharin caused cancer in rats, but epidemiologic studies showed later that it didn't cause cancer in humans.
- Beware of press conferences and other hype. Scientists, not to mention the editors of medical journals, love to make the front page of major newspapers and hear their studies mentioned on the evening news. The fact that the study in question may have been flawed or inconclusive or old news may not seem worth mentioning. This doesn't mean you shouldn't believe anything. Truth, too, may be accompanied by hype.
- Notice the number of study participants and the study's length. The smaller the number of subjects and the shorter the time, the greater the possibility that the findings are erroneous.

This is sound advice for medical and science writers, but the more experienced reporters in this field learned these lessons years ago and seldom are caught off base.

In fact, they don't even show up at some press conferences because they know the report will be rehashed material or is coming from a dubious source. Moreover, following a news conference, they begin using the phone to get comments from other experts on the validity of what they've heard. Then they're ready to write.

The late Alton Blakeslee, a longtime science writer for the Associated Press, once said that the essence of his work was a "simple lead followed by the clear explanation."

Science can be tougher to write about than any other field, he added, because the reporter can't assume that the reader has a common knowledge about the subject. "You have to have respect for the innocence of the reader," he said. "Make it meaningful to people. Use technical terms only if you immediately explain them. Then, in later stories, don't expect readers to remember your previous explanations. Explain again."

John Fried, a former science writer for *Life* magazine and several newspapers, said that when interviewing a scientist, "I keep asking questions until I fully understand what he or she is talking about. If I find the explanations beyond me, I ask them to cover it again."

Fried, who has written eight books on scientific subjects as well as articles for the *Reader's Digest* and other magazines, said he gets many of his ideas for articles from reading scientific journals, which doctors later "translate" for him.

Science is becoming increasingly specialized, making it harder for journalists, "even journalists with advanced training, to know what is important and what is not important," writes *New York Times* Science Editor Cornelia Dean in *Nieman Reports* magazine, which is published by the Nieman Foundation for Journalism at Harvard University. She warns that, "If we are not sufficiently vigilant we can be sold on something whose true significance is far from clear. Or we might be so cautious that we miss truly important developments, or muffle them in a blanket of cautionary caveats."

In the same magazine, Douglas Starr, co-director of the Knight Center for Science and Medical Journalism at Boston University, advises students that the traditional practice of balancing a story by giving equal space to both sides might work in political coverage but rarely does in science writing. "Many science issues have more than two sides," he points out. "Others cannot be posited as equal and opposite sides of an argument. The answer is not merely to *present* these opinions, but to *weigh* them."

The medical beat also includes the public health sector in which the well-being of perhaps millions of people is affected. In these stories, sources may include nonmedical public officials as well as health officers. Outbreaks of *E. coli* or salmonella, both deadly infections from food, are the basis of crucial stories that will name the restaurant where the bad food was served and contain warnings on how to avoid the illness.

One of the most recent issues in medical reporting is national health insurance that goes beyond Medicare. It's estimated that 45 million Americans are without any health care insurance. The problem is as much political as medical and has fostered debate between Republican and Democratic politicians.

Another hot topic is the soaring popularity of HMOs (health maintenance organizations), which stress preventive care and take a business approach to medicine to lower costs. The system has spurred controversy among doctors as well as in the public arena.

A science writer may be called on to take over a story on an accidental spill of toxic chemicals that could create life-threatening dangers for a community. At the same time, it's important not to create a panic. A seasoned science reporter knows how to gather sound, accurate information from experts to put the danger in proper perspective while explaining what residents can do to avoid contamination. Of course, if necessary, authorities will evacuate whole neighborhoods near the spill. At this moment, science reporters in the U.S. and Russia are seeking to learn what kind of gas Russian troops used when they stormed a theater in which terrorists held about 700 persons hostage. The gas is believed to have caused the death of some 100 hostages. Experts at universities and other research facilities are being tapped for their theories on the type of gas sprayed into the theater. The important point here is that the writers know what experts to call and where they are located.

AP science writer Bob Locke got into his field because he believes it's important. He commented:

> Science and technology are more and more affecting every part of day-to-day living. That really began after World War II but we're only now becoming acutely aware of it. Revolutions are occurring in many fields, from genetic engineering with its wide-ranging impacts through medicine to the faint beginnings of commerce and industry in space. From birth control pills that prevent conception and test tubes for infertile couples to death at a later age, but sometimes related to the sea of chemicals we have created—and almost everything in between, science is involved.

Locke noted that his job is not to provide answers, "which I don't have, but to suggest questions and help give the public enough information to make decisions based on facts rather than blind trust or unreasoning fear."

An example of readable writing necessary in a science or medical story is demonstrated in this piece:

By Misti Crane

A genetic mutation appears to be responsible for some cancer cases previously considered random, an international team of scientists reports in today's *New England Journal of Medicine.*

The finding could prompt testing in people considered at risk for the mutation and lead scientists to develop better medicines for certain cancers, including leukemia and breast cancer, researchers say.

The work was led by Dr. Carlo Croce, director of Ohio State University's human cancer genetics program.

Researchers analyzed tumor and blood samples from 216 people with various sporadic cancers, 109 people with cancer in the family or multiple types of the disease, and 475 cancer-free people. The National Cancer Institute, the Italian Ministry of Public Health and the Italian Association for Cancer Research paid for the study.

A gene named ARLTS1, which normally works to deter tumors, was mutated and rendered ineffective in a significant number of cancer patients, the study found.

The genetic mutation was three times as likely to be found in patients with cancer in the family and two times as likely to be found in those with random cases of cancer than in the cancer-free people.

About 2 percent of the population appears to carry the mutation that may predispose them to a variety of cancers.

Such mutations don't guarantee an eventual cancer diagnosis, but they do warn of an increased risk.

Ideally, the discovery of genetic links to cancer will lead researchers to develop drugs that more efficiently and successfully fight it.

"The more we learn about such factors that contribute to cancer, the better idea we have how to interfere with those factors," said Dr. Thomas Kipps, who worked on the study at the University of California, San Diego, where he is deputy director of research for the cancer center.

"The Holy Grail of cancer biology is to try to develop specific drugs that can interfere with specific pathways."

Identification of genetic links also helps people make wise lifestyle decisions and have more frequent screenings to look for disease, Croce said.

Perhaps the most well-known mutations to date are in the so-called breast-cancer genes—called BRCA1 and BRCA2. Some healthy women who have breast cancer in the family seek genetic testing and counseling and opt for mastectomies and other preventive treatment.

"The genes that are involved in cancer susceptibility are many, but they are difficult to discover," Croce said, explaining that a relatively small number of people may suffer from genetic defects.

"We were lucky that we found one that tends to be very interesting."

The link was made after a failed attempt to locate a gene responsible for the most common type of leukemia, Croce said.

For now, the researchers don't know how many of those with the genetic mutation actually get cancer or what percentage of cancers are linked to the gene.

—The Columbus (Ohio) *Dispatch*

The beauty of this story is the clear expression of a technical subject and one important to readers. The story has special significance since Dr. Croce, director of Ohio State University's human cancer genetics program, is involved in the research. But reporters in any community could have landed the assignment to write this story. Most communities have medical or research facilities within their circulation area, so reporters need to be able to understand complicated scientific issues and explain them in laymen's terms.

If a newspaper's library doesn't have all the information you need, start working the phone for "the usual suspects"—experts who can fill you in on what's missing for a coherent article. Where do you find experts? Experienced science and medical writers keep a list of people they have previously interviewed or know about. There also are reference books like *American Men and Women of Science, Current Biography,* and the American Medical Association's *Directory of Medical Specialists,* which may be in the paper's library and might even be available online.

Education News

Education is a major beat in the nation's press. The little red schoolhouse has been replaced by a massive concentration of buildings, a huge bureaucratic superstructure and millions of students from kindergarten through graduate school. The growth has brought enormous problems in funding, educational philosophy, racial integration, schoolyard safety, tenure, prayer in schools and athletic eligibility, to name a few. Education reporters can no longer fulfill their function by merely covering school board meetings and writing about the year's honor students.

There also is an awareness in the media that education cannot be separated from the mainstream of society as an institution answerable only to itself. Issues such as school prayer, crime, lunch-program funding and busing spill over into politics and the country's social fabric. Page One stories, for instance, tell of controversies over the influx of immigrants and their effect on school systems, guns on campus and new school construction. Whether there should be bilingual education arouses hot rhetoric from both sides of the question. Teachers strike for higher pay, and universities struggle to hold down the rising cost of tuition.

Education reporters deal with all this on a daily basis. In a smaller community, the education beat might include all school levels: K–12 and beyond if there is a college in the community. On large newspapers, the beat may be divided among three or four education specialists, one or two dealing with elementary and high schools and the others with colleges and universities. Their sources include teachers, principals, school board officials, college department chairpersons, university presidents, deans, PTA leaders, students, building engineers and, often, publicists for a school district or college.

Aggressive education reporters, who know their field inside out, don't wait for news to break. Using this knowledge, they develop stories, perhaps from tips or a sense that some aspect of their beat cannot be accommodated in a straight news story and should be told in depth.

Whether writing a standard news article or an in-depth one, the education reporter must take what is often a complex subject and bring it home to the reader. One headache for such a reporter is the tendency for education professionals to talk in the kind of jargon they use among themselves and in the never-ending stream of articles they write for journals in their field. Reporters hear such terms as "competency-based education," "full-time equivalent," "teaching units" and "bell curve." In writing the story, care must be taken to convert these phrases into lucid English.

The following is an example of an enterprise story dealing with education. It's the kind of information that doesn't come off a press release.

By David J. Smollar

Chemistry textbook:

$74.70.

Ka-ching!

Physics textbook:

$80.

Ka-ching!

Technology of Machine Tools:

$61.

Ka-ching!

Elementary Linear Algebra:

$61.50.

Ka-ching!

Once again, the book-buying season is upon college students, and the cash register totals are awesome. Phat Chiem, a University of California, Irvine, senior, debited his credit card for $263.32 last week. Junior Brian Shea charged $215.76. Freshman Vivian Lee plunked down plastic for $248.89.

Hour after hour, these muscular dollar figures flash across the UCI Bookstore sales terminals as students lined up resignedly to fork over large sums.

Students are cogs in a massive machine: college textbook sales, which last year totaled $2.75 billion nationwide. At UCI, sales of new and used books ran about $6 million; at California State University, Fullerton, the tab topped $6.5 million.

And everywhere, students complain about the prices, so much so that Cal State Fullerton bookstore employees slip a paper inside each textbook, detailing where each dollar goes. It lists the store's profit margin at 3.9 cents on the dollar—so students don't think of the store manager as a modern-day King Midas.

"It's just something we have to face as students," UCI freshman Daniel Choi said. "You don't like the prices but you have to buy textbooks."

Students can find savings with used books. Up to half of all books purchased, new and used, will be resold to bookstores and book wholesalers.

"The price of books means a lot of students now 'rent' their books and don't keep them," said James Danzinger, a UCI political science professor and textbook author.

Danzinger explains the economics of textbooks to his students in the first day of class—"a pre-emptive strike," he says, against complaints about his own book assignments.

But even used-book prices strike many students as unreasonable, since most are bought from students for 20 percent or less of their current price and resold for about 75 percent of the original sticker.

"Sure we sell books back, but (bookstores) don't give you that much, say only $8 on a $25 book," said UCI sophomore Leticia Solorzano.

Everyone involved in the textbook business—professors, publishers, store managers—agrees that the prices are outrageous. But there's no consensus as to whether the prices really are too high and, if so, why and who's responsible.

Publishers point out that textbook prices, indexed for inflation, have risen less than those of many other commodities, from candy bars to pianos to Cal State fees. If prices seem high, the publishers blame the bookstores—for selling too many used books, forcing the publishers to print new, updated editions more frequently to redraw their profit curves.

Bookstore managers say the issue just isn't price, but value: If students find a book central to success in the classroom, they won't find the cost out of line. If prices seem high, the managers blame the publishers—for printing new and higher-priced editions too often, forcing students to clamor for used textbooks, which only begins the cost cycle again.

Professors say they are powerless. If prices seem high, they lament not receiving royalties on used books and say publishers give them no choice but to write new editions.

"There's no short answer I can give students as to prices," said David Holcomb, bookstore manager at Orange Coast College and a board member with the National Association of College Stores.

"Most students don't really want to know why," Holcomb said. "But based on the two courses I've taken, I agree with students that prices can often seem high."

To illustrate the complexities that leave students at the end of the line with the book bag, take a popular textbook by Orange Coast College marine-biology instructor Tom Garrison. His textbook,

Oceanography is—in the parlance of Holcomb—a "home run." It's into its second edition with more than 20,000 copies in print, and it's assigned nationwide, from Stanford University and the University of Nebraska to the U.S. Naval Academy and the University of Massachusetts.

While 20,000 is an impressive number, matched by few textbooks, Garrison's book has high production costs, with four-color charts and photographs, high-quality paper and a cloth binding.

"Given the nature of oceanography, good visuals and graphics are a must," Garrison said.

Campus bookstores typically mark up a book 33 percent, meaning one bought from a publisher for $7.50 sells for $10, said a spokesman for the National Association of College Bookstores. Since Garrison's text retails for $59 at most bookstores, the publisher wholesales it for about $44. Garrison is paid 10 percent of the wholesale cost, or about $4.40.

"I realize the price is high—my own daughter spends a couple of hundred dollars on her college texts—but I also know the effort and time that goes into making a good textbook that will actually motivate students," Garrison said. "I just decided I wanted the very best possible book—I'm not getting rich off of this."

Professors who author textbooks have resigned themselves to the fact that their books will be repurchased and resold an average of four times—with royalties paid only on the first sale.

"The publisher and author make practically nothing after the first year," said Ronald Pynn, political-science professor at the University of North Dakota.

Pynn, acting director of the Text and Academic Authors Association, said his organization has tried unsuccessfully to arrange royalty payments on the sale of used textbooks.

Because of lost profits, he said, there's pressure on publishers and authors to issue new editions earlier than normal. Professors generally assign the latest edition because they believe students want up-to-date textbooks.

"My (U.S. presidents) book is in its fourth edition, but to be honest, maybe only a second was justified," Pynn said. "Really, does a change of presidents justify a new edition? Presidential governance has pretty much remained the same, whether it's Reagan or Clinton."

Garrison said a few professors have told him they prefer the first edition of *Oceanography* because the changes in the second edition don't justify the higher price.

"I understand that point, but on the other hand, I want students to have the benefit of the latest information," Garrison said.

One reason for the conformity in textbook prices is that college bookstores face little competition.

Nevertheless, some entrepreneurs believe they can undercut the campus store and turn a profit through high-volume sales of the most popular textbooks.

John Abdol, a former Cal State San Bernardino business professor, operates five off-campus textbook stores. His newest branch, at the Marketplace in Irvine, prices textbooks about 13 percent cheaper than the UCI bookstore.

"I'm looking for sales volume and if I get enough students, we can make money," Abdol said.

UCI's textbook manager, Mike Kiley, said Abdol's store might skim some business as students become aware of the competitor. But so far, UCI has not had to change its pricing.

"To do so would mean that our original pricing structure was not legitimate," Kiley said. "Given his prices and the costs involved, I'm not sure he can stay in business."

—Orange County Register

The lead points up the fact that education stories—as is true of any specialty writing—can be informal. The cash register rings at the start were meant to grab readers' attention, and they undoubtedly did. Never be afraid to try different approaches to a story, as long as they're accurate and clear. Don't be so bowled over by the serious nature of the subject that your writing becomes stiff and dull. There are all kinds of opportunities for creativity in journalism. Take advantage of them. In a singular departure from standard style, Cara Mia DiMassa of the *Los Angeles Times* went to poetry for her light treatment of a story involving stolen props from the set the movie, "The Cat in the Hat." The second stanza read: "Was it a thief?/Was it a prank?/Police have to say,/They are drawing a blank."

The textbook article was right on the button for these other reasons:

- There was a good mix of sources, from students to bookstore managers to professors.
- There was an array of solid facts: prices, royalties, how markups work and one salient example of the path of a book from author to publisher to bookstore.
- The quotes were revealing and believable. Most students could identify with the resignation of buyers in the checkout line.
- The writer did not attempt to put any slant on the story. The issue was examined fairly from the different sides.
- The writing was tight and clear.

Two other points: The copydesk fell in with the offbeat lead. The headline on the story read: "$250 a Semester for a Textbook? You Can Believe It." Second, as in many expanded stories, the piece included a sidebar, a separate story alongside the main story that gives the reader more insight into an issue or controversy. Sidebar material usually cannot be crammed easily into the main story because it would risk disrupting the main story's continuity.

The textbook sidebar pictured a dollar bill split with the overline "Where Does Your Textbook Dollar Go?" The addition also compared prices for specific books at the UCI bookstore and the independent, off-campus store.

Business and Financial Writing

Newspaper editors and business executives have one wish in common: that more journalism graduates come in with at least a basic knowledge of business and finance. Business news is as likely to land on Page One as in the business section because a growing number of stories have a business angle. Sports is one example. Even if you don't plan to be a business writer, it would be a wise idea to take some courses in economics, business and marketing. And if you are thinking of specializing in this area, such courses are virtually a must. The world turns on the economy, which must be explained fully and fairly to a waiting audience. The problems of Enron and other troubled companies are regularly making Page One.

Business is news—often big news. Industrial downsizing, mergers, trade differences between the United States and Japan, tax relief for businesses, new product development and stock market fluctuations are no longer just the concern of industry moguls and major shareholders. They also affect the person on the street. A big aircraft contract to Boeing means hundreds of jobs in the Seattle and Long Beach, California, areas. The merger of two large banks will mean job losses and affect depositors who may find that their neighborhood bank branch has disappeared. The advent of the 21st century brought huge stock losses that affected millions of small shareholders and major corporate mergers that left thousands without jobs. These developments often were front-page stories.

The problem for newspapers is finding qualified journalists who have the background and aptitude for this kind of writing and who understand what they're writing about. Financial specialists must know how the stock market works, what forces influence it, and how the American and world economies operate. They must comprehend and interpret a company's annual report, the actions and influence of the Federal Reserve Board and the intricacies of the commodities market. Other business stories include bond issues, takeovers, consumer credit, antitrust actions, advertising campaigns, new business ventures and the human side of the economy. The *Wall Street Journal* has featured articles on the lifestyle of young executives, depressed factory towns in New England and the trauma of families who move frequently because of company transfers.

Generally, business stories fall into three categories: breaking news, explanatory articles and analysis. We examine two, the first being a story that made Page One on a number of newspapers because of its news value:

By Peter Stinton

After fending off Wells Fargo & Co. in the banking industry's most contentious takeover battle, Los Angeles-based First Interstate Bancorp agreed yesterday to sell out to its San Francisco rival in a deal valued at $11.6 billion—the most ever paid for a U.S. bank.

The acquisition will create the eighth-largest bank in the nation, with $108 billion in assets. The Wells Fargo name will remain and after 92 years, First Interstate will disappear. But in recognition of the commercial clout of Southern California, the combined bank will maintain dual headquarters in San Francisco and Los Angeles.

The big winners in the deal will be the shareholders. Under terms of the agreement, First Interstate shareholders will receive two-thirds of a share of Wells Fargo stock for each share of First Interstate in a tax-free swap.

Wells Fargo shares rose 1 to 229 1/2 yesterday. At that closing price, the deal is worth about $153 per First Interstate share. That is 44 percent more than the $106 price of First Interstate shares before Wells Fargo made its initial offer October 18. First Interstate shares closed up 2 1/4 at $149 yesterday.

By consolidating operations in 13 states—mainly in California, where there is considerable overlap of branches—Wells Fargo anticipates that it will be able to wring at least $800 million in annual cost savings out of the combined bank. That should translate into higher earnings and returns to shareholders.

The big losers in the deal are likely to be the employees. Both banks said it is too early to give an exact figure on the human toll. The deal is unlikely to close before April and it will take 18 months to fully merge the two organizations. But Wells Fargo president Bill Zuendt estimated that there could be 8,000 to 9,000 fewer jobs or up to 19 percent of the two banks' combined work force of 47,000.

As many as 5,000 of the job losses could occur in California, where Wells Fargo has most of its 19,500 employees and First Interstate has about 6,000 of its 27,000 workers. At a press conference in Los Angeles, Wells Fargo Chief Executive Officer Paul Hazen and First Interstate CEO William Siart said they will not try to "sugar coat" the impact on employees, although both hope that hiring freezes and attrition will reduce the number of layoffs.

But many will lose their jobs as Wells Fargo combines data processing and other back-office operations and closes perhaps 350 California branches. Wells Fargo currently operates 983 branches in the state, close to half of them in supermarkets. First Interstate has 406 branches in California.

The decision on which First Interstate and Wells branches to close will be based on their location, parking facilities, cost of real estate and other factors. In addition, the U.S. Department of Justice is likely to require the sale of branches in cities where the combined bank would have an overwhelming share, such as in Sacramento, where the two banks have a total of 51 offices.

Wells Fargo Chief Financial Officer Rod Jacobs said antitrust concerns could prompt the sale of $1 billion in assets.

Wells Fargo does not need the excuse of a mega-merger to close large, stand-alone branches. It and other banks have found that they can deliver banking services more cheaply through automated teller machines, 24-hour phone call centers and mini-branches at supermarkets.

Consumer response to the merger was mixed. Danette Rutts, who was using an ATM machine at Wells Fargo's main branch in San Francisco, said: "I look forward to more teller machines." Her companion, Elizabeth Carter, a First Interstate customer, said, "I'm thinking of changing banks. I think smaller banks put more emphasis on smaller accounts."

First Interstate's Siart will leave the bank when the deal closes, but he will take along $4.6 million in severance benefits.

For three months, the 48-year-old executive vigorously opposed a combination with Wells. Instead, he sought out a white knight in the form of First Bank System of Minneapolis, which agreed to buy First Interstate for about $10 billion in stock—more than a billion less than Wells was willing to pay.

A deal with the Minnesota bank would have resulted in far fewer layoffs than a merger with Wells.

But a critical turning point came Friday, when the Securities and Exchange Commission ruled that First Interstate could not repurchase any of its own shares for two years following a merger. To make the deal work, First Interstate had to raise its earnings per share after the merger, and the main way it planned to do that was by buying back shares.

After the SEC delivered its blow, First Interstate's board of directors met in Los Angeles and instructed Siart to negotiate with Wells.

Siart flew to the Oakland airport Saturday for five hours of discussions with Hazen. First Interstate's board convened again Sunday afternoon and after two hours called Wells Fargo to say they had a preliminary agreement. The boards of both banks met separately Tuesday and agreed on the final terms, which included adding seven of First Interstate's directors to the 14-person Wells board.

First Bank System may have lost its bid but it will be lavishly compensated for playing the favored suitor role for three months. It will receive a record $200 million in "breakup" as stipulated by a November 5 agreement with First Interstate. After investment banking and other expenses, it will make about $190 million before taxes.

Wells Fargo will also pay out about $30 million in fees, mainly to investment banks Montgomery Securities and CS First Boston and to law firms Cravath, Swaine & Moore and Sullivan & Cromwell. First Interstate will pay about $20 million in fees.

Employees of Wells Fargo and First Interstate will not fare so well. However, Wells Fargo will double its normal severance pay to workers who lose their jobs to four weeks for every year of service. First Interstate will also offer four weeks of severance per year of service.

Wells has also started paying $2,000 bonuses and moving expenses to workers who take new jobs at different locations.

—San Francisco Chronicle

The account is about as well crafted as a story can be. The merger is solidly explained, the impact on consumers, employees and communities is presented clearly and there are precise figures to flesh it out. It's obvious the writer had a pipeline to key sources and used them to the advantage of the reader. One mark of a well-written story is whether it answers the major questions of its audience. This one left no major holes. The qualifying "major" is used because no reporter can include everything in a story. Business reporting aside, Stinton's article stands as a model for any multifaceted story.

As previously noted, today's business pages are far ranging, as this story illustrates:

By Karen Hanna

Hands shoot up when Karrie Steinmetz's practical nursing students are asked whether they've lost their jobs.

More than half.

The Career Center has become a home away from home for a group of women well acquainted with factory work's revolving door. Moving on wasn't easy, but looking back isn't an option. For them, economic development is just getting by.

Deborah Piacent says she has always felt a certain comfort in the idea of factory work—generations of people working side by side, giving an honest day's labor and earning a pay check like clock work.

"And any way you look at it, a job is a lot easier than a career, whether you're working it or pursuing it," Piacent, 51, of Hayesville said.

She and long-time friend Sharon Burkholder are studying to be nurses.

They have rung up 60 years of factory work between them, a string that includes a series of factory shutdowns—four years at Hedstrom Corp., 10 years at Liqui-Box Corp., nine years at Bosch Rexroth Corp.

"I think a lot of people are just dealing with the blows, you know, the economy, the best way they can. I know, I was always brought up you get knocked down, you pick yourself up again," Burkholder, whose parents grew up in the Depression, said.

Recovery, triage-style

According to David Kleinschmidt, director of the Career Center's adult-education department, more than 1,000 displaced workers had been served by triage responses organized when companies such as Hedstrom, General Hone Corp. and Pentair Pump Group's South Facility (Hydromatic) closed.

At Ashland County Department of Job and Family Services' One-Stop, people who are unemployed or looking for new jobs can take advantage of free resume and job-search services. People who have been laid off, meet income-eligibility requirements or are military veterans may qualify for financial aid for schooling or re-training.

Piacent had no funding for her course—she says the aid from the Workforce Investment Act came with too many strings attached—and she could not turn down work when Bosch called her back. If she had, she would have lost her eligibility for unemployment benefits.

Instead, she juggled both, allowing her husband the opportunity to finish out his clinicals—the home-improvement salesman is back in school for radiology. According to Piacent, Tom's decision to leave sales after he was laid off was fine when she was working; it's become harder since she lost her job. Piacent's wages were slashed about $6 an hour over the past three years she was at Bosch.

"I had a classified job. There were only four people who could bump me, but I didn't get bumped, I got reduced," Piacent said as members of her class acted out the roles of patients and nurses in admission interviews. She made $13.88 an hour by the time she was laid off.

From job to career

According to Kleinschmidt and financial aid officer RaeAnn Smith, the Career Center administers work skills, math and reading tests to incoming students. Even so, some students can't manage the rigors of work, home and family lives. A handful each year drop out because they find jobs or can't afford to stay in school without work.

Smith said some programs require a high school diploma or General Equivalency Examination—preparation classes and math and literacy refreshers are offered free—and students must demonstrate they have overcome one other potential obstacle on their own—they have to show they have sitters lined up, if they have children.

That isn't a problem for single mother Lynn Bailey—her baby just turned 18.

In going back to school, Bailey, who worked alongside Piacent and Burkholder at Bosch, hopes she can be an example for her son.

"That's what his attitude is: Just get a diploma and get out, and I tell him there's more to it than that in this world," said Bailey, who has spent the last 24 years in a factory.

Being laid off, she said, "it's like the bottom dropped out of your world."

She's currently studying business office technologies.

"Yeah, you go from pretty OK to being in the welfare line—they don't call it that anymore—but yeah, I was embarrassed, I never asked for help before," said Bailey, 43.

She qualified for a Pell Grant and aid from the Workforce Investment Act, which was designed to help workers displaced by overseas manufacturing.

Good employment, good pay

According to Kleinschmidt, the Career Center is responsible for tracking its graduates and offering programs that provide in-demand skills. Some funding is based on job-outlook studies.

Lawson, Piacent and Burkholder attend class in a room that adjoins the business office technologies class. Lawson defines economic development as "decent employment, decent pay."

With two daughters, ages 2 and 6, 29-year-old Rachelle Lawson and her husband struggle to pay their bills. She said she wouldn't complain if Ashland was able to attract more stores and restaurants—that's one of the plans for the U.S. 250 corridor—but that isn't enough.

"I think the Super Wal-Mart is a good idea because I've been there, a lot of stuff is cheaper, but it's going to hurt the mom and pop stores, and I feel for them . . . because they're going to be out, and I know what it's like to be out," Lawson said.

Losing her job, Lawson said, has given her the motivation she needed to go back to school—she always wanted to be a nurse, anyway. "I liked it," Lawson said of working at Bosch, "but this was my blessing in disguise, my ticket out of there."

Despite the uncertainties of factory work, the women said they always gave 100 percent at any job they worked.

"It was always I do this for me because I didn't want to hear, 'Boy, poor Deb, she's about as worthless as lips on a chicken,' " Piacent said. "I always figured for what I get paid, they deserve a decent day's work."

Coming back from setback

Piacent said her wages have fallen from about $51,000 a year to $24,000 a year—that's from working on call-back at Bosch.

No matter, she said. She manages.

She was trained to. Her father always believed in working and saving while he had job, preparing for the possibility he wouldn't.

"The year calculators came out," Piacent said, "I think we got five of them."

Dad punched in his wages and figured out his expenses. His children followed suit. They learned the more they worked, the more they would have.

"So we were programmed for overtime and figuring out overtime," Piacent said.

She and her former coworkers are survivors.

"And me, I believe failure is not an option, and by hook or crook, I'll make it," Piacent pledged. "Come hell or high water."

—*Ashland* (Ohio) *Times-Gazette*

It should be said here that the business section is no longer closed to female journalists. The era when female reporters were consigned to cover society news on the "women's page" has long since passed.

Sports Reporting

In households across America there are untold numbers of subscribers who read the sports pages before anything else in the newspaper. It's also true that many fans who watch athletic contests on TV or on-site still avidly read the newspaper's account of the game the next day. Baseball particularly may be the national pastime, but sports in general are a national obsession. And, in recent years, women's sports, although not yet getting the newspaper play of the men's games, are climbing steadily in that direction.

Participation sports, too, are rapidly rising in popularity. The burgeoning affluence of the middle class has produced a booming market in skiing, running, boating and gymnastics. Papers in certain parts of the country provide detailed information on ski conditions, and big-city marathon races, which attract mostly amateurs, are major events worthy of generous space.

All this promises a bright career for the budding sports journalist, both male and female. Women sportswriters are becoming so common that they are taken in stride by most athletes, even when they go into the locker rooms of some teams after a basketball or football game. Also keep in mind that in sportswriting there are specializations within that specialization. Major dailies and sports magazines can field experts in baseball, football, tennis, skiing and so on. On smaller papers, one or two sports reporters cover everything. One way ambitious sportswriters get to the top is by covering high school sports for community newspapers, all the while looking for opportunities on major dailies.

The newcomer, however, should realize (and some no doubt do) that sportswriting has evolved from a who won/who lost kind of coverage to reporting that takes a much more in-depth approach in writing about players, coaches and the millionaire owners of the franchises. On a few papers, athletes are still treated reverentially, but the trend, in professional sports especially, is to cut them down to size—to show them as merely human beings who, because of their skills, make bags of money and aren't always models for kids. There also is an awareness among editors and writers that sports are dominated by big businesses whose owners make decisions that usually are more in the interest of their bank accounts than the fans and the communities that support them. Cleveland Browns fans learned that their loyalty to the team meant little or nothing when the owners decided to move the club to Baltimore, which years earlier had suffered the same loss when the Colts moved to Indianapolis. Los Angeles waved goodbye to both the Raiders and the Rams.

All this is reported daily, sometimes to the ire of athletes and their coaches and corporate bosses. Basketball and football players, whose talents have come under criticism in the press, have assaulted more than one sportswriter or barred them from the locker room.

In short, sports pages no longer function as a public relations outlet for the home team. Reporting is often sharp-edged. The financial side of sports is major news, and athletes who break the law or are accused of enhancing their prowess with steroids can expect to see the information in print. Sportswriters can be the most irreverent journalists on the paper, who never duck a controversial issue.

This is not to say that traditional reporting has been tossed aside. Sports reporters are themselves sports fans, and their writing strives to bring the excitement and passion on the field to the reader. What's missing are the old clichés and banalities that were part of sportswriting for many years. Sports pages try to avoid bromides like "power hitter," "scrappy third baseman," "hoopsters" and "goal line stand." Frenzied adjectives also are passé, although a few diehards insist on using them.

While sportswriting has changed, it must still be combined with a thorough knowledge of the game. At the outset of their careers, sportswriters should be familiar with several sports, particularly if they start on smaller newspapers, where they may be covering everything from tennis to football. And even on metro dailies with 40 or more sportswriters, there is a slew of men and women who can comfortably cover football, track, baseball, soccer, hockey and downhill skiing. Bob Broeg, former sports editor of the *St. Louis Post-Dispatch,* who began his career covering sports for a college paper, commented:

> I think it's important that someone who wants to get into sportswriting makes certain that it's not just a desire to watch sports that has motivated him, but a true desire to report and write. If, in addition, he will familiarize himself with all sports, not only those for which he has the greatest interest, and if he will evaluate a good performance from a bad one in all the sports and know the general rules, if not necessarily all the fine points, he will be well on his way.

Broeg also recommended that new sports staffers "write for the wastebasket," meaning that writing should be practiced until craftsmanship is achieved.

Los Angeles Times sports editor Bill Dwyre believes that sportswriting has entered a new era, saying: "We're about at the end of a generation of sportswriters who could get by simply by going to games and press conferences and regurgitating what they were told. Sports reporters will have to be much more curious, will have to ask a lot of questions and have better instincts. They also will have to be more attuned to consumer needs."

As to motivation for seeking jobs as sportswriters, Dwyre observed: "There are many young men and women who want to get into this business because they like sports. That's not enough. They should want to be sportswriters because they like journalism; there is a big difference."

Dwyre said that with the growth in the number of leagues and new sports gaining popularity, "The potential for stories is larger than ever but it will take the new generation of sportswriters and astute editors to spot the stories that will transcend all audiences. We don't write just for Laker fans or Dodger fans. We also have to write for readers interested in the human side of sports."

Sportswriting ranges from the straight to a feature style in which almost anything goes. Certainly, it has more latitude than the general news sections. This might be called a typical nuts-and-bolts story that appeared in the Sacramento State (Calif.) University student newspaper, the *Hornet.*

By Jimmy Spencer

Weber State University used to own Sacramento State basketball. Now they just rent them out for the playoffs.

The Hornets (12–15, 8–6) are looking to change history this time around, however, as Weber State (12–15, 7–7) visits the

Hornets Nest for the second-straight year in the Big Sky Conference Tournament quarterfinals.

The Hornets finally solved its 18-game winless streak against Weber with a home win last season and earned a second program victory against the Wildcats at home again this season. But in the playoffs, beating Weber hasn't been easy.

The Wildcats have knocked the Hornets out of the program's first two Big Sky Conference tournaments the past two seasons. Last year, the Wildcats beat the Hornets 68–62 in Sac State's first-ever tournament home game.

The season before that, in Sac State's first tournament appearance, Weber State beat the Hornets in Utah in the semifinals, after the Hornets won at Montana in the first round. That year, the Wildcats would become Big Sky champions, advancing to the NCAA Tournament as a No. 12 seed, ultimately falling 81–74 in the first round to the No. 5 seed, University of Wisconsin.

"They are our nemesis," said Sac State head coach Jerome Jenkins. "It's only right that we have to go through them."

This season, the rivals have split in conference play, with both teams winning its home game. Weber State's victory came through a controversial call on a last-second layup that resulted in the suspension of Jenkins and reports that freshman Randy Adams was challenging spectators to fight him on the floor and senior E.J. Harris made inappropriate gestures at Weber State fans.

"I think there is an intense amount of animosity and emotional ties against Weber State," said senior guard Jameel Pugh. "Our team is going to come out like a pack of wild dogs ready to rip them apart.

"They're not ready to take on the amount of intensity we're going to bring to the floor with our crowd, on our court."

The home game will be last for both Pugh and E.J. Harris, the team's only seniors. Pugh averaged 17.6 points in conference and led the Hornets in scoring in its last four conference games, averaging 24.8 points in that span.

"This is going to be an emotional game for me," Pugh said. "Obviously I want to extend my career and leave my last game knowing that I won in the playoffs. E.J. and I want to go out on a high note."

Former Hornets guard Joseth Dawson said he still dwells on last season's tournament loss to Weber State—his last game with the Hornets.

"It was disappointing," said Dawson, who led the Hornets in scoring and was named to the all-Big Sky first team last season. "We could have made more history, but we just couldn't pull it out.

"I put my legacy down already; it's time to pass the torch."

Now it's up to Pugh and the rest of the new generation of Hornets to take the program to the next level.

"I understand the program is happy to be in the playoffs, but we've been here for three years in a row," Jenkins said. "We want to win the Big Sky."

—The State Hornet

That the writer knows basketball well is displayed in the story. His use of background on the team is helpful to the reader, and the quotes ring true. Note that the writer uses direct quotes from players and the coach that have a ring to the reader's ear, and keep advancing the story. The last direct quote, from Coach Jenkins, is effective at ending the story on a positive and forward-looking note. The writer uses the quotes to show, rather than tell, the readers in his own words without attribution what the game means.

This technique allows the writer to give the story a focus, and to some extent analyze the significance of the sports event, without losing his objectivity. Seemingly, sports fans have an insatiable appetite for analysis, commentary and just plain facts about the sports world whether their teams are playing or not.

Next up is an example of a loose, informal style that cloaks numerous sports articles.

By Mark Zeigler

Think about this for a moment: The United States . . . favored in an international men's soccer tournament.

Very strange.

Very true.

The CONCACAF Gold Cup opens today with a doubleheader in Anaheim, and it is hard to scan the rosters of the nine national teams and not pick the United States to win the biennial championship for the region (North and Central America and the Caribbean).

Yes, that's the same United States that in 1994 won its first World Cup match in 44 years.

Mexico is here. Brazil is here. Honduras and Canada are here. But on paper, at least, Team USA is the most experienced, most proven and—gasp—maybe the most talented.

The F-word. Favorite.

"With our success over the past couple years comes a new responsibility," says defender Alexi Lalas, who doesn't appear to have cut his hair over the past couple of years. "For the first time I can think of, we're one of the favorites. I mean, we've got the underdog thing down.

"The mark of great teams is to sustain that level."

If you're holding a soccer tournament and Brazil is entered, then Brazil is the favorite. That would hold true here if Brazil sent Romario and Bebeto and the rest of its A team, or even its B or C team. But Brazil is using Southern California as a proving ground for its Olympic team, and no one wearing the yellow and blue here is older than 22. No experience.

Mexico? It beat Team USA 4–0 in the last Gold Cup final, but that was before 130,800 at Azteca Stadium in Mexico City and that was in 1993. Since then, the Tricolor has fired coach Miguel Meja Baron, been eliminated by the Americans in the Copa America last summer and lost to Slovenia's under-23 team at home last month. No momentum.

The United States has experience and momentum. Coach Steve Sampson vowed to bring his best 20 players, and he has. The average age is 26 1/2, and 15 played on the '94 World Cup team. They won the U.S. Cup last summer, then reached the semifinals for the treacherous Copa America in Uruguay on their first try.

Oh, and they have good chemistry.

"The best it's ever been for a national team," says Sampson, the one-time interim replacement for Bora Milutinovic who never stopped winning. "The players enjoy seeing each other. There are no cliques on this team, and you couldn't always say that. These guys play for each other."

About the only thing they don't have is the enormous home-field advantage.

They are playing in Southern California, where Mexico and even El Salvador routinely outdraw them. And the tournament has been plagued by poor organization and minimal promotion—Sampson has told the team to expect attendance closer to intimate gatherings than large crowds.

There also is the matter of the draw, which basically puts Mexico—the best box office attraction—through to the Jan. 21 final.

"Until the Gold Cup is a pure draw instead of a placement," Sampson says, "there are going to be some inequities, and inequities in sports are not well-received by the players or by the fans. Having said that, I understand why they're doing it, and it's to make money."

The heaviest cash cow, of course, would be a U.S.-Mexico final, their first meeting since Milutinovic was fired by the former and hired by the latter. Mexico shouldn't have any trouble getting here, thanks to its draw. Neither might the United States, thanks to its team.

—*San Diego Union-Tribune*

In sports, as in any other subject, writing style is determined by the nature of the story. Although there is more leeway in sportswriting, serious stories crop up, and a newspaper would look silly trying to make them funny or trivializing them in other ways. The 1995 major league baseball strike and 2005 steroids scandal are serious issues. The strike left fans feeling bitter toward both the players and management and created economic hardship for hundreds of people like food and souvenir vendors, who make their living from the ballparks. And the steroids scandal casts a shadow over the many records set by modern-day sluggers. Do today's players hit the ball farther because they're better conditioned, or is it due to performance-enhancing drugs?

John Hohenberg, a professor of journalism at Columbia University, in his book *The Professional Journalist* said today's sportswriters face greater pressure to make their writing lively since fans aren't turning to the newspaper for scores. Fans get that information more quickly, he said, through radio and television (not to mention a source Hohenberg doesn't mention, the Internet).

"What becomes important is how and why the result was achieved, which means the techniques of the feature writer have now become all important on the sports page," Hohenberg said. That leaves plenty of room for lively writing, and even some editorialization, Hohenberg added.

Foreign Correspondence

No other job in journalism, with the possible exception of investigative reporting, carries the glamour of foreign correspondence. The term evokes memories of such famous and colorful correspondents as Richard Harding Davis, Homer Bigart, Web Miller, Leland Stowe, Marguerite Higgins, Ed Murrow and Ernest Hemingway (before he began writing novels).

It's still a desirable assignment. Staff correspondents live well abroad, are usually given a housing allowance and paid transportation from their base on business travel. This author interviewed the AP correspondent in Beijing in her huge, lavishly furnished apartment in a protected compound while millions of Chinese were cramming two or three families into one small abode. Similarly, the agency's reporter in Nairobi, Kenya, lived in an eight-room house with two servants in one of the city's best neighborhoods. In addition, of course, correspondents' work often involves interviewing high government officials and covering wars and other major stories that often land on Page One.

Still, there doesn't seem to be the same interest among young journalists in overseas reporting as in the past. The then-foreign editor of the *Los Angeles Times* told the author that he had difficulty recruiting promising staffers on the paper for foreign assignments. The reason, he explained, was that many of them were married with children, owned their homes and otherwise had deep roots in the community. They did not want to be separated from their families for long periods of time, and possibly putting themselves in danger. In the halcyon days of foreign correspondents—the 1920s, '30s and '40s—most of them were single and had moved around a lot in stateside jobs. Some, like Robert St. John, went overseas looking for jobs with American news bureaus. He was hired by AP as World War II broke out.

The danger is real for correspondents in foreign lands. Some have been killed in wars and by terrorists in recent years. One recent casualty in Pakistan was Daniel Pearl, 38, of the *Wall Street Journal,* who was murdered by terrorists. Also, it's an assignment that can create a high stress level. As reported in the *Columbia Journalism Review*, a study, partly funded by the Freedom Forum, of 170 correspondents revealed that war journalists "had significantly more post-traumatic stress disorder (PTSD), depression and psychological distress," with photographers being "particularly vulnerable." Reporters can sometimes fashion a story from behind the lines in a war, but to get dramatic photos, photographers must be on the battleground. Robert Capa, a famous war photographer, once commented: "If your pictures aren't any good, you're not close enough." AP's Joe Rosenthal, who shot the celebrated flag-raising photo by Marines on Iwo Jima's Mount Suribachi in World War II, was close enough, so close, in fact, that bullets were zipping by him as he aimed his camera.

Yet, the opportunities are there for those adventurous enough to want the job and have the skills to qualify for them. Virtually all foreign correspondents have proved themselves as stateside reporters for as long as 10 years. It's not an assignment that is handed to recent journalism graduates. Nevertheless, if that is your goal, prepare for it by being the best reporter you can be, becoming competent in at least one foreign language—French, German or Russian for a European assignment, and Chinese or Japanese for Asia duty. At some point in your career, move to a major newspaper or wire service with overseas bureaus, although some newspapers without standing bureaus send reporters abroad on limited assignments.

Other Specialties

Beginning in the 1970s, newspapers, facing stiff competition from TV for audience attention, began expanding their editorial menu to embrace new content or expand the old. Lifestyle sections began blossoming on big and small papers, arts and entertainment got a face-lift, fashion writers were hired and kids' pages were added.

Today, the opportunity for specialization is greater than ever as newspapers try to win readers, particularly those in the 18 to 35 age group. Surveys have shown that the most loyal and dependable newspaper readers are older, middle- or upper-class Americans, who renew their subscriptions year after year. Of course, thousands of newspapers are sold in vending machines, but single-copy buyers are not as dear to the hearts of publishers and advertisers as home-delivery subscribers.

The studies also have indicated that subscribers are generally better-educated than the population as a whole, which translates into the creation of sections that appeal to them. Thus, newspapers, mainly on Sunday, offer information about travel, real estate, automobiles, computer developments, gardening, photography, careers and increased world news. Real estate sections, as one example, are widely read for tips and advice on buying or selling a house, apartment renting, fixing up old homes, condominium living, choosing a real estate agent and dealing with mortgage lenders. Travel writers go beyond destination pieces with articles on trip health precautions, how to pack, where the air and cruise bargains are and techniques for traveling with children. Arts and cultural sections—for some the most desired part of the paper—are awash with personality profiles, insider glimpses into movie and theater production, movie, TV and book reviews and dozens of other features that range from financing of the arts to the emergence of new pop music groups. Automotive writers can praise or skewer a new model without worrying about the reaction of auto dealer advertisers.

On the hard news side of the larger papers, there are specialists in labor, housing, foreign affairs, the media (a hot topic these days), automobiles and aviation. In addition, some columnists focus on particular subjects.

Most of the specialists in these areas started on newspapers as general-assignment reporters, waited for an opportunity in the specialty that appealed to them and managed to convince an editor they deserved a shot at it.

As with the previous, more traditional specialties listed in this chapter, those just mentioned require a thorough knowledge of the subject and the ability to write about it in a lively, absorbing way. Read all you can about the field. If the theater is your passion, see all the plays you can afford and read those you can't. If, as likely, you begin on a smaller paper, volunteer to review local high school or college plays to learn the craft. Ditto for movies and TV programs.

Once you land on a newspaper, we see no reason why you should not be able to attain the role of specialist—if that's what you want. Opportunities are endless.

Investigative Reporting

It may be a stretch to include investigative reporting in this chapter. Former *Washington Post* executive editor Ben Bradlee, who, as mentioned, orchestrated the Watergate probe, once asserted that investigative reporting "begins with the fourth or fifth question asked. A reporter doesn't need a neon sign saying, 'I'm an investigative reporter.'"

Other editors and reporters maintain that all reporting is investigative—or should be. Maybe it should, but it's our opinion that true investigative reporters are a special breed who have the temperament, patience and curiosity that enables them to spend long, plodding hours poring through documents and interviewing perhaps dozens of individuals to arrive at the truth. They may also have a sense of outrage that impels them to make the world, or at least their community, a better place.

Few newspeople have these qualities. Genuine investigative reporting can mean irregular hours, a chaotic home life, consorting with unsavory characters and immense frustration when leads do not pan out. Weeks or months of snooping may end in a blank wall or leave the reporter with material that is tantalizing but not strong enough to print. The paper's attorney, fearing a libel suit, might turn thumbs down on your efforts.

The idea of investigative journalism is indeed a romantic one with rewards thrown in. Each year, the Pulitzer Prizes, the highest awards in journalism, include at least one investigative reporter. Yet you must ask yourself if you're the kind of person who would be comfortable with this kind of life. Most of a newspaper's editorial content does not consist of investigative revelations. Providing readers with straight news, information, background, opinion and interpretation continues to be the main function of the press. You can have a very satisfying career meeting these needs. Although Watergate propelled many college-bound students into journalism, very few J-school graduates became investigative reporters. Pulitzer Prize winners Donald L. Bartlett and James Steele of the *Philadelphia Inquirer* and later of *Time* magazine, two of the best investigative reporters in the nation, know from experience that the road to success in their specialty involves long, plodding hours of hard work. This is how they described one of their investigations in *Quill* magazine:

> The two of us trudged up a narrow wooden stairway at the rear of Philadelphia's labyrinthine City Hall to an isolated alcove nestled under one of the building's great domes.
>
> There, in row after row of brown, aging, legal-size folders, stacked seven to eight feet high on dusty metal shelves above a concrete floor, was the record of violent crime in Philadelphia for the last quarter century.
>
> Occupying an aged, wooden desk and two disabled chairs, we began to read, take notes and systematically extract information from the files of murders, rapes, robberies and assaults which took place in Philadelphia during one year. . . .
>
> For nearly six months, we repeated this ritual, arriving at 9 a.m. each day to begin work, taking a brief luncheon break at 1 p.m., then returning to our secluded garret for a few more hours of research. Late in the afternoon, we would walk four blocks north to the [newspaper] building to study the day's cases, type notes of the more interesting ones and jot down those that might require a follow-up.
>
> Such is the glamorous life of an investigative reporter.

The pair conceded, though, that the results of such labors can be "quite dramatic." Drudgery notwithstanding, if you see investigative reporting as your future and are willing to pay your training dues to get there, by all means go for it. This kind of journalism has righted wrongs and improved the quality of life. Reporting leaking toxins from a chemical plant in your town is surely a good deed. So is uncovering abuses of patients in nursing homes or lifting the lid on a securities scam.

Not all investigative reporting leads to someone going to jail or being fired. The *Sacramento Bee* produced a fine series on ocean pollution, and other newspapers have investigated overcrowded prison conditions, political campaign spending, teenage pregnancy, immigration problems, nursing homes and inadequate schools. The reporter's satisfaction can come from an effort that improved society in some way. The amount of work is about the same as going after the bad guys, but the risks of libel are less.

In any event, the groundwork for investigative reporting lies in learning the basic skills as a general assignment or beat reporter. Becoming familiar with the criminal justice system, the courts and city hall is the best education you can get if investigative journalism is your goal.

The Arts

Some student journalists who have been theater, music or dance critics on their college newspapers want the same kind of assignment in their first professional jobs. It's not likely to happen. In the first place, that first job probably will be on a small paper, which cannot afford the luxury of an arts reviewer and, even if it can, there are not enough artistic events in the community to merit a full-time staffer to report on them. What the editor wants from a newcomer is the ability to cover city hall and the school board. But that should not discourage an applicant who is truly serious about hoping to make such journalism a career. There may not be a plethora of plays and concerts to cover, but there are some—a local theater group, school plays, a string quartet or a performance by dance school students. The aspiring critic can carry out his city hall duties while pestering the editor to let him take a crack at reviewing a play—or perhaps movies. Thus, when he moves to a big-city daily he will have some clips to show an editor that he has qualifications for writing about the metropolitan arts scene.

But besides having clips, a would-be critic should thoroughly immerse herself in the area that interests her most, whether it be theater, dance, film, or something else. Critics for major news media have devoted a good part of their lives to acquiring knowledge and background in their field. A theater critic, for instance, should be familiar not only with contemporary plays but also the works of George Bernard Shaw and Berthold Brecht. The background enables a reviewer to put a play—or movie— in perspective.

Now read this review published in a small California newspaper.

By Lewis Brand

Neil Labute's "The Shape of Things to Come," which had its West Coast premiere Friday at the Laguna Playhouse, involved four students whose lives become entangled in ways that are sometimes funny but more often corrosive as their relationships veer toward the edge and over.

For older viewers, the play might call up memories of George Bernard Shaw's "Pygmalion" or the movie "Bob & Carol & Ted & Alice." Any parallel to the latter disappears quickly under Labute's whiplash dialogue and much franker approach to sex. The "Pygmalion" analogy holds up better but in converse order.

In the opening scene, Evelyn (Stacy Solodkin), an aspiring sculptress and MFA candidate at a small Midwestern college, is preparing to spray paint a nude sculpture at a local museum. She is not against nudity in art, just this particular nude. Adam (Michael Eric Strickland), another student who is a part-time attendant at the museum, makes a half-hearted attempt to halt her mischief but Evelyn convinces him of the purity of her motive. "I'm a straightforward person," she later proclaims, a line that Adam eventually hurls back at her with no little justification.

Adam, initially portrayed as a shy, stodgy loner, is smitten by this free spirit, who engulfs him. Cunning and manipulative, Evelyn embarks on a makeover with him as her subject. She convinces him to wear hippier clothes, switch hairstyles, get a nose job (although it's hard to imagine he needs one), lose 25 pounds, which is cleverly achieved in passing, and introduces him to performance art and her bedroom. Adam, who previously had trouble even getting a date, is transformed and transported.

Still, both briefly stray—Adam with a former girlfriend (Robyn Cohen), and Evelyn with Philip (Jay Boyer), Adam's ex-roommate and Jenny's fiance. Philip, cynical and caustic, is a match for Evelyn as he suspects that she vandalized the statue, an act that she and Adam have kept secret.

Despite their liaison, which seems like an act of revenge, Philip and Evelyn clearly despise each other, engaging in a verbal clash that is a dramatic highlight.

Relationships shatter amid bitter recriminations and accusations of infidelity. Adam, no longer quite the naif, now flips barbs with as much acidity as Evelyn but crumbles when she demands an agonizing price for her continued affections.

The play climaxes in a brutally emotional and revelatory scene. As in his film, "The Company of Men," LaBute examines society with a baleful eye.

All four actors are perfectly cast for their roles, turning in excellent performances. I look forward to seeing them again on stage. The play runs for two hours and 15 minutes or so without an intermission. Under Richard Stein's deft direction, pace and timing hold up well. Nevertheless, I think one break would not harm its effectiveness.

The settings are minimal, appearing in quick shifts on a bare stage with a mobile backdrop. The play runs through June 30.

—*Laguna News-Post,* Laguna Beach, Calif.

Covering the Beats

The beat reporter is both reporter and editor. Away from the mainstream of newsroom general assignment, such reporters often decide what and what not to cover on a beat, be it the police station or the White House. Their desks are not in the city room but at the police station, city hall or courthouse pressrooms. They might be called the local "foreign correspondents" of the newspaper since their contacts with home-office editors are usually by phone or computer.

They generally determine their own assignments, using their editorial judgment on what to cover. A courthouse reporter, for example, may have to pick one of six trials or other court proceedings scheduled on a particular day. Police reporters on metro dailies are likely to pass on minor burglaries or misdemeanor drug arrests in a city plagued by drive-by shootings and other homicides, carjackings, arson and bank robberies.

Some newspapers have eliminated traditional beats in favor of "topic" reporters or team reporting of various sectors, while other papers hew to them as highly necessary functions. Depending on the size of the paper, beats now include such areas as transportation, military affairs, suburban bureaus, merchant shipping and education. For these, however, the reporter generally works out of the main office.

Bob Burdick, former editor of the *Rocky Mountain News* in Denver, Colorado, believes strongly in maintaining the beat structure, notably the police beat.

"They are extremely important," he said. "People want to know if there's a problem in their neighborhood—whether they should take security precautions."

At the same time, Burdick continued, standard beats are evolving in keeping with changing times.

"We now want to know how city hall interacts with suburban city halls. And we want reporters to cover not just meetings but to look into common problems like air pollution. The beginning staffer benefits from beats because they teach responsibility. The mental discipline involved in knowing that you are responsible for everything connected with your beat has great value. As I look around and talk to other editors, I see a lot of beats still operating."

The late Marcia McQuern, former editor and publisher of the *Riverside* (Calif.) *Press-Enterprise,* said her paper also relies on beat reporters to maintain a steady and reliable news flow from governmental agencies. "We also field teams of reporters for certain kinds of coverage, but a staffed beat is one of our mainstays," she disclosed.

The beat reporter also benefits from getting a thorough, inside look at how the police or city hall system works. (In covering the federal courts and agencies in a major city, we learned a tremendous amount about the law, information that was to be helpful throughout our careers.)

A vital part of the beat reporter's task is to maintain close relations with news sources without getting chummy to the point where they expect favorable treatment in the paper. The relationship should be a businesslike one with both parties being aware of the other's obligations and responsibilities. The reporter is responsible to her readers and her newspaper. She is not part of the city hall or police department establishment and should not represent its interests, although she should treat it fairly. Many beat reporters are on a first-name basis with their regular sources without letting that fact affect their objectivity. Other journalists have been pulled off beats because they identified too much with the people they covered.

Above all, the reporter cannot develop a "handout" mentality—depending solely on press releases and self-serving statements from news sources for story material. Nor will the reporter get much by merely sticking his head into an official's door each morning to ask whether there is any news. Time must be spent with news makers to extract stories. Often a source is unaware of an important story until so convinced by a reporter.

Questions to sources should be specifically worded, as in these examples:

- To the mayor: Do you agree with Councilman Kern's suggestion that the city should ban new housing developments?
- To the police chief: Are the bullet-proof vests ordered by your department unsafe as claimed by the Police Benevolent Association?
- To the district attorney: Will you seek an indictment in connection with Palmer's arrest?
- To the school superintendent: How do you account for the fact that the State Education Association ranked the system as the lowest in the state in verbal and math test scores?
- To a defense lawyer in a murder case: What will be your defense strategy in the trial?

In his perceptive book *On Press,* ex-*New York Times* columnist Tom Wicker discusses the knack of phrasing questions to force interviewees into giving substantive answers. Instead of, for example, asking the president at a news conference to comment on reports that aid to Africa may be revised — a tactic that may elicit a filibuster from a skilled politician — the reporter could instead ask:

> "Mr. President, is it true that the State Department has informed the appropriations subcommittee in the House that no further aid beyond what's in the pipeline should go to Uganda? And if it is true, why did you order this action?"

This technique is much more likely to result in the president's answering the question directly to avoid perhaps having a hostile member of a House subcommittee leak his own version of events. Wicker notes that a reporter might ask the question that way even if he had no such "leak" from the subcommittee.

You don't have to be interviewing a president to use this technique. The way you frame a question often determines the kind of answer you'll get from any official. Suggesting to an interviewee that you know more than you actually do is a time-honored ploy for getting a source to talk. The idea is that the source, thinking that the reporter knows more than she does, will decide there's no point in holding back. The strategy doesn't always work, but try to acquire at least a morsel of knowledge about the subject before beginning an interview. Your own newspaper library is a good place to start.

The news in this story from the education beat sprang from the action of government, through the No Child Left Behind learning standards mandated by Congress and the U.S. Education Department. But the reporter gave the story more meaning and depth through interviews.

By Karen Hanna

Many of the children at the Tri-County Cooperative Preschool know their colors; some can write the letters of their names. Classroom songs and activities all carry a hidden message that explains how teachers manage to make academics child's play.

"I talked to a dad, and I told him how we taught through play, and he said, 'Oh, then, you just sneak learning in?'" teacher Pat Kenyon said between sessions at the school.

The public preschool, which is housed in a wing of Dale-Roy School, provides early-education experiences for children ages 3–5 who have been identified with special needs.

Like teachers throughout the state, Tri-County Cooperative Preschool's instructors are now responsible for addressing specific content standards mandated by the state. Coloring, singing and pasting must all have a purpose.

"The [preschool-kindergarten] standards were put in place because now more than ever before we're expecting children to learn at high levels," Ohio Department of Education spokesperson J.C. Benton said of the standards set forth by the state to prescribe age-appropriate expectations. The preschool standards include the abilities to use language to express an idea, sort like objects, recognize simple patterns and follow instructions.

All those were on display Monday when teacher Barb Dreher's class counted up the number of "L's" in each student's name. Bright inflatable egg-shaped "letter people" hung from a clothesline above cubbies where students store their coats; charts illustrated the day's date and weather.

"It's creating an atmosphere and providing them with opportunities to grow," Dreher said of the preschool's mission during a pause in the class, when students played quietly on their own. One boy at the discovery table—home to the hermit crab cage—placed black buttons down the center of snowmen according to numbers written on their top hats.

Since the state adopted standards for all grade levels—testing is now required periodically throughout students' careers—preschool teachers have begun meeting with their colleagues at Ashland City Schools to determine how well their curriculum aligns with what children need to succeed in kindergarten.

Kindergarten teachers are required to collect base-line data about each student within six weeks of the start of school, Terri Jewett, who oversees the district's elementary curriculum, said.

Preschool experiences mean many students are coming to school better prepared, Jewett said, but parents who choose to keep their children at home can make sure their school years start off positively by keeping them engaged—teaching them through fun.

The standards, she said, "are just things that parents can easily help their children with"—students should be eager to learn and able to interact with others. Jewett believes children can be best prepared for school by being exposed to reading—the standards stipulate that they recognize letters, understand the right direction to hold a book and be able to respond to stories.

"You know, as educators, our job is to be ready for the child, not necessarily have the child ready for us," Jewett said. She is impressed by how well the preschool standards relate to children's later learning—and by how well their preschool experiences align with what they'll need to know in kindergarten.

Tri-County Cooperative Preschool teachers say their focus is still behavior—each morning, Dreher gently reminds her class of little "friends" to say "please" and "thank-you" when they're offered breakfast—but the academic standards, which were published in 2002, have always been important.

"Preschool helps give them a head start," Michele Espy, a volunteer in Pam Bradley's class, said as she and a student played with blocks. Espy's two sons have each had Bradley as their teacher; 5-year-old Gage will attend kindergarten next year, and his older brother, who has experienced speech delays, is currently a first grader at Taft Elementary School.

"There's just so much they have to learn that I don't remember ever having to learn," mused Espy, who admires Bradley's gift for engaging both students with special needs and youngsters like Gage, who is typically developing. Espy believes since she was in public school—she never had preschool—the educational demands have increased.

"They have to read, they have spelling words . . ." Espy said of her older son's first-grade curriculum. "I don't remember ever having to do spelling words in first grade."

Preschool teacher Joyce Picking said she was skeptical about applying state standards to children as young as 3—it's sometimes hard enough to have them sit still—but realized the new mandates simply confirmed what she was already teaching.

Her first reaction, though, can be recalled with a head shake: "What's going to be next? Proficiency tests for 4-year-olds?"

Picking said she believes she's always met the standards, though after meetings with elementary school teachers this summer, she's worked to eliminate some inconsistencies in her curriculum. She offered the word "oval" as an example—since that shape is called an "ellipse" by first-grade teachers, she's introduced a new term in her lessons. "Some of the kids," she said, "will pick up on that word, 'ellipse,' because it's so different from anything they've ever heard before."

According to Joyce Picking's colleague down the hall, sneaking learning in can be as simple as giving a child bubble wrap—popping the packaging material exercises the same muscles children will need when they hold a pencil—or making up silly rhymes. The standards, she said, don't take anything away from preschool's childish games and songs because "no matter what term they put on it, we've done it."

—*Ashland* (Ohio) *Times-Gazette*

Although a beat is an excellent place to learn journalism basics and acquire a thorough grounding in police, courts and government systems, it may not be your best career path. The police beat, particularly, can become a dead end offering little chance for writing, however exciting the reporting. Most young reporters opt to move on to general assignment or a more prestigious specialty after one to three years in the "cop shop." One problem with a beat—primarily the pressroom kind—is that it becomes repetitive after a year or so, and one day you realize that you've learned just about everything you can from the assignment. You should then examine your options before burnout and boredom set in.

Don't wait for an editor to relieve you from the post, especially if you are doing a good job. Editors are loathe to make any staff changes when a beat is well-served. In all probability you will have to initiate your switch—by making a pest of yourself, if necessary. Tell your boss that you enjoyed the experience and benefited from it but now feel it's time to move on. Conversely, some journalists do decide to make a career of their beat with successful results. Edna Buchanan, longtime crack police reporter for the *Miami Herald,* won a Pulitzer Prize and became nationally known through TV. She is currently a top-selling crime novelist, using her police beat experience for plot and character material. Equally famous was Jim Hagerty, who, after distinguishing himself as a statehouse correspondent in Albany, N.Y., went on to become President Dwight Eisenhower's press secretary.

After mulling it over, make your choice. If you grow unhappy on a beat, it's best that you seek other challenges. If the beat leaves you with a satisfied feeling after a few years, it may be the place for you. Those who elect to spend their careers on small-town papers will, of course, always have a variety of stories to cover.

Suggested Assignments

1. Request permission to spend a day with a beat reporter for your local paper. Cover the same stories that he does and write one of them.
2. Cover an intercollegiate sporting event and write a straight story on the outcome.

3. Do a profile of an athlete or coach or write an interpretive story about an aspect of a college team or athletic program. You might go down one of these avenues:
   a. How much revenue do sports contribute to the institution and how is it used?
   b. How much is the football or basketball coach paid and what is the extent and source of the coach's outside income? How does his income compare with that of other coaches?
   c. How does the athletic scholarship program work (or not work) and does it meet NCCA rules?
4. If your interest lies in movies, theater or TV criticism, select a film, show or play and turn in a review.
5. Focus on what might be a problem area in the local school system and write an in-depth piece about it. Problems might be overcrowding, non-English–speaking pupils, a shortage of teachers (both regular and bilingual), campus safety, dilapidated buildings, outdated lab equipment, conflict between liberal and conservative school board members or a controversy over the use of certain textbooks. Stick with one subject. Don't attempt to jam several problems into one story.

13

Problems and Issues

In terms of coverage, thoroughness and professionalism, newspapers outshine the rest of the mass media. For 50 cents (average cost of a daily paper), the reader gets a package that can include local, national and international news as well as special-interest sections on sports, business, entertainment, health, real estate and even automobiles, depending on the size of the newspaper. Television and radio, whatever their merits, can, at best, offer only a headline service. Some magazines provide excellent in-depth examination of certain subjects but they, too, do not deal in current news. Notable exceptions are *Time, Newsweek, U.S. News & World Report,* and *The Economist,* a British newsweekly that extensively covers U.S. politics and culture as well as economic affairs. All four publish high-grade weekly roundups and do some investigative reporting.

Yet for the past 20 years, newspapers have been losing readers and advertisers. Worse, they have generally failed to lure enough younger readers—aged 18–35—into embracing the newspaper habit. One bright spot is the program called Newspapers in Education (NIE), a cooperative program between newspapers and schools that puts newspapers in the classroom as study tools. Newspapers know their long-term survival depends on a new crop of readers. Their most loyal customers now are in the 45–65 age group.

The recession of the early 1990s hurt newspaper revenues at a time when the industry already had started to lose circulation and advertising, which, for newspapers, is largely driven by circulation. The dwindling market has prompted newspapers to search for new revenue streams and to revamp content to appeal to segmented audiences as well as the general population. Beyond their newsprint product, many newspapers have expanded into Internet communication services whose financial success has yet to be achieved—more about this in a moment. The metro dailies also have stepped up their zoning practice: making over the news and advertising content to target readers in various neighborhoods and suburbs. In addition to its downtown metro edition, the *Los Angeles Times* prints zoned editions for populous Orange County, the San Fernando Valley and Ventura County and special sections tailored to other areas in sprawling Los Angeles County. Other large papers such as the *Chicago Tribune, Boston Globe* and the *New Orleans Times-Picayune* follow the same policy. Suburban or neighborhood bureaus, incidentally, are where beginning reporters and photographers are often placed, much to their advantage. They're excellent venues to get a solid grounding in daily coverage, especially in the city and county government sectors.

In a further effort to attract and hold young readers, hundreds of newspapers have launched the program mentioned previously, NIE (Newspaper in Education), in which copies are distributed free or at reduced cost to school classrooms as a teaching tool. In some communities, local businesses underwrite or share in the cost of the program, whose purpose is to convert youngsters to newspaper reading so that they grow up to become subscribers.

None of this should lead you to believe that newspapers are in desperate trouble. Profit margins are down from the high-flying 1980s, but the papers are still making money and, in some cases, building new printing facilities and buying state-of-the-art equipment. But for an industry that once routinely counted on a 25 percent to 30 percent profit margin, the new reality is a bitter pill.

Still, newspapers are far from the poverty line. *Editor & Publisher,* the industry trade magazine, reported in a recent issue that ". . . one thing is clear: newspapers may still be climbing out the hole that is the advertising recession, but investors couldn't love them more right now." The article went on to say that publicly traded newspaper companies were outperforming the Standard and Poor's 500 Index during most of 2002, resulting in higher than usual values, making for "pricey" stocks. *E&P* also noted that newspapers were expecting a rise in advertising.

Newspapers Online

The "Information Superhighway" has become part of the language, and newspapers are traveling down that road, although no one is exactly sure where it's leading.

One thing is sure: Scores of papers—small ones as well as big ones—have set up interactive communication systems whereby anyone with a telephone and/or personal computer can access news, sports, stock reports, weather reports, restaurant listings, local events, entertainment sites, classified ads, ski conditions, tourist options and other information. Electronic publishing is so much a part of the information landscape that *Editor & Publisher* runs a weekly section on it, and it has been the focus of several national conferences.

Scores of newspapers have put large chunks of their content on the Internet. *The San Jose Mercury News* invested $15 million in Mercury Center, an online service for its circulation area. The *Lexington (Ky.) Herald-Leader* offers an interactive package that includes a computer version of the newspaper "KY Hoops," specializing in University of Kentucky basketball, and plans to provide a full-text search of the daily paper. The *York* (Pa.) *Daily Record,* in the face of a severe blizzard, introduced a page on the World Wide Web for readers who could not get delivery of the paper.

Some of this information is free because of advertising support. There are fees for other material or a monthly service charge. At this writing, no newspaper has reported sizable profits from its interactive operations (some are enduring losses), but most consider it an investment in a future in which online journalism will play an even more prominent role.

So prominent that it will replace the traditional newspaper? Not in the foreseeable future, according to experts. It's interesting to note that Knight Ridder Newspapers abandoned a project that was intended to produce a "flat panel" electronic newspaper, a device that could be carried in a briefcase and enable the user to punch up any particular piece of information she desired, including making reservations at a restaurant or reserving theater tickets. Something like this may emerge in the years ahead, but it would seem that now is not the time. Newspapers still serve a need that cannot be entirely met by electronic publishing. They are, for instance, considered by advertisers the best home for grocery and department and discount store ads, a major revenue source for newspapers. Newspapers also have a pass-along value that the computer cannot duplicate. Computer printouts are seldom seen lying around the house or handed to friends and neighbors. In pitching their product to advertisers, newspapers stress circulation and readership, which means five to 10 people may read one issue.

In an interview concerning the effect of online information and cable TV on the future of newspapers, the aforementioned Ben Bradlee, erstwhile executive editor of the *Washington Post,* commented, "I think we should look at them, but my God, there are 500 TV stations out there. Wherever the information highway is going, it seems to me that people will need newspapers to make sense out of it all. You can't surf 500 channels. I am more optimistic about newspapers than ever before. They may be fewer in number, but the good ones will survive with bells on."

One development, however, is significant. Several newspapers have separate staffs for their interactive service. There also is a budding trend toward creating a particular writing style for this kind of communication, a style terser and targeted for a segmented audience. If online information systems continue to flourish, it could mean more editorial staff jobs on newspapers. The Mercury Center has about 22 employees separate from the main paper.

William B. Ketter, editor of the *Quincy* (Mass.) *Patriot Ledger* and former president of the American Society of Newspaper Editors (ASNE), predicted in an interview with *Editor & Publisher* that newspapers' involvement with electronic news transmission will intensify over time.

"The journalist of tomorrow," he continued, "will be a multimedia reporter, working not only for the paper but for all its information enterprises."

He, too, foresees a future in which newspapers will survive, terming them an "important part of the democratic process. They allow people to make critical decisions relating to their communities and themselves, and that's something editors need to give more thought to. If we lose track of that purpose, if our compass gets off course, then I think newspapers might well become an endangered species."

Although the end of the printed newspaper is nowhere in sight, there are many indications that the number of persons relying on the Internet for at least a part of their information needs will continue to expand. Nielsen Net Ratings reported that in 2005, 140.58 million Americans were Internet users. Newspapers around the country are introducing innovative techniques to increase the figure. The *Denver Post* and

Rocky Mountain News, for example, offer e-mail and online promotions of the daily lunch specials in the area by way of OrdersUP.com. The Tribune Company of Chicago, which owns the *Chicago Tribune* and *Los Angeles Times,* has a site called BlackVoices.com that provides easy access to black entertainment and news as well as a BlackVoices Career Center. Knight Ridder, one of the nation's largest newspaper chains, has developed a Real Cities network of more than 30 owned-and-operated sites serving both consumers and advertisers with a variety of options in local communities, including making restaurant reservations. Boston Works, run by the *Boston Globe,* is a job recruitment service for technology professionals. And major papers are not the only players in the online game. *The Anderson (S.C.) Independent, Presstime* magazine reported, has initiated a book club for readers, who can meet at the local library with the paper's lifestyle editor for a discussion of a new book or comment on a volume via their computers. In fact, most small dailies and some weeklies have an online presence. Southwest Surburban Publishing of Shakopee, Minn., fields seven community newspapers in the Minneapolis area, each with its own site. Mark Weber, director of the company's Internet operations, told *Presstime* that users, 11 percent of them from out of town, log into the sites for breaking news, obituaries or services.

The expanding number of online services calls for more and more writers and editors who can adapt to this kind of journalism. Barbara Chuck, who edited medical content for a health care Web site and also has several years of traditional newspaper experience, said good writing is valued regardless of the medium.

"Most tools work in all media: active verbs, a clear concept, pithy quotes, conversational tone and so forth." Chuck stressed, however, that writers must "know your audience. You have to know for whom you are writing, Who's visiting the site? How can your writing serve those online readers, and how can it attract others?" Chuck also suggested quickly making one's point, keeping sentences to about 10 words and avoiding dense paragraphs. Only the main story should fill more than one computer screen, she said.

"Remember, all it takes is a click and they're gone," Chuck said. "Splitting your story into two or three shorter ones will target readers rather than turn them off."

Tabloidization

Supermarket tabloids represent for some critics, both public and professional, the worst that journalism has to offer. And recently, critics have found reason to believe that mainstream newspapers are embracing the same kind of sensationalism.

Two murder trials, those of O.J. Simpson and William Skakel, the nephew of the late Robert Kennedy, revived this issue. Some daily newspapers were charged with exploiting both trials with superheated reporting and, in the case of the Skakel trial, blowing up the Kennedy-family connection.

Newspapers also get rapped for running gory photos, reporting vivid details of brutal murders and wallowing in scandal. Recently, more than 150 readers complained when the *Springfield* (Mass.) *Union-News* published a picture of local high school students looking at cats they had just dissected in a biology class. Earlier, the *Sacramento Bee* and several other newspapers were bombarded with objections about a picture of a woman who hanged herself from a tree in war-torn Bosnia. The *Bee* ran it in color.

All this has left many people wondering—and worrying—as to whether daily newspapers are irrevocably wrapping themselves in sleaze.

James P. Gannon, former Washington bureau chief for the *Detroit News,* is one of them. In an *Editor & Publisher* essay, he wrote:

> There are powerful forces reshaping the news media in this country. In an age when newspaper readership is declining and the audiences for network news programs are shrinking, owners and managers of media properties are rightfully concerned about their future. In a desperate search for audience, they are increasingly substituting entertainment for news values. . . . The new media reality is this: If a story can get into the tabloids or on the talk shows, it can and will get into the mainstream press, including daily newspapers. The new rules of the media are simple: There are no rules.

Gannon pointed out, though, that there are still plenty of outstanding newspapers, adding, "So we have not lost our souls. But there is a struggle under way for the soul of journalism—and many respected veterans of our business believe the struggle is being lost."

The late David Shaw, Pulitzer Prize–winning media critic of the *Los Angeles Times,* shared that view to some degree. In an interview with the authors, he observed that "over the last several years we have increasingly been inclined to share story interest with what we think of as the tabloid press. On smaller newspapers, this results in pushing out of the mainstream news information that the readers ought to have."

Dwindling readership, he maintained, "has caused newspapers to lower their barriers to some extent on what they will and will not use. The explosion in the number of media outlets and the compression of the news cycle have made it much more difficult for gatekeepers to exercise traditional controls."

Thus, when tabloid broadcasters or CNN airs a sensational story for hours on end, editors begin worrying that readers or viewers will think they're covering up the story "so they go ahead and print it or broadcast it without bothering to have their reporters check it out," Shaw said.

There is no question that competition is a factor in the trend toward tabloid journalism. One had only to observe the media swarm in connection with the O.J. Simpson trial, the Oklahoma City bombing and the drowning of two children by a South Carolina mother to realize that newspapers and broadcast stations believe there is a huge public appetite for this kind of news. And however the tabloids trumpet these stories, they are still legitimate publications. But is the same air of legitimacy involved in celebrity news coverage, which often focuses on off and on again relationships and paternity suits?

Donna Balancia, who has been a reporter for both the national *Star,* a checkout-stand tabloid, and "legitimate" daily newspapers in New York and California, has a simple explanation for the media's fascination with spicy journalism: "Sensationalism sells."

"For the tabloids," she went on, "it's a race to beat everybody else in getting sensational stories on the cover, and they have the money to pay for exclusive interviews. The mainstream press is following along because they don't want to be left behind. It's becoming harder to distinguish between real news and what the tabloids are putting out."

Perhaps, but a couple of things should be kept in mind before engaging in too much handwringing over tabloidization of daily newspapers. For one thing, the phenomenon primarily affects large, metropolitan papers, and not all of those. There are hundreds of small- and medium-size dailies and weeklies that are as sober as ever. Second, a brief scan of the tabloids *National Enquirer, Globe* and *Star* should assure anyone that they bear only a faint resemblance to the paper you have delivered to your home or buy at a newsstand. It's true that accounts of leading politicians having illicit sexual relations or stories of the latest scandals in Britain's royal family sometimes find their way into the hometown paper, but how often has your local newspaper displayed such headlines as "Jack Wagner's Naughty Nude," "Which Celeb Paid 15g for Hookers?" "I Keep Seeing Nicole's Body" (reputed O.J. Simpson report to his psychiatrist) and "Gary Busey, My Psycho Lover"? There were stories to match in the tabloid *Globe.*

Actual news in the tabloids is as scarce as daisies in the Arctic Circle. So, even when mainline newspapers jump on a story featured in the tabloids, it doesn't signal the death of responsible journalism. If you want to learn what's really happening in your city, state, nation or the world, the standard newspaper is still the best place to look.

By the way, care should be taken not to put all tabloids in the same bucket. The term "tabloid" basically refers to the half size of the paper. A regular-size newspaper is called a broadsheet. There are several conventional tabloid dailies, including the *Chicago Sun-Times, Newsday,* the *Rocky Mountain News* in Denver, the *New York Post* and the *Boston Herald.*

The main differences are that the supermarket variety thrives on lurid, often weird, content and that it pays for information and candid pictures of celebrities. Mainstream newspapers don't—with an occasional exception made for free-lance photos tied to a legitimate news story.

Still, in a democratic society, sensational journalism has its place. Judging by the empty tabloid racks near the checkout stands at the end of the day, there is certainly a market for them. In addition, they sporadically keep the dailies on their toes by breaking a bona fide news story that the latter must chase.

Of more concern to the media is the criticism heaped on them for reputedly dwelling on negative news and conflict and not digging deep enough into society's problems. In his book *Breaking the News,* Washington journalist James Fallows indicted the media for putting too much emphasis on entertainment and celebrity reporting and also for "presenting a crisis or issue with the volume turned all the way up, only to drop that issue and turn to the next emergency. . . . And while they do these things, they will constantly be more hated and constantly less useful to the public whose attention they are trying to attract."

Commenting in a *Newsweek* magazine forum, Thomas Patterson, a political science professor at Syracuse University, lamented that "Journalists are obsessed with the underbelly of American politics. Negative news stories more than doubled since 1970 and now exceed positive coverage."

In the same issue, writer Susan Faludi accuses the media of reporting in terms of "two extremes—the 'conventional' view that enforces the status quo and the most 'radical' opinion, which the media dub a lunatic fringe, then the media sic the two against each other in a fixed fight in which the conventional always wins. Our press is hooked on gotcha journalism, where new ideas are met with cynicism and knocked down."

Adding to the chorus was Donna Shalala, former secretary of the U.S. Department of Health and Human Services, who said the press focuses on "conflicts more than healers. We investigate less and pontificate more. We pounce on politicians' every little mistake, yet reverently give private corporations a pass."

Harsh assessments, but how valid are they? And how much of them apply to TV rather than newspapers? How much of it is an age-old tendency to blame the messenger for bad news?

In our view, most of it. With due respect to Secretary Shalala's opinion, many newspapers are heavily engaged in investigative reporting, which does not spare the private sector. And certainly, the press has not given a "pass" in its coverage of the corruption and other misdeeds of Enron, World Com and other corporations.

Fallows implied that the media do not adequately address the nation's social and moral concerns, yet newspapers have published hundreds of stories about gun control, gangs, teenage pregnancy, impoverished schools, AIDS awareness, the evils of narcotics, assaults on the environment and other problems that clearly fall into the categories of "social and moral concerns." To a lesser extent, the better TV stations also have reported on these issues.

"Good" news can also be found in newspapers. Anthony Marquez, managing editor of the *West County Times* in Richmond, California, got so tired of complaints that the newspaper printed only bad news that he and other staffers put together a 12-page special section broadsheet called "Good Times" filled with "positive" stories the paper had run during the past year.

"And we published only a small portion of the stories we had available," Marquez said in an interview. The special issue featured stories about a vocational program that teaches carpentry to at-risk youngsters, a former gangbanger who founded an activities club to take gang members off the streets and a group of parishioners who pitched in to rebuild their burned-out church.

Sacramento Bee columnist William Endicott put the subject into proper perspective when he wrote:

> It's fashionable right now to bash the media for the sorry state of American politics and to suggest that if reporters didn't dwell so much on the negative, things would somehow get better.
>
> Such criticism is not completely without merit. Political reporters can sometimes be like motorists braking for a better look at a freeway pile-up. They gravitate toward conflict like sharks toward blood in the water.
>
> But the broader question is whether politics reflects the press coverage it gets, or the press reflects the politics it covers.

Endicott pointed out that politics is polarized with extremes on the right and left. "The press did not create this state of affairs and would be derelict in not reporting on it," he contended.

That observation could cover developments at city hall or the board of education as well as Washington, D.C. Journalism is not a perfect science; its practitioners are less than perfect. Yet the United States has the freest media system in the world, and this freedom is frequently used to right wrongs, put crooks in jail, spotlight societal needs and problems and, most important, inform, explain and entertain every day.

The Chains: Pro and Con

Some academicians and self-styled newspaper critics view with alarm the trend toward control of multiple newspapers by corporate giants like Knight Ridder, Gannett and MediaNews Group, which own approximately 80% of the daily newspapers in the United States. They regret the passing of the "hometown" newspaper and its local publisher who cared about the community he served. The traditionalists see chain newspapers as being run by faceless executives in faraway headquarters whose only interest in newspapers is their capability for profit.

Actually, the above scenario is more myth than reality. There are still several viable, independently owned newspapers such as the *Seattle Times* and the *Columbus* (Ohio) *Dispatch,* in addition to many small dailies and weeklies around the country. Moreover, group owners are not the villains they are often portrayed. In some instances, they have saved a newspaper from extinction by acquiring it; the *Oakland* (Calif.) *Tribune,* which was bought by Media General, is a case in point. As a major chain, with its assets and expertise, it has made a number of local papers better than they were through superior management, a higher degree of professionalism, and more modern, cost-saving equipment. Unfortunately, not all community papers are paragons of good journalism or effective marketing.

It's also a fact that the more astute chains give their local publishers and editors a great deal of autonomy in day-to-day production on the theory that the latter have a more grounded insight on local affairs. For editorials, however, some group masters insist on a paper following the corporate line, particularly on national issues.

However, the critics are not entirely off base. In recent years, the big outfits like Knight Ridder and Gannett have taken a hard look at the bottom line and found it wanting. The result has been severe cost-cutting moves, including staff layoffs and a trimming of editorial content as advertising declines. Newspapers, even in tough times, are generally profitable but some tend to panic when profits fall below the 25–30 percent to which they had become accustomed.

To young job hunters, the chains represent the best chance of keeping newspapers alive. An added benefit is that they offer the opportunity to move up from a smaller to a larger paper or to make a stab at management to become themselves arbiters of what gets printed. And for those who prefer the pace of a small-town, locally owned daily or weekly, the opportunities are still here.

Public Journalism

Its advocates believe public journalism can ease some of the press criticism while its opponents fear that it will jeopardize newspapers' independence and integrity by diluting the papers' time-honored objectivity.

A concept that took root in the mid-1990s following publication of a book on the subject by New York University journalism professor Jay Rosen, public journalism lends itself to different interpretations. Basically, it's a process by which newspapers (broadcasters and magazines have not signed on at this point) take a leadership role in their communities to help solve problems they face. This can take the form of organizing town meetings on particular issues, interacting with readers, opening a newspaper's pages to more ideas from the public and generally facilitating public dialogue on civic matters.

Gannett Newspapers, the nation's largest chain, is in the forefront of the public journalism movement, as is the Knight Ridder group. The Gannett-owned *Shreveport* (La.) *Times* published a monthly series of reports on area neighborhoods. Each report began with a public meeting co-sponsored by the paper and neighborhood residents at which city officials answered questions about particular problems. In preparation for the sessions, *Times* reporters walked the neighborhood asking about householders' concerns. One result was the mayor's vow to make city government more responsive to citizens.

In Sioux Falls, South Dakota, the *Argus Leader* teamed up with the University of South Dakota for a project called "Community on the Rise" to halt the decline of rural communities because of people moving out. The town of Tyndall (population 1,200) was selected and a rural specialist from the university was assigned to help get the hamlet back on its feet. Reported Phil Currie, Gannett's senior vice president/news: "Goal-setting brainstorming sessions got residents involved, stimulating public debate. Among results: Work continues toward getting a defibrillator for the local hospital and 911 service for the area; funds were raised for youth activities, seminars have been held on farm and ranch management."

To cut down on local crime, the *Poughkeepsie* (N.Y.) *Journal* launched "SafeStreets" with city residents and community leaders. The newspaper developed four eight-page reports examining what the city was doing to cope with crime. According to Currie, "big changes" took place, including the introduction of civilian patrols on city streets, the formation of a police anti-drug unit and a street cleanup program.

Currie views public journalism as a revival of what old-time newspapers did toward helping their communities.

"They took stronger positions. They had leadership roles," he explained in Gannett's internal publication, the Gannetteer. ". . . However, I think what's new is the blending of these traits with much more involvement by the people in the community. For example, when we set out to do stories, we look to citizens to help determine the critical questions and issues. As we report on problems, we also try to find solutions—and many times citizens are involved in that search."

Here is the way Davis "Buzz" Merritt, editor of the *Wichita* (Kan.) *Eagle,* a Knight Ridder paper, justified public journalism in an *Editor & Publisher* article: "Public life, including politics, is in trouble; the nation and its communities cannot seem to solve or even talk civilly about their most basic problems. Journalism also is in trouble: pick just about any statistic. The viability of public life and the value of journalism are inextricably bound together. If people continue to withdraw from public life, if they are not interested in it, they have no need for journalism or journalists."

Information alone cannot make public life viable, Merritt asserted. And if journalists continue to insist that their job is solely providing and interpreting information, they "will not be particularly helpful to public life or our profession."

Another public journalism advocate, Christopher Peck, editor of the *Memphis Commercial Appeal,* put it this way: "We must realize that if the newspaper does not have a viable community in which to publish and people do not have a public life, there will be no need for a newspaper. Public journalism helps give citizens a sense of place."

In sharp contrast to those supporters, Michael Gartner, publisher and editor of *The* (Ames, Iowa) *Tribune* and former president of NBC News, described public journalism as a "menace" in a speech at a convention of the Society of Professional Journalists. He blasted it as wrong "journalistically or morally or philosophically. . . . Newspapers are not to take sides—even for Mom and apple pie. . . . That stuff should be saved for the editorial pages. It will ultimately cost newspapers their credibility."

At the same convention, humor writer Garrison Keillor, turning serious, advised journalists to steer clear of public journalism. The future of newspapers, he asserted, lies "not in good works, not in doing color graphics, but stories, which newspapers tell better than anybody else."

They are not alone in their distaste for public journalism. Some editors and publishers regard it as pandering to their audience. They feel that their job is to report community problems, not to solve them.

In a speech at the University of California, Riverside, former *New York Times* managing editor Gene Roberts described public journalism as a "fad," adding,

> Not all of it is bad, but much of it has more to do with public relations than with journalism. . . . I believe in public journalism, too. But my definition of it involves covering public meetings, not sponsoring them. It involves informing the community thoroughly and diligently about all aspects of community life. . . . It involves supplying readers with the information they need to pass judgment on the community's government, its leadership, its schools and public services.

Currie refers to these critics as "obstinate journalists who don't respect their public enough." He dismisses the notion that public journalism will contaminate journalists' ethics and objectivity.

"In fact," he said, "our readers care a great deal about very significant and important topics, and they want us to carry out our watchdog role. To include them in finding solutions only makes sense."

A number of newly minted journalism graduates will undoubtedly find themselves on newspapers that practice public journalism. The decision to engage in this activity will be made by editors and publishers, but reporters will be the foot soldiers who help make it work. Some beginning reporters and photographers may find this role objectionable. If that is the case, they should disclose their attitude to their supervising editor and ask to be excused from the assignment. This may or may not work.

For young journalists who entered the field with the expectation of helping to make life better for their fellow citizens, public journalism should yield a great deal of personal satisfaction.

Credibility Crisis?

Media credibility is coming under more fire today than, perhaps, any other time since the rip-roaring days of no-holds-barred journalism of the late 19th and early 20th centuries. The subject has been covered in other parts of this book, but perhaps it should be examined in a wider perspective.

Addressing a group of journalists, Los Angeles attorney Robert Shapiro, who has defended many clients in high-profile cases, said he doubted that the Bill of Rights would be approved if put to a popular vote. The Bill of Rights, of course, begins with the First Amendment that protects freedom of the press, speech and religion.

But it was clear that Shapiro believed it is the press that would turn voters away from the bill, which has long been held sacred by journalists—and by most lawyers.

The attorney delivered this gloomy prediction after castigating the media, both print and electronic, for what he termed its frenzied and sometimes inaccurate coverage of the O.J. Simpson trial, in which he was one of the lead defense lawyers. He particularly berated tabloid TV and its print counterpart for its "cash-for-trash" reporting, a reference to paying for information.

Shapiro is not alone in warning the media that they are an endangered species in the court of public opinion, as well as in the eyes of some judges and legislators.

Nor do we have to rely solely on the personal views of lawyers and politicians, who may have a bone to pick with certain newspapers or broadcasters. Various surveys have revealed that journalists rank rather low in terms of credibility and honesty compared with other professions. One poll showed them slightly above used car dealers in trustworthiness. Another placed TV newscasters well ahead of newspaper reporters in believability.

This response is not hard to understand. People can see TV broadcasters, who also, for the most part, happen to be handsome men and women. They appear to impart a sense of reliability and trust. A newspaper byline, on the other hand, is impersonal by comparison. Unless a reader has followed the stories of a certain reporter and is convinced of his accuracy and fairness, the person will glean little from a byline, although the same story she saw and heard on the air will be treated in much greater depth in the newspaper. A story with no byline is even more impersonal.

We do not mean to denigrate broadcast journalism as a conveyer of news and information. Some TV and radio reporters do an excellent job within the limitations of the medium. Moreover, TV can bring a dimension to a story that is impossible for the print media. The devastation of Hurricane Katrina, famine in Africa, scenes from a battlefield and other pictorially enhanced reports make TV news watching almost a must for those who want the story in all its dimensions. There is hardly a newspaper editor or managing editor who does not have at least one TV set in his or her office for news monitoring. And Monday would be a much slower news day were it not for the Sunday talk shows that frequently produce Page One stories. But even the popularity of TV cannot dispel the public malaise concerning the media.

Evidence is plentiful that the crux of the credibility problem lies in the fact that people don't like bad news and are prone to blame the media for it. Then, too, journalism is instant history. Under the crush of deadlines, some mistakes and distortions occur. The news media would rather they didn't and take enormous fail-safe measures to prevent them. And when reporting goes wrong, newspapers are quick to make next-day corrections. This action and other steps newspapers take, such as hiring ombudsmen, using focus groups and following the trend toward public journalism, do help make the press more credible. There are still millions of people who rely on their daily newspapers and quote from them at the barbershop, hairdresser, gym and backyard barbecue.

In judging newspapers, it should also be kept in mind that information is only as good as its source. If a reporter's source is unreliable or untruthful, the story will suffer. Reliability usually depends on the nature and relationship of the journalist and the source. Veteran investigative reporters have relied on some sources for years because they have been dependable. Many such contacts have personal axes to grind, a fact that should not deter you from using their information if you believe it to be sound. You can also double-check his or her statement with other sources.

Journalists are trained to confirm facts, double-check reports and use the most reliable sources they can. Still, there are officials who lie, cover up or exaggerate, people who mistakenly give out wrong information, and situations that change quickly after a deadline has passed. That's why the past tense is employed so frequently in stories. The reporter can only report what he believed to be true at the time he was covering the event.

Credibility crisis? Not really, in our opinion. This does not mean that there is not room for improvement in journalism. Of course there is, a fact that is recognized in virtually every convention, conference, workshop and seminar held by the media—and there are a lot of them. Every so often, a major story with a huge emotional impact like the Saddam Hussein trial in Iraq, the arrest of alleged terrorists or the Washington, D.C., area sniper killings, comes along, setting off a media blitz. In this competitive atmosphere, some journalists will cross an ethical line, and some newspapers will hype the story to the point where comparisons with supermarket tabloids are not unwarranted. But they are a minority, and they will be scorned as much by their media brethren as by the public.

A better way to judge newspapers, in our opinion, is how they cover city hall, community problems and issues and the picture they present of the nation and world. In the United States, newspapers do that as well as or better than the press of any other country in the world.

14

Preparing for a Career in the Media

Basic reporting skills, graphic literacy, critical thinking, enterprise and hard work add up to success in the media industry. Without them, you'll get nowhere fast.

But even if you have what it takes, you have to know how to parlay those skills into a job. First and foremost: Get an internship. To assist in this, seek out a mentor as quickly as possible and make sure that person has experience in your chosen field. An English professor who has never worked for a TV station may not be the best mentor if you're dreaming of entering broadcast journalism. Instead, seek out the journalism instructor, schedule an appointment and interview her about jobs and internships in your chosen field as thoroughly as you would a source for a story. The same holds true for public relations or print journalism. Your college or university has connections in the media industry—alumni working in the field, public relations professionals in the media relations department, full-time journalists who teach part-time. Ask lots of questions, collect names and numbers of their friends in the profession and call to ask about opportunities. It takes only one person to know about an opening and to pass the information along.

Media professionals in a position to hire new recruits expect them to exhibit the same tenacity in job seeking as they would in pursuing a story. Make finding an internship your full-time job until you've succeeded. In today's competitive media market, only the best prepared get the plum jobs; without a few internships on your résumé, you won't have the experience you need to land a good job out of college.

Some hints for finding an internship:

1. **Work on the college newspaper or at the radio or TV station.** For whatever field you plan to enter, experience on the college paper is probably the most essential to your future success. The paper—whether a weekly or daily—forces you to learn and practice the skills you'll need in any media internship. It also gives you published writing samples called clips. Most media employers want evidence of writing skills and rarely consider academic papers as suitable proof.
2. **Plan ahead.** After you've written some decent clips for a student publication, find an internship at a small PR firm, newspaper, radio or TV outlet. Generally expect to receive no pay; most universities give college credit for a job well done.

Try to land your first internship in the summer after your freshman year, no later than the sophomore year. It serves two important purposes: You find out whether you like the work. If you do, and you've received high marks from your supervisor, you're well-positioned to land a paid internship the next time. And you've honed your skills and added a professional credit to your list of references.

3. **Get organized.** Don't rely on anyone else to do the work for you. Your journalism, public relations or advertising instructor may keep a file of openings or post them on a bulletin board, but it's up to you to seek out the opportunity. If the sheer number of opportunities available is daunting, seek advice from your mentor. Don't expect to work for CBS News or the *Wall Street Journal* immediately. You're not ready. There's nothing worse than landing an internship only to discover you lack the skills you need to perform the job. The best training ground is a small market, where you can make mistakes and learn from them in relative obscurity.

4. **Apply widely.** Identify as many places as are geographically convenient to you and fit your career interests. Call each and ask for information about internship programs. If there is no formal internship program, ask for the name and number of someone you could talk to about setting up an informal program. Write down the names of the people you speak with and their titles and phone numbers. When you call the editor in charge of internships, you can leave the message: "Mr. Human Resource suggested that I call you about a possible internship." Try to research the place so that you can tell your prospective employer how you think you'll help the organization and why he should take a chance on you. Remember, employers want to know what you can do for *them*.

5. **Send résumé, cover letter and five of your best pieces of published writing.** The pieces should be photocopied on similarly sized paper. Never send originals. A cover letter should include specific examples of how you have met and exceeded professional expectations in the past. Never send a résumé or cover letter with errors, especially in spelling, style or grammar. After all, you want a job working with words. What you send to prospective employers tells them how likely you are to succeed.

The following is a copy of the information one major U.S. newspaper gathers from an applicant's reference when evaluating college students for internships and job training programs:

> In each performance category below, please rank the applicant's work. Circle the number of the designation that best applies and underline any comments you feel are relevant. If you do not feel qualified to answer a question, please write NA (for "not applicable") beside it.
>
> **Applicant's written expression:**
> 1 — Exceptional (superior organization; able to master complex subject matter in clear, concise fashion)
> 2 — Above average (clear, clean copy; few grammatical, spelling errors)

3—Adequate (can communicate ideas, but work sometimes rambles)

4—Improvement needed (work lacks focus; thoughts are often muddled; language use is poor)

Comments/examples:

Oral expression:

1—Exceptional (articulate; quick on his/her feet; poised under pressure)

2—Above average (expresses self with clarity, depth; generally poised)

3—Adequate (able to exchange ideas and thoughts clearly, but without distinction)

4—Improvement needed (inarticulate; lacks basic oral communication skills; too withdrawn or too pushy)

Comments/examples:

Ability to handle stress or deadline pressure:

1—Exceptional (handles unexpected problems in mature manner; able to complete assignments under pressure without problems)

2—Above average (generally cool under pressure; not easily upset)

3—Adequate (generally competent, but some lapses under pressure; occasionally frazzled by deadlines)

4—Improvement needed (often lacks concentration; likely to freeze or blow up under pressure)

Comments/examples:

Productivity:

1—Exceptional (consistently delivers more and higher quality work than required; volunteers for extra work; delivers work on or before deadline)

2—Above average (usually does more or higher quality work than required; willing to assume additional duties; meets deadlines)

3—Adequate (carries own share of workload; production meets the standard)

4—Improvement needed (does not complete work in required time; difficulty working at same pace as others)

Comments/examples:

Persistence:

1—Exceptional (always sticks with assignments to completion; dogged in pursuit of information needed to resolve problems)

2—Above average (willing to make repeated attempts to solve problems; enjoys following up when additional information is needed)

3—Adequate (perseveres with projects despite problems; willing to follow up to resolve problems when asked)

4—Improvement needed (easily sidetracked when pursuing assignments; tends to abandon projects that don't go smoothly)

Comments/examples:

Curiosity:

1—Exceptional (consistently tries to understand the "why"; has questioning attitude)

2—Above average (probes beneath the surface of assignments; asks lots of questions)

3—Adequate (generally interested in what goes on around him/her)

4—Improvement needed (accepts most things at face value; fails to recognize or try to resolve inconsistencies in information presented)

Comments/examples:

Resourcefulness/Initiative:

1—Exceptional (not deterred by obstacles; frequently initiates own projects; finds new and creative ways to solve problems)

2—Above average (willing to tackle difficult assignments; able to resolve most problems without direction)

3—Adequate (follows through on assignments, but needs some guidance when problems occur)

4—Improvement needed (stymied by problems; shows little follow-through)

Comments/examples:

Adaptability:

1—Exceptional (consistently seeks new challenges; views change as opportunity to learn)

2—Above average (adapts readily to new situations; applies lessons learned in past to new situations)

3—Adequate (accepts change; learns skills with reasonable amount of instruction)

4—Improvement needed (inability or unwillingness to accept new procedures or assignments; resists change and suggestions)

Comments/examples:

Attitude toward job or classroom:

1—Exceptional (exerts maximum energy; frequently makes valuable contributions; consistently enthusiastic; strives for continual improvement)

2—Above average (does required work with enthusiasm; self-motivated; willing to take on additional work when asked)

3—Adequate (exerts required effort; cooperative)

4—Improvement needed (very little effort to meet job or class standards; frequent absences and/or lapses in attention)

Comments/examples:

Relationships with others:

1—Exceptional (relates easily to many different types of people; deals fairly with those with whom he/she disagrees; enjoys helping to resolve conflicts)

2—Above average (accepts individual differences and adjusts to them; tries to understand those with whom he/she disagrees)

3—Adequate (can work with others to meet mutual objectives; fair and reasonable; tends to avoid conflict)

4—Improvement needed (difficult to get along with; indifferent to the needs and feelings of others)

Comments/examples:

General knowledge of news and current events:

1—Exceptional (extremely interested in the news and its ramifications; understands significance of current events)

2—Above average (consistently reads newspapers and/or listens to broadcast news reports; tries to understand and relate news events to life around him/her)

3—Adequate (can discuss current events with reasonable understanding and perspective)

4—Improvement needed (shows little interest in, awareness of news and current events)

Comments/examples:

Has the applicant demonstrated an interest in a newspaper career? In what ways?

6. **Find mentors.** Mentors are exceedingly important in the media business; you need someone to vouch for you, especially when it comes to writing letters of recommendation, landing that first internship and keeping you informed of opportunities suited to your career aspirations. Often, a mentor will make the difference between getting the job and getting passed over for it. Remember, mentors put their reputations on the line when they recommend you for a position. If you fail to perform and disappoint your employer, you harm your mentor's reputation and the chances of other students following you into the internship. If for some reason you realize you can't do the job, be honest about it and seek help from your supervisor or mentor. It's much better to fix the problem as soon as it occurs than to wait until the end of your tenure and receive a bad evaluation.

7. **Show initiative on the job.** Lack of initiative is the biggest problem students face while on the job. Talking to a prospective editor about an internship, one student became chagrined when the editor asked her flatly, "What can you do for me?"

"Imagine," the student said. "He wanted to know what I could do for *him*."

Welcome to the real world. You must prove to a prospective employer that you will be an asset, not a liability. Though many employers feel it is their responsibility to train the next generation, few have the time, inclination or money to institute formal training programs. Especially at smaller- and medium-size papers, PR firms or TV stations, editors and supervisors expect students to hit the ground running. Far too many students wait for assignments and then fail to complete them well, blaming supervisors for lack of direction or for refusing to give them adequate time to complete the task.

Employers want results, not excuses. They don't care why you failed to complete an assignment. But they will always remember that you didn't come through for them and will be reluctant to recommend you when asked.

Interns most often founder because they fail to budget their time well enough to do their best work or they fail to ask enough questions or the right questions of their supervisor when given a task. Let's say, for example, your internship supervisor says: "I need you to research a story we're doing about women, minorities and the job market." The successful intern asks questions to get an idea of the sort of research needed. If you come back with an armload of books on the subject when your editor wanted newspaper articles from the *Los Angeles Times, Washington Post* and *New York Times* written in the last two years, you will have failed.

Or let's say your editor wants you to do a database search, to pull relevant articles and then to create a source list with phone numbers. Does your editor want to see a record of the search terms used, the time frame considered and the date and citations of each article? If you come back with anything less, you've failed.

Because professional supervisors are often so busy trying to finish the job the intern was supposed to do, they never take the time to explain to the intern what went wrong. The end result is a bad experience for both student and supervisor. The best way to avoid failing is to remain scrupulously honest with supervisors. Let them know as soon as humanly possible if you can't meet a deadline. Always seek help, work hard, show enterprise and above all—deliver.

"I go to my internship every day, but there's never anything for me to do so I just sit there," one student whined recently. Be forewarned: This sort of lack of initiative is precisely what employers despise. It is not at all uncommon for interns to arrive on the job and discover nobody expected them and there's nothing for them to do. Worse, nobody has time, it seems, to even answer questions. Smaller agencies, stations and newspapers tend to have too few people doing too much work. That, in part, may be the reason they gave you the internship. Go in expecting little to no assistance. Then, if you get help, you'll be pleasantly surprised. Otherwise, have a game plan on how to get the most out of your internship. Figure out what you want to learn and do your best to pitch assignments you can reasonably complete that will help you reach your goal.

Let's say you land an internship on a weekly and you want to eventually become a political reporter. Volunteer to cover a night city council meeting or dig around for overlooked stories. It's a given in journalism that there are far more great stories than anyone in the media knows about or bothers to cover. Start finding and pitching them.

8. **Seek an internship at a larger organization.** After successfully completing an internship at a small agency, station or newspaper, you're ready to consider applying to a more formal program at a larger venue. These internships, often highly competitive, draw from a nationwide pool of applicants and will likely offer you a salary or stipend. Follow the same steps that led you to your first internship: Send the best of the published work you did in your first internship along with recommendations from your professional supervisors and your mentor.

Once you've successfully completed an internship at a prestigious media company—say, a network affiliate in a major metropolitan market or a medium-to-big city daily or a large public relations firm—you're well-positioned to parlay the professional work you did into a full-time job. When applying for full-time positions, don't overlook training programs. Some of the major media outlets, for example, have special programs for recent college graduates with potential but in need of more experience. These programs run one to two years, pay less than a full-time staff position would, have few if any benefits and won't necessarily lead to a permanent spot. But they provide inexperienced journalists the chance to work with highly skilled professionals on all sorts of stories, major and minor.

Don't despair if you're graduating in the spring and you've yet to complete an internship. The aim is to build a portfolio, résumé and contacts in the industry. You can start doing that anytime. If you're job hunting without an internship behind you, or if you have only one internship at a small weekly or daily, it's best to use the saturation approach to finding employment, regardless of which media field you plan to enter. If, for instance, you want to work in newspapers, pick a geographic location where you'd like to be. Then go to the library and consult the *Editor & Publisher International Yearbook* for all the newspapers operating in that geographical location. Call each one and ask for the title and correct spelling of the name of the person in charge of editorial hiring. Send a cover letter, résumé and clips to each, indicating you'll call to inquire about employment opportunities within the week. Even if the editor flatly tells you, "We have no openings," ask if she wouldn't mind spending a few minutes with you to discuss your intended career. Most media professionals want to help their youthful counterparts; they'll likely admire your spunk and will set up an appointment. Your aim is to get your foot in the door and make a professional contact.

Dress professionally, arrive promptly and don't be disappointed if the manager forgets about you or is late. Politely remind the receptionist that you have an appointment. When you meet, shake hands firmly, look the editor in the eye and be prepared with lots of questions. Ask what you need to do to get hired. Ask if the editor knows of other managers looking to hire someone with your qualifications. Ask if the editor might give you the names and phone number of other editors in town. Write everything down. After the appointment, write a thank you note and follow that up periodically with samples of your latest work and a cover letter explaining you're still interested in working for the publication. If you follow that prescription 100 times at 100 places—that's right, 100 places—you will find a job. Tracking down 100 potential employers is full-time work. So is looking for a job. Don't stop until you find something.

Once you're working, employers expect steady performance and constant improvement. Compliments are as rare as big raises. To gauge your progress, most employers use annual evaluations, in which you're graded on a laundry list of skills, including enterprise, accuracy, ability to meet deadlines, ideas, writing, use of the library and other resources, teamwork and general knowledge about the community and world. At many places, performance evaluations help supervisors award raises. It's best to inquire about the job's expectations on the first day by asking to see a copy of guidelines for the annual evaluation and attempting to meet and exceed as many of them as possible during your probationary period.

Salaries and Opportunities

Smaller companies offer media graduates the best hope for jobs, but they also pay quite a bit less. Salaries begin at $19,000 a year for an entry-level professional position at a small weekly, public relations firm or independent station or cable operation and go as high as $50,000 to $60,000 a year for those few lucky and talented enough to land a job at a network affiliate or a major metropolitan daily. But opportunity abounds, especially for students willing to travel to another state or go to a more rural area. Journalismjobs.com, a Web site offered in a partnership with the *Columbia Journalism Review,* offers a listing of internships as well as jobs on newspapers and all media industries.

Regardless of which media specialty you wish to eventually pursue, your best chances of getting hired remain in print, where a plethora of small publications throughout the country means lots of entry-level openings. Even students considering a career in public relations should think about a stint on a small daily; many public relations firms prefer hiring staff members with writing and reporting experience.

Before you accept a job, you'll negotiate a salary. Negotiating a fair salary, though difficult, is extremely important. Do a little digging first. The industry trade magazine *Editor & Publisher,* for instance, routinely publishes survey results of industry averages for salaries at various-size newspapers. Go to the library and get the clips on salaries or call the Newspaper Guild of America and ask for the current "top minimum" pay for union journalists. (Top minimum usually means the reporter has at least two to six years' experience.)

You'll find a wide range of salaries, depending on experience. The latest salary figures available from the Guild shows a reporter with five years experience earning $570 a week at the *Bakersfield Californian,* $1,260 a week at the *Boston Globe,* $767 a week at the *Bremerton Sun* in Washington, $1,069 at the *Baltimore Sun,* $1,147 a week at the *Minneapolis Star Tribune* and $496 a week at the *Norristown Pennsylvania Times Herald.*

Let's say you're offered a $10,000 annual salary to work for a small, nonunion daily. According to the most recent Illinois State University survey, the average entry-level pay at small dailies is just under $20,000. It will help your negotiations to inquire about the disparity and ask for more money. Asking for more money rarely offends employers; employers want to hire you as cheaply as possible, so they tend to make lowball offers. Make a counter offer based on the research you've done and see what happens. Having several job offers also helps salary negotiations. Remember, though, any threat you make might backfire. If you tell your prospective employer, "I have an offer for $20,000 at the *Daily Bugle,* and if you don't match it, I'm outta here," the employer might well say, "See you later." If you don't really have another offer, you're unemployed. If you have another offer, but really have no desire to work for the *Daily Bugle,* you're stuck.

Remember, too, that you'll likely work at two or three small companies before you find a place large enough to keep you challenged longer than a few years. That's when salary negotiations become extremely important. Expect to earn $30,000 or less a year for the few years you'll need to gain experience. Soon enough, though, you'll jump to a larger corporation with deeper pockets and starting salaries of $40,000 and $50,000 a year. At those places, salary negotiations are a delicate dance; remember, you need and want the job, so try hard not to offend anyone. On the other hand, if you accept too low an offer at a place where you'd like to stay for a while, it will become extremely difficult for you to reach parity with other employees who started at the same time but negotiated a better deal. Getting a fair salary is your responsibility and right. At metro dailies, annual salaries for experienced reporters are often in the $40,000- to $70,000-a-year bracket.

And just what are media employers looking for? According to the Illinois State University survey, media employers want students with basic journalism skills plus "a good academic grounding in history, political science, economics and English." Employers encourage students to "work on campus news media that emphasize writing and editing," and they rated "experience with desktop publishing an important quality." Said the survey director: "Most (employers) want plenty of hands-on experience and good knowledge of language and government."

Where the TV News Jobs Are: Fox, Cable

By Lou Prato

So much gloom has permeated TV news in recent years that many young people contemplating a career in the business are being advised to think about another profession.

They should if they're entering TV news for the glamour, money and prestige, say several of the industry's experts in job placement.

But if they're willing to work hard for moderate—sometimes inadequate—wages and find satisfaction in the life of a reporter or producer, there are plenty of opportunities, now and in the future.

The opportunities, however, are no longer concentrated in the traditional jobs at local network affiliates or on network news staffs. Independent stations and cable operations—local, regional and national—are the growth areas for TV news. And news delivered into homes by direct broadcast satellite (DBS) is on the horizon.

"The next generation of television journalists may be narrow-casters," says Don Fitzpatrick, who runs one of the industry's top job referral services. "With fiber optics cable or DBS people may be able to dial up to 500 outlets. TV news will become like magazines. Instead of covering a fire or city hall, the reporter will be covering the latest in architecture for the architecture channel."

Fitzpatrick and others believe the best opportunities in the near future will be in local cable and at independent broadcast stations affiliated with the Fox Network.

Perhaps the biggest myth about TV news is that jobs are disappearing. Certainly, staff reductions at the networks and many local stations have strained the traditional marketplace. But jobs are available. It's the pay and advancement that are limited.

"There are the same number of jobs today as there were 20 years ago," says Sherlee Barish, who has her own career placement and talent agency. "They're just in different areas.

"What makes it seem like there are less jobs is that people are not changing stations that much. And when positions are eliminated, people can't find similar jobs at the same pay."

As a result, she says, many take jobs that once went to less experienced applicants. That makes it more difficult for someone at the entry-level . . . But even during this tight job environment at local stations, there are opportunities for producers, assignment editors and other behind-the-camera personnel. But too many young people want to be reporters in a market glutted with reporters, many of whom are experienced and unemployed.

Whenever a local news director has an opening for a reporter, he or she is inundated with audition tapes and resumes. It's not unusual for a station to get 150 to 200 tapes, no matter the size of the market or its location.

"I haven't had a reporter opening for more than a year," says Ed Wickenheiser, veteran news director at WGAL-TV in

Lancaster, Pennsylvania, "but I still get a couple of unsolicited tapes each week.

"Finding producers is another matter. My counterparts in Philadelphia and Pittsburgh tell me the same thing. We're all starting to hire kids and train them. A good producer can move on to a bigger market quickly."

Perhaps the best advice for young people getting into TV news is to be flexible. Technology is changing so rapidly that fewer people are needed in the technical areas; individuals who have multiple skills and not simply air presence are at a premium.

"Not everyone is cut out to be in radio and TV news," says Rod Gelatt, the long-time head of broadcast journalism programs at the University of Missouri. "We tell our students they may want to focus on other careers where they can use the same skills of writing, reporting and videography, like corporate video, public relations and marketing.

"But if they're still determined to work in TV news, they can find a job," Gelatt says. "Good people always do."

—American Journalism Review

On the Job: Diversity

Diversity, according to a recent report in the *New York Times,* "may be the most explosive issue inside American newsrooms." In the last decade, many newsroom managers have hired more minorities and changed coverage to reflect their influence, prompting strong reactions from journalists. During the 1990s, while newsroom managers pushed to hire more racially diverse journalists, one of the industry's worst recessions was prompting layoffs and cutbacks among veteran staffers.

Despite this, said Alicia Shepard, a former senior writer for the *American Journalism Review,* the push remained among white newsroom managers to hire minorities. This push naturally resulted in newsroom tensions, as white males felt their traditional dominance threatened amidst the affirmative action push. Conversely, minorities dismissed this concern as "white male angst," contending that newspapers still were not doing enough to attract people of color and other minorities.

The drive to diversity began in the late 1970s, when surveys showed that only 4 percent of those working in newsrooms were minorities, not because they had no interest in the media, but because the establishment systematically denied them entry. Thanks to an industry-sponsored diversity campaign, minorities now make up more than 11 percent of the journalists working in America's newsrooms. (A continuing problem for newspapers, *Editor & Publisher* reported, "is that 96 percent of minority college students don't choose journalism as a career.")

Throughout the country, press clubs, the traditional bastion of the old boys' network, are being supplanted by journalism associations for minorities of all kinds—

the National Association of Black Journalists, the Native American Journalists Association, the National Association of Minority Media Executives, the Asian American Journalists Association, the National Association of Hispanic Journalists, and the National Lesbian and Gay Journalists Association. The associations sponsor job fairs and assist members in networking, advancing their careers and monitoring the content of the media to make them more sensitive to minority concerns and issues.

At the Poynter Institute, a journalism education organization devoted to media research and training, researchers want to find ways to "institutionalize diversity, to make it part of the newspaper's corporate structure so that it remains a priority no matter who's in charge," the *American Journalism Review* reports. Most of the ideas being studied have been attempted at various newspapers, including:

- Having all managers, including the publisher, attend cultural awareness seminars that deal with the value of diversity.
- Making progress toward diversity a factor in job evaluations, raises and promotions.
- Having at least one minority among the finalists for all job openings.
- Including minorities on planning committees on design, reorganizing the newsroom and other issues.
- Sending all reporters and editors, not just minority affairs writers, into minority communities to get to know the people and issues.

The greatest changes are taking place at newspapers with circulations of 500,000 or more. "At those papers, managers are under fierce pressure to increase minority staff and are often rewarded with bonuses for every percentage point increase," according to the *American Journalism Review*.

Though the number of minorities working at larger dailies has increased, progress is still slow at smaller newspapers. Recent figures show 45 percent of American papers have all-white newsrooms, representing one-third of the nation's daily circulation, "The most ambitious journalists, white and non-white, want to work at large metropolitan newspapers. And a white male's chance of getting a job at one of these papers—which are cutting staff and trying to hire minorities—is diminishing," according to an *American Journalism Review* survey.

Newspapers in major metropolitan areas that are home to large numbers of minorities—Atlanta, New York, Washington, D.C., Cincinnati, Portland, Hartford, Connecticut, Los Angeles, to name a few—have changed the way they hire journalists and the way they cover the news in an effort to become more diverse. The *Seattle Times* has a manager of development and diversity. It also has a diversity committee of reporters, editors and photographers who meet regularly to evaluate the paper's coverage of minorities.

The *St. Petersburg* (Fla.) *Times* has required newsroom managers to include a woman, a minority or both among their top three finalists for any job opening. Even managers at some small papers, such as the *Merced* (Calif.) *Sun-Star,* have dramatically increased minority hires. The *Sun-Star* went from 4 percent to 20 percent minority hires in about two years, thanks to the efforts of a new managing editor who went to job fairs in nearby San Francisco and San Jose to recruit. One of the longest running programs is the *Los Angeles Times'* Minority Editorial Training Program (METPRO) in reporting, photography and copyediting.

Despite these efforts, the National Association of Black Journalists says the push for African-American diversity is lagging. In the middle of the first decade of the 21st century, the association said newspaper editors are nearly a decade behind meeting the goals they set in the early 1990s for recruiting black journalists. At the current rate of hiring, the survey found "it would take nearly 50 years for newsrooms to reach parity with the populations they serve."

"Once again, this is pitiful. We have many, many black journalists ready, willing and able to work in our nation's newspapers," NABJ President Herbert Lowe said in a prepared statement. "So why is it that our numbers are not increasing? It's clear that not enough editors are willing to do what it takes to make the numbers grow. Why aren't their results consistent with their intentions?"

NABJ Vice President-Print Bryan Monroe, assistant vice president-news at Knight Ridder, one of the nation's largest and most influential media chains, said the industry should be dissatisfied with its progress in hiring qualified blacks on major newspapers. "At the current rate, for editors to meet their parity goal, they must double not just their efforts, but their results," Monroe said.

Editors often complain that they cannot find enough journalists of color to hire. However, Lowe, who is a reporter at *Newsday,* said student membership of NABJ has doubled in recent years. "I don't buy the argument that you can't find talent out there," Lowe said. "The editors just aren't trying enough."

Another recent survey reveals that the media fall short of the oft-stated goal of racial parity with America at large: 19 percent of newsroom workers at English-speaking television stations are people of color, while 31 percent of all Americans are non-white. In radio news, eight percent of the journalists are African American, Latino, Asian-American or Native American. At the nation's daily newspapers, 12 of the staff members are people of color. But among America's 200 largest newspapers, 20 exceed racial parity.

Women

Women work in every aspect of media and have been steadily gaining power and position since the first pioneers broke through the gender barrier in the 1960s and 1970s. "Ask most publishers about women's advancement in the newsroom and brace yourself for a litany that is equal parts statistics and verve," writes Dorothy Giobbe in *Editor & Publisher.*

Giobbe said it is true that women have made significant gain in the management ranks in the past 10 or 15 years. But she said the lack of women in newspapers' top ranks indicates that a glass ceiling still exists in promotions. "Only a fraction occupy the very highest spot: editor or executive editor," Giobbe told *Editor & Publisher.*

Time and demographics, many women say, will soon right the gender imbalance. Those who currently are second- or third-in-command believe they have a fair shot at the top job when it opens up.

Though more and more women are landing top spots at newspapers, and they constitute nearly 50 percent of the journalists working for America's newspapers, they have yet to achieve parity with men in salary and promotions. The number of top editor positions held by women at major dailies has dropped from 34 in 2000 to 26 in 2002, a five percent decrease, according to a study released in June 2002 by Northwestern University's Media Management Center. The study surveyed 137 newspapers with more than 85,000 circulation. Researchers found a variety of reasons that fewer women wind up with the editor's job, from sexism and discrimination to their own conscious decisions to forgo promotions to spend more time with family.

Other problems for women persist, the study found. Male culture at newspapers "tends to be self-perpetuating. Those in control hire and promote others like themselves," the study reported. Of the 15 CEOs and presidents interviewed for the study, 10 said the informal network at newspapers still favors men. "Guys have the advantage," says Gregory Moore, chair of the American Society of Newspaper Editors diversity committee and editor of the *Denver Post,* "because guys make the decisions."

Editor & Publisher discovered another reason as well: women have limited social access to higher-ranking executives who hire editors. Because men have yet to share equally in the burdens of family life and child rearing, women spend less time networking and more time at home. Ann Marie Lipinski, editor of the *Chicago Tribune,* and Julia Wallace, editor of the *Atlanta Journal-Constitution,* recalled for *Editor & Publisher* some of the difficulties they had combining family and newspapers: Lipinski felt compelled to reject a promotion after the birth of a child, and Wallace carted her kids to the newsroom on many occasions so that she could work. "My kids were raised on many a copy desk," she said. "After Sept. 11 (2001), they didn't see Mom for a month."

Another, more recent study shows many more women than men feel they will never be promoted in their current jobs. In a survey of editors, managing editors and assistant managing editors at newspapers with daily circulation of 50,000 or more, 66 percent of the women said they felt blocked from advancing at their papers; of those, nearly two-thirds said they felt it was because their employers favored male candidates. The survey, conducted by the American Press Institute and the Pew Center for Civic Journalism, also reported that 27 percent of the female respondents predicted they would leave the newspaper industry prematurely, while only 6 percent of the male respondents said they would depart early. Of the women, 35 percent said their current newspaper was unlikely to promote them, compared to 24 percent of the men. Of the women, 40 percent said they felt they lacked the political savvy to move ahead, compared to 12 percent of the men. Only 20 percent of the women—compared to 36 percent of the men—said they "definitely" want to seek promotion in the newspaper business.

"This brings to light a whole class of women struggling to move up," Ann Selzer, the study's author, told *Editor & Publisher.* "They don't feel like they have the tools to make it happen."

One bit of good news from the Northwestern study: The percentage of women publishers has increased from 8 percent in 2000 to 14 percent in 2002. Some newspaper companies, such as McClatchy and Gannett, use monetary incentives to encourage executives to hire more women publishers. The McClatchy-owned *Sacramento Bee* has a day care center and allows parents flexible scheduling to spend more time with their families. "It's a high priority for us," says Gary Pruitt, chairman and CEO of McClatchy newspapers.

Other newspapers need to follow the *Bee*'s lead becoming "more family-friendly," if they wish to encourage and support reporters and editors to stay in the business, says Gregory Moore, editor of the *Denver Post.* "Create an environment where someone with commitments to family can do it without sacrificing careers."

Another bright spot researchers found: 39 percent of the country's largest dailies have women managing editors, a position considered the training ground for the top editor's post. To become the executive editor of a major daily "requires a certain amount of training and time," says Allen H. Neuharth, retired chairman and CEO of Gannett, though he adds, "there are still some decision makers who don't believe women should be in those positions." With time, though, Neuharth says he believes that will change.

While some younger women insist they have never seen cases where women intending to enter a particular profession were prevented from doing so because of gender, older women not only remember discrimination, they lived it. Only 30 years ago, women sportswriters, TV news correspondents and political commentators were rare not because women had no interest in entering the profession but because the men in authority refused to let them.

Before the 1970s and the women's movement, newsrooms nationwide were overwhelmingly male and white. It took losing a court battle in the late 1970s, for instance, to persuade sports teams to allow women reporters equal access to the workplace, namely the locker room. Without access to the locker room, women reporters were unable to fairly compete with their male colleagues for stories. By 1980, there were few women managing editors and editorial page editors at the nation's newspapers. There were virtually no top editors at over-100,000 circulation newspapers.

The situation was not so different for women in TV news. Affirmative action laws and the threat of losing lawsuits provoked TV networks to hire female correspondents in the 1970s. And though women now anchor prime-time newsmagazines, earn multimillion-dollar salaries and land plum assignments, "It is still problematic for women to be middle-aged in television," TV news anchor Jane Pauley told the *Los Angeles Times.* "There is not a single woman in this business who has not experienced sexism . . . from the emphasis on looks and youth . . . to the inherent rivalry between management and on-air 'talent' that causes some male executives to pitch an anchorwoman out on camera, with or without a career track, to see if she fails or is an overnight sensation."

Despite the battles women have had to fight for desks in the nation's newsrooms, their presence has, to some extent, changed media coverage in the last two decades. "The women's movement was beginning to focus more attention on family and child-care issues in the early '70s," explains journalist Susan Jacoby. "Many newswomen were also mothers of young children. They began to cover stories generated by their own lives. Even without the women's movement, the old distinction between 'hard' and 'soft' news—hard news meaning high-level politics—was already breaking down."

In TV news, women have been advancing steadily after stagnating in the 1980s, the *Los Angeles Times* reported recently. "Women make up close to 33 percent of the correspondents (on newscasts and news magazines combined) at the major broadcast networks. At ABC, that's double the amount 16 years ago."

While professional women today no longer have to fight as hard to enter their chosen profession, and more are breaking into the ranks of their career's upper echelons, they still have to battle sexual harassment, discrimination and income disparities, problems that if not overcome often prevent women from advancing. Recent surveys indicate that women still have a long way to go before they win parity with men in the workplace.

Almost 40 percent of women journalists say their employer had discriminated against them on the basis of gender; 36 percent say they had personally experienced sexual harassment on the job, according to a recent study. A few years ago, the Advertising Women of New York released the results of a survey of media professionals showing a gender gap in the industry: 65 percent of the women surveyed said "an old-boy network and a sexist cultural climate were inhibiting their chances to succeed." The survey also showed a wide disparity in income: Men earned roughly $7,000 more than women at the beginning of their careers and an average of $32,000 more after 20 years. These findings underscore the need for women to take control of their careers from the outset, to research salaries before accepting a rate of pay lower than what others receive for doing the same job.

Why It's Not Working for Minority Journalism Students
By Ernest L. Wiggins

With 10 years of daily newspapers behind me, I packed up my files and notebooks, my handy desk references and bric-a-brac, hopped in my car and roared off for the academy.

A tenure-track position at the University of South Carolina College of Journalism and Mass Communications was calling me. Apparently, my work in urban affairs and multiculturalism, my experiences as a reporter and editor, together with my M.A. and research into minority portrayals in the media, and, to be honest, my gender and race alchemically combined to create a golden opportunity.

And I responded but not without consternation.

Would I adapt to the academy's glacial pace or to its unique pressures?

Would scaling the ivory tower prove to be an enormous overestimation of my abilities?

Looking back, my first semester was stressful and revelatory.

It was stressful for all of the expected reasons—classes and committees, students' demands and crises, my own inexperience and the connivance of well-smelted goldbricks who couldn't find the time to read assignments. I got good evaluations on my teaching and much-appreciated "attaboys" from colleagues.

The semester was revelatory because I discovered why the print medium is not further along in its quest for proportionate representation of minorities in newsrooms and in the news.

If the University of South Carolina is representative, and I believe it is, few students of color major in print journalism. Of those who do, many, energetic and resourceful as they are, have writing deficiencies serious enough to slow their progress and deny them success in reporting and editing classes.

I do not know if in general white journalism students are better prepared than students of color. Conventional wisdom would suggest that they are.

However, I would suggest that students of color who are trying to get into mainstream newsrooms need weak writing and editing skills like they need a hole in the head. While mediocrity in a white candidate might be overlooked, because public perception of African-Americans and Latinos already detracts from their perceived competence and effectiveness, measurable language deficiencies are certain death to a career in mainstream newspapers.

Few newsrooms have the time or inclination to provide remedial assistance to staffers. And in the age of corporate downsizing, the pool of talented reporters and editors is getting wider and deeper daily.

Individual attention from college instructors is needed, but it is nearly impossible to get this at large colleges. Faculty members, especially eager and energetic junior faculty, are pulled in five directions as they finish dissertations, write for journals, conduct community service projects, serve on committees and teach classes. Senior faculty are busy with administrative duties and their own research and higher-level classes.

In the end, the students most deserving of attention, and most in need, are frequently those who get the least. Students of color get shut out and candidates for the newsrooms of the future drop journalism for other, more accommodating fields.

In light of this, I would challenge newsroom managers to offer selected staffers a couple of hours of free time a month to coach students of color at area high schools and colleges who have an interest in newspaper journalism.

Many companies have worker incentives for employees who volunteer for Laubach tutoring or CPR training. To do likewise for these students would lend valuable support to journalism schools suffering their own cutbacks and downsizing.

My second revelation: Colleges aren't teaching European-American students what they need to move newspapers to more balanced coverage of minority communities.

White students aren't routinely challenged to pursue stories in minority communities. This experience is essential to their formal training because newsrooms cannot wait to get reporters of color to report the issues and concerns in those communities. Or rather, they should not wait.

Making black stories the exclusive territory of black reporters, however logical the reasoning, is undermanaging human resources.

In the past, I had editors say to me, "We want you to move into a public housing project for a week and write the story. We can't send [a white colleague]. He'll stand out like a sore thumb. You're the only one who can do it."

This was different from what I heard said to my European-American colleagues: "We want you to go to the statehouse to get a reading on the budget debate. You're the only one who can do it."

In the latter case, it appeared that the decision was based on experience; in the former, on color.

To deny a white reporter the opportunity to tell that minority story, in whatever manner he or she could get it, is a dreadful waste of human capital.

To deny reporters of color the opportunity to stretch out and pursue stories all across the map is equally unwise and could result in the eventual demoralization and loss of that valued employee.

Journalism schools are committed to creating total journalists, i.e., those who can report, write, edit, shoot photographs and develop graphics.

Colleges must add: "And who will go wherever the story is."

I hope newsrooms will join colleges in this commitment.

—Editor & Publisher

Glossary

AAJA   Asian American Journalists Association.

ad   Advertisement.

add   Additional copy to the first part of the story.

advertorial   A made-up word designating advertising in news- or feature-story form. Responsible newspapers always label it as advertising.

agate   5 1/2 point type; also agate line, a unit of measured advertising.

Al Jazeera   Private, worldwide news service specializing in coverage of the Arab world.

all caps   Material set entirely in capital letters.

AP   Associated Press, worldwide wire service cooperative supported mainly by its newspaper membership.

art   Photographs, graphics, drawings and other illustrations accompanying editorial matter.

assignment   A story a reporter or photographer is given to cover.

attribution   The act of telling readers the source of information the writer is using.

backgrounder   Usually off-the-record material given to a reporter by an informed source.

banner   A headline that stretches across a page.

BBC   British Broadcasting Corporation.

beat   An agency or department regularly covered by reporters, such as police, courts or city hall; also a scoop by one reporter over another or by one newspaper over others.

blog   A posting or series of postings on a Web site that can summarize a writer's views on news events or serve as a diary. Also known as a Weblog, and updated frequently.

blow-up   An enlarged picture or other piece of art.

boil down   To shorten or tighten a story.

boldface   Heavy, black type.

box   A ruled border enclosing a story or announcement; often used for a short, amusing feature.

brightener   A short feature, usually funny, ironic or offbeat.

budget   A summary of upcoming news stories provided by a wire service.

bulldog   The first edition of a newspaper; also, a tenacious reporter.

byline   A writer's name at the head of the story or the photographer's name with a photo. The latter also is called a "credit line."

caps   All capital letters.

caption   Identification for a photo or other art; also a cutline.

clip   A story clipped from the paper and stored in the newspaper library, usually in an electronic database or online. Entire newspapers are often microfilmed. Reporters requesting a story from the library will likely get a printout.

color   Human interest, anecdotes and other material that enliven a story.

copy   All material written before publication.

copydesk   The place where stories are edited, given headlines and sometimes page layouts are prepared. Today, nearly all copydesks are computerized.

copyperson   All-around helper in the newsroom, carrying editorial matter, mail, coffee, etc.

copyright   Protection from the government to those who produce literary or artistic works.

correspondent   A reporter who covers for a newspaper from out of town or a foreign country.

crop   To trim photos for size or to remove unwanted faces or background.

CRT   Cathode ray tube for use in electronic editing.

cub   An old term for a beginning reporter.

dateline   The line at the start of a story stating the place of the story and sometimes the date. Wire services include their initials, for example, AP.

deadline   For reporters, the time their copy must be in the hands of an editor to make the press run.

deck   One headline or a multiheadlined story.

disk storage   The capacity for storing memory data on a computer's magnetic disk.

dupe   Carbon copy; gone the way of the Linotype machine as new technology takes over newspapers. Also, unneeded because of photocopying machines.

ear   Boxed weather report or other announcement at the top of front page.

editing   The process of reworking or refining news copy to make it better.

edition   One of two or more editions published in a daily cycle, usually by metropolitan newspapers; for example, the first edition, city edition, afternoon final, sports final and late final.

editorial   Comment or opinion representing a newspaper's viewpoint; also any material in the paper other than advertising is considered "editorial material." News department is often referred to as "editorial."

embargo   Time hold on a story set by the source; it sets the time that the story can be published.

file   To send a story by computer, Telex, phone or other means from place or origin by a reporter.

filler   A brief item to fill space at the end of a page column.

flag   The name of the newspaper atop the front page.

Fourth Estate   The press or media. The term traces back to feudal times when the first three estates were the clergy, the nobility, and the commoners.

free-lancer   A writer or photographer who submits material to a newspaper or magazine on speculation or assignment; not a staff member.

galley   A long, narrow tray in which type is stored after being set. With offset printing and new technology, this, too, has become a relic except at a few small weeklies that still use type.

galley proof   Strips of the first printing of type used to check for mistakes.

halftone   A cut made from a paragraph.

handout   A press release.

head   Abbreviation for headline, the few words in a print publication or on a Web site that tell the reader what the story is about.

hold for release   An instruction accompanying a press release; or an editor's order on a story; see *embargo*.

HTML   Short for Hypertext Mark-Up Language. These are tags that instruct Web browsers on how to display text and images.

insert   A paragraph or more to be inserted in a story already written.

inverted pyramid   Traditional newswriting standard that puts the most important information at the beginning of a story. This is standard in writing stories for the Web.

jump   An inside page where a story continues.

kicker   A small, introductory headline above or to the left of the main head.

kill   Delete all or part of a story.

layout   A ruled diagram of the newspaper page on which editors mark places for story and art.

lead   The first paragraph of a story.

legman, legwoman   A reporter who covers an event and phones the facts to a rewrite person in the main office.

libel   Printed defamation of a person that can lead to a lawsuit against the newspaper and the reporter.

lifestyle   A generic term referring to a newspaper's section on trends, fashion, health and behavior.

line printer   A machine that prints "hard copy" from a computer.

logo   A newspaper's nameplate; also, a *flag*.

make over   To change the layout of a page for a new edition.

managing editor   The editor who directs the paper's entire news operation.

masthead   A section usually on the editorial page and listing the paper's publisher and other top business and editorial executives.

memory   News stories and other information stored in a computer.

metro editor   An editor who is responsible for coverage of the metropolitan area, which can include nearby suburbs and other outlying sections.

morgue   An outdated term for a newspaper's library and reference room.

mug shot   A full-face photo; sometimes called "head and shoulders shot."

NAA   Newspaper Association of America; a publishers' group.

NABJ   National Association of Black Journalists.

NAHJ   National Association of Hispanic Journalists.

news editor   The editor who works under the managing editor in selecting and determining news layout.

newshole   The daily space allotted to news content as opposed to advertising.

news peg   An element or angle on which the news story can hang; for example, the discovery of a toxic waste dump could be a peg for a story on waste sites in the county or state.

newsprint   The rolls of paper on which a newspaper is printed.

news source   One who supplies information to reporters.

NLGJA   National Lesbian and Gay Journalists Association.

objectivity   The idea that journalists should give readers unbiased information that presents all sides of an issue without any slant. Some argue this is difficult to do, and that fairness is a more reachable target in news gathering.

offset   A printing method that does away with letterpress printing by a method in which material is printed on a rubber roller that takes an impression from a metal plate and transfers it to paper.

off-the-record   Information given to a reporter by a source who wants it kept confidential. Usually given for background purposes, but the reporter can confirm the information from other sources if the original source has no objection. Reporter must agree to confidentiality for it to be valid.

op-ed   Columns or opinion essays on the page opposite the editorial page.

overset   Copy that did not get into the paper.

pad   To lengthen a story with unneeded material.

page proof   A sample impression of a whole page.

pagination   Laying out full pages with electronic editing devices.

paste-up   Stories and art pasted on sheets; called "copy camera," used in offset printing.

plagiarism   Using ideas or writing of others without attribution, that is, without giving credit to the source of that information.

play   Emphasis and placement given to a story.

P.M.   An afternoon newspaper.

precede   Late-breaking development that tops a story already in print; also called "lead-all."

proofreader   A person who reads galley proofs for errors; position virtually eliminated with the advent of computerized editing.

puff   Free advertising in the form of a news story.

replate   To make over a page for a major news break.

Reuters   Worldwide news service specializing in financial reporting.

rewrite   To put together a story from facts taken from a reporter, wire service or press releases; rewrite person is a highly skilled and fast writer.

rim   The outside of a horseshoe-shaped copydesk, where copy editors work; traditional copydesk changed with electronic editing.

ROP   Run of press; used mainly for advertising content.

rule   A metal strip used in separating columns.

running story   A news event that calls for several stories over a period of days or weeks.

second front   The first page of section 2 of a newspaper.

SEJ   Society of Environmental Journalists.

sidebar   A facet of a major story that usually runs on the same page or jump page; features angles not covered in main story.

slot   Inside of the copydesk, where the chief copy editor or "slot man/woman" sits.

soft news   Usually human interest, humorous or service feature; as opposed to "hard news" such as crime, accidents, meetings, demonstrations and other developments.

SPJ   Society of Professional Journalists.

string book   A book of pasted news clippings; valuable in job hunting.

stringer   Part-time correspondent; usually paid on space rate or by the story.

subhead   A one-line head used to break up parts of a long story.

supplement   An editorial or advertising insert in the newspaper.

tabloid   A newspaper formatted in half size.

take   Part of a story written under deadline pressure; an editor may want the story in "short takes" to move it as quickly as possible into production.

tearsheet   A whole page torn out of a newspaper.

UPI   United Press International, a U.S. wire service that used to be AP's chief U.S. competitor.

wire editor   The editor who handles AP and other wire copy.

wraparound   A special feature or advertising section that is wrapped around the main newspaper.

Recommended Reading

Beasley, Maurine H., and Sheila J. Gibbons, *Taking Their Place: A Documentary History of Women and Journalism,* The American University Press, Washington, D.C., 1993.

Boynton, Robert S., *The New Journalism: Conversations With America's Best Writers on Their Craft,* Vintage Books, New York, 2005.

Bradlee, Ben, *A Good Life, Newspapering and Other Adventures,* Simon and Schuster, New York, 1995.

Brooks, Brian S, and Jack Z. Sissors, *The Art of Editing,* Allyn and Bacon, Needham Heights, Mass., 2001.

Emery, Michael C., Edwin Emery and Nancy Roberts, *The Press and America: An Interpretive History of the Mass Media,* Allyn & Bacon, Needham Heights, Mass., 2000.

Franklin, Jon, *Writing for Story,* Atheneum, New York, 1986.

Gillmor, Dan, *We the Media: Grassroots Journalism by the People, for the People,* O'Reilly and Associates, Sebastapol, Calif., 2004.

Goldstein, Norm, *The Associated Press Stylebook and Briefing on Media Law: Fully Revised and Updated with a New Internet Guide and Glossary,* Perseus Press, Cambridge, Mass., 2002.

Hay, Vicky, *The Essential Feature: Writing for Magazines and Newspapers,* Columbia University Press, New York, N.Y., 1990.

Heider, Don, ed., *Class and News,* Rowman & Littlefield, Lanham, Md., 2004.

Hess, Stephen, *News and Newsmaking,* Brookings Institution, Washington, D.C., 1996.

Larousse, *Dictionary of Twentieth Century History,* ed. Min Lee, Larousse, New York, 1994.

Lovell, Ronald P., *Freelancing,* Waveland Press, Inc., Prospect Heights, Ill., 1996.

Merrill, John C., *Journalism Ethics,* St. Martin's Press, New York, N.Y., 1996.

Mitchell, Dave, Cathy Mitchell and Richard Ofshe, *The Light on Synanon,* Seaview Books, New York, 1980.

Mollenhoff, Clark R., *Investigative Reporting: From Courthouse to White House,* Macmillan, New York, 1981.

Mott, Frank Luther, *American Journalism,* 3rd ed., Macmillan, New York, 1962.

Overbeck, Wayne, *Major Principles of Media Law,* Thomson Wadsworth, Belmont, Calif., 2004.

Pember, Don R. *Mass Media Law,* McGraw-Hill, Boston, 2001.

Rosenbaum, Mort, *Who Stole the News? Why We Can't Keep Up With What Happens in the World and What We Can Do About It,* John Wiley & Sons, New York, 1993.

Schiffrin, Anya, and Amer Bisat, eds., *Globalization: A Handbook for Reporters,* Columbia University Press, New York, 2004.

Shertzer, Margaret, *The Elements of Grammar,* Macmillan Publishing Company, New York, N.Y., 1996.

Sims, Norman, *Literary Journalism,* Oxford University Press, New York, N.Y., 1990.

Sloan, William David, *The Media in America,* Vision Press, Northport, Ala., 2005.

Stein, M.L., *How to Write Plain English,* Monarch Press, New York, 1984.

Stein, M.L., Susan Paterno, *Talk Straight, Listen Carefully: The Art of Interviewing,* Iowa State University Press, Ames, Iowa, 2001.

Streitmatter, Rodger, *Mightier Than the Sword: How the News Media Have Shaped American History,* Westview Press, Boulder, Colo, 1997.

Strunk, William Jr., E.B. White, *The Elements of Style,* 2nd ed., Macmillan Publishing Company, New York, N.Y., 1972.

Weinberg, Steve, *The Reporter's Handbook: A Guide to Documents, Databases and Techniques,* Bedford/St. Martin's, Boston, 2002.

Wicker, Tom, *On The Record: An Insider's Guide to Journalism,* Bedford/St. Martin's, Boston, 2002.

Wilstein, Steve, *Sportswriting Handbook,* McGraw-Hill, New York, 2002.

Yocum, Robin, *Dead Before Deadline—And Other Tales from the Police Beat,* University of Akron Press, Akron, Ohio, 2004.

Zinsser, William, *On Writing Well,* Harper Collins, New York, N.Y., 1998.

Index